COMPLETE BOOK OF
BAKING

COMPLETE BOOK OF
BAKING

Over 400 recipes for pies, tarts, buns, muffins, breads,
cookies and cakes, shown in 1800 step-by-step photographs

MARTHA DAY

southwater

This edition is published by Southwater,
an imprint of Anness Publishing Ltd,
Blaby Road, Wigston, Leicestershire LE18 4SE;
info@anness.com

www.southwaterbooks.com; www.annesspublishing.com

If you like the images in this book and would like to investigate using them for publishing, promotions
or advertising, please visit our website www.practicalpictures.com for more information.

Publisher: Joanna Lorenz
Project Editor: Felicity Forster
Text: Carole Clements
Designer: Sheila Volpe
Photography, Styling: Amanda Heywood
Food Styling: Elizabeth Wolf-Cohen, Carla Capalbo, steps by Cara Hobday, Teresa Goldfinch, Nicola Fowler
Additional Recipes: Carla Capalbo and Laura Washburn, Frances Cleary, Norma MacMillan
Illustrations: Anna Koska
Index: Dawn Butcher

PUBLISHER'S NOTE
Although the advice and information in this book are believed to be accurate and true at the time of going to
press, neither the authors nor the publisher can accept any legal responsibility or liability for any errors or
omissions that may have been made nor for any inaccuracies nor for any loss, harm or injury that comes about
from following instructions or advice in this book.

Previously published as *Complete Baking*

NOTES
• Bracketed terms are intended for American readers.
• For all recipes, quantities are given in both metric and imperial measures and,
where appropriate, in standard cups and spoons.
Follow one set of measures, but not a mixture, because they are not interchangeable.
• Standard spoon and cup measures are level. 1 tsp = 5ml, 1 tbsp = 15ml, 1 cup = 250ml/8fl oz.
Australian standard tablespoons are 20ml. Australian readers should use 3 tsp in
place of 1 tbsp for measuring small quantities.
American pints are 16fl oz/2 cups. American readers should use 20fl oz/2.5 cups in place
of 1 pint when measuring liquids.
• Electric oven temperatures in this book are for conventional ovens. When using a fan oven,
the temperature will probably need to be reduced by about 10–20°C/20–40°F. Since ovens vary, you
should check with your manufacturer's instruction book for guidance.
• The nutritional analysis given for each recipe is calculated per portion (i.e. serving or item),
unless otherwise stated.
If the recipe gives a range, such as Serves 4–6, then the nutritional analysis will be
for the smaller portion size, i.e. 6 servings.
Measurements for sodium do not include salt added to taste.
• Medium (US large) eggs are used unless otherwise stated.

CONTENTS

INTRODUCTION

Nothing equals the satisfaction of home baking. No commercial cake mix or store-bought cookie can match one that is made from the best fresh ingredients with all the added enjoyment that baking at home provides – the enticing aromas that fill the house and stimulate appetites, the delicious straight-from-the-oven flavour, as well as the pride of having created such wonderful goodies yourself.

This book is filled with familiar favourites as well as many other lesser known recipes. Explore the wealth of cookies, buns, teabreads, yeast breads, pies, tarts, and cakes within these pages. Even if you are a novice baker, the easy-to-follow and clear step-by-step photographs will help you achieve good results. For the more experienced home baker, this book will provide some new recipes to add to your repertoire.

Baking is an exact science and needs to be approached in an ordered way. First read through the recipe from beginning to end. Set out all the required ingredients before you begin. Medium eggs are assumed unless specified otherwise, and they should be at room temperature for best results. Sift the flour after you have measured it, and incorporate other dry ingredients as specified in the individual recipes. If you sift the flour from a fair height, it will have more chance to aerate and lighten.

When a recipe calls for folding one ingredient into another, it should be done in a way that incorporates as much air as possible into the mixture. Use either a large metal spoon or a long rubber or plastic scraper. Gently plunge the spoon or scraper deep into the centre of the mixture and, scooping up a large amount of the mixture, fold it over. Turn the bowl slightly so each scoop folds over another part of the mixture.

No two ovens are alike. Buy a reliable oven thermometer and test the temperature of your oven. When possible bake in the centre of the oven where the heat is more likely to be constant. If using a fan-assisted oven, follow the manufacturer's guidelines for baking. Good-quality baking tins (pans) can improve your results, as they conduct heat more efficiently.

Practice, patience and enthusiasm are the keys to confident and successful baking. The recipes that follow will inspire you to start sifting flour, breaking eggs and stirring up all sorts of delectable homemade treats – all guaranteed to bring great satisfaction to both the baker and those lucky enough to enjoy the results.

INGREDIENTS, EQUIPMENT & TECHNIQUES

KEEPING YOUR KITCHEN STOCKED
WITH THE RIGHT INGREDIENTS
AND EQUIPMENT, AS WELL AS
MASTERING THESE BASIC
TECHNIQUES, WILL ENSURE
BAKING SUCCESS EVERY TIME.

BAKING INGREDIENTS

This guide highlights a few of the most essential items that every baker should keep in their store cupboard and refrigerator.

BUTTER AND MARGARINE

Butter gives the best flavour for baking and should be used whenever possible, especially when there is a high fat content, as in shortbread.

Butter needs to be at room temperature before being used. It is usually melted or diced before being worked into the other ingredients to make a batter. This is then beaten by hand or in an electric mixer. For some bread recipes, the butter is kneaded into the dough after the initial rising, since larger quantities of butter can inhibit the action of the yeast.

For a low-fat alternative to butter, try polyunsaturated margarine instead. Low-fat spreads are ideal for spreading on breads and tea breads, but are unfortunately not suitable for baking because they have a high water content.

EGGS

Eggs are a staple ingredient in most baking recipes. They should be stored and used at room temperature, so if you keep them in the refrigerator, remove the number you want at least 30 minutes before making a recipe.

Above: Properly fed hens lay the best and tastiest eggs.

Above: There are many different types of flour, each with different properties, so make sure you select the one that is best for your recipe.

FLOURS

Mass-produced, highly refined flours are fine for most baking purposes, but for the very best results choose organic stone-ground flours because they will add flavour as well as texture to your baking.

Strong flour

Made from hard wheat, which contains a high proportion of gluten, this flour is the one to use for bread-making.

Soft flour

This flour, sometimes called sponge flour, contains less gluten than strong flour and is ideal for light cakes and biscuits (cookies).

Wholemeal (wholewheat) flour

Because this flour contains the complete wheat kernel, it gives a coarser texture and a good wholesome flavour to bread.

Rye flour

This dark-coloured flour has a low gluten content and gives a dense loaf with a good flavour. It is usually best mixed with strong wheat flour to give a lighter loaf.

SWEETENERS

Sugars

Most baking recipes call for sugar. Granulated (white) sugar is the best sweetener to use for the creaming method because the crystals dissolve easily and quickly when creamed with the fat. Granulated sugar can also be used for rubbed-in mixtures and when the sugar is heated with the fat or liquid until it dissolves.

Demerara (raw) sugar can be used when the sugar is dissolved over heat before being added to the dry ingredients. Soft light and dark brown sugars are used when a richer flavour and colour are called for.

Raw sugar is unrefined sugar that is uncoloured and pure – it also has more flavour than refined sugars, and contains some minerals.

Fruit juice

Concentrated fruit juices are very useful for baking. They have no added sweeteners or preservatives and can be diluted as required. Use them in their concentrated form for baking or for sweetening fillings.

Pear and apple spread

This is a very concentrated fruit juice spread with no added sugar. It has a

Above: Fruits add natural sweetness to baked goods.

sweet-sour taste and can be used as a spread or blended with fruit juice and added to baking recipes as a sweetener.

Dried fruits

These are a traditional addition to cakes and teabreads and there is a very wide range available, including more unusual varieties such as peach, pineapple, banana, mango and papaya. The natural sugars add sweetness to baked goods and keep them moist, making it possible to use less fat.

Chop and add dried fruits to breads by hand rather than putting them in an electric mixer or food processor, as the blades will blend the fruit and spoil the appearance and flavour of the loaf.

Honey

Good honey has a strong flavour so you can use less of it than the equivalent amount of sugar. It also contains traces of minerals and vitamins.

Malt extract

This is a sugary by-product of barley. It has a strong flavour and is good to use in bread, cakes and tea breads as it adds a moistness of its own.

Molasses

This is the residue left after the first stage of refining sugar cane. It has a strong, smoky and slightly bitter taste that gives a good flavour to cakes and bakes. Black treacle can often be used as a substitute for molasses.

MILK

Teabreads, sweet breads and cakes are often made with milk, whereas savoury loaves tend to be made using water. Breads made with milk are softer both in the crumb and the crust than those using water.

There are low-fat alternatives to full-fat (whole) milk: skimmed milk and semi-skimmed (low-fat) milk have a much lower fat content and don't taste as rich as the full-fat type.

HERBS AND SPICES

Chopped fresh herbs lend interest to baking, adding flavour to breads, scones (biscuits) and soda breads. In the absence of fresh herbs, dried ones can be used; less is needed but the flavour is generally not as good.

Spices can add either strong or subtle flavours depending on the amount and variety used. The most commonly used sweet spices for baking are cinnamon, nutmeg, cloves and ginger, and the savoury spices are cumin, fennel, caraway and anise. Mace, pepper and coriander seeds can be used for both sweet and savoury bakes. Spices can be added with the flour or kneaded in with other ingredients.

SALT

Many baking recipes add salt at the beginning, stirring or sifting it into the flour. Salt is one of the few essential ingredients in bread-making, both for flavour and for the effect it has on the yeast and dough.

Above: Check that your store cupboard supplies are kept fresh and plentiful, and stock up on the ingredients you use most often.

Baking Equipment

Baking sheet
Choose a large, heavy baking sheet
that will not warp at high temperatures.

Cake boards
Silver cake boards are perfect for
presenting finished cakes. They come
in a variety of shapes and sizes, in
circles, squares and rectangles.

Cake tester
A simple implement that, when
inserted into a cooked cake, will
come out clean if the cake is ready.

Cook's knife
This has a heavy, wide blade and is
ideal for chopping.

Deep round cake tin (pan)
A deep tin is useful for baking
fruit cakes.

Electric whisk
Perfect for whisking egg whites and
incorporating air into light mixtures.

Honey twirl
For spooning honey without making
a mess!

Icing smoother
This will give a wonderfully uniform
finish to fondant-covered cakes.

Juicer
Used for squeezing the juice from
citrus fruits.

Loaf tin (pan)
Available in various sizes and used
for making loaf-shaped breads and
teabreads.

Measuring jug (cup)
Absolutely essential for measuring any
kind of liquid accurately.

Measuring spoons
Standard measuring spoons are
essential for measuring small quantities.

Mixing bowls
A set of different-sized mixing bowls
is essential in any kitchen for
whisking and mixing.

Non-stick baking paper
For lining tins and baking sheets to
ensure that cakes, meringues and
biscuits do not stick.

Nylon sieve (strainer)
Suitable for most baking purposes,
and particularly for sieving foods that
react adversely with metal.

Palette knives and metal spatulas
These are used for loosening pies,
tarts and breads from baking
sheets and for smoothing icing
over cakes.

Pastry brush
Useful for brushing excess flour
from pastry and brushing glazes over
pastries, breads and tarts.

Pastry cutters
A variety cutters is useful when
stamping out pastry, biscuit (cookies)
and scone (biscuit) doughs.

Plastic chopping board
Use this as a smooth, flat surface for
cutting or rolling ingredients.

Plastic scrapers
These can be used to create all
sorts of "combing" patterns in
butter icing.

Rectangular cake tin (pan)
For making tray cakes and other
bakes served cut into slices.

Ring mould
Perfect for making angel cakes and
other ring-shaped cakes.

Rolling pin
Use a heavy rolling pin for rolling
out dough, marzipan and fondant.

Sable paint brushes
These are expensive, but are well
worth the extra cost when painting
fine details on to cakes.

Serrated knives
Sharp knives are essential for cutting
fruit and vegetables, and those with
a serrated edge will allow you to
cut cakes without them breaking
into pieces.

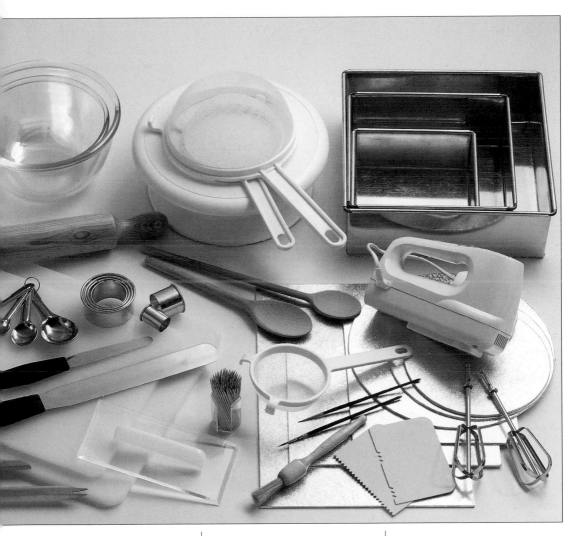

Square cake tin (pan)
Used for making square cakes or cakes served cut into smaller squares.

Vegetable knife
A useful knife for preparing fruit and vegetables for your bakes.

Weighing scales
These are essential for accuracy when weighing ingredients for baking.

Wooden cocktail sticks (toothpicks)
These can be used to make designs on cakes, or to support pieces of cake to make a particular shape. Always remove them before serving.

Wooden spoons
Essential for mixing ingredients for baking and for creaming mixtures. These are available in a wide variety of sizes.

Above: To be able to bake efficiently and with pleasure, you need good equipment. That is not to say that you should invest in an extensive and expensive collection of tins (pans), tools and gadgets, but a basic range is essential. In addition, buy the best equipment you can afford, adding more as your budget allows. Well-made equipment lasts and is a sound investment; inexpensive tins are likely to dent or break.

Baking Techniques

Baking your own muffins and breads is easy and satisfying, even if you're a beginner. Just follow the recipes and the tips, hints, and step-by-step techniques and you'll get perfect results every time.

1 ▲ For liquids measured in jugs (cups): Use a glass or clear plastic measuring jug. Put the jug on a flat surface and pour in the liquid. Bend down and check that the liquid is exactly level with the marking on the jug, as specified in the recipe.

2 ▲ For measuring dry ingredients in a spoon: Fill the spoon with the ingredient. Level the surface with the rim of the spoon, using the straight edge of a knife.

3 ▲ For liquids measured in spoons: Pour the liquid into the measuring spoon, to the brim, and then pour it into the mixing bowl.

4 ▲ For measuring flour in a cup or spoon: Scoop the flour from the canister in the measuring cup or spoon. Hold it over the canister and level the surface.

5 ▲ For measuring butter: Cut with a sharp knife and weigh, or cut off the specified amount following the markings on the wrapping paper.

6 ▲ For rectangular and square cake tins (pans): Fold the paper and crease it with your nail to fit snugly into the corners of the tin. Then press the bottom paper lining into place.

7 ▲ To line muffin tins: Use paper cases of the required size. Or grease and flour the tins.

MAKING SCONES

Scone (biscuit) dough may be rolled out and cut into shapes for baking in the oven or cooking on a griddle. To ensure light, well-risen scones, do not handle the dough too much and do not roll it out too thinly.

Drop scones are made from a batter that has the consistency of thick cream. The batter is dropped in spoonfuls on to a hot griddle or frying pan.

1 Sift the dry ingredients into a bowl (flour, baking powder with or without bicarbonate of soda (baking soda), salt, sugar, ground spices, etc).

2 ▲ Add the fat (butter, margarine, vegetable fat, etc). With a pastry blender or two knives used scissor-fashion, cut the fat into the dry ingredients until the mixture resembles fine crumbs, or rub in the fat with your fingertips.

3 ▲ Add the liquid ingredients (milk, cream, buttermilk, eggs) to the flour mixture. Stir with a fork until the dry ingredients are thoroughly moistened and will come together in a ball of fairly soft dough in the centre of the bowl.

Date Oven Scones
Sift 225g/8oz/2 cups self-raising (self-rising) flour with a pinch of salt and rub in 50g/2oz/¼ cup butter. Add 50g/2oz chopped dates. Mix to a soft dough with 150ml/ ¼ pint/⅔ cup milk. Roll out and cut 5cm/2in rounds. Glaze with egg or milk. Bake at 230°C/450°F/Gas 8 for 8–10 minutes or until risen and golden brown. *Makes about 12.*

4 ▲ Turn the dough on to a lightly floured surface. Knead it very lightly, folding and pressing, to mix evenly – about 30 seconds. Roll or pat out the dough to 2cm/¾in thickness.

6 ▲ For griddle scones: If using a well-seasoned cast iron griddle, there is no need to grease it. Heat it slowly and evenly. Put scone triangles or rounds on the hot griddle and cook for 4–5 minutes on each side or until golden brown and cooked through.

5 ▲ For oven-baked scones: With a floured, sharp-edged cutter, stamp out rounds or other shapes, or cut triangles with a floured knife. Arrange the scones on an ungreased baking sheet so they are not touching. Brush the tops with beaten egg, milk or cream if the recipe specifies. Bake until risen and golden brown.

Cutting tips
- Be sure the cutter or knife is sharp so that the edges of the scone shapes are not compressed; this would inhibit rising.
- Cut the shapes close together so that you won't have to reroll the dough more than once.
- If necessary, a short, sturdy drinking glass can be pressed into service as a cutter. Flour the rim well and do not press too hard.

MAKING TEABREADS AND MUFFINS

These sorts of bread are very quick and easy to make. The raising agent reacts quickly with moisture and heat to make the breads and muffins rise, without the need for a rising (or proving) period before baking.

The raising agent is usually bicarbonate of soda (baking soda) or baking powder, which is a mixture of bicarbonate of soda and an acid salt such as cream of tartar. Many recipes use self-raising (self-rising) flour, which includes a raising agent. Remember that the raising agent will start to work as soon as it comes into contact with liquid, so don't mix the dry and liquid ingredients until just before you are ready to fill the tin (pan) or tins and bake the mixture.

1 ▲ **For muffins:** Combine the dry ingredients in a bowl. It is a good idea to sift the flour with the raising agent, salt and any spices to mix them evenly. Add the liquid ingredients and stir just until the dry ingredients are moistened; the mixture will not be smooth. Do not overmix by attempting to remove all the lumps. If you do, the muffins will be tough and will have air holes in them.

2 ▲ Divide the mixture evenly among the greased muffin tins or deep bun tins lined with paper cases, filling them about two-thirds full. Bake until golden brown and a wooden skewer inserted in the centre comes out clean. To prevent the muffins having soggy bottoms, remove the muffins immediately from the tins to a wire rack. Cool, and serve warm or at room temperature.

Crunchy Muesli Muffins
Make the mixture from 150g/5oz/ 1¼ cups plain (all-purpose) flour, 12.5ml/2½ tsp baking powder, 30ml/ 2 tbsp caster (superfine) sugar, 250ml/8fl oz/1 cup milk, 50g/2oz melted butter or corn oil, and 1 egg, adding 200g/7oz toasted oat cereal with raisins to the dry ingredients. Pour into muffin tins (pans) or deep bun tins. Bake in a 200°C/400°F/ Gas 6 oven for 20 minutes or until golden brown. *Makes 10.*

3 ▲ **For fruit and/or nut teabreads:** Method 1: Stir together all the liquid ingredients. Add the dry ingredients and beat just until smoothly blended. Method 2: Beat the butter with the sugar until the mixture is light and fluffy. Beat in the eggs followed by the other liquid ingredients. Stir in the dry ingredients. Pour the mixture into a prepared tin (typically a loaf tin). Bake until a wooden skewer inserted in the centre comes out clean. If the bread is browning too quickly, cover the top with foil.

4 ▲ Cool in the tin for 5 minutes, then turn out on to a wire rack to cool completely. A lengthways crack on the surface is characteristic of teabreads. For easier slicing, wrap the bread in baking parchment and overwrap in foil, then store overnight at room temperature.

MAKING SIMPLE MERINGUE

There are two types of this egg white and sugar foam: a soft meringue used as an insulating topping for pies and baked Alaska and a firm meringue that can be shaped into containers for luscious fillings.

Take care when separating the egg whites and yolks because even the smallest trace of yolk will prevent the whites from being whisked to their maximum volume. All equipment must be scrupulously clean and free of grease.

Meringue Nests
Make a firm meringue using 2 egg whites and 115g/4oz/½ cup caster (superfine) sugar. Scoop spoonfuls of meringue on to a baking sheet lined with baking parchment. Slightly hollow out the centre of each with the back of the spoon,to make a nest shape. Alterna-tively, put the meringue into a piping bag fitted with a 1cm/½ in plain nozzle and pipe the nest shapes. Sprinkle lightly with a little extra sugar. Dry in a 110°C/225°F/Gas ¼ oven for 3–4 hours or until crisp and firm but not brown. Leave to cool. To serve, fill with sweetened whipped cream and fresh fruit. *Makes 4–6.*

1 ▲ Put the egg whites in a large, scrupulously clean and grease-free bowl. With a whisk or electric mixer, whisk the whites until they are foamy. If not using a copper bowl, add a pinch of cream of tartar.

3 ▲ **For a soft meringue:** Sprinkle the sugar over the whites, whisking constantly. Continue whisking for about 1 minute or until the meringue is glossy and holds stiff peaks when you lift the whisk or beaters. The meringue is now ready to be spread on a pie filling or used for baked Alaska.

Sweetened whipped cream
This is used as a topping and filling for many hot and cold desserts. Whip 300ml/½ pint/ 1¼ cups chilled whipping or double (heavy) cream until it starts to thicken. Add 30ml/2 tbsp sifted icing (confectioners') sugar and continue whipping until the cream holds a soft peak on the beaters. The cream may be flavoured with 2.5ml/½ tsp vanilla or almond extract or 10ml/2 tsp brandy or liqueur, added with the sugar.

2 ▲ Continue whisking until the whites hold soft peaks when you lift the whisk or beaters (the tips of the peaks will flop over).

4 ▲ **For a firm meringue:** Add a little of the sugar (about 7.5ml/1½ tsp for each egg white). Continue whisking until the meringue is glossy and will hold stiff peaks.

5 ▲ Add the remaining sugar to the bowl, with any flavouring the recipe specifies. With a rubber spatula, fold the sugar into the meringue as lightly as possible by cutting down with the spatula to the bottom of the bowl and then turning the mixture over. The meringue is now ready to be shaped into containers or gâteau layers.

MAKING SHORTCRUST PASTRY

A meltingly short, crumbly pastry sets off any filling to perfection, whether sweet or savoury. The dough can be made with half butter or margarine and half white vegetable fat (shortening) or with all one kind of fat.

FOR A 23CM/9IN PASTRY CASE

225g/8oz/2 cups plain (all-purpose) flour

1.25ml/¼ tsp salt

115g/4oz/½ cup fat, chilled and diced

45–60ml/3–4 tbsp iced water

1 ▲ Sift the flour and salt into a bowl. Add the diced fat. Rub it into the flour with your fingertips until the mixture is crumb-like.

2 ▲ Sprinkle 45ml/3 tbsp water over the mixture. With a fork, toss gently to mix and moisten it.

Pastry making tips

- It helps if the fat is cold and firm, particularly if making the dough in a food processor. Cold fat has less chance of warming and softening too much when it is being rubbed into the flour, resulting in an oily pastry. Use block margarine rather than the soft tub-type.
- When rubbing the fat into the flour, if it begins to soften and feel oily, put the bowl in the refrigerator to chill for 20–30 minutes. Then continue making the dough.
- Liquids used should be ice-cold so that they will not soften or melt the fat.
- Take care when adding the water: start with the smaller amount (added all at once, not in a dribble), and add more only if the mixture will not come together into a dough. Too much water will result in tough pastry.
- When gathering the mixture together into a ball of dough, handle it as little as possible: overworked pastry will be tough.
- To avoid shrinkage, refrigerate the pastry dough before rolling out and baking. This 'resting time' will allow any elasticity developed during mixing to relax.

3 ▲ Press the dough into a ball. If it is too dry to form a dough, add the remaining water.

5 ▲ To make pastry in a food processor: Combine the flour, salt and cubed fat in the work bowl. Process, turning the machine on and off, just until the mixture is crumbly. Add the iced water and process again briefly – just until the dough starts to pull away from the sides of the bowl. It should still look crumbly. Remove the dough from the processor and gather it into a ball. Wrap and refrigerate.

4 ▲ Wrap the ball of dough with clear film (plastic wrap) and refrigerate it for at least 30 minutes.

Shortcrust pastry variations

- For *Nut Shortcrust:* Add 30ml/ 2 tbsp finely chopped walnuts or pecan nuts to the flour mixture.
- For *Rich Shortcrust:* Use 225g/ 8oz/2 cups flour and 175g/6oz/¾ cup fat (preferably all butter), plus 15ml/ 1 tbsp caster (superfine) sugar if making a sweet pie. Bind with 1 egg yolk and 30–45ml/2–3 tbsp water.
- For a *Two-crust Pie,* increase the proportions by 50 per cent thus the amounts needed for basic shortcrust pastry are: 350g/12oz/3 cups flour, 2.5ml/½ tsp salt, 175g/6oz/ 1½ cups fat, 75–90ml/5–6 tbsp water. For Nut Shortcrust, as above with 60ml/4 tbsp nuts. For Rich Shortcrust, as above but 250g/9oz/ generous 1 cup fat, 60–75ml/3–4 tbsp water and 1 egg yolk.

MAKING FRENCH FLAN PASTRY

The pastry for tarts, flans and quiches is made with butter or margarine, giving a rich and crumbly result. The more fat used, the richer the pastry will be – almost like a biscuit (cookie) dough – and the harder to roll out. If you have difficulty rolling it, you can press it into the tin (pan) instead, or roll it out between sheets of clear film (plastic wrap). Flan pastry, like short-crust, can be made by hand or in a food processor. Tips for making, handling and using shortcrust pastry apply equally to French flan pastry.

FOR A 23CM/9IN FLAN CASE

225g/8oz/2 cups plain (all-purpose) flour
2.5ml/½ tsp salt
115g/4oz/½ cup butter or margarine, chilled and cubed
1 egg yolk
1.25ml/¼ tsp lemon juice
30–45ml/2–3 tbsp iced water

1 ▲ Sift the flour and salt into a bowl. Add the butter or margarine. Rub into the flour until the mixture resembles fine crumbs.

2 ▲ In a small bowl, mix the egg yolk, lemon juice and 30ml/2 tbsp water. Add to the flour mixture. With a fork, toss gently to mix and moisten.

3 ▲ Press the dough into a rough ball. If it is too dry to come together, add the remaining water. Turn on to the work surface or a pastry board.

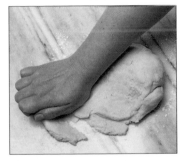

4 ▲ With the heel of your hand, push small portions of dough away from you, smearing them on the surface or board.

Flan pastry variations
- For *Sweet Flan Pastry:* Reduce the amount of salt to 1.25ml/¼ tsp; add 15ml/1 tbsp caster (superfine) sugar with the flour.
- For *Rich Flan Pastry:* Use 225g/8oz/2 cups flour, 2.5ml/½ tsp salt, 150g/5oz/10 tbsp butter, 2 egg yolks, and 15–30ml/1–2 tbsp water.
- For *Rich Sweet Flan Pastry:* Make rich flan pastry, adding 45ml/3 tbsp caster (superfine) sugar with the flour and 2.5ml/½ tsp vanilla extract with the egg yolks.

5 ▲ Continue mixing the dough in this way until it feels pliable and can be peeled easily off the surface.

6 ▲ Press the dough into a smooth ball. Wrap in clear film and chill for at least 30 minutes.

ROLLING OUT AND LINING A TIN

A neat pastry case that doesn't distort or shrink in baking is the desired result. The key to success is handling the dough gently. Use the method here for lining a round pie or tart tin (pan) that is about 5cm/2in deep.

Remove the chilled dough from the refrigerator and allow it to soften slightly at room temperature. Unwrap and put it on a lightly floured surface. Flatten the dough into a neat, round disc. Lightly flour the rolling pin.

Rolling out and lining tips

- Reflour the surface and rolling pin if the dough starts to stick.
- Should the dough tear, patch with a piece of moistened dough.
- When rolling out and lining the pie or tart tin, do not stretch the dough. It will only shrink back during baking, spoiling the shape of the pastry case.
- Once or twice during rolling out, gently push in the edges of the dough with your cupped palms, to keep the circular shape.
- A pastry scraper will help lift the dough from the work surface, to wrap it around the rolling pin.
- Tins (pans) made from heat-resistant glass or dull-finish metal such as heavyweight aluminium will give a crisp crust.
- When finishing the edge, be sure to hook the dough over the rim all the way round or to press the dough firmly to the rim. This will prevent the dough pulling away should it start to shrink.
- If covering a pie dish, roll the dough to a round or oval 5cm/2in larger than the dish. Cut a 2.5cm/1in strip from the outside and lay this on the moistened rim of the dish. Brush the strip with water and lay the sheet of dough on top. Press edges to seal, then trim even with the rim. Knock up the edge with a knife.

1 ▲ Using even pressure, start rolling out the dough, working from the centre to the edge each time and easing the pressure slightly as you reach the edge.

3 ▲ Continue rolling out until the dough circle is about 5cm/2in larger all round than the tin. The dough will be about 3mm/⅛in thick.

5 ▲ Hold the roliing pin over the tin and gently unroll the pastry dough so it drapes into the tin, centring it as much as possible.

2 ▲ Lift up the dough and give it a quarter turn from time to time during the rolling. This will prevent the dough sticking to the surface, and will help keep the thickness even.

4 ▲ Set the rolling pin on the dough, near one side of the circle. Fold the outside edge of dough over the pin, then roll the pin over the dough to wrap the dough round it. Do this gently and loosely.

6 ▲ With your fingertips, lift and ease the dough into the tin, gently pressing it over the bottom and up the side. Turn excess dough over the rim and trim it with a knife or scissors, depending on the edge to be made.

LINING A FLAN TIN OR RING

A flan tin (pan) is shallow, with no rim. Its straight sides (smooth or fluted) give a tart or flan the traditional shape. The most useful tins have removable bases, making it very easy to turn out a tart. Flan rings are straight-sided metal rings that are set on a baking sheet.

In addition to flan tins and rings, there are porcelain quiche dishes and small, individual tartlet tins, both plain and fluted.

Pecan Nut Tartlets
Line six 10cm/4in tartlet tins (pans) with flan pastry. Place 25g/1oz pecan nut halves in each. In a bowl, beat 3 eggs to mix. Add 25g/ 1oz/2 tbsp melted butter, 275g/10oz golden (light corn) syrup and 2.5ml/ ½ tsp vanilla extract. Sift together 90g/3½ oz/½ cup caster (superfine) sugar and 15ml/1 tbsp plain (all-purpose) flour. Add to the egg mixture and stir until evenly blended. Fill the tartlet cases and leave until the nuts rise to the surface. Bake in a 180°C/350°FGas 4 oven for 35–40 minutes or until a knife inserted near the centre comes out clean. Cool in the tins for 15 minutes, then turn on to a wire rack.

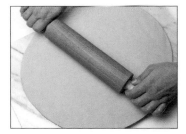

1 ▲ Remove the chilled dough from the refrigerator and let it soften slightly at room temperature. Roll out to a circle about 5cm/2in larger all round than the tin or ring. It will be about 3mm/⅛in thick.

3 ▲ With your fingertips, ease the dough into the tin or ring, gently pressing it smoothly over the bottom, without stretching it.

5 ▲ Roll the rolling pin over the top of the tin or ring to cut off excess dough and leave a neat edge. Smooth the cut edge and press it against the side of the tin or ring, if necessary, to keep it in place.

2 ▲ Roll up the dough round the rolling pin, then unroll it over the tin or ring, draping it gently.

4 ▲ Fold the overhanging dough down inside the tin or ring, to thicken the side of the pastry case. Smooth and press the side of the case against the side of the tin or ring.

6 ▲ For tartlet tins: Arrange them close together and unroll the dough over them, draping it loosely. Roll the rolling pin over the top to cut off excess pastry. Press into the bottom and sides of the tins.

FINISHING THE EDGE

1 ▲ **For a forked edge:** Trim the dough even with the rim and press it flat. Firmly and evenly press the prongs of a fork all round the edge. If the fork sticks, dip it in flour.

2 ▲ **For a crimped edge:** Trim the dough to leave an overhang of about 1cm/½in all round. Fold the extra dough under. Put the knuckle or tip of the index finger of one of your hands inside the edge, pointing directly out. With the thumb and index finger of your other hand, pinch the dough edge around your index finger into a 'V' shape. Continue all round the edge.

3 ▲ **For a ruffled edge:** Trim the dough to leave an overhang of about 1cm/½in all round. Fold the extra dough under. Hold the thumb and index finger of one of your hands about 2.5cm/1in apart, inside the edge, pointing directly out. With the index finger of your other hand, gently pull the dough between them, to the end of the rim. Continue all the way round the edge.

Apple and Cherry Crumble Pie
Mix together 350g/12oz peeled, cored and sliced eating apples, 275g/10oz stoned cherries and 115g/4oz/½ cup soft light brown sugar. Put into a 23cm/9in pastry case. For the topping, combine 115g/4oz/1 cup plain (all-purpose) flour, 115g/4oz/½ cup soft light brown sugar and 5ml/1 tsp ground cinnamon. Rub in 75g/3oz/6 tbsp butter until the mixture resembles coarse crumbs. Sprinkle over the fruit. Bake in a 190°C/375°F/Gas 5 oven for about 45 minutes or until golden. *Serves* 6.

4 ▲ **For a cutout edge:** Trim the dough even with the rim and press it flat on the rim. With a small pastry cutter, cut out decorative shapes from the dough trimmings. Moisten the edge of the pastry case and press the cutouts in place, overlapping them slightly if you like.

5 ▲ **For a ribbon edge:** Trim the dough even with the rim and press it flat on the rim. Cut long strips about 2cm/¾in wide from the dough trimmings. Moisten the edge and press one end of a strip on to it. Twist the strip gently and press it on to the edge again. Continue all the way round the edge.

BAKING BLIND

Baked custard and cream fillings can make pastry soggy, so the cases for these flans and tarts are often given an initial baking before the filling is added and the final baking is done. Such pre-baking is referred to as baking 'blind'. The technique is also used for pastry cases that are to be filled with an uncooked or precooked mixture, such as quiches.

The purpose of using weights such as baking beans is to prevent the bottom of the pastry case from rising too much and becoming distorted, thus keeping its neat shape.

1 ▲ Set the pie or flan tin (pan), or flan ring, on a sheet of baking parchment or foil. Draw or mark around its base. Cut out a circle about 7.5cm/3in larger all round than the drawn or marked one.

2 ▲ Roll out the pastry dough and use to line the tin or ring set on a baking sheet. Prick the bottom of the pastry case all over with a fork.

Fresh Strawberry Flan
Make the case using sweet flan pastry or rich sweet flan pastry. Bake it blind fully, then cool. Beat 400g/14oz/1¾ cups full-fat soft cheese with 50g/2oz/¼ cup caster (superfine) sugar, 1 egg yolk and 60ml/4 tbsp whipping cream until smooth. Fold in 1 stiffly whisked egg white. Pour into the case and spread evenly. Bake at 180°C/350°F/Gas 4 for 15–20 minutes or until the filling is softly set; it will set further as it cools. When cool, arrange halved strawberries on top in concentric circles. Melt 150g/5oz redcurrant jelly and brush over the berries to glaze them. Leave the flan to cool before serving. *Serves 6.*

3 ▲ Lay the circle of parchment or foil in the pastry case and press it smoothly over the bottom and up the side.

4 ▲ Put enough dried beans or baking beans in the case to cover the bottom thickly.

5 ▲ **For partially baked pastry:** Bake the case in a 200°C/400°F/Gas 6 oven for 15–20 minutes or until it is slightly dry and set. Remove the baking parchment or foil and beans. The pastry is now ready to be filled and baked further.

6 ▲ **For fully baked pastry:** After baking for 15 minutes, remove the paper or foil and beans. Prick the bottom again with a fork. Return to the oven and bake for 5–10 minutes or until golden brown. Cool completely before adding the filling.

MAKING A TWO-CRUST PIE

Two succulent pastry layers enveloping a sweet filling – what could be nicer? Use the same method for making small pies, such as mince pies.

American-style Apple Pie
Combine 900g/2lb peeled, cored and thinly sliced eating apples, 15ml/1tbsp plain (all-purpose) flour, 90g/3½oz/½ cup caster (superfine) sugar and 3.75ml/¾ tsp mixed (apple pie) spice. Toss to coat the fruit evenly. Use to fill the two-crust pie. Bake in a 190°C/375°F/ Gas 5 oven for about 45 minutes or until the pastry is golden brown and the fruit is tender (test with a skewer through a slit in the top crust). Cool on a rack.

1 ▲ Roll out half of the pastry dough on a floured surface and line a pie tin (pan) that is about 5cm/2in deep. Trim the dough even with the rim.

2 ▲ Put in the filling. Brush the edge of the pastry case evenly with water to moisten it.

3 ▲ Roll out a second piece of dough to a circle that is about 2.5cm/1in larger all round than the tin. Roll it up around the rolling pin and unroll over the pie. Press the edges together.

4 ▲ Trim the edge of the lid to leave a 1cm/½in overhang. Cut slits or a design in the centre. These will act as steam vents during baking.

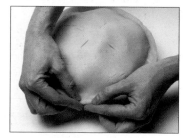

5 ▲ Fold the overhang of the lid under the edge of the case. Press the two together gently and evenly to seal. Finish the edge as wished.

6 ▲ Brush the top of the pie with milk or cream for a shiny finish. Or brush with 1 egg yolk mixed with 5ml/1 tsp water for a glazed golden brown finish. Or brush with water and then sprinkle with sugar or cinnamon and sugar for a sugary crust.

7 ▲ If you like, cut out decorative shapes from the dough trimmings, rolled out as thinly as possible. Moisten the cutouts with a little water and press them on to the top. Glaze the decorations before baking.

MAKING A LATTICE TOP

A woven pastry lattice is a very attractive finish for a pie. Prepare shortcrust for a two-crust pie.

Roll out half of the pastry dough and line the pie tin (pan). Trim the dough to leave a 1cm/½in overhang all round. Put in the filling. Roll out the second piece of dough into a circle that is about 5cm/2in larger all round than the pie tin.

Apricot Lattice Pie
Toss together 1kg/2¼lb peeled, stoned and thinly sliced apricots, 30ml/2 tbsp plain (all-purpose) flour and 90g/3½oz sugar. Fill the pastry case and make a lattice top. Glaze with milk and bake in a 190°C/375°F/Gas 5 oven for about 45 minutes or until the pastry is golden and the filling is bubbling. Cool on a wire rack.

1 ▲ With the help of a ruler, cut neat straight strips of dough that are about 1cm/½in wide, using a knife or fluted pastry wheel.

3 ▲ Fold back every other strip from the centre. Lay another strip across the centre, on the flat strips, at right angles to them. Lay the folded strips flat again.

2 ▲ For a square woven lattice: Lay half of the strips across the pie filling, keeping them neatly parallel and spacing them evenly.

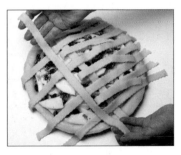

4 ▲ Now fold back those strips that were not folded the first time. Lay another strip across those that are flat now, spacing this new strip evenly from the centre strip.

5 ▲ Continue folding the strips in this way until half of the lattice is completed. Repeat on the other half of the pie.

6 ▲ Trim the ends of the strips even with the rim of the pie tin. Moisten the edge of the pastry case and press the strips gently to it to seal. Finish the edge.

7 ▲ For a diamond lattice: Weave as above, laying the intersecting strips diagonally instead of at right angles. Or lay half the strips over the filling and the remaining strips on top.

Making a Biscuit Case

A biscuit (cookie) case is one of the simplest bases to make, and the variations in flavouring are almost endless. Crumbs from any dry biscuit can be used, both sweet and savoury. You can also use breadcrumbs and cake crumbs. Most biscuit cases are sweet, to hold sweet fillings, but there are also unsweetened biscuit cases for savoury cheesecakes.

Makes a 20–23cm/8–9in case

225g/8oz/4 cups crushed biscuits (cookies)

115g/4oz/½ cup butter, melted

45–60ml/3–4 tbsp caster (superfine) sugar (optional)

Biscuit (cookie) case flavourings
● Use digestive biscuits (graham crackers). Sweeten with sugar to taste, if liked. Add 5ml/1 tsp ground cinnamon or ginger or mixed (apple pie) spice, or 2.5ml/½ tsp grated nutmeg.
● Use digestive biscuits and sweeten with sugar to taste, if liked. Add 5ml/1 tsp grated lemon zest or 10ml/2 tsp grated orange zest.
● Use 200g/7oz/3½ cups digestive biscuits and 40g/1½oz ground or finely chopped nuts.
● Use shortbread, ginger nut biscuits (gingersnaps), amaretti or crisp almond macaroons. No sugar is needed.
● Use water biscuits (crackers) or other savoury crackers, without adding sugar, for a savoury filling.

Crushing the biscuits (cookies)
To make fine biscuit crumbs, break the biscuits into small pieces. Put them, a small batch at a time, in a heavy plastic bag and roll over or bash them with a rolling pin. Alternatively, grind them finely in a blender or food processor.

1 ▲ Combine the biscuits, melted butter and sugar, plus any other flavourings, if using in a large bowl. Stir well to mix.

2 ▲ Turn the biscuit mixture into a buttered 20cm/8in springform cake tin (pan) or 34cm/9in tart tin. Spread it over the bottom and up the side.

3 ▲ With the back of a large smetal poon or your fingers, press the biscuit mixture firmly against the tin, to pack the crumbs into a solid crust in an even layer around the tin.

4 ▲ According to the recipe, refrigerate the case to set it, usually at least 1 hour. Or bake the case in a 180°C/350°F/Gas 4 oven for 8–10 minutes; cool before filling.

Easy Chocolate Tart
Prepare the biscuit (cookie) case using ginger nut biscuits (gingersnaps) and press it into a 23cm/9in tin (pan). Bake and cool. Melt 175g/6oz plain (semi-sweet) chocolate with 60ml/4 tbsp milk; cool. Whip 450ml/¾ pint/scant 2 cups double (heavy) or whipping cream until thick. Fold into the cooled chocolate. Spread evenly in the case. Cover and refrigerate until firm. Just before serving, garnish with chocolate curls or grated chocolate. *Serves 6.*

MAKING CHOUX PASTRY

Unlike other pastries, where the fat is rubbed into the flour, with choux pastry the butter is melted with water and then the flour is added, followed by eggs. The result is more of a paste than a pastry. It is fairly easy to make, but care must be taken in measuring the ingredients.

FOR 18 PROFITEROLES OR 12 ECLAIRS

115g/4oz/½ cup butter, cut into small pieces
250ml/8fl oz/1 cup water
10ml/2 tsp caster (superfine) sugar (optional)
1.25ml/¼ tsp salt
150g/5oz/1¼ cups plain (all-purpose) flour
4 eggs, beaten to mix

Shaping choux pastry
• For *large puffs*: Use two large spoons dipped in water. Drop the paste in 5–6cm/2–2½in wide blobs on the paper-lined baking sheet, leaving 4cm/1½in between each. Neaten the blobs as much as possible. Alternatively, for well-shaped puffs, pipe the paste using a piping bag fitted with a 2cm/¾in plain nozzle.
• For *profiteroles*: Use two small spoons or a piping bag fitted with a 1cm/½in nozzle and shape 2.5cm/1in blobs.
• For *éclairs*: Use a piping bag fitted with a 2cm/¾in nozzle. Pipe strips 10–12cm/4–5in long.
• For *a ring*: draw a circle with a diameter of 30cm/12in on the paper. Spoon the paste in large blobs on the circle to make a ring. Or pipe two rings round the circle and a third on top.

Baking times for choux pastry
Bake large puffs and éclairs 30–35 minutes, profiteroles 20–25 minutes, rings 40–45 minutes.

1 ▲ Combine the butter, water, sugar, if using, and salt in a large, heavy pan. Bring the mixture to the boil over moderately high heat, stirring occasionally.

3 ▲ Return the pan to moderate heat and cook, stirring, until the mixture will form a ball, pulling away from the side of the pan. This will take about 1 minute. Remove from the heat again and allow to cool for 3–5 minutes.

5 ▲ While still warm, shape large choux puffs, éclairs, profiteroles or large rings on a baking sheet lined with baking parchment.

2 ▲ As soon as the mixture is boiling, remove the pan from the heat. Add the flour all at once and beat vigorously with a wooden spoon to mix the flour into the liquid.

4 ▲ Add a little of the beaten egg and beat well with the spoon or an electric mixer to incorporate. Add a little more egg and beat in well. Continue beating in the eggs until the mixture becomes a smooth, shiny paste thick enough to hold its shape.

6 ▲ Glaze with 1 egg beaten with 5ml/1 tsp cold water. Put into a 220°C/425°F/Gas 7 oven, then reduce the heat to 200°C/400°F/Gas 6. Bake until puffed and golden brown.

MAKING CAKES BY THE CREAMING METHOD

The Victoria sandwich, with its tender crumb and rich, moist flavour, is always popular. It is delicious enough to be served plain, with just a dusting of sugar, or it can be filled and iced.

To make cakes by the creaming method, the fat and sugar are 'creamed' – or beaten – together before the eggs and dry ingredients are added. The fat (usually butter or margarine) should be soft enough to be beaten, so if necessary remove it from the refrigerator and leave it at room temperature for at least 30 minutes. For best results, the eggs should be at room temperature.

Mocha Victoria Sponge
Make the mixture using 175g/6oz/ ¾ cup fat, 175g/6oz/scant 1 cup caster (superfine) sugar and 175g/6oz/ 1½ cups self-raising (self-rising) flour and 3 eggs. Divide between two bowls. To one add 15ml/1 tbsp strong black coffee; to the other add 15ml/1 tbsp unsweetened cocoa powder mixed to a paste with 15–30ml/1–2 tbsp boiling water. Place alternate spoonfuls of each flavour, side by side, in two greased and bottom-lined 18cm/7in round sandwich tins (pans). Smooth the top. Bake at 180°C/350°F/Gas 4 for 25–30 minutes. Turn out on to a wire rack and leave to cool. Sandwich the cakes together with coffee buttercream. Cover the top, or top and sides, with buttercream.

1 ▲ Sift the flour with the salt, raising agent(s) and any other dry ingredients, such as ground spices or unsweetened cocoa powder. Set aside.

3 ▲ Add the sugar to the creamed fat gradually. With the mixer at medium-high speed, beat it into the fat until the mixture is pale and very fluffy. The sugar should be completely incorporated. This will take 4–5 minutes. During this process, air will be beaten into the mixture, which will help the cake to rise.

5 ▲ Add the dry ingredients to the mixture, beating at low speed just until smoothly combined. Or fold in with a large metal spoon.

2 ▲ Put the fat in a large, deep bowl and beat with an electric mixer at medium speed, or a wooden spoon, until the texture is soft and pliable.

4 ▲ Add the eggs or egg yolks, one at a time, beating well after each addition (about 45 seconds). Scrape the bowl often so all the ingredients are evenly combined. When adding the eggs, the mixture may begin to curdle, especially if the eggs are cold. If this happens, add 15ml/1 tbsp of the measured flour.

6 ▲ If the recipe calls for any liquid, add it in small portions alternately with portions of the dry ingredients.

7 ▲ If the recipe specifies, whisk egg whites separately until frothy, add sugar and continue whisking until stiff peaks form. Fold into the mixture.

8 ▲ Pour the mixture into a cake tin (pan) or tins, prepared according to the recipe, and bake as specified in a preheated oven.

9 ▲ To test creamed-method cakes, insert a metal skewer or wooden cocktail stick (toothpick) into the centre; it should come out clean.

Making American Frosting

This fluffy white frosting has an attractive gloss and a texture like meringue. It is a delicious filling and icing for sanwich cakes.

Makes enough to fill and ice a 23cm/9in sandwich cake

300g/10oz/1½ cups sugar
1.25ml/¼ tsp cream of tartar
2 egg whites
60ml/4 tbsp cold water
15ml/1 tbsp liquid glucose
10ml/2 tsp vanilla extract

1 ▲ Combine the sugar, cream of tartar, egg whites, water and glucose in a large heatproof bowl or the top of a double pan. Stir just to mix.

2 ▲ Set the bowl over a pan of boiling water. The base of the bowl should not touch the water.

Frosting variations

For *Orange Frosting*: Use orange juice instead of water and add 5ml/ 1 tsp grated orange zest. Reduce the vanilla to 2.5ml/½ tsp.

For *Lemon Frosting*: Use 30ml/ 2 tbsp each lemon juice and water and add 2.5ml/½ tsp grated lemon zest. Reduce the vanilla extract to 2.5ml/½ tsp.

3 ▲ Beat with a hand-held electric mixer at high speed for about 7 minutes or until the frosting is thick and white and will form stiff peaks.

4 ▲ Remove from the heat. Add the vanilla and continue beating for about 3 minutes or until the frosting has cooled slightly. Use immediately.

MAKING CAKES BY THE ALL-IN-ONE METHOD

Many cakes are made by an easy all-in-one method where all the ingredients are combined in a bowl and beaten thoroughly. The mixture can also be made in a food processor, but take care not to over-process. A refinement on the all-in-one method is to separate the eggs and make the mixture with the yolks. The whites are whisked separately and then folded in.

1 ▲ Sift the dry ingredients (flour, salt, raising agent, spices and so on) into a bowl.

2 ▲ Add the liquid ingredients (eggs, melted or soft fat, milk, fruit juices and so on) and beat until smooth, with an electric mixer for speed. Pour into the prepared tins (pans) and bake as specified in the recipe.

MAKING SIMPLE BUTTERCREAM

Quick to make and easy to spread, buttercream is ideal for all kinds of cakes, from simple ones to gâteaux. The basic buttercream can be varied with many other flavours, and it can be tinted with food colouring, too.

MAKES ENOUGH TO COVER THE TOP AND SIDE OF A 17–20CM/7–8IN CAKE

115g/4oz/½ cup butter, preferably unsalted, at room temperature

225g/8oz/2 cups icing (confectioners') sugar, sifted

5ml/1 tsp vanilla extract

about 30ml/2 tbsp milk

1 ▲ Put the butter in a deep mixing bowl and beat it with an electric mixer at medium speed, or a wooden spoon, until it is soft and pliable.

2 ▲ Gradually add the icing sugar and beat at medium-high speed. Continue beating until the mixture is pale and fluffy.

3 ▲ Add the vanilla extract and 15ml/1 tbsp milk. Beat until smooth and of a spreading consistency. If it is too thick, beat in more milk. If too thin, beat in more sugar.

Buttercream variations
● For *Orange or Lemon Buttercream*, grate the zest from 1 small orange or ½ lemon; squeeze the juice. Beat in the zest with the sugar; use the juice instead of the vanilla and milk.
● For *Chocolate Buttercream*, add 60ml/4 tbsp unsweetened cocoa powder, beating it in with the sugar. Increase the milk to 45–60ml/3–4 tbsp.

● For *Mocha Buttercream:* Warm the milk and dissolve 5ml/1 tsp instant coffee powder in it; cool and use to make chocolate buttercream, adding more milk if needed.
● For *Coffee Buttercream*, warm the milk and dissolve 15ml/1 tbsp of instant coffee powder in it; cool before adding to the buttercream.

MAKING CAKES BY THE MELTING METHOD

Cakes made by the melting method are wonderfully moist and keep quite well. Ingredients such as sugar, syrup (black treacle (molasses), honey or golden (light corn) syrup) and fat melted together and combined before being added to the dry ingredients.

Fruit Cake

Sift 225g/8oz/2 cups self-raising (self-rising) flour, a pinch of salt and 5ml/1 tsp mixed (apple pie) spice. Melt together 115g/4oz/½ cup butter or margarine, 115g/4oz/½ cup soft light brown sugar, 150ml/¼ pint/ ⅔ cup water and the grated zest and juice of 1 orange. When smooth, add 115g/4oz/⅔ cup each sultanas (golden raisins), currants and raisins and simmer gently for about 10 minutes, stirring occasionally. Cool. Add the fruit mixture to the dry ingredients. Add 50g/2oz/¼ cup each chopped glacé (candied) cherries and mixed chopped (candied) peel, 15ml/1 tbsp orange marmalade and 2 beaten eggs. Mix thoroughly. Pour into a lined 20cm/8in round cake tin (pan). Bake at 170°C/325°F/ Gas 3 for 1½ hours or until firm and golden; a skewer inserted in the centre should come out clean. Cool in the tin for 30 minutes before turning out on to a wire rack.

1 ▲ Sift the dry ingredients (such as flour, raising agent, salt, ground spices) into a large bowl.

2 ▲ Put the sugar and/or syrup and fat in a pan with any other ingredients specified in the recipe. Warm over a low heat, stirring occasionally, until the fat has melted and sugar dissolved. The mixture should not boil.

3 ▲ If the recipe instructs, warm fruit in the syrup mixture. Remove from the heat and leave to cool slightly (if too hot, it will not combine well with dry ingredients).

4 ▲ Make a well in the centre of the dry ingredients and pour in the cooled melted mixture. Add beaten eggs and any other liquid ingredients (milk, water, etc) and beat to a smooth, thick batter.

5 ▲ If called for in the recipe, stir in fruit and/or nuts (if these have not been warmed in the syrup). Turn the cake mixture into a lined tin (pan) and bake according to the recipe.

Maturing for flavour
Melting-method cakes taste best if they are allowed to 'mature' be-fore serving. After the cake has cooled completely, wrap it in baking parchment and then over-wrap in foil. Keep it in a cool place for 1–2 days before cutting into slices.

MAKING A CLASSIC WHISKED SPONGE

The classic whisked sponge contains no fat and no raising agents – just eggs, sugar and flour. The light, airy texture of the finished cake depends on the large quantity of air beaten into the mixture.

Sometimes the eggs are separated for a whisked sponge and sometimes the cake is enriched with butter. American angel cake uses egg whites only.

A whisked sponge can be simply dusted with icing (confectioners') or caster (superfine) sugar, filled with sweetened whipped cream, jam or fruit, or used to make a Swiss roll (jelly roll).

If you use a table-top electric mixer to beat the eggs and sugar, or if using separated eggs, there is no need to set the bowl over a pan of simmering water.

Whisked Sponge
Make the mixture using 4 eggs, 150g/5oz/¾ cup caster (superfine) sugar and 115g/4oz/1 cup plain (all-purpose) flour. Pour into a greased, bottom-lined and floured 23cm/9in round cake tin (pan). Bake in a 180°C/350°F/Gas 4 oven for 25–30 minutes. Cool in the tin for 10 minutes, then turn out on to a wire rack and cool completely. Before serving, peel off the paper. Dust the top with sifted icing (confectioners') sugar.

1 ▲ In a heatproof bowl, combine the eggs (at room temperature) and sugar. Set the bowl over a pan of simmering water; the base of the bowl should not touch the water.

3 ▲ Lift out the beaters; the mixture on the beaters should trail back on to the surface of the remaining mixture in the bowl to make a ribbon that holds it shape.

5 ▲ Sift the flour and fold it into the mixture, cutting in to the bottom of the bowl with a rubber spatula or large metal spoon and turning the mixture over, working gently yet thoroughly to retain the volume of the whisked egg and sugar mixture.

2 ▲ Beat with a hand-held electric mixer at medium-high speed, or a rotary beater or whisk, until the mixture is very thick and pale – about 10 minutes.

4 ▲ Remove the bowl from over the pan of water and continue beating for a further 2–3 minutes or until the mixture is cool.

6 ▲ Pour the mixture into the prepared tin (pan) or tins and bake as directed in the recipe in a preheated oven. To test whether a whisked sponge is cooked, press the centre lightly with your fingertip: the cake should spring back.

MAKING A SWISS ROLL

A rolled sponge reveals an attractive spiral of filling when it is sliced. The filling could be sweetened whipped cream, ice cream, fruit jam or buttercream.

The whisked sponge mixture can be made using whole or separated eggs, as preferred.

Line the tin (pan) with greaseproof (waxed) paper or baking parchment, grease the paper and dust with flour.

Chocolate Ice Cream Roll
Make the sponge mixture using 4 eggs, separated, 115g/4oz/generous ½ cup caster (superfine) sugar and 115g/4oz/1 cup plain (all-purpose) flour sifted with 45ml/3 tbsp unsweetened cocoa powder. Pour into a prepared 37.5 × 25cm/15 × 10in Swiss roll tin (jelly roll pan). Bake in a 190°C/375°F/Gas 5 oven for about 15 minutes. Turn out, roll up and cool. When cold, unroll the cake and spread with 600ml/1 pint/2½ cups softened vanilla or chocolate ice cream. Roll up the cake again, wrap in foil and freeze until firm. 30 minutes before serving, transfer the cake to the refrigerator. Sprinkle with sugar before serving. If you like, serve with warm bittersweet chocolate sauce. *Serves 8.*

1 ▲ Pour the mixture into the prepared tin and spread it evenly into the corners with a palette knife or metal spatula. Bake as specified in the recipe.

3 ▲ Carefully peel off the lining paper from the cake. If necessary, trim off any crisp edges from the side of the cake.

5 ▲ Once cold, remove the towel and unroll the cake. Remove the lining paper. Spread the chosen filling over the cake.

2 ▲ Spread a dish towel flat and lay a sheet of baking parchment on top. Sprinkle the paper, as specified, with caster sugar, unsweetened cocoa powder or a sugar and spice mixture. Invert the cake on to the paper.

4 ▲ Carefully roll up the cake, with the paper inside, starting from a short side. Wrap the towel round the cake roll and leave to cool on a wire rack.

6 ▲ Roll up the cake again, using the paper to help move it forward. Sprinkle with sugar or ice the cake, as the recipe specifies.

PREPARING CAKE TINS

Instructions vary from recipe to recipe for preparing cake tins (pans). Some are simply greased, some are greased and floured, some are lined with baking parchment or greased greaseproof (waxed) paper. The preparation depends on the type of cake mixture and the length of the baking time. Proper preparation aids turning out.

Flavourful coatings
Some cake recipes specify that the greased tin (pan) be coated with sugar, unsweetened cocoa powder or ground nuts. Follow the method given for flouring.

1 ▲ To grease a tin: Use butter, margarine, or a mild or flavourless oil. If using butter or margarine, hold a small piece in a kitchen paper (or use your fingers), and rub it all over the bottom and up the side of the tin to make a thin, even coating. If using oil, brush it on with a pastry brush.

2 ▲ To flour a tin: Put a small scoopful of flour in the centre of the greased tin. Tip and rotate the tin so that the flour spreads and coats all over the bottom and up the side. Turn the tin over and shake out excess flour, tapping the base of the tin to dislodge any pockets of flour.

3 ▲ To line the bottom of a tin: Set the tin on the sheet of baking parchment or greaseproof paper and draw round the base. Cut out this circle, square or rectangle, cutting just inside the drawn line. Press the paper smoothly on to the bottom of the tin.

4 ▲ To line the sides of a tin (for rich mixtures and fruit cakes): Cut a strip of paper long enough to wrap round the outside of the tin and overlap by 4cm/1½in. The strip should be wide enough to extend 2.5cm/1in above the rim of the tin.

5 ▲ Fold the strip lengthways at the 2.5cm/1in point and crease firmly. With scissors, snip at regular intervals along the 2.5cm/1in fold, from the edge to the crease. Line the side of the tin, with the snipped part of the strip on the bottom.

6 ▲ For square and rectangular cake tins, fold the paper and crease it with your fingernail to fit snugly into the corners of the tin. Then press the bottom paper lining into place.

7 ▲ If the recipe specifies, grease the paper using a brush or a piece of greaseproof paper before you put it in the tin. If the tin is to be floured, do this after the paper is in place.

8 ▲ To line bun and muffin tins: Use paper liners of the required size. Or grease and flour the tins.

9 ▲ To line a Swiss roll tin (jelly roll pan): Cut a rectangle of paper 5cm/2in larger all round than the tin. Grease the bottom of the tin lightly to prevent the paper from slipping.

10 ▲ Lay the paper evenly in the tin. With a table knife, press the paper into the angle all round the bottom of the tin, creasing the paper firmly but not cutting it.

11 ▲ With scissors, snip the paper in the corners, from top to bottom, so it will fit neatly into them. Grease the paper according to recipe instructions, unless using baking parchment.

USING SEPARATED EGGS FOR A WHISKED SPONGE

This version of whisked sponge is easier to make than the classic one that uses whole eggs, but the results are no less light and delicious. There is no need to set the bowl over a pan of simmering water for whisking, although if you are using a balloon whisk rather than an electric mixer or rotary beater you may want to do so to speed up the thickening of the egg yolk and sugar mixture and to increase its volume. All bowls and beaters used with egg whites must be scrupulously clean.

1 ▲ Separate the eggs, taking care that there is no trace of yolk with the whites. Put the yolks and whites in separate large bowls.

2 ▲ Add most of the sugar to the yolks. With a hand-held or table-top electric mixer, whisk at medium-high speed until the mixture is very thick and pale. Lift out the beaters: the mixture on the beaters should trail back on to the surface of the remaining mixture in the bowl to make a ribbon that holds its shape.

3 ▲ Whisk the egg whites until they form soft peaks (if not using a copper bowl, add a pinch of cream of tartar once the whites are frothy). Add the remaining sugar and continue whisking until the whites will form stiff peaks.

4 ▲ With a rubber spatula, fold the sifted flour into the egg yolk mixture, then fold in the whisked egg whites. Fold gently but thoroughly. Pour the mixture into the prepared tin (pan) and bake as instructed.

A Genoese sponge
This whisked sponge, made with whole or separated eggs, is more rich and trickier to make, as melted butter is folded in just before pouring into the tin (pan).

MAKING YEAST DOUGH

Making bread is a very enjoyable and satisfying culinary experience – with no other preparation do you have such 'hands-on' contact. And from the kneading through to the shaping of the risen (or proven) dough, you are working with a living organism, yeast, not a chemical raising agent. You can use either fresh yeast or dried yeast, which is available in an easy-blend (rapid-rise) variety too.

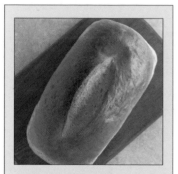

Everyday White Bread
Sift 700g/1½lb/6 cups strong white bread flour into a large bowl with 7.5ml/1½ tsp salt and 15ml/1 tbsp caster (superfine) sugar. Stir in 10ml/2 tsp easy-blend (rapid-rise) dried yeast. Make a well in the centre and add 450ml/¾ pint/scant 2 cups mixed warm water and milk and 25g/1oz/2 tbsp melted and cooled butter. Mix to a soft dough, adding more flour or liquid if necessary, then knead until smooth and elastic. Leave to rise until doubled in bulk. Knock back the dough to deflate. Divide it in half and shape each piece into a loaf, tucking the ends under. Put in two greased 21 × 11cm/8½ × 4½in loaf tins (pans). Leave in a warm place to rise for 30–45 minutes. Glaze the tops of the loaves with 1 egg beaten with 15ml/1 tbsp milk. Bake in a 230°C/450°F/Gas 8 oven for 30–35 minutes. *Makes 2 loaves.*

1 ▲ If using ordinary dried yeast, put it in a small bowl, add some of the warm liquid (40–43°C/105–110°F) called for in the recipe and whisk with a fork until dissolved. Add a little sugar if the recipe specifies it.

3 ▲ Using your fingers or a spoon, gradually draw the flour into the liquids. Mix until all the flour is incorporated and the dough pulls away from the sides of the bowl. If the dough feels too soft and wet, work in a little more flour. If it doesn't come together, add a little more liquid.

5 ▲ Shape the dough into a ball. Put it in a lightly greased bowl and turn the dough to grease all over. Cover the bowl with a towel or clear film (plastic wrap). Set it aside in a warm, draught-free place (about 27°C/80°F).

2 ▲ Sift the flour into a large warm bowl (with other dry ingredients such as salt). Make a well in the centre and add the yeast mixture plus any other liquid ingredients.

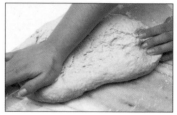

4 ▲ Turn the dough on to a lightly floured surface. Fold the dough over on to itself towards you and then press it down away from you with the heels of your hands. Rotate the dough slightly and fold and press it again. Knead until the dough looks satiny and feels elastic, about 10 minutes.

6 ▲ Leave to rise until about doubled in bulk, 1–1½ hours. To test if it is sufficiently risen, press a finger about 2.5cm/1in into the dough and withdraw it quickly; the indentation should remain.

7 ▲ Gently punch the centre of the dough with your fist to deflate it and fold the edges to the centre. Turn the dough on to a lightly floured surface and knead it again for 2–3 minutes. If instructed, shape the dough into a ball again and rise a second time.

8 ▲ Shape the dough into loaves, rolls or other shapes as instructed in the recipe. Put into prepared tins (pans) or on to baking sheets. Cover and leave to rise in a warm place for ¼–1 hour. If the recipe instructs, glaze the loaves or rolls.

9 ▲ Bake in the centre of a heated oven until well risen and golden brown. To test, tip the loaf out of the tin and tap the base with your knuckle. If it sounds hollow, like a drum, it is fully cooked. Immediately transfer to a wire rack for cooling.

SHAPING ROLLS

A basket of freshly baked bread rolls, in decorative shapes, is a delightful accompaniment for soups or salads. After shaping, arrange the rolls on a baking sheet, leaving space around each roll for spreading, and leave to rise for 30 minutes before baking.

Working with yeast
Easy-blend (rapid-rise) yeast is the most readily available dried yeast. Unlike ordinary dried yeast, there is no need to mix it with liquid. Just combine it with the flour and other dry ingredients and then add the warm liquids.

If using fresh yeast, allow 15g/½oz to each 15ml/1 tbsp dried. Crumble it into a small bowl, add warm liquid and mash the yeast with a fork until blended.

If you are in any doubt about the freshness of ordinary dried or fresh yeast, set the mixture aside in a warm place; after 10 minutes or so it should be foamy. If it isn't, discard it.

1 ▲ For Parker House rolls: Roll out the risen dough to 5mm/¼in thickness and cut out 6–7cm/2½–3in rounds using a floured cutter. Brush the rounds with melted butter. Fold them in half, slightly off-centre so the top overlaps the bottom. Press the folded edge firmly. Arrange the rolls on a greased baking sheet.

2 ▲ For crescent rolls: Roll out the risen dough to a large round 5mm/¼in thick. Brush with melted butter. With a sharp knife, cut into wedges that are 6–7cm/2½–3in at their wide end. Roll up each wedge, from the wide end. Set the rolls on a greased baking sheet, placing the points underneath.

3 ◀ For bowknot rolls: Divide the risen dough into pieces. Roll each with your palms on a lightly floured surface to make ropes that are about 1cm/½in thick. Divide the ropes into 23cm/9in lengths. Tie each rope loosely into a knot, tucking the ends under. Arrange the rolls on a greased baking sheet.

MAKING PIZZA DOUGH

The range of toppings for a pizza is virtually limitless. Although you can buy pizza bases, it's very easy to make your own at home, and takes much less time than you would expect.

MAKES A 35CM/14in PIZZA BASE

10ml/2 tsp dried yeast
175ml/6fl oz/¾ cup warm water
350g/12oz/3 cups strong white bread flour
5ml/1 tsp salt
22.5ml/1½ tbsp olive oil

Tomato and Mozzarella Pizza
Thinly spread 300ml/½ pint/1¼ cups tomato-garlic sauce over the pizza base, not quite to the edges. Scatter 115g/4oz/1 cup grated mozzarella cheese over the sauce (plus thinly sliced pepperoni or salami if you like). Sprinkle over freshly grated Parmesan cheese and then add a drizzle of olive oil. Bake in a 240°C/475°F/Gas 9 oven for 15–20 minutes.

Food processor pizza dough
Combine the flour, salt, yeast mixture and olive oil in the processor container. Process briefly, then add the rest of the warm water. Work until the dough begins to form a ball. Process 3–4 minutes to knead the dough, then knead it by hand for 2–3 minutes.

1 ▲ Put the yeast in a small bowl, add 60ml/4 tbsp of the water and soak for 1 minute. Whisk lightly with a fork until dissolved.

3 ▲ Using the fingers of one hand, gradually draw the flour into the liquid from the side of the bowl. Continue mixing until all the flour is incorporated and the dough will just hold together.

5 ▲ Cover the bowl with clear film (plastic wrap). Set aside in a warm place to rise about 1 hour or until doubled in bulk. Turn the dough on to the lightly floured surface again. Gently knock back to deflate it, then knead lightly until smooth.

2 ▲ Sift the flour and salt into a large warm bowl. Make a well in the centre and add the yeast mixture, olive oil and remaining warm water.

4 ▲ Turn the dough on to a lightly floured surface. Knead it until it is smooth and silky, about 5 minutes. Shape the dough into a ball. Put it in an oiled bowl and rotate to coat the surface evenly with oil.

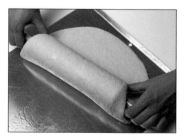

6 ▲ Roll out the dough into a round or square about 5mm/¼in thick. Transfer it to a lightly oiled metal pizza tin (pan) or baking sheet. Add the topping as specified in the recipe. Bake until the pizza crust is puffy and well browned. Serve hot.

MAKING FOCACCIA AND BREAD STICKS

Italian flatbreads, such as focaccia, and bread sticks can be topped with herbs and seeds for tasty accompaniments or starters. Personalize them with combinations of your favourite ingredients for unusual snacks, or split and fill flatbreads with ham or cheese for an Italian-style sandwich.

This basic dough can be used for other recipes, such as pizza. The dough may be frozen before it is baked, and thawed before filling.

1 ▲ **For focaccia:** Warm a mixing bowl by swirling some hot water in it. Drain the water. Place the yeast in the bowl and pour on the warm water. Stir in the sugar, mix with a fork, and allow the mixture to stand until the yeast has dissolved and starts to foam, 5–10 minutes.

Different types of focaccia
Focaccia makes an ideal base for a wide range of different toppings, from simple enhancement such as a sprinkling of sea salt, sesame seeds or finely chopped herbs such as rosemary or thyme, to more complex additions such as sun-dried tomatoes, sliced onions or cubes of cheese such as mozzarella, or a combination, such as garlic, black olives and sliced onions.

The basic dough mixture can also be enhanced by the addition of dried herbs and strong flavours such as soaked saffron, which lends the bread a lovely colour as well as flavour.

2 ▲ Use a wooden spoon to mix in the salt and about one-third of the flour. Mix in another third of the flour, stirring with the spoon until the dough forms a mass and begins to pull away from the sides of the bowl.

3 ▲ Sprinkle some of the remaining flour on to a smooth work surface. Remove the dough from the bowl and begin to knead it, working in the remaining flour a little at a time. Knead for 8–10 minutes. By the end the dough should be elastic and smooth. Form it into a ball.

4 Lightly oil a mixing bowl. Place the dough in the bowl. Stretch a damp dish towel or clear film (plastic wrap) across the top of the bowl, and leave it to stand in a warm place until the dough has doubled in volume, about 40–50 minutes or more, depending on the type of yeast used. To test whether the dough has risen enough, poke two fingers into the dough. If the indentations remain, the dough is ready to use.

5 ▲ Punch the dough down with your fist to release the air. Knead for 1–2 minutes.

6 ▲ Brush a tin (pan) with oil. Press the dough into the tin with your fingers to a layer 2cm/1in thick. Cover and leave to rise for 30 minutes. Preheat the oven. Make indentations all over the focaccia with your fingers. Brush with oil, add filling and bake until pale golden brown.

7 ▲ **For bread sticks:** There's no need for the first rising. Divide dough into walnut-size pieces and roll out on a floured surface with your hands, into thin sausage shapes. Transfer to a greased baking tray, cover and leave in a warm place for 10–15 minutes. Bake until crisp.

BISCUITS & BARS

KEEP THE BISCUIT (COOKIE) JAR
FILLED WITH THIS WONDERFUL
ARRAY OF BISCUITS AND BARS —
SOME SOFT AND CHEWY, SOME
CRUNCHY AND NUTTY, SOME
RICH AND SINFUL, AND SOME
PLAIN AND WHOLESOME. ALL
ARE IRRESISTIBLE.

Farmhouse Biscuits

Makes 18

115g/4oz/1/2 cup butter or margarine, at room temperature

90g/31/2oz/1/2 cup soft light brown sugar

65g/21/2oz/1/4 cup crunchy peanut butter

1 egg

50g/2oz/1/2 cup plain (all-purpose) flour

2.5ml/1/2 tsp baking powder

2.5ml/1/2 tsp ground cinnamon

0.6ml/1/8 tsp salt

175g/6oz/11/2 cups muesli

50g/2oz/scant 1/2 cup raisins

50g/2oz chopped walnuts

1 Preheat a 180°C/350°F/Gas 4 oven. Grease a baking sheet.

2 With an electric mixer, cream the butter or margarine and sugar until light and fluffy. Beat in the peanut butter. Beat in the egg.

3 ▲ Sift the flour, baking powder, cinnamon and salt over the peanut butter mixture and stir to blend. Stir in the muesli, raisins and walnuts. Taste the mixture to see if it needs more sugar, as muesli varies.

4 ▲ Drop rounded tablespoonfuls of the mixture on to the prepared baking sheet about 2.5cm/1in apart. Press gently with the back of a spoon to spread each mound into a circle.

5 Bake in the preheated oven for about 15 minutes, until lightly coloured. With a metal spatula, transfer to a wire rack to cool. Store in an airtight container.

Crunchy Oatmeal Biscuits

MAKES 14

175g/6oz/3/4 cup butter or margarine, at room temperature

175g/6oz/scant 1 cup caster (superfine) sugar

1 egg yolk

175g/6oz/11/2 cups plain (all-purpose) flour

5ml/1 tsp bicarbonate of soda (baking soda)

2.5ml/1/2 tsp salt

50g/2oz/scant 1/2 cup rolled oats

50g/2oz small crunchy nugget cereal

1 ▲ With an electric mixer, cream the butter or margarine and sugar together for about 5 minutes, until light and fluffy. Add the egg yolk and beat to combine well.

2 Sift over the flour, bicarbonate of soda and salt, then stir into the butter mixture. Add the oats and cereal and stir to blend thoroughly. Refrigerate for at least 20 minutes.

3 Preheat a 190°C/375°F/Gas 5 oven. Grease a baking sheet.

4 ▲ Roll the mixture into balls. Place them on the sheet and flatten with the bottom of a floured glass.

5 Bake until golden, 10–12 minutes. With a metal spatula, transfer to a rack to cool completely. Store in an airtight container.

~ VARIATION ~

For Nutty Oatmeal Biscuits, substitute an equal quantity of chopped walnuts or pecans for the cereal, and prepare as described.

Farmhouse: Energy 165kcal/688kJ; Protein 2.9g; Carbohydrate 16.9g, of which sugars 10.1g; Fat 10g, of which saturates 4.1g; Cholesterol 24mg; Calcium 25mg; Fibre 1.1g; Sodium 94mg.
Crunchy: Energy 220kcal/923kJ; Protein 2.3g; Carbohydrate 27.6g, of which sugars 14.3g; Fat 11.9g, of which saturates 6.8g; Cholesterol 41mg; Calcium 33mg; Fibre 0.8g; Sodium 81mg.

Oaty Coconut Biscuits

MAKES 48

175g/6oz/1³/4 cups rolled oats

75g/3oz desiccated (dry unsweetened shredded) coconut

225g/8oz/1 cup butter or margarine, at room temperature

115g/4oz/generous ¹/2 cup caster sugar, plus 30ml/2 tbsp

50g/2oz/4 tbsp soft dark brown sugar

2 eggs

60ml/4 tbsp milk

7.5ml/1¹/2 tsp vanilla extract

115g/4oz/1 cup plain (all-purpose) flour

2.5ml/¹/2 tsp bicarbonate of soda (baking soda)

2.5ml/¹/2 tsp salt

5ml/1 tsp ground cinnamon

1 Preheat a 200°C/400°F/Gas 6 oven. Lightly grease two baking sheets.

2 ▲ Spread the oats and coconut on an ungreased baking sheet. Bake for 8–10 minutes, until golden brown, stirring occasionally.

3 With an electric mixer, cream the butter or margarine and both sugars until light and fluffy. Beat in the eggs, one at a time, then the milk and vanilla. Sift over the dry ingredients and fold in. Stir in the oats and coconut.

4 ▼ Drop spoonfuls of the mixture 2.5–5cm/1–2in apart on the prepared sheets and flatten with the bottom of a greased glass dipped in sugar. Bake for 8–10 minutes, until golden. Transfer to a rack to cool.

Crunchy Jumbles

MAKES 36

115g/4oz/¹/2 cup butter, at room temperature

225g/8oz/generous 1 cup caster (superfine) sugar

1 egg

5ml/1 tsp vanilla extract

150g/5oz/1¹/4 cups plain (all-purpose) flour

2.5ml/¹/2 tsp bicarbonate of soda (baking soda)

0.6ml/¹/8 tsp salt

50g/2oz crisped rice cereal

175g/6oz/2 cups chocolate chips

~ VARIATION ~

Add 45ml/3 tbsp chopped walnuts, with the cereal and chocolate chips.

---

1 Preheat a 180°C/350°F/Gas 4 oven. Lightly grease two baking sheets.

2 ▲ With an electric mixer, cream the butter and sugar until light and fluffy. Beat in the egg and vanilla. Sift over the flour, bicarbonate of soda and salt and fold in carefully.

3 ▼ Add the cereal and chocolate chips. Stir to mix thoroughly.

4 Drop spoonfuls of the mixture 2.5–5cm/1–2in apart on the prepared baking sheets. Bake until golden, 10–12 minutes. Transfer to a wire rack to cool.

Biscuits: Energy 84kcal/352kJ; Protein 1.1g; Carbohydrate 8.3g, of which sugars 3.8g; Fat 5.4g, of which saturates 3.4g; Cholesterol 18mg; Calcium 11mg; Fibre 0.5g; Sodium 34mg.
Jumbles: Energy 95kcal/398kJ; Protein 0.9g; Carbohydrate 14.2g, of which sugars 9.8g; Fat 4.2g, of which saturates 2.5g; Cholesterol 12mg; Calcium 18mg; Fibre 0.3g; Sodium 31mg.

Ginger Biscuits

MAKES 36

225g/8oz/generous 1 cup caster
  (superfine) sugar

100g/3½oz/scant ½ cup soft light
  brown sugar

115g/4oz/½ cup butter,
  at room temperature

115g/4oz/½ cup margarine,
  at room temperature

1 egg

90ml/6 tbsp black treacle (molasses)

250g/9oz/2¼ cups plain
  (all-purpose) flour

10ml/2 tsp ground ginger

2.5ml/½ tsp grated nutmeg

5ml/1 tsp ground cinnamon

10ml/2 tsp bicarbonate of soda
  (baking soda)

2.5ml/½ tsp salt

1 Preheat a 170°C/325°F/Gas 3 oven.
Line serveral baking sheets with
baking parchment and grease lightly.

2 ▲ With an electric mixer, cream
half of the caster sugar, the brown
sugar, butter and margarine until
light and fluffy. Add the egg and
continue beating to blend well.
Add the treacle.

3 ▲ Sift the flour, spices and
bicarbonate of soda three times,
then stir into the butter mixture.
Refrigerate for 30 minutes.

4 ▲ Place the remaining sugar in a
shallow dish. Roll tablespoonfuls of
the biscuit mixture into balls, then
roll the balls in the sugar to coat.

5 Place the balls 5cm/2in apart
on the prepared sheets and flatten
slightly. Bake until golden around the
edges but soft in the middle, 12–15
minutes. Let stand for 5 minutes
before transferring to a rack to cool.

~ VARIATION ~

To make Gingerbread Men, increase
the amount of flour by 25g/1oz. Roll
out the mixture and cut out shapes
with a special cutter. Decorate with
icing, if wished.

Energy 57kcal/239kJ; Protein 0.6g; Carbohydrate 10.3g, of which sugars 6.8g; Fat 1.7g, of which saturates 1g; Cholesterol 7mg; Calcium 16mg; Fibre 0.1g; Sodium 15mg.

Orange Biscuits

MAKES 30

115g/4oz/¹/₂ cup butter, at room temperature
200g/7oz/1 cup sugar
2 egg yolks
15ml/1 tbsp fresh orange juice
grated rind of 1 large orange
190g/6¹/₂oz/1²/₃ cups plain (all-purpose) flour
15ml/1 tbsp cornflour (cornstarch)
2.5ml/¹/₂ tsp salt
5ml/1 tsp baking powder

1 ▲ With an electric mixer, cream the butter and sugar until light and fluffy. Add the yolks, orange juice and rind, and continue beating to blend. Set aside.

2 In another bowl, sift together the flour, cornflour, salt and baking powder. Add to the butter mixture and stir until it forms a dough.

4 Preheat the oven to 190°C/375°F/ Gas 5. Grease two baking sheets.

6 ▼ Press down with a fork to flatten. Bake until golden brown, 8–10 minutes. With a metal spatula transfer to a wire rack to cool.

3 ▲ Wrap the dough in baking parchment and refrigerate for 2 hours.

5 ▲ Roll spoonfuls of the dough into balls and place 2.5–5cm/1–2in apart on the prepared sheets.

Energy 83kcal/350kJ; Protein 0.9g; Carbohydrate 12.6g, of which sugars 7.1g; Fat 3.6g, of which saturates 2.1g; Cholesterol 22mg; Calcium 15mg; Fibre 0.2g; Sodium 25mg.

Cinnamon-Coated Cookies

MAKES 30

115g/4oz/¹/₂ cup butter, at room
   temperature

250g/12oz/scant 2 cups caster
   (superfine) sugar

5ml/1 tsp vanilla extract

2 eggs

50ml/2fl oz/¹/₄ cup milk

400g/14oz/generous 3¹/₃ cups plain
   (all-purpose) flour

5ml/1 tsp bicarbonate of soda
   (baking soda)

50g/2oz finely chopped walnuts

FOR THE COATING

75ml/5 tbsp sugar

30ml/2 tbsp ground cinnamon

1 Preheat a 190°C/375°F/Gas 5 oven.
Grease two baking sheets.

2 With an electric mixer, cream the
butter until light. Add the sugar and
vanilla and continue mixing until
fluffy. Beat in the eggs, then the milk.

3 ▲ Sift the flour and bicarbonate of
soda over the butter mixture and stir
to blend. Stir in the nuts. Refrigerate
for 15 minutes.

4 ▲ For the coating, mix the sugar
and cinnamon. Roll tablespoonfuls
of the mixture into walnut-size balls.
Roll the balls in the sugar mixture.
You may need to work in batches.

5 Place 5cm/2in apart on the
prepared sheets and flatten slightly.
Bake until golden, about 10 minutes.
Transfer to a rack to cool.

Chewy Chocolate Biscuits

MAKES 18

4 egg whites

275g/10oz/2¹/₂ cups icing
   (confectioners') sugar

115g/4oz/1 cup unsweetened cocoa powder

30ml/2 tbsp plain (all-purpose) flour

5ml/1 tsp instant coffee powder

15ml/1 tbsp water

115g/4oz finely chopped walnuts

1 Preheat a 180°C/350°F/Gas 4 oven.
Line two baking sheets with baking
parchment and grease the paper.

~ VARIATION ~

If wished, add 75g/3oz/5 tbsp
chocolate chips with the nuts.

2 With an electric mixer, beat the
egg whites until frothy.

3 ▼ Sift the sugar, cocoa, flour and
coffee into the whites. Add the water
and continue beating on low speed to
blend, then on high for a few minutes
until the mixture thickens. With a
rubber spatula, fold in the walnuts.

4 ▲ Place generous spoonfuls of
the mixture 2.5cm/1in apart on the
prepared sheets. Bake until firm and
cracked on top but soft on the inside,
12–15 minutes. With a metal spatula,
transfer to a rack to cool.

Cookies: Energy 124kcal/519kJ; Protein 2g; Carbohydrate 18g, of which sugars 8g; Fat 5g, of which saturates 2g; Cholesterol 24mg; Calcium 33mg; Fibre 1g; Sodium 31mg.
Biscuits: Energy 136kcal/573kJ; Protein 3g; Carbohydrate 19g, of which sugars 17g; Fat 6g, of which saturates 1g; Cholesterol 0mg; Calcium 18mg; Fibre 0g; Sodium 77mg.

Chocolate Pretzels

3 ▲ Roll the dough into 28 small balls. Refrigerate the balls until needed. Preheat the oven to 190°C/375°F/Gas 5.

4 ▲ Roll each ball into a rope about 25cm/10in long. With each rope, form a loop with the two ends facing you. Twist the ends and fold back on to the circle, pressing in to make a pretzel shape. Place on the sheets.

5 ▲ Brush the pretzels with the egg white. Sprinkle sugar crystals over the tops and bake until firm, 10–12 minutes. Transfer to a rack to cool.

MAKES 28

150g/5oz/1¹/₄ cups plain (all-purpose) flour

0.6ml/¹/₈ tsp salt

25g/1oz/¹/₄ cup unsweetened cocoa powder

115g/4oz/¹/₂ cup butter, at room temperature

150g/5oz/³/₄ cup sugar

1 egg

1 egg white, lightly beaten, for glazing

sugar crystals, for sprinkling

2 ▲ With an electric mixer, cream the butter until light. Add the sugar and continue beating until light and fluffy. Beat in the egg. Add the dry ingredients and stir to blend. Gather the dough into a ball, wrap in clear film (plastic wrap), and refrigerate for 1 hour or freeze for 30 minutes.

1 Sift together the flour, salt and cocoa powder. Set aside. Grease two baking sheets.

Energy 72kcal/303kJ; Protein 1g; Carbohydrate 9.1g, of which sugars 5g; Fat 3.8g, of which saturates 2.3g; Cholesterol 16mg; Calcium 13mg; Fibre 0.3g; Sodium 37mg.

Cream Cheese Spirals

MAKES 32

225g/8oz/1 cup butter,
  at room temperature

225g/8oz/1 cup cream cheese

10ml/2 tsp caster (superfine) sugar

225g/8oz/2 cups plain
  (all-purpose) flour

1 egg white beaten with 15ml/1 tbsp
  water, for glazing

caster sugar, for sprinkling

FOR THE FILLING

115g/4oz finely chopped walnuts

115g/4oz/1/2 cup soft light brown sugar

5ml/1 tsp ground cinnamon

1 With an electric mixer, cream the butter, cream cheese and sugar until soft. Sift over the flour and mix until combined. Gather into a ball and divide in half. Flatten each half, wrap in greaseproof (waxed) paper and refrigerate for at least 30 minutes.

2 Meanwhile, make the filling. Mix together the chopped walnuts, the brown sugar and the cinnamon and set aside.

3 Preheat a 190°C/375°F/Gas 5 oven. Grease two baking sheets.

4 ▲ Working with one half of the mixture at a time, roll out thinly into a circle about 28cm/11in in diameter. Trim the edges with a knife, using a dinner plate as a guide.

5 ▼ Brush the surface with the egg white glaze and then sprinkle evenly with half the filling.

6 Cut the circle into quarters, and each quarter into four sections, to form 16 triangles.

7 ▲ Starting from the base of the triangles, roll up to form spirals.

8 Place on the sheets and brush with the remaining glaze. Sprinkle with caster sugar. Bake until golden, 15–20 minutes. Cool on a rack.

Energy 150kcal/621kJ; Protein 1.7g; Carbohydrate 9.7g, of which sugars 4.3g; Fat 11.8g, of which saturates 6g; Cholesterol 28mg; Calcium 24mg; Fibre 0.3g; Sodium 67mg.

Vanilla Crescents

MAKES 36

175g/6oz/1 cup unblanched almonds

115g/4oz/1 cup plain (all-purpose) flour

pinch of salt

115g/4oz/¹/₂ cup unsalted butter

115g/4oz/scant ³/₄ cup sugar

5ml/1 tsp vanilla extract

icing (confectioners') sugar for dusting

1 Grind the almonds with a few tablespoons of the flour in a food processor, blender or nut grinder.

2 Sift the remaining flour with the salt into a bowl. Set aside.

3 With an electric mixer, cream together the butter and sugar until light and fluffy.

4 ▼ Add the almonds, vanilla extract and the flour mixture. Stir to mix well. Gather the dough into a ball, wrap in baking parchment, and chill for at least 30 minutes.

5 Preheat the oven to 170°C/325°F/ Gas 3. Lightly grease two baking sheets with butter.

6 ▲ Break off walnut-size pieces of dough and roll into small cylinders about 1cm/¹/₂in in diameter. Bend into small crescents and place on the prepared baking sheets.

7 Bake for about 20 minutes until dry but not brown. Transfer to a wire rack to cool only slightly. Set the rack over a baking sheet and dust with an even layer of icing sugar. Leave to cool completely.

Walnut Crescents

MAKES 72

115g/4oz/²/₃ cup walnuts

115g/4oz/¹/₂ cup unsalted butter

115g/4oz/scant ³/₄ cup sugar

2.5ml/¹/₂ tsp vanilla extract

225g/8oz/2 cups plain (all-purpose) flour

1.25ml/¹/₄ tsp salt

icing (confectioners') sugar, for dusting

1 Preheat the oven to 180°C/350°F/ Gas 4.

2 Grind the walnuts in a food processor, blender or nut grinder until they are almost a paste. Transfer to a bowl.

3 Add the butter to the walnuts and mix with a wooden spoon until blended. Add the sugar and vanilla extract and stir to blend.

4 ▼ Sift the flour and salt into the walnut mixture. Work into a dough.

5 Shape the dough into small cylinders about 4cm/1¹/₂in long. Bend into crescents and place evenly spaced on an ungreased baking sheet.

6 ▲ Bake until lightly browned, about 15 minutes. Transfer to a rack to cool only slightly. Set the rack over a baking sheet and dust lightly with icing sugar.

Vanilla: Energy 100kcal/414kJ; Protein 1g; Carbohydrate 6g, of which sugars 4g; Fat 8g, of which saturates 3g; Cholesterol 13mg; Calcium 18mg; Fibre 1g; Sodium 39mg.
Walnut: Energy 51kcal/213kJ; Protein 1g; Carbohydrate 4g, of which sugars 2g; Fat 4g, of which saturates 2g; Cholesterol 7mg; Calcium 7mg; Fibre 0g; Sodium 26mg.

Pecan Puffs

MAKES 24

115g/4oz/¹/₂ cup unsalted butter

30ml/2 tbsp sugar

pinch of salt

5ml/1 tsp vanilla extract

115g/4oz/²/₃ cup pecans

115g/4oz/1 cup plain (all-purpose)
  flour, sifted

icing (confectioners') sugar,
  for dusting

1 Preheat the oven to 150°C/300°F/
Gas 2. Grease two baking sheets.

2 ▲ Cream the butter and sugar
until light and fluffy. Stir in the salt
and vanilla extract.

3 Grind the nuts in a food processor,
blender or nut grinder. Stir several
times to prevent nuts becoming oily.
If necessary, grind in batches.

4 ▲ Push the ground nuts through
a sieve (strainer) set over a bowl to
aerate them. Pieces too large to go
through can be ground again.

5 ▲ Stir the nuts and flour into the
butter mixture to make a firm,
springy dough.

6 Roll the dough into marble-size
balls between the palms of your
hands. Place on the prepared baking
sheets and bake for 45 minutes.

7 ▲ While the puffs are still hot,
roll them in icing sugar. Leave to cool
completely, then roll once more in
icing sugar.

Energy 90kcal/373kJ; Protein 1g; Carbohydrate 5g, of which sugars 2g; Fat 7g, of which saturates 3g; Cholesterol 10mg; Calcium 12mg; Fibre 0g; Sodium 30mg.

Pecan Tassies

MAKES 24

115g/4oz/¹/2 cup cream cheese
115g/4oz/¹/2 cup butter
115g/4oz/1 cup plain (all-purpose) flour
FOR THE FILLING
2 eggs
115g/4oz/¹/2 cup soft dark brown sugar
5ml/1 tsp vanilla extract
pinch of salt
30ml/2 tbsp butter, melted
115g/4oz/1 cup pecans

1 Place a baking sheet in the oven and preheat to 180°C/350°F/Gas 4. Grease 24 mini-muffin tins (pans).

2 Chop the cream cheese and butter into cubes. Put them in a mixing bowl. Sift over half the flour and mix. Add the remaining flour and continue mixing to form a dough.

3 ▲ Roll out the dough thinly. With a floured fluted pastry cutter, stamp out 24 7cm/2¹/2in rounds. Line the tins with the rounds and chill.

~ **VARIATION** ~

To make Jam Tassies, fill the cream cheese pastry shells with raspberry or blackberry jam, or other fruit jams. Bake as described.

4 To make the filling, lightly whisk the eggs in a bowl. Gradually whisk in the brown sugar, and add the vanilla extract, salt and butter. Set aside until required.

5 ▼ Reserve 24 undamaged pecan halves and chop the rest coarsely with a sharp knife.

6 ▲ Place a spoonful of chopped nuts in each muffin tin and cover with the filling. Set a pecan half on the top of each.

7 Bake on the hot baking sheet for about 20 minutes, until puffed and set. Transfer to a wire rack to cool. Serve at room temperature.

Energy 140kcal/582kJ; Protein 2g; Carbohydrate 9g, of which sugars 5g; Fat 11g, of which saturates 5g; Cholesterol 37mg; Calcium 23mg; Fibre 0g; Sodium 60mg.

Lady Fingers

MAKES 18

90g/3¹/₂oz/³/₄ cup plain (all-purpose) flour

pinch of salt

4 eggs, separated

115g/4oz/scant ³/₄ cup sugar

2.5ml/¹/₂ tsp vanilla extract

icing (confectioners') sugar, for sprinkling

1 Preheat the oven to 150°C/300°F/ Gas 2. Grease two baking sheets, then coat lightly with flour, and shake off the excess.

2 Sift the flour and salt together twice in a bowl.

~ COOK'S TIP ~

To make the biscuits (cookies) all the same length, mark parallel lines 10cm/4in apart on the greased baking sheets.

3 With an electric mixer beat the egg yolks with half of the sugar until thick enough to leave a ribbon trail when the beaters are lifted.

4 ▲ In another bowl, beat the egg whites until stiff. Beat in the remaining sugar until glossy.

5 Sift the flour over the yolks and spoon a large dollop of egg whites over the flour. Carefully fold in with a large metal spoon, adding the vanilla extract. Gently fold in the remaining whites.

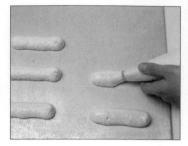

6 ▲ Spoon the mixture into a piping bag fitted with a large plain nozzle. Pipe 10cm/4in long lines on the prepared baking sheets about 2.5cm/1in apart.

7 Sift over a layer of icing sugar. Turn the sheet upside down to dislodge any excess sugar.

8 Bake for about 20 minutes until crusty on the outside but soft in the centre. Cool slightly on the baking sheets before transferring to a wire rack to cool completely.

Walnut Cookies

MAKES 60

115g/4oz/¹/₂ cup butter

175g/6oz/scant 1 cup caster (superfine) sugar

115g/4oz/1 cup plain (all-purpose) flour,

10ml/2 tsp vanilla extract

115g/4oz walnuts, finely chopped

~ VARIATION ~

To make Almond Cookies, use an equal amount of finely chopped unblanched almonds instead of walnuts. Replace half the vanilla with 2.5ml/ ¹/₂ tsp almond extract.

1 Preheat the oven to 150°C/300°F/ Gas 2. Grease two baking sheets.

2 ▲ With an electric mixer, cream the butter or margarine until soft. Add 50g/2oz/¹/₄ cup of the sugar and continue beating until light and fluffy. Stir in the flour, vanilla and walnuts.

3 Drop teaspoonfuls of the batter 2.5–5cm/1–2in apart on the prepared baking sheets and flatten slightly. Bake for about 25 minutes.

4 ▼ Transfer to a wire rack set over a baking sheet and sprinkle with the remaining sugar.

Fingers: Energy 62kcal/263kJ; Protein 2g; Carbohydrate 11g, of which sugars 7g; Fat 2g, of which saturates 0g; Cholesterol 52mg; Calcium 16mg; Fibre 0g; Sodium 19mg.
Cookies: Energy 45kcal/190kJ; Protein 0g; Carbohydrate 5g, of which sugars 3g; Fat 3g, of which saturates 1g; Cholesterol 4mg; Calcium 5mg; Fibre 0g; Sodium 12mg.

Italian Almond Biscotti

MAKES 48

200g/7oz/scant 2 cups whole unblanched almonds
225g/8oz/2 cups plain (all-purpose) flour
90g/3¹/₂oz/¹/₂ cup sugar
0.6ml/¹/₈ tsp salt
0.6ml/¹/₈ tsp saffron powder
2.5ml/¹/₂ tsp bicarbonate of soda (baking soda)
2 eggs
1 egg white, lightly beaten

~ COOK'S TIP ~

Serve biscotti after a meal, for dunking in glasses of sweet white wine, such as an Italian *Vin Santo* or a French *Muscat de Beaumes-de-Venise*.

1 Preheat a 190°C/375°F/Gas 5 oven. Grease and flour two baking sheets.

2 ▲ Spread the almonds in a baking tray and bake until lightly browned, about 15 minutes. When cool, grind 50g/2oz/¹/₂ cup of the almonds in a food processor, blender, or coffee grinder until pulverized. Coarsely chop the remaining almonds in two or three pieces each. Set aside.

3 ▲ Combine the flour, sugar, salt, saffron, bicarbonate of soda and ground almonds in a bowl and mix to blend. Make a well in the centre and add the eggs. Stir to form a rough dough. Transfer to a floured surface and knead until well blended. Knead in the chopped almonds.

4 ▲ Divide the dough into three equal parts. Roll into logs about 2.5cm/1in diameter. Place on one of the prepared sheets, brush with the egg white and bake for 20 minutes. Remove from the oven.

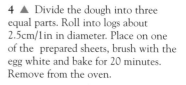

5 ▲ With a very sharp knife, cut into each log at an angle making 1cm/¹/₂in slices. Return the slices on the baking sheets to a 140°C/275°F/Gas 1 oven and bake for 25 minutes more. Transfer to a wire rack to cool.

Energy 53kcal/222kJ; Protein 2g; Carbohydrate 6g, of which sugars 2g; Fat 3g, of which saturates 0g; Cholesterol 10mg; Calcium 18mg; Fibre 1g; Sodium 22mg.

Christmas Cookies

MAKES 30

175g/6oz/³/4 cup unsalted butter,
  at room temperature

300g/10oz/1¹/2 cups caster (superfine) sugar

1 egg

1 egg yolk

5ml/1 tsp vanilla extract

grated rind of 1 lemon

1.25ml/¹/4 tsp salt

275g/10oz/2¹/2 cups plain (all-purpose) flour

FOR DECORATING (OPTIONAL)

coloured icing and small decorations

1 Preheat a 180°C/350°F/Gas 4 oven.

2 ▲ With an electric mixer, cream the butter until soft. Add the sugar gradually and continue beating until light and fluffy.

3 ▲ Using a wooden spoon, slowly mix in the whole egg and the egg yolk. Add the vanilla, lemon rind and salt. Stir to mix well. Add the flour and stir until blended.

4 Gather the mixture into a ball, wrap in greaseproof (waxed) paper or clear film (plastic wrap) paper, and refrigerate for at least 30 minutes.

5 ▼ On a floured surface, roll out the mixture about 3mm/¹/8in thick.

6 ▲ Stamp out shapes or rounds with pastry cutters.

7 Bake until lightly coloured, about 8 minutes. Transfer to a wire rack and let cool completely before icing and decorating, if wished.

Energy 118kcal/495kJ; Protein 1.3g; Carbohydrate 17.3g, of which sugars 10.1g; Fat 5.3g, of which saturates 3.2g; Cholesterol 26mg; Calcium 21mg; Fibre 0.3g; Sodium 39mg.

Toasted Oat Meringues

MAKES 12

50g/2oz/scant 1/2 cup rolled oats
2 egg whites
0.6ml/1/8 tsp salt
7.5ml/1 1/2 tsp cornflour (cornstarch)
175g/6oz/scant 1 cup caster (superfine) sugar

1 Preheat a 140°C/275°F/Gas 1 oven. Spread the oats on a baking sheet and toast until golden, about 10 minutes. Lower the heat to 130°C/250°F/Gas 1/2. Grease and flour a baking sheet.

~ VARIATION ~

Add 2.5ml/1/2 tsp ground cinnamon with the oats, and fold in gently.

---

2 ▼ With an electric mixer, beat the egg whites and salt until they start to form soft peaks.

3 Sift over the cornflour and continue beating until the whites hold stiff peaks. Add half the sugar and whisk until glossy.

4 ▲ Add the remaining sugar and fold in, then fold in the oats.

5 Gently spoon the mixture onto the prepared sheet and bake for 2 hours.

6 When done, turn off the oven. Lift the meringues from the sheet, turn over, and set in another place on the sheet to prevent sticking. Leave in the oven as it cools down.

Meringues

MAKES 24

4 egg whites
0.6ml/1/8 tsp salt
300g/10oz/1 1/2 cups caster (superfine) sugar
2.5ml/1/2 tsp vanilla or almond extract (optional)
250ml/8fl oz/1 cup whipped cream (optional)

1 Preheat a 110°C/225°F/Gas 1/4 oven. Grease and flour two large baking sheets.

2 With an electric mixer, beat the egg whites and salt in a very clean metal bowl on low speed. When they start to form soft peaks, add half the sugar and continue beating until the mixture holds stiff peaks.

3 ▲ With a large metal spoon, fold in the remaining sugar and vanilla or almond extract, if using.

4 ▼ Pipe the meringue mixture or gently spoon it on the prepared sheet.

5 Bake for 2 hours. Turn off the oven. Loosen the meringues, invert, and set in another place on the sheets to prevent sticking. Leave in the oven as it cools. Serve sandwiched with whipped cream, if wished.

Oat: Energy 78kcal/334kJ; Protein 1.1g; Carbohydrate 18.9g, of which sugars 15.2g; Fat 0.4g, of which saturates 0g; Cholesterol 0mg; Calcium 10mg; Fibre 0.3g; Sodium 13mg.
Meringues: Energy 87kcal/364kJ; Protein 0.7g; Carbohydrate 12.3g, of which sugars 12.3g; Fat 4.2g, of which saturates 2.6g; Cholesterol 11mg; Calcium 12mg; Fibre 0g; Sodium 13mg.

Traditional Sugar Biscuits

3 ▲ Add the flour mixture alternately with the milk, stirring with a wooden spoon to make a soft dough. Wrap the dough in clear film (plastic wrap) and refrigerate at least 30 minutes, or overnight.

4 ▲ Preheat a 180°C/350°F/Gas 4 oven. Roll out the dough on a lightly floured surface to 3mm/⅛in in thickness. Cut into rounds or other shapes with pastry cutters.

5 ▲ Transfer the biscuits (cookies) to ungreased baking trays. Sprinkle each one with a little coloured or demerara sugar.

6 Bake until golden brown, for about 10–12 minutes. With a slotted spatula, transfer the biscuits to a wire rack and let cool.

MAKES 36

350g/12oz/3 cups plain (all-purpose) flour

5ml/1 tsp bicarbonate of soda (baking soda)

10ml/2 tsp baking powder

1.25ml/¼ tsp grated nutmeg

115g/4oz/½ cup butter or margarine, at room temperature

225g/8oz/generous 1 cup caster (superfine) sugar

2.5ml/½ tsp vanilla extract

1 egg

120ml/4fl oz/½ cup milk

coloured or demerara (raw) sugar, for sprinkling

1 Sift the flour, bicarbonate of soda, baking powder and nutmeg into a small bowl. Set aside.

2 ▲ With an electric mixer, cream the butter or margarine, caster sugar and vanilla together until the mixture is light and fluffy. Add the egg and beat to mix well.

Energy 85kcal/359kJ; Protein 1.2g; Carbohydrate 14.3g, of which sugars 6.9g; Fat 3g, of which saturates 1.8g; Cholesterol 12mg; Calcium 22mg; Fibre 0.3g; Sodium 23mg.

Chocolate Chip Nut Biscuits

MAKES 36

115g/4oz/1 cup plain (all-purpose) flour

5ml/1 tsp baking powder

1.25ml/¼ tsp salt

90g/3½oz/½ cup butter or margarine, at room temperature

115g/4oz/scant ¾ cup sugar

50g/2oz/4 tbsp soft light brown sugar

1 egg

5ml/1 tsp vanilla extract

150g/5oz chocolate chips

50g/2oz/⅓ cup hazelnuts, chopped

1 ▲ Preheat a 180°C/350°F/Gas 4 oven. Grease two or three baking trays.

2 Sift the flour, baking powder and salt into a small bowl. Set aside.

3 ▲ With an electric mixer, cream the butter or margarine and sugars together. Beat in the egg and vanilla.

4 Add the flour mixture and beat well with the mixer on low speed.

5 ▼ Stir in the chocolate chips and half of the chopped hazelnuts using a wooden spoon.

6 Drop teaspoonfuls of the biscuit (cookie) mixture onto the prepared baking trays, to form 2cm/¾in mounds. Space the biscuits 2–5cm/1–2in apart so they do not spread into each other.

7 ▲ Flatten each mound lightly with a wet fork. Sprinkle the remaining hazelnuts on top of the biscuits and press into the surface.

8 Bake until golden brown, about 10–12 minutes. With a slotted spatula, transfer the biscuits to a wire rack and let cool.

Energy 77kcal/323kJ; Protein 1g; Carbohydrate 10g, of which sugars 7g; Fat 4g, of which saturates 2g; Cholesterol 12mg; Calcium 12mg; Fibre 0g; Sodium 44mg.

Chocolate Macaroons

MAKES 24

50g/2oz plain (semisweet) chocolate

175g/6oz/1 cup blanched almonds

225g/8oz/generous 1 cup caster (superfine) sugar

2 egg whites

2.5ml/¹/₂ tsp vanilla extract

1.25ml/¹/₄ tsp almond extract

icing (confectioners') sugar, for dusting

1 Preheat a 150°C/300°F/Gas 2 oven. Line two baking sheets with baking parchment and grease the paper.

2 ▼ Melt the chocolate in the top of a double boiler, or in a heatproof bowl set over a pan of hot water.

3 ▲ Grind the almonds finely in a food processor, blender or grinder. Transfer to a mixing bowl.

4 ▲ In a mixing bowl, whisk the egg whites until they form soft peaks. Fold in the sugar, vanilla and almond extracts, ground almonds and cooled melted chocolate. Refrigerate for 15 minutes.

5 ▲ Use a teaspoon and your hands to shape the mixture into walnut-size balls. Place on the sheets and flatten slightly. Brush each ball with a little water and sift over a thin layer of icing sugar. Bake until just firm, about 20–25 minutes. With a palette knife or metal spatula, transfer to a wire rack to cool.

> ### ~ VARIATION ~
> For Chocolate Pine Nut Macaroons, spread 75g/3oz/¹/₂ cup pine nuts in a shallow dish. Press the chocolate macaroon balls into the nuts to cover one side and bake as described, nut-side up.

Coconut Macaroons

MAKES 24

40g/1¹/₂oz/¹/₃ cup plain (all-purpose) flour

0.6ml/¹/₈ tsp salt

225g/8oz desiccated (dry unsweetened shredded) coconut

175ml/6fl oz/³/₄ cup sweetened condensed milk

5ml/1 tsp vanilla extract

1 Preheat a 180°C/350°F/Gas 4 oven. Grease two baking sheets. Sift the flour and salt into a bowl. Stir in the coconut.

2 ▲ Pour in the milk. Add the vanilla and stir from the centre to make a very thick mixture.

3 ▼ Drop heaped tablespoonfuls of mixture 2.5cm/1in apart on the sheets. Bake until golden brown, about 20 minutes. Cool on a rack.

Chocolate: Energy 93kcal/390kJ; Protein 2g; Carbohydrate 12g, of which sugars 12g; Fat 5g, of which saturates 1g; Cholesterol 0mg; Calcium 19mg; Fibre 1g; Sodium 7mg.
Coconut: Energy 87kcal/360kJ; Protein 1g; Carbohydrate 6g, of which sugars 5g; Fat 7g, of which saturates 5g; Cholesterol 3mg; Calcium 25mg; Fibre 2g; Sodium 22mg.

Almond Tuiles

MAKES 40

50g/2oz/¹/₃ cup blanched almonds
115g/4oz/scant ³/₄ cup sugar
50g/2oz/¹/₄ cup unsalted butter
2 egg whites
40g/1¹/₂oz/¹/₃ cup plain (all-purpose) flour
2.5ml/¹/₂ tsp vanilla extract
115g/4oz/1 cup slivered almonds

1 Grind the blanched almonds with 30ml/2 tbsp of the sugar in a food processor, blender or nut grinder. If necessary, grind in batches.

2 Preheat the oven to 220°C/425°F/Gas 7. Grease two baking sheets.

3 ▲ Put the butter in a large bowl and mix in the remaining sugar, using a metal spoon. With an electric mixer, cream them together until light and fluffy.

4 Add the egg whites and stir until blended. Sift over the flour and fold in with a metal spoon. Fold in the ground almonds and vanilla extract.

5 ▲ Working in small batches, drop tablespoonfuls of the mixture 7.5cm/3in apart on one of the prepared sheets. With the back of a spoon, spread out into thin, almost transparent circles about 6cm/2¹/₂in in diameter. Sprinkle each circle with some of the slivered almonds.

6 Bake until the outer edges have browned slightly, about 4 minutes.

7 ▲ Remove from the oven. With a metal spatula, quickly drape the biscuits (cookies) over a rolling pin to form a curved shape. Transfer to a wire rack when firm. If the biscuits harden too quickly to shape, reheat briefly. Repeat the baking and shaping process until the mixture is used up. Store in an airtight container.

Energy 42kcal/175kJ; Protein 1g; Carbohydrate 4g, of which sugars 3g; Fat 2g, of which saturates 0g; Cholesterol 0mg; Calcium 12mg; Fibre 1g; Sodium 4mg.

Florentines

MAKES 36

50g/2oz/¹/₄ cup butter

120ml/4fl oz/¹/₂ cup whipping cream

130g/4¹/₂oz/scant ³/₄ cup sugar

130g/4¹/₂oz/ 1 cup flaked (sliced) almonds

50g/2oz/²/₃ cup chopped mixed
(candied) peel

40g/1¹/₂oz glacé (candied) cherries, chopped

65g/2¹/₂oz/9 tbsp plain (all-purpose)
flour, sifted

225g/8oz plain (semisweet) chocolate

5ml/1 tsp vegetable oil

1 Preheat the oven to 180°C/350°F/
Gas 4. Grease two baking sheets.

2 ▲ Melt the butter, cream and
sugar together and slowly bring to
the boil. Take off the heat and stir
in the almonds, chopped peel,
cherries and flour until blended.

3 Drop teaspoonfuls of the batter
2.5–5cm/1–2in apart on the prepared
sheets and flatten with a fork.

4 Bake until the cookies brown at
the edges, about 10 minutes. Remove
from the oven and correct the shape
by quickly pushing in any thin uneven
edges with a knife or a round pastry
cutter. Work fast or they will cool and
harden while still on the sheets. If
necessary, return to the oven for a
few moments to soften. While still
hot, use a metal spatula to transfer
the florentines to a clean, flat surface.

5 Melt the chocolate in the top of a
double boiler or in a heatproof bowl
set over a pan of hot water. Add the
oil and stir to blend.

6 ▲ With a palette knife or metal
spatula, spread the smooth underside
of the cooled florentines with a thin
coating of the melted chocolate.

7 ▼ When the chocolate is about to
set, draw a serrated knife across the
surface with a slight sawing motion to
make wavy lines. Store in an airtight
container in a cool place.

Energy 80kcal/337kJ; Protein 1g; Carbohydrate 11g, of which sugars 9g; Fat 4g, of which saturates 3g; Cholesterol 6mg; Calcium 10mg; Fibre 0g; Sodium 14mg.

Nut Lace Wafers

MAKES 18

65g/2¹/₂oz/generous ¹/₂ cup whole
blanched almonds

50g/2oz/¹/₄ cup butter

40g/1¹/₂oz/¹/₃ cup plain (all-purpose) flour

90g/3¹/₂oz/¹/₂ cup sugar

30ml/2 tbsp double (heavy) cream

2.5ml/¹/₂ tsp vanilla extract

1 Preheat the oven to 190°C/375°F/
Gas 5. Grease several baking sheets.

2 Finely chop the almonds with a
sharp knife, food processor, blender,
or coffee grinder.

3 ▼ Melt the butter in a pan over
low heat. Remove from the heat and
stir in the remaining ingredients
and the almonds.

4 Drop teaspoonfuls 6cm/2¹/₂in apart
on the prepared sheets. Bake until
golden, about 5 minutes. Cool on
the baking sheets briefly, just until the
wafers are stiff enough to remove.

5 ▲ Using a palette knife or metal
spatula, transfer the biscuits (cookies)
to a wire rack to cool.

> **~ VARIATION ~**
> Add 50g/2oz/²/₃ cup finely chopped
> orange peel to the mixture.

Oatmeal Lace Rounds

MAKES 36

150g/5oz/10 tbsp butter or margarine

130g/4¹/₂oz/1¹/₃ cups rolled porridge oats

165g/5¹/₂oz/scant ³/₄ cup soft dark
brown sugar

150g/5oz/³/₄ cup caster (superfine) sugar

40g/1¹/₂oz/¹/₃ cup plain
(all-purpose) flour

1.25ml/¹/₄ tsp salt

1 egg, lightly beaten

5ml/1 tsp vanilla extract

75g/3oz/¹/₂ cup pecans or walnuts,
finely chopped

1 Preheat the oven to 180°C/350°F/
Gas 4. Grease two baking sheets.

2 Melt the butter in a pan over low
heat. Set aside.

3 In a mixing bowl, combine the
oats, brown sugar, caster sugar, flour
and salt.

4 ▲ Make a well in the centre and
add the butter or margarine, beaten
egg and vanilla extract.

5 ▼ Mix until blended, then stir in
the chopped nuts.

6 Drop rounded teaspoonfuls of the
mixture about 5cm/2in apart on the
prepared sheets. Bake until lightly
browned on the edges and bubbling,
5–8 minutes. Let cool on the sheet for
2 minutes, then transfer to a rack to
cool completely.

Wafers: Energy 78kcal/327kJ; Protein 1g; Carbohydrate 7.2g, of which sugars 5.5g; Fat 5.2g, of which saturates 2.2g; Cholesterol 8mg; Calcium 16mg; Fibre 0.3g; Sodium 18mg.
Rounds: Energy 103kcal/432kJ; Protein 1g; Carbohydrate 13.2g, of which sugars 9.7g; Fat 5.5g, of which saturates 2.5g; Cholesterol 15mg; Calcium 11mg; Fibre 0.4g; Sodium 32mg.

Raspberry Sandwich Biscuits

MAKES 32

175g/6oz/1 cup blanched almonds
175g/6oz/1½ cups plain (all-purpose) flour
175g/6oz/¾ cup butter, at room temperature
115g/4oz/scant ¾ cup caster (superfine) sugar
grated rind of 1 lemon
5ml/1 tsp vanilla extract
1 egg white
0.6ml/⅛ tsp salt
25g/1oz/¼ cup flaked (sliced) almonds
250ml/8fl oz/1 cup raspberry jam
15ml/1 tbsp fresh lemon juice

1 Place the almonds and 45ml/3 tbsp of the flour in a food processor, blender or coffee grinder and process until finely ground. Set aside.

2 With an electric mixer, cream the butter and sugar together until light and fluffy. Stir in the lemon rind and vanilla. Add the ground almonds and remaining flour and mix well until combined. Gather into a ball, wrap in baking parchment, and refrigerate for at least 1 hour.

3 Preheat a 170°C/325°F/Gas 3 oven. Line two baking sheets with baking parchment. Grease the paper.

4 Divide the biscuit mixture into four equal parts. Working with one section at a time, roll out to a thickness of 3mm/⅛in on a lightly floured surface. With a 6cm/2½in fluted pastry cutter, stamp out circles. Gather the scraps, roll out and stamp out more circles. Repeat with the remaining sections.

5 ▲ Using a 2cm/¾in piping nozzle or pastry cutter, stamp out the centres from half the circles. Place the rings and circles 2.5cm/1in apart on the prepared sheets.

6 ▲ Whisk the egg white with the salt until just frothy. Chop the flaked almonds. Brush only the rings with the egg white, then sprinkle over the almonds. Bake until very lightly browned, 12–15 minutes. Let cool for a few minutes on the sheets before transferring to a rack.

7 ▲ In a pan, melt the jam with the lemon juice until it comes to a simmer. Brush the jam over the circles and sandwich together with the rings. Store in an airtight container with sheets of greaseproof (waxed) paper between the layers.

Energy 133kcal/554kJ; Protein 2g; Carbohydrate 13.9g, of which sugars 9.5g; Fat 8.1g, of which saturates 3.1g; Cholesterol 12mg; Calcium 27mg; Fibre 0.6g; Sodium 39mg.

Brandysnaps

MAKES 18

50g/2oz/¹/₄ cup butter, at room temperature

150g/5oz/³/₄ cup caster (superfine) sugar

15ml/1 tbsp golden (light corn) syrup

40g/1¹/₂oz/¹/₃ cup plain (all-purpose) flour

2.5ml/¹/₂ tsp ground ginger

FOR THE FILLING

250ml/8fl oz/1 cup whipping cream

30ml/2 tbsp brandy

1 With an electric mixer, cream together the butter and sugar until light and fluffy, then beat in the golden syrup. Sift over the flour and ginger and mix together.

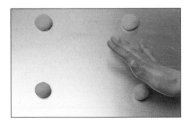

2 ▲ Transfer the mixture to a work surface and knead until smooth. Cover and refrigerate for 30 minutes.

3 Preheat a 190°C/375°F/Gas 5 oven. Grease a baking sheet.

4 ▲ Working in batches of four, form the mixture into walnut-size balls. Place these far apart on the prepared baking sheet and flatten slightly. Bake until golden and bubbling, about 10 minutes.

5 ▼ Remove from the oven and let cool a few moments. Working quickly, slide a metal spatula under each one, turn over, and wrap around the handle of a wooden spoon (have four spoons ready). If they firm up too quickly, reheat for a few seconds to soften. When firm, slide the snaps off and place on a rack to cool.

6 ▲ When all the brandy snaps are completely cold, prepare the filling. Whip the cream and brandy until soft peaks form. Fill a piping bag fitted with a star nozzle with the brandy cream. Pipe into each end of the brandy snaps to fill completely just before serving.

Energy 122kcal/508kJ; Protein 1g; Carbohydrate 11g, of which sugars 9g, Fat 8g, of which saturates 5g; Cholesterol 21mg; Calcium 13mg; Fibre 0g; Sodium 25mg.

Spicy Pepper Biscuits

MAKES 48

190g/6½oz/1⅔ cups plain (all-purpose) flour

50g/2oz/½ cup cornflour (cornstarch)

10ml/2 tsp baking powder

2.5ml/½ tsp ground cardamom

2.5ml/½ tsp ground cinnamon

2.5ml/½ tsp grated nutmeg

2.5ml/½ tsp ground ginger

2.5ml/½ tsp ground allspice

2.5ml/½ tsp salt

2.5ml/½ tsp freshly ground black pepper

225g/8oz/1 cup butter or margarine, at room temperature

90g/3½oz/½ cup soft light brown sugar

2.5ml/½ tsp vanilla extract

5ml/1 tsp finely grated lemon rind

50ml/2fl oz/¼ cup whipping cream

75g/3oz/¾ cup finely ground almonds

30ml/2 tbsp icing (confectioners') sugar

1 Preheat a 180°C/350°F/Gas 4 oven.

2 Sift the flour, cornflour, baking powder, spices, salt and pepper into a bowl. Set aside.

3 With an electric mixer, cream the butter or margarine and brown sugar together until light and fluffy. Beat in the vanilla and lemon rind.

4 ▲ With the mixer on low speed, add the flour mixture alternately with the cream, beginning and ending with flour. Stir in the ground almonds.

5 ▲ Shape the dough into 2cm/¾in balls. Place them on ungreased baking trays about 2.5cm/1in apart. Bake until the biscuits (cookies) are golden brown underneath, 15–20 minutes.

6 Let the biscuits cool on the baking trays about 1 minute before transferring them to a wire rack to cool completely. Before serving, sprinkle them lightly with icing sugar.

Chocolate and Coconut Slices

MAKES 24

175g/6oz/3 cups crushed digestive biscuits (graham crackers)

50g/2oz/¼ cup caster (superfine) sugar

0.6ml/⅛ tsp salt

115g/4oz/½ cup butter or margarine, melted

75g/3oz/1 cup desiccated (dry unsweetened shredded) coconut

250g/9oz plain (semisweet) chocolate chips

250ml/8fl oz/1 cup sweetened condensed milk

115g/4oz/⅔ cup walnuts, chopped

1 Preheat a 180°C/350°F/Gas 4 oven.

2 ▼ In a bowl, combine the crushed biscuits (cookies), sugar, salt and butter or margarine. Press the mixture evenly over the bottom of an ungreased 33 × 23cm/13 × 9in baking dish.

3 ▲ Sprinkle the coconut over the biscuit base, then scatter over the chocolate chips. Pour the condensed milk evenly over the chocolate. Sprinkle the walnuts on top.

4 Bake 30 minutes. Unmould on to a wire rack and leave to cool, preferably overnight. When cooled, cut into slices.

Biscuits: Energy 75kcal/314kJ; Protein 0.8g; Carbohydrate 6.8g, of which sugars 2.6g; Fat 5.2g, of which saturates 2.8g; Cholesterol 11mg; Calcium 12mg; Fibre 0.2g; Sodium 30mg.
Slices: Energy 217kcal/907kJ; Protein 2.8g; Carbohydrate 20g, of which sugars 15.8g; Fat 14.6g, of which saturates 7.5g; Cholesterol 18mg; Calcium 48mg; Fibre 1g; Sodium 89mg.

Shortbread

MAKES 8

150g/5oz/10 tbsp unsalted butter,
   at room temperature

90g/3½oz/½ cup caster (superfine) sugar

175g/6oz/1½ cups plain (all-purpose) flour

50g/2oz/½ cup rice flour

1.25ml/¼ tsp baking powder

0.6ml/⅛ tsp salt

1 Preheat the oven to 170°C/325°F/
Gas 3. Grease a shallow 20cm/8in
cake tin (pan), preferably with a
removable bottom.

2 With an electric mixer, cream the
butter and sugar together until light
and fluffy. Sift over the flours, baking
powder and salt and mix well.

3 ▲ Press the dough neatly into the
prepared tin, smoothing the surface
with the back of a spoon.

4 Prick all over with a fork, then
score into eight equal wedges.

5 ▲ Bake until golden, 40–45
minutes. Leave in the tin until cool
enough to handle, then turn out and
recut the wedges while still hot. Store
in an airtight container.

Flapjacks

MAKES 8

50g/2oz/¼ cup butter

15ml/1 tbsp golden (light corn) syrup

75g/3oz/6 tbsp soft dark brown sugar

90g/3½oz/1 cup rolled porridge oats

0.6ml/⅛ tsp salt

1 ▲ Preheat a 180°C/ 350°F/Gas 4
oven. Line a 20cm/8in cake tin (pan)
with baking parchment and grease.

2 ▼ Place the butter, golden syrup
and sugar in a pan over a low heat.
Cook, stirring, until everything has
melted and combined.

~ **VARIATION** ~

If wished, add 5ml/1 tsp ground
ginger to the melted butter.

3 ▲ Remove from the heat and add
the oats and salt. Stir to blend.

4 Spoon into the prepared tin and
smooth the surface. Place in the
centre of the oven and bake until
golden brown, 20–25 minutes. Leave
in the tin until cool enough to handle,
then turn out and cut into wedges
while still hot.

Shortbread: Energy 290kcal/1212kJ; Protein 2.5g; Carbohydrate 36.2g, of which sugars 15.4g; Fat 15.7g, of which saturates 9.8g; Cholesterol 40mg; Calcium 39mg; Fibre 0.8g; Sodium 116mg.
Flapjacks: Energy 144kcal/604kJ; Protein 1.9g; Carbohydrate 21g, of which sugars 10.5g; Fat 6.4g, of which saturates 3.3g; Cholesterol 13mg; Calcium 14mg; Fibre 1g; Sodium 50mg.

Chocolate Delights

5 ▲ Stir in the chocolate, then the flour. Stir in the nuts.

6 ▲ Divide the mixture into four equal parts, and roll each into 5cm/2in diameter logs. Wrap tightly in foil and refrigerate or freeze until firm.

7 Preheat a 190°C/375°F/Gas 5 oven. Grease two baking sheets.

8 With a sharp knife, cut the logs into 5mm/¹/₄in slices. Place the rounds on the prepared sheets and bake until lightly coloured, about 10 minutes. Transfer to a rack to cool.

MAKES 50

25g/1oz plain (semisweet) chocolate

25g/1oz dark (bittersweet) chocolate

225g/8oz/2 cups plain (all-purpose) flour

2.5ml/¹/₂ tsp salt

225g/8oz/1 cup unsalted butter, at room temperature

225g/8oz/generous 1 cup caster (superfine) sugar

2 eggs

5ml/1 tsp vanilla extract

115g/4oz/²/₃ cup walnuts, finely chopped

1 Melt the chocolates in the top of a double boiler, or in a heatproof bowl set over a pan of gently simmering water. Set aside.

2 ▼ In a small bowl, sift together the flour and salt. Set aside.

3 With an electric mixer, cream the butter until soft. Add the sugar and continue beating until the mixture is light and fluffy.

4 Mix the eggs and vanilla, then gradually stir into the butter mixture.

~ VARIATION ~

For two-tone biscuits, melt only half the chocolate. Combine all the ingredients, except the chocolate, as above. Divide the mixture in half. Add the chocolate to one half. Roll out the plain mixture to a flat sheet. Roll out the chocolate mixture, place on top of the plain one and roll up. Wrap, slice and bake as described.

Energy 90kcal/377kJ; Protein 1.1g; Carbohydrate 8.9g, of which sugars 5.5g; Fat 5.8g, of which saturates 2.7g; Cholesterol 17mg; Calcium 13mg; Fibre 0.2g; Sodium 31mg.

Cinnamon Treats

MAKES 50

250g/9oz/2¼ cups plain (all-purpose) flour

2.5ml/½ tsp salt

10ml/2 tsp ground cinnamon

225g/8oz/1 cup unsalted butter,
    at room temperature

225g/8oz/generous 1 cup caster
    (superfine) sugar

2 eggs

5ml/1 tsp vanilla extract

1 In a bowl, sift together the flour, salt and cinnamon. Set aside.

2 ▲ With an electric mixer, cream the butter until soft. Add the sugar and continue beating until the mixture is light and fluffy.

3 Beat the eggs and vanilla, then gradually stir into the butter mixture.

4 ▲ Stir in the dry ingredients.

5 ▲ Divide the mixture into four equal parts, then roll each into 5cm/2in diameter logs. Wrap tightly in foil and refrigerate or freeze until firm.

6 Preheat a 190°C/375°F/Gas 5 oven. Grease two baking sheets.

7 ▼ With a sharp knife, cut the logs into 5mm/¼in slices. Place the rounds on the prepared sheets and bake until lightly coloured, about 10 minutes. With a metal spatula, transfer to a rack to cool.

Energy 71kcal/298kJ; Protein 0.8g; Carbohydrate 8.6g, of which sugars 4.8g; Fat 4g, of which saturates 2.4g; Cholesterol 17mg; Calcium 11mg; Fibre 0.2g; Sodium 31mg.

Coffee Ice Cream Sandwiches

MAKES 8

115g/4oz/¹/₂ cup butter or margarine,
   at room temperature

50g/2oz/¼ cup caster (superfine) sugar

115g/4oz/1 cup plain (all-purpose) flour,

30ml/2 tbsp instant coffee powder

icing (confectioners') sugar,
   for sprinkling

475ml/16fl oz/2 cups coffee ice cream

30ml/2 tbsp unsweetened cocoa powder,
   for sprinkling

1 Lightly grease two or three baking trays with butter.

2 With an electric mixer or wooden spoon, beat the butter or margarine until soft. Beat in the caster sugar.

3 ▲ Add the flour and coffee and mix by hand to form an evenly blended dough. Wrap in a plastic bag and refrigerate at least 1 hour.

4 Lightly sprinkle the work surface with icing sugar. Knead the dough on the sugared surface for a few minutes to soften it slightly.

5 ▼ Using a rolling pin dusted with icing sugar, roll out the dough to 3mm/¹/₈in thickness. With a 6cm/2½in fluted pastry cutter, cut out 16 rounds. Transfer the rounds to the prepared baking trays. Refrigerate for at least 30 minutes.

6 Preheat a 150°C/300°F/Gas 2 oven. Bake the biscuits (cookies) until they are lightly golden, about 30 minutes. Let them cool and firm up before removing them from the trays to a wire rack to cool completely.

7 Remove the ice cream from the freezer and let soften 10 minutes at room temperature.

8 ▲ With a metal spatula, spread the ice cream evenly on the flat side of eight of the biscuits, leaving the edges clear. Top with the remaining biscuits, flat-side down.

9 Arrange the ice cream sandwiches on a baking tray. Cover and freeze at least 1 hour, longer if a firmer sandwich is desired. Sift the cocoa powder over the tops before serving.

Energy 258kcal/1078kJ; Protein 3g; Carbohydrate 28g, of which sugars 16g; Fat 16g, of which saturates 10g; Cholesterol 40mg; Calcium 68mg; Fibre 1g; Sodium 135mg.

Hazelnut Squares

MAKES 9

50g/2oz plain (semisweet) chocolate

75g/3oz/6 tbsp butter or margarine

225g/8oz/generous 1 cup caster
  (superfine) sugar

50g/2oz/½ cup plain (all-purpose) flour

2.5ml/½ tsp baking powder

2 eggs, beaten

2.5ml/½ tsp vanilla extract

115g/4oz/⅔ cup skinned hazelnuts,
  roughly chopped

1 Preheat the oven to 180°C/350°F/
Gas 4. Grease a 20cm/8in square
baking tin (pan).

2 ▲ In a heatproof bowl set over a
pan of barely simmering water, or in a
double boiler, melt the chocolate and
butter or margarine. Remove the bowl
from the heat.

4 ▼ Pour the mixture into the
prepared tin. Bake 10 minutes, then
sprinkle the reserved hazelnuts over
the top. Return to the oven and
continue baking until firm to the
touch, about 25 minutes.

3 ▲ Add the sugar, flour, baking
powder, eggs, vanilla and half the
hazelnuts to the melted mixture and
stir well with a wooden spoon.

5 ▲ Let cool in the tin, set on a wire
rack, for 10 minutes, then unmould
onto the rack and let cool completely.
Cut into squares for serving.

Energy 299kcal/1252kJ; Protein 4.2g; Carbohydrate 34.8g, of which sugars 30.2g; Fat 16.9g, of which saturates 5.7g; Cholesterol 58mg; Calcium 48mg; Fibre 1.1g; Sodium 62mg.

Peanut Butter Biscuits

MAKES 24

150g/5oz/1¹/4 cups plain (all-purpose) flour

2.5ml¹/2 tsp bicarbonate of soda (baking soda)

2.5ml¹/2 tsp salt

115g/4oz/¹/2 cup butter, at room temperature

165g/5¹/2oz/scant ³/4 cup soft light brown sugar

1 egg

5ml/1 tsp vanilla extract

275g/10oz crunchy peanut butter

1 Sift together the flour, bicarbonate of soda and salt and set aside.

2 With an electric mixer, cream the butter and sugar together until light and fluffy.

3 In another bowl, mix the egg and vanilla, then gradually beat into the butter mixture.

4 ▲ Stir in the peanut butter and blend thoroughly. Stir in the dry ingredients. Refrigerate for at least 30 minutes, or until firm.

5 Preheat the oven to 180°C/350°F/Gas 4. Grease two baking sheets.

6 Spoon out rounded teaspoonfuls of the dough and roll into balls.

7 ▲ Place the balls on the prepared sheets and press flat with a fork into circles about 6cm/2¹/2in in diameter, making a criss-cross pattern. Bake until lightly coloured, 12–15 minutes. Transfer to a rack to cool.

> ### ~ VARIATION ~
> Add 75ml/5 tbsp peanuts, chopped, with the peanut butter.

Chocolate Chip Cookies

MAKES 24

115g/4oz/¹/2 cup butter or margarine, at room temperature

50g/2oz/¹/4 cup caster (superfine) sugar

115g/4oz/¹/2 cup soft dark brown sugar

1 egg

2.5ml/¹/2 tsp vanilla extract

175g/6oz/1¹/2 cups plain (all-purpose) flour

2.5ml/¹/2 tsp bicarbonate of soda (baking soda)

0.6ml/¹/8 tsp salt

275g/6oz chocolate chips

50g/2oz/¹/3 cup walnuts, chopped

1 Preheat the oven to 180°C/350°F/Gas 4. Grease two large baking sheets.

2 ▼ With an electric mixer, cream the butter or margarine and two sugars together until light and fluffy.

3 In another bowl, mix the egg and vanilla, then gradually beat into the butter mixture. Sift over the flour, bicarbonate of soda and salt and stir.

4 ▲ Add the chocolate chips and walnuts, and mix to combine well.

5 Place heaped teaspoonfuls of the dough 5cm/2in apart on the prepared sheets. Bake until lightly coloured, 10–15 minutes. Transfer to a wire rack to cool.

Biscuits: Energy 154kcal/641kJ; Protein 3.4g; Carbohydrate 13.7g, of which sugars 8.3g; Fat 9.9g, of which saturates 4g; Cholesterol 18mg; Calcium 19mg; Fibre 0.8g; Sodium 71mg.
Cookies: Energy 139kcal/582kJ; Protein 1.7g; Carbohydrate 16.7g, of which sugars 11.1g; Fat 7.7g, of which saturates 3.9g; Cholesterol 19mg; Calcium 20mg; Fibre 0.5g; Sodium 33mg.

Apple-sauce Biscuits

Apple-sauce Biscuits (top), Toffee Bars

MAKES 36

90g/3½oz/½ cup sugar

50g/2oz/¼ cup butter or vegetable fat, at room temperature

175ml/6fl oz/¾ cup thick apple sauce

0.6ml/⅛ tsp grated lemon rind

115g/4oz/1 cup plain (all-purpose) flour,

2.5ml/½ tsp baking powder

1.25ml/¼ tsp bicarbonate of soda (baking soda)

1.25ml/¼ tsp salt

2.5ml/½ tsp ground cinnamon

75g/3oz/½ cup chopped walnuts

~ COOK'S TIP ~

If the apple sauce is runny, put it in a strainer over a bowl and let it drain for 10 minutes.

---

1 Preheat oven to 190°C/375°F/Gas 5.

2 In a medium bowl, beat together the sugar and butter or vegetable fat until well mixed. Beat in the apple sauce and lemon rind.

3 ▲ Sift the flour, baking powder, bicarbonate of soda, salt and cinnamon into the mixture, and stir to blend. Fold in the chopped walnuts.

4 ▲ Drop teaspoonfuls of the dough on a lightly greased baking sheet, spacing them about 5cm/2in apart.

5 Bake the biscuits (cookies) in the centre of the oven until they are golden brown, 8–10 minutes. Transfer the biscuits to a wire rack to cool.

Toffee Bars

MAKES 32

450g/1lb/2 cups soft light brown sugar, firmly packed

450g/1lb/2 cups butter or margarine, at room temperature

2 egg yolks

7.5ml/1½ tsp vanilla extract

450g/1lb/4 cups plain (all-purpose) or wholemeal (whole-wheat) flour

2.5ml/½ tsp salt

115g/4oz milk chocolate, broken in pieces

115g/4oz/⅔ cup chopped walnuts or pecans

1 Preheat the oven to 180°C/350°F/ Gas 4.

2 Beat together the sugar and butter or margarine until light and fluffy. Beat in the egg yolks and vanilla. Stir in the flour and salt.

3 ▼ Spread the dough in a greased 33 × 23 × 5cm/13 × 9 × 2in tin (pan). Bake until lightly browned, 25–30 minutes. The texture will be soft.

4 ▲ Remove from the oven and immediately place the chocolate pieces on the hot biscuit (cookie) base. Let stand until the chocolate softens, then spread it evenly with a spatula. Sprinkle with the nuts.

5 While still warm, cut into bars about 5 × 4cm/2 × 1½in.

Biscuits: Energy 58kcal/243kJ; Protein 1g; Carbohydrate 6g, of which sugars 4g; Fat 4g, of which saturates 1g; Cholesterol 3mg; Calcium 9mg; Fibre 0g; Sodium 33mg.
Bars: Energy 234kcal/979kJ; Protein 2g; Carbohydrate 26g, of which sugars 15g; Fat 15g, of which saturates 8g; Cholesterol 43mg; Calcium 36mg; Fibre 1g; Sodium 122mg.

Chocolate Chip Brownies

MAKES 24

115g/4oz plain (semisweet) chocolate
115g/4oz/¹/₂ cup butter
3 eggs
200g/7oz/1 cup sugar
2.5ml/¹/₂ tsp vanilla extract
pinch of salt
150g/5oz/1¹/₄ cups plain (all-purpose) flour
175g/6oz chocolate chips

1 ▼ Preheat a 180°C/350°F/Gas 4 oven. Line a 33 × 23cm/13 × 9in tin (pan) with baking parchment; grease.

2 ▲ Melt the chocolate and butter in the top of a double boiler, or in a heatproof bowl set over a pan of gently simmering water.

3 ▲ Beat together the eggs, sugar, vanilla and salt. Stir in the chocolate mixture. Sift over the flour and fold in. Add the chocolate chips.

4 ▲ Pour the mixture into the prepared tin and spread evenly. Bake until just set, about 30 minutes. Do not overbake; the brownies should be slightly moist inside. Cool in the pan.

5 To turn out, run a knife all around the edge and invert onto a baking sheet. Remove the paper. Place another sheet on top and invert again so the brownies are right-side up. Cut into squares for serving.

Energy 160kcal/672kJ; Protein 2g; Carbohydrate 21g, of which sugars 16g; Fat 8g, of which saturates 5g; Cholesterol 40mg; Calcium 18mg; Fibre 0g; Sodium 40mg.

Marbled Brownies

MAKES 24

225g/8oz plain (semisweet) chocolate

75g/3oz/6 tbsp butter

4 eggs

300g/10oz/1½ cups sugar

150g/5oz/1¼ cups plain (all-purpose) flour

2.5ml/½ tsp salt

5ml/1 tsp baking powder

10ml/2 tsp vanilla extract

115g/4oz/⅔ cup chopped walnuts

FOR THE PLAIN MIXTURE

50g/2oz/¼ cup butter, at room temperature

175g/6oz/¾ cup cream cheese

90g/3½oz/½ cup sugar

2 eggs

25g/1oz/¼ cup plain (all-purpose) flour

5ml/1 tsp vanilla extract

1 Preheat a 180°C/350°F/Gas 4 oven. Line a 33 × 23cm/13 × 9in tin (pan) with baking parchment, and grease.

2 Melt the chocolate and butter over very low heat, stirring constantly. Set aside to cool.

3 Meanwhile, beat the eggs until light and fluffy. Gradually add the sugar and continue beating until blended. Sift over the flour, salt and baking powder and fold to combine.

4 ▲ Stir in the cooled chocolate mixture. Add the vanilla and walnuts. Measure and set aside 450ml/¾ pint/ scant 2 cups of the chocolate mixture.

5 ▲ For the plain mixture, cream the butter and cream cheese with an electric mixer.

6 Add the sugar and continue beating until blended. Beat in the eggs, flour and vanilla.

7 Spread the unmeasured chocolate mixture in the tin. Pour over the plain mixture. Drop spoonfuls of the reserved chocolate mixture on top.

8 ▲ With a metal spatula, swirl the mixtures to marble. Do not blend completely. Bake until just set, 35–40 minutes. Turn out when cool, then cut into squares for serving.

Energy 259kcal/1083kJ; Protein 3.8g; Carbohydrate 28.8g, of which sugars 23.1g; Fat 15.1g, of which saturates 7.1g; Cholesterol 66mg; Calcium 42mg; Fibre 0.6g; Sodium 73mg.

Nutty Chocolate Squares

MAKES 16

2 eggs

10ml/2 tsp vanilla extract

0.6ml/¹/₈ tsp salt

175g/6oz/1 cup pecan nuts, chopped

50g/2oz/¹/₂ cup plain (all-purpose) flour

50g/2oz/¹/₄ cup caster (superfine) sugar

120ml/4fl oz/¹/₂ cup golden
 (light corn) syrup

75g/3oz plain (semisweet) chocolate,
 finely chopped

25g/1oz/2 tbsp butter

16 pecan halves, for decorating

1 Preheat a 170°C/325°F/Gas 3 oven.
Line the bottom and sides of a 20cm/
8in square baking tin (pan) with
baking parchment and grease lightly.

2 ▼ Whisk together the eggs,
vanilla and salt. In another bowl, mix
together the pecans and flour. Set
both aside.

3 In a pan, bring the sugar and
golden syrup to a boil. Remove from
the heat and stir in the chocolate and
butter and blend thoroughly with a
wooden spoon.

4 ▲ Mix in the beaten eggs, then
fold in the pecan mixture.

5 Pour the mixture into the prepared
tin and bake for about 35 minutes,
until set. Leave to cool in the tin for
10 minutes before unmoulding. Cut
into 5cm/2in squares and press pecan
halves into the tops while warm. Cool
completely on a wire rack.

Raisin Brownies

MAKES 16

115g/4oz/¹/₂ cup butter or margarine

50g/2oz/¹/₂ cup unsweetened cocoa powder

2 eggs

225g/8oz/generous 1 cup caster
 (superfine) sugar

5ml/1 tsp vanilla extract

40g/1¹/₂oz/¹/₃ cup plain (all-purpose) flour

75g/3oz/¹/₂ cup chopped walnuts

75g/3oz/generous ¹/₂ cup raisins

1 Preheat the oven to 180°C/350°F/
Gas 4. Line the bottom and sides of a
20cm/8in square baking tin (pan)
with baking parchment and grease
the parchment.

2 ▼ Gently melt the butter or
margarine in a small pan. Remove
he pan from the heat and stir in the
cocoa powder.

3 With an electric mixer, beat the
eggs, sugar and vanilla together until
light. Add the cocoa mixture and stir
to blend.

4 ▲ Sift the flour over the cocoa
mixture and gently fold in. Add
the walnuts and raisins and scrape the
mixture into the prepared tin.

5 Bake in the centre of the oven for
30 minutes. Do not overbake. Leave
in the tin to cool before cutting into
5cm/2in squares and removing. The
brownies should be soft and moist.

Squares: Energy 172kcal/719kJ; Protein 2.4g; Carbohydrate 15.2g, of which sugars 12.7g; Fat 11.8g, of which saturates 2.9g; Cholesterol 29mg; Calcium 19mg; Fibre 0.7g; Sodium 45mg.
Brownies: Energy 181kcal/759kJ; Protein 2.5g; Carbohydrate 20.4g, of which sugars 18.1g; Fat 10.5g, of which saturates 4.6g; Cholesterol 39mg; Calcium 26mg; Fibre 0.7g; Sodium 86mg.

Chocolate Walnut Bars

MAKES 24

50g/2oz/½ cup walnuts

50g/2oz/¼ cup caster (superfine) sugar

115g/4oz/1 cup plain (all-purpose)
flour, sifted

75g/3oz/6 tbsp cold unsalted butter,
cut into pieces

FOR THE TOPPING

25g/1oz/2 tbsp unsalted butter

90ml/6 tbsp water

25g/1oz/¼ cup unsweetened cocoa powder

90g/3½oz/½ cup caster (superfine) sugar

5ml/1 tsp vanilla extract

0.6ml/⅛ tsp salt

2 eggs

icing (confectioners') sugar, for dusting

1 Preheat a 180°C/350°F/Gas 4 oven.
Grease a 20cm/8in square tin (pan).

2 ▼ Grind the walnuts with a few
tablespoons of the sugar in a food
processor, blender or coffee grinder.

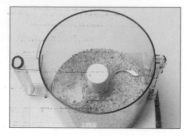

3 In a bowl, combine the ground
walnuts, remaining sugar and flour.
With your fingertips, rub in the butter
until the mixture resembles coarse
breadcrumbs. Alternatively, place all
the ingredients in a food processor
and process until the mixture
resembles coarse breadcrumbs.

4 ▲ Pat the walnut mixture into the
bottom of the prepared tin in an even
layer. Bake for 25 minutes.

5 ▲ Meanwhile, for the topping,
melt the butter with the water. Whisk
in the cocoa and sugar. Remove from
the heat, stir in the vanilla and salt
and let cool for 5 minutes. Whisk in
the eggs until blended.

6 ▲ Pour the topping over the crust
when baked.

7 Return to the oven and bake until
set, about 20 minutes. Set the tin on a
rack to cool. Cut into 6 × 2.5cm/
2½ × 1in bars and dust with icing
sugar. Store in the refrigerator.

Energy 97kcal/407kJ; Protein 1.5g; Carbohydrate 9.8g, of which sugars 6.5g; Fat 6.1g, of which saturates 2.9g; Cholesterol 26mg; Calcium 16mg; Fibre 0.3g; Sodium 45mg.

Pecan Squares

MAKES 36

225g/8oz/2 cups plain (all-purpose) flour

pinch of salt

115g/4oz/scant ³/4 cup sugar

225g/8oz/1 cup cold butter or
   margarine, chopped

1 egg

finely grated rind of 1 lemon

FOR THE TOPPING

175g/6oz/³/4 cup butter

75ml/5 tbsp honey

50g/2oz/¼ cup sugar

115g/4oz/½ cup soft dark brown sugar

75ml/5 tbsp whipping cream

450g/1lb/2²/3 cups pecan halves

1 Preheat the oven to 190°C/375°F/
Gas 5. Grease a 40 × 28 × 2.5cm/16 ×
11 × 1in Swiss roll tin (jelly roll pan).

2 ▲ Sift the flour and salt into a
mixing bowl. Stir in the sugar. Cut
and rub in the butter or margarine
until the mixture resembles coarse
crumbs. Add the egg and lemon rind
and blend with a fork until the
mixture just holds together.

3 ▼ Spoon the mixture into the
prepared tin. With floured fingertips,
press into an even layer. Prick the
pastry all over with a fork and chill
for 10 minutes.

4 Bake the pastry crust in the oven
for 15 minutes. Remove the tin from
the oven, but keep the oven on while
making the topping.

5 ▲ To make the topping, melt the
butter, honey and both sugars. Bring
to the boil. Boil, without stirring, for
2 minutes. Off the heat, stir in the
cream and pecans. Pour over the
crust, return to the oven and bake
for 25 minutes. Leave to cool.

6 When cool, run a knife around the
edge. Invert on to a baking sheet,
place another sheet on top and invert
again. Dip a sharp knife into very hot
water and cut into squares for serving.

Energy 245kcal/1017kJ; Protein 3g; Carbohydrate 15g, of which sugars 10g; Fat 20g, of which saturates 8g; Cholesterol 35mg; Calcium 27mg; Fibre 1g; Sodium 72mg.

Figgy Bars

MAKES 48

350g/12oz/2 cups dried figs

3 eggs

175g/6oz/scant 1 cup caster (superfine) sugar

75g/3oz/⅔ cup plain (all-purpose) flour

5ml/1 tsp baking powder

2.5ml/½ tsp ground cinnamon

1.25ml/¼ tsp ground cloves

1.25ml/¼ tsp grated nutmeg

1.25ml/¼ tsp salt

75g/3oz/½ cup finely chopped walnuts

30ml/2 tbsp brandy or cognac

icing (confectioners') sugar, for dusting

1 Preheat a 170°C/325°F/Gas 3 oven.

2 Line a 30 × 20 × 3cm/12 × 8 × ½in tin (pan) with baking parchment and grease the parchment.

3 ▲ With a sharp knife, chop the figs roughly. Set aside.

4 In a bowl, whisk the eggs and sugar until well blended. In another bowl, sift together the dry ingredients, then fold into the egg mixture in several batches.

5 ▼ Stir in the figs, walnuts and brandy or cognac.

6 Scrape the mixture into the prepared tin and bake until the top is firm and brown, 35–40 minutes. It should still be soft underneath.

7 Let cool in the tin for 5 minutes, then unmould and transfer to a sheet of baking parchment lightly sprinkled with icing sugar. Cut into bars.

Lemon Bars

MAKES 36

50g/2oz/½ cup icing (confectioners') sugar

175g/6oz/1½ cups plain (all-purpose) flour

2.5ml/½ tsp salt

175g/6oz/¾ cup butter, cut in small pieces

FOR THE TOPPING

4 eggs

350g/12oz/1¾ cups caster (superfine) sugar

grated rind of 1 lemon

120ml/4fl oz/½ cup fresh lemon juice

175ml/6fl oz/¾ cup whipping cream

icing (confectioners') sugar, for dusting

1 Preheat a 170°C/325°F/Gas 3 oven.

2 Grease a 33 × 23cm/13 × 9in baking tin (pan).

3 Sift the sugar, flour and salt into a bowl. With a pastry blender, cut in the butter until the mixture resembles coarse breadcrumbs.

4 ▲ Press the mixture into the bottom of the prepared tin. Bake until golden brown, about 20 minutes.

5 Meanwhile, for the topping, whisk the eggs and sugar together until blended. Add the lemon rind and juice and mix well.

6 ▲ Lightly whip the cream and fold into the egg mixture. Pour over the still warm base, return to the oven, and bake until set, about 40 minutes.

7 Cool completely before cutting into bars. Dust with icing sugar.

Figgy: Energy 53kcal/224kJ; Protein 1g; Carbohydrate 8.9g, of which sugars 7.7g; Fat 1.6g, of which saturates 0.2g; Cholesterol 12mg; Calcium 26mg; Fibre 0.7g; Sodium 9mg.
Lemon: Energy 124kcal/519kJ; Protein 1.3g; Carbohydrate 15.7g, of which sugars 12g; Fat 6.6g, of which saturates 3.9g; Cholesterol 37mg; Calcium 20mg; Fibre 0.2g; Sodium 39mg.

Apricot Specials

3 ▲ Transfer to a 20cm/8in square cake tin (pan) and press level. Bake for 15 minutes. Remove from the oven but leave the oven on.

4 Meanwhile, for the topping, combine the apricots and water in a saucepan and simmer until soft, about 10 minutes. Strain the liquid and reserve. Chop the apricots.

5 ▲ Return the apricots to the pan and add the lemon rind, caster sugar, cornflour, and 60ml/4 tbsp of the apricot soaking liquid. Cook for 1 minute.

MAKES 12

90g/3¹/₂oz/¹/₂ cup soft light
   brown sugar

75g/3oz/²/₃ cup plain (all-purpose) flour

75g/3oz/6 tbsp cold unsalted butter,
   cut in pieces

FOR THE TOPPING

150g/5oz/generous ¹/₂ cup dried apricots

250ml/8fl oz/1 cup water

grated rind of 1 lemon

65g/2¹/₂ oz/5 tbsp caster (superfine) sugar

10ml/2 tsp cornflour (cornflour)

50g/2oz/¹/₃ cup chopped walnuts

1 Preheat a 180°C/350°F/Gas 4 oven.

2 ▲ In a bowl, combine the brown sugar and flour. With a pastry blender, cut in the butter until the mixture resembles coarse breadcrumbs.

6 ▲ Cool slightly before spreading the topping over the base. Sprinkle over the walnuts and continue baking for 20 minutes more. Let cool in the tin before cutting into bars.

Energy 169kcal/711kJ; Protein 1.8g; Carbohydrate 23.9g, of which sugars 18.3g; Fat 8.1g, of which saturates 3.5g; Cholesterol 13mg; Calcium 30mg; Fibre 1.1g; Sodium 41mg.

Almond-Topped Squares

MAKES 18

75g/3oz/6 tbsp butter

50g/2oz/¼ cup sugar

1 egg yolk

grated rind and juice of ½ lemon

2.5ml/½ tsp vanilla extract

30ml/2 tbsp whipping cream

115g/4oz/1 cup plain (all-purpose) flour

FOR THE TOPPING

225g/8oz/generous 1 cup sugar

75g/3oz/¾ cup flaked (sliced) almonds

4 egg whites

2.5ml/½ tsp ground ginger

2.5ml/½ tsp ground cinnamon

1 ▲ Preheat the oven to 190°C/375°F/
Gas 5. Line a 33 × 23cm/13 × 9in
Swiss roll tin (jelly roll pan) with
baking parchment; grease.

2 Cream the butter and sugar. Beat
in the egg yolk, lemon rind and juice,
vanilla extract and cream.

3 ▲ Gradually stir in the flour.
Gather into a ball of dough.

4 With lightly floured fingers, press
the dough into the prepared tin.
Bake for 15 minutes. Remove from
the oven but leave the oven on.

5 ▲ To make the topping, combine
all the ingredients in a heavy pan.
Cook, stirring until the mixture
comes to the boil.

6 Continue boiling until just golden,
about 1 minute. Pour over the dough,
spreading evenly.

7 ▲ Return to the oven and bake
for about 45 minutes. Remove and
score into bars or squares. Cool
completely before cutting into
squares and serving.

Energy 158kcal/661kJ; Protein 2g; Carbohydrate 21g, of which sugars 16g; Fat 8g, of which saturates 3g; Cholesterol 24mg; Calcium 25mg; Fibre 1g; Sodium 42mg

Spiced Raisin Bars

MAKES 30

115g/4oz/1 cup plain (all-purpose) flour,

7.5ml/1¹/₂ tsp baking powder

5ml/1 tsp ground cinnamon

2.5ml/¹/₂ tsp grated nutmeg

1.25ml/¹/₄ tsp ground cloves

1.25ml/¹/₄ tsp ground allspice

215g/7¹/₂oz/1¹/₂ cups raisins

115g/4oz/¹/₂ cup butter or margarine,
     at room temperature

90g/3¹/₂oz/¹/₂ cup sugar

2 eggs

165g/5¹/₂oz molasses

50g/2oz/¹/₃ cup walnuts, chopped

1 Preheat a 180°C/350°F/Gas 4 oven. Line a 33 × 23cm/13 × 9in tin (pan) with baking parchment and grease.

2 Sift together the flour, baking powder and spices.

3 ▲ Place the raisins in another bowl and toss with a few tablespoons of the flour mixture.

4 ▲ With an electric mixer, cream the butter or margarine and sugar together until light and fluffy. Beat in the eggs, one at a time, then the molasses. Stir in the flour mixture, raisins and walnuts.

5 Spread evenly in the tin. Bake until just set, 15–18 minutes. Let cool in the tin before cutting into bars.

Toffee Meringue Bars

MAKES 12

50g/2oz/¹/₄ cup butter

215g/7¹/₂oz/sacnt 1 cup soft dark
     brown sugar

1 egg

2.5ml/¹/₂ tsp vanilla extract

65g/2¹/₂oz/9 tbsp plain (all-purpose) flour

2.5ml/¹/₂ tsp salt

1.25ml/¹/₄ tsp grated nutmeg

FOR THE TOPPING

1 egg white

0.6ml/¹/₈ tsp salt

15ml/1 tbsp golden (light corn) syrup

90g/3¹/₂oz/¹/₂ cup caster (superfine) sugar

50g/2oz/¹/₃ cup walnuts, finely chopped

1 ▲ Combine the butter and brown sugar in a pan and heat until bubbling. Set aside to cool.

2 Preheat the oven to 180°C/350°F/ Gas 4. Line the bottom and sides of a 20cm/8in square cake tin (pan) with baking parchment and grease.

3 Beat the egg and vanilla into cooled sugar mixture. Sift over the flour, salt and nutmeg and fold in. Spread in the bottom of the tin.

4 ▲ For the topping, beat the egg white with the salt until it holds soft peaks. Beat in the golden syrup, then the sugar. Continue beating until the mixture holds stiff peaks. Fold in the nuts and spread on top. Bake for 30 minutes. Cut into bars when cool.

Spiced: Energy 102kcal/429kJ; Protein 1.2g; Carbohydrate 14.6g, of which sugars 12g; Fat 4.7g, of which saturates 2.2g; Cholesterol 21mg; Calcium 45mg; Fibre 0.3g; Sodium 34mg.
Toffee: Energy 189kcal/797kJ; Protein 2g; Carbohydrate 31.9g, of which sugars 27.8g; Fat 6.8g, of which saturates 2.5g; Cholesterol 25mg; Calcium 28mg; Fibre 0.3g; Sodium 42mg.

Strawberry Shortcake

SERVES 6

450g/1lb strawberries, hulled and halved or quartered, depending on size

45ml/3 tbsp icing (confectioners') sugar

250ml/8fl oz/1 cup whipping cream

mint leaves, for garnishing

FOR THE SHORTCAKE

225g/8oz/2 cups plain (all-purpose) flour

90g/3¹/₂oz/¹/₂ cup caster (superfine) sugar

15ml/1 tbsp baking powder

2.5ml/½ tsp salt

250ml/8fl oz/1 cup whipping cream

1 Preheat a 200°C/400°F/Gas 6 oven. Lightly grease a baking tray.

2 ▲ For the shortcake, sift the flour into a mixing bowl. Add 50g/2oz/ ¹/₄ cup of the caster sugar, the baking powder and salt. Stir well.

3 ▲ Gradually add the cream, tossing lightly with a fork until the mixture forms clumps.

4 ▲ Gather the clumps together, but do not knead the dough. Shape the dough into a 15cm/6in log. Cut into six slices and place them on the prepared baking tray.

5 ▲ Sprinkle with the remaining 25g/1oz/2 tbsp caster sugar. Bake until light golden brown, about 15 minutes. Let cool on a wire rack.

6 ▲ Meanwhile, combine one-quarter of the strawberries with the icing sugar. Mash with a fork. Stir in the remaining strawberries. Let stand 1 hour at room temperature.

7 ▲ In a bowl, whip the cream until soft peaks form.

8 ▲ To serve, slice each shortcake in half horizontally using a serrated knife. Put the bottom halves on individual dessert plates. Top each half with some of the whipped cream. Divide the strawberries among the six shortcakes. Replace the tops and garnish with mint. Serve with the remaining whipped cream.

~ COOK'S TIP ~

For best results when whipping cream, refrigerate the bowl and beaters until thoroughly chilled. If using an electric mixer, increase speed gradually, and turn the bowl while beating to incorporate as much air as possible.

Energy 436kcal/1811kJ; Protein 3.2g; Carbohydrate 33.2g, of which sugars 17.3g; Fat 32.9g, of which saturates 20.2g; Cholesterol 107mg; Calcium 60mg; Fibre 1.1g; Sodium 101mg.

BUNS & TEABREADS

EASY TO MAKE AND SATISFYING TO
EAT, THESE BUNS AND TEABREADS
WILL FILL THE HOUSE WITH
MOUTHWATERING SCENTS AND LURE
YOUR FAMILY AND FRIENDS TO
LINGER OVER BREAKFAST, COFFEE OR
TEA – AND THEY ARE GREAT FOR
SNACKS OR LUNCH.

Raisin Bran Buns

MAKES 15

50g/2oz/¹/4 cup butter or margarine

40g/1¹/2oz/¹/3 cup plain (all-purpose) flour

50g/2oz/¹/2 cup wholemeal
(whole-wheat) flour

7.5ml/1¹/2 tsp bicarbonate of soda
(baking soda)

0.6ml/¹/8 tsp salt

5ml/1 tsp ground cinnamon

25g/1oz/¹/4 cup bran

75g/3oz/¹/2 cup raisins

75g/3oz/6 tbsp soft dark brown sugar

50g/2oz/¹/4 cup caster (superfine) sugar

1 egg

250ml/8fl oz/1 cup buttermilk

juice of ¹/2 lemon

1 Preheat a 200°C/ 400°F/Gas 6 oven.
Grease 15 bun-tray cups.

2 ▲ Place the butter or margarine
in a pan and melt over gentle heat.
Set aside.

3 In a mixing bowl, sift together the
flours, bicarbonate of soda, salt and
ground cinnamon.

4 ▲ Add the bran, raisins and sugars
and stir until blended.

5 In another bowl, mix together the
egg, buttermilk, lemon juice and
melted butter.

6 ▲ Add the buttermilk mixture to
the dry ingredients and stir lightly and
quickly just until moistened; do not
mix until smooth.

7 ▲ Spoon the mixture into the
prepared bun tray, filling the cups
almost to the top. Half-fill any empty
cups with water.

8 Bake until golden, 15–20 minutes.
Serve warm or at room temperature.

Energy 89kcal/373kJ; Protein 2g; Carbohydrate 13.4g, of which sugars 8.9g; Fat 3.4g, of which saturates 1.9g; Cholesterol 20mg; Calcium 34mg; Fibre 1.1g; Sodium 36mg.

Raspberry Crumble Buns

MAKES 12

175g/6oz/1¹/₂ cups plain (all-purpose) flour

50g/2oz/¼ cup caster (superfine) sugar

50g/2oz/¼ cup soft light brown sugar

10ml/2 tsp baking powder

0.6ml/¹/₈ tsp salt

5ml/1 tsp ground cinnamon

115g/4oz/¹/₂ cup butter, melted

1 egg

120ml/4fl oz/¹/₂ cup milk

150g/5oz/scant 1 cup fresh raspberries

grated rind of 1 lemon

FOR THE CRUMBLE TOPPING

25g/1oz/2 tbsp finely chopped pecan nuts
    or walnuts

50g/2oz/4 tbsp soft dark brown sugar

45ml/3 tbsp plain (all-purpose) flour

5ml/1 tsp ground cinnamon

45ml/3 tbsp butter, melted

1 Preheat a 180°C/350°F/Gas 4 oven.
Lightly grease a 12-cup bun tray or use
paper cases.

2 Sift the flour into a bowl. Add
the sugars, baking powder, salt and
cinnamon and stir to blend.

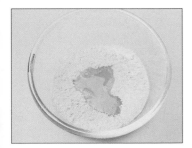

3 ▲ Make a well in the centre.
Place the butter, egg and milk in
the well and mix until just combined.
Stir in the raspberries and lemon rind.
Spoon the mixture into the prepared
bun tray, filling the cups almost
to the top.

4 ▼ For the crumble topping, mix
the nuts, dark brown sugar, flour and
cinnamon in a bowl. Add the melted
butter and stir to blend.

5 ▲ Spoon some of the crumble over
each bun. Bake until browned, about
25 minutes. Transfer to a rack to cool
slightly. Serve warm.

Energy 225kcal/940kJ; Protein 2.7g; Carbohydrate 25.2g, of which sugars 14.1g; Fat 13.3g, of which saturates 7.3g; Cholesterol 45mg; Calcium 48mg; Fibre 0.9g; Sodium 93mg.

Carrot Buns

MAKES 12

175g/6oz/³/4 cup margarine,
   at room temperature

100g/3³/4oz/ scant ¹/2 cup soft dark
   brown sugar

1 egg, at room temperature

15ml/1 tbsp water

225g/8oz carrots, grated

150g/5oz/1¹/4 cups plain (all-purpose) flour

5ml/1 tsp baking powder

2.5ml/¹/2 tsp bicarbonate of soda

5ml/1 tsp ground cinnamon

1.25ml/¹/4 tsp grated nutmeg

2.5ml/¹/2 tsp salt

1 Preheat an oven to 180°C/350°F/
Gas 4. Grease a 12-cup bun tray or use
paper cases.

2 With an electric mixer, cream the
margarine and sugar until light and
fluffy. Beat in the egg and water.

3 ▲ Stir in the carrots.

4 Sift over the flour, baking powder,
bicarbonate of soda, cinnamon,
nutmeg and salt. Stir to blend.

5 ▼ Spoon the mixture into the
prepared bun tray, filling the cups
almost to the top. Bake until the tops
spring back when touched lightly,
about 35 minutes. Let stand for
10 minutes, then transfer to a rack.

Dried Cherry Buns

MAKES 16

250ml/8fl oz/1 cup natural (plain) yogurt

175g/6oz/¹/2 cup dried cherries

115g/4oz/¹/2 cup butter, at room temperature

175g/6oz/scant 1 cup caster
   (superfine) sugar

2 eggs, at room temperature

5ml/1 tsp vanilla extract

190g/6¹/2oz/1²/3 cups plain
   (all-purpose) flour

10ml/2 tsp baking powder

5ml/1 tsp bicarbonate of soda
   (baking soda)

0.6ml/¹/8 tsp salt

1 Combine the yogurt and cherries
in a large mixing bowl. Cover and let
stand for 30 minutes.

2 Preheat a 180°C/350°F/Gas 4 oven.
Grease a 16 bun tray or use paper cases.

3 With an electric mixer, cream the
butter and sugar together until light
and fluffy.

4 ▼ Add the eggs, one at a time,
beating well after each addition. Add
the vanilla and the cherry mixture and
stir to blend. Set aside.

5 ▲ In another bowl, sift together
the flour, baking powder, bicarbonate
soda and salt. Fold into the cherry
mixture in three batches.

6 Fill the prepared cups two-thirds
full. For even baking, half-fill any
empty cups with water. Bake until
the tops spring back when touched
lightly, about 20 minutes. Transfer to
a wire rack to cool.

Carrot: Energy 190kcal/793kJ; Protein 2g; Carbohydrate 19g, of which sugars 10g; Fat 12g, of which saturates 3g; Cholesterol 20mg; Calcium 36mg; Fibre 1g; Sodium 278mg.
Cherry: Energy 165kcal/692kJ; Protein 2g; Carbohydrate 26g, of which sugars 16g; Fat 7g, of which saturates 4g; Cholesterol 17mg; Calcium 60mg; Fibre 1g; Sodium 199mg.

Blueberry Muffins

MAKES 12

175g/6oz/1½ cups plain (all-purpose) flour
65g/2½oz/generous ¼ cup sugar
10ml/2 tsp baking powder
1.25ml/¼ tsp salt
2 eggs
50g/2oz/¼ cup butter, melted
175ml/6fl oz/¾ cup milk
5ml/1 tsp vanilla extract
5ml/1 tsp grated lemon rind
175g/6oz/1½ cups fresh blueberries

1 Preheat a 200°C/400°F/Gas 6 oven.

2 ▼ Grease a 12-cup muffin tin (pan) or use paper cases.

3 ▲ Sift the flour, sugar, baking powder and salt into a bowl.

4 In another bowl, whisk the eggs until blended. Add the melted butter, milk, vanilla and lemon rind and stir to combine.

5 Make a well in the dry ingredients and pour in the egg mixture. With a large metal spoon, stir just until the flour is moistened, not until smooth.

6 ▲ Fold in the blueberries.

7 ▲ Spoon the batter into the cups, leaving room for the muffins to rise.

8 Bake until the tops spring back when touched lightly, 20–25 minutes. Let cool in the pan for 5 minutes before turning out.

Energy 129kcal/543kJ; Protein 3.1g; Carbohydrate 19.6g, of which sugars 7.6g; Fat 4.8g, of which saturates 2.6g; Cholesterol 41mg; Calcium 47mg; Fibre 0.8g; Sodium 44mg.

Apple and Cranberry Muffins

MAKES 12

50g/2oz/¹/₄ cup butter

1 egg

90g/3¹/₂oz/¹/₂ cup sugar

grated rind of 1 large orange

120ml/4fl oz/¹/₂ cup freshly squeezed
    orange juice

150g/5oz/1¹/₄ cups plain (all-purpose) flour

5ml/1 tsp baking powder

2.5ml/¹/₂ tsp bicarbonate of soda
    (baking soda)

5ml/1 tsp ground cinnamon

2.5ml/¹/₂ tsp grated nutmeg

2.5ml/¹/₂ tsp ground allspice

2.5ml/¹/₂ tsp ground ginger

1.25ml/¹/₄ tsp salt

1–2 eating apples

175g/6oz/1¹/₂ cups cranberries

50g/2oz/¹/₃ cup walnuts, chopped

icing (confectioners') sugar,
    for dusting (optional)

1 Preheat the oven to 180°C/350°F/Gas 4. Grease a 12-cup muffin tin (pan) or use paper cases.

2 Melt the butter or margarine over gentle heat. Set aside to cool.

3 ▲ Place the egg in a bowl and whisk. Add the melted butter or margarine and whisk to combine.

4 Add the sugar, orange rind and juice. Whisk to blend, then set aside.

5 In a large bowl, sift together the flour, baking powder, bicarbonate of soda, cinnamon, nutmeg, allspice, ginger and salt. Set aside.

6 ▲ Quarter, core and peel the apples. With a sharp knife, chop them coarsely.

7 Make a well in the dry ingredients and pour in the egg mixture. With a spoon, stir until just blended.

8 ▲ Add the apples, cranberries and walnuts and stir to blend.

9 Fill the cups three-quarters full and bake until the tops spring back when touched lightly, 25–30 minutes. Transfer to a wire rack to cool. Dust with icing sugar, if desired.

Energy 149kcal/624kJ; Protein 2.5g; Carbohydrate 20.4g, of which sugars 10.8g; Fat 6.9g, of which saturates 2.6g; Cholesterol 25mg; Calcium 30mg; Fibre 0.9g; Sodium 34mg.

Chocolate Chip Muffins

MAKES 10

115g/4oz/¹/₂ cup butter or margarine, at room temperature

75g/3oz/6 tbsp caster (superfine) sugar

25g/1oz/2 tbsp soft dark brown sugar

2 eggs, at room temperature

215g/7¹/₂ oz/scant 2 cups plain (all-purpose) flour

5ml/1 tsp baking powder

125ml/4fl oz/¹/₂ cup milk

175g/6oz plain (semisweet) chocolate chips

1 Preheat the oven to 190°C/375°F/ Gas 5. Grease 10 muffin cups or use paper cases.

2 ▼ With an electric mixer, cream the butter until soft. Add both sugars and beat until light and fluffy. Beat in the eggs, one at a time.

3 Sift together the flour and baking powder, twice. Fold into the butter mixture, alternating with the milk.

4 ▲ Divide half the mixture between the muffin cups. Sprinkle several chocolate chips on top, then cover with a spoonful of the batter. To ensure even baking, half-fill any empty cups with water.

5 Bake until lightly coloured, about 25 minutes. Let stand 5 minutes before turning out.

Chocolate Walnut Muffins

MAKES 12

175g/6oz/³/₄ cup unsalted butter

150g/5oz plain (semisweet) chocolate

200g/7oz/1 cup caster (superfine) sugar

50g/2oz/4 tbsp soft dark brown sugar

4 eggs

5ml/1 tsp vanilla extract

1.25ml/¹/₄ tsp almond extract

115g/4oz/1 cup plain (all-purpose) flour,

15ml/1 tbsp unsweetened cocoa powder

115g/4oz/²/₃ cup walnuts, chopped

1 Preheat the oven to 180°C/350°F/ Gas 4. Grease a 12-cup muffin pan or use paper cases.

2 ▼ Melt the butter with the chocolate in the top of a double boiler or in a heatproof bowl set over a pan of hot water. Transfer to a large mixing bowl.

3 Stir both the sugars into the chocolate mixture. Mix in the eggs, one at a time, then add the vanilla and almond extracts.

4 Sift over the flour and cocoa.

5 ▲ Fold in and stir in the walnuts.

6 Fill the prepared cups almost to the top and bake until a skewer inserted in the centre barely comes out clean, 30–35 minutes. Let stand 5 minutes before turning out onto a rack to cool completely.

Chip: Energy 306kcal/1281kJ; Protein 5g; Carbohydrate 38g, of which sugars 22g; Fat 16g, of which saturates 10g; Cholesterol 74mg; Calcium 65mg; Fibre 1g; Sodium 142mg.

Walnut: Energy 374kcal/1563kJ; Protein 6g; Carbohydrate 37g, of which sugars 30g; Fat 24g, of which saturates 11g; Cholesterol 108mg; Calcium 44mg; Fibre 1g; Sodium 118mg.

Oat and Raisin Muffins

MAKES 12

90g/3¹/₂oz/1 cup rolled porridge oats

250ml/8fl oz/1 cup buttermilk

115g/4oz/¹/₂ cup butter, at room temperature

100g/3³/₄oz/ scant ¹/₂ cup soft dark
    brown sugar

1 egg, at room temperature

115g/4oz/1 cup plain (all-purpose) flour,

5ml/1 tsp baking powder

2.5ml/¹/₂ tsp bicarbonate of soda
    (baking soda)

1.25ml/¹/₄ tsp salt

25g/1oz/2 tbsp raisins

~ COOK'S TIP ~

Instead of buttermilk. add 15ml/
1 tbsp lemon juice to milk. Leave
for a few minutes to curdle.

1 ▲ In a bowl, combine the oats and buttermilk and let soak for 1 hour.

2 ▲ Lightly grease a 12-cup muffin tin (pan) or use paper cases.

3 ▲ Preheat the oven to 200°C/ 400°F/Gas 6. With an electric mixer, cream the butter and sugar until light and fluffy. Beat in the egg.

4 In another bowl, sift the flour, baking powder, bicarbonate of soda and salt. Stir into the butter mixture, alternating with the oat mixture. Fold in the raisins. Do not overmix.

5 Fill the prepared cups two-thirds full. Bake until a skewer inserted in the centre comes out clean, 20–25 minutes. Transfer to a rack to cool.

Pumpkin Muffins

MAKES 14

115g/4oz/¹/₂ cup butter, at room temperature

150g/5oz/generous ¹/₂ cup soft dark
    brown sugar

60ml/4 tbsp molasses

1 egg, at room temperature, beaten

225g/8oz cooked or canned pumpkin

225g/8oz/2 cups plain (all-purpose) flour

1.25ml/¹/₄ tsp salt

5ml/1 tsp bicarbonate of soda (baking soda)

7.5ml/1¹/₂ tsp ground cinnamon

5ml/1 tsp grated nutmeg

25g/1oz/2 tbsp currants or raisins

1 Preheat the oven to 200°C/400°F/ Gas 6. Grease 14 muffin cups or use paper cases.

2 With an electric mixer, cream the butter in a large bowl until soft. Add the sugar and molasses and beat until light and fluffy.

3 ▲ Add the egg and pumpkin and stir until well blended.

4 Sift over the flour, salt, bicarbonate of soda, cinnamon and nutmeg. Fold just enough to blend; do not overmix.

5 ▼ Fold in the currants or raisins.

6 Spoon the mixture into the prepared muffin cups or paper cases, filling them three-quarters full.

7 Bake until the tops of the muffins spring back when touched lightly, 12–15 minutes. Remove from the oven and let cool on a wire rack. Serve warm or cold.

Oat: Energy 190kcal/795kJ; Protein 3g; Carbohydrate 24g, of which sugars 11g; Fat 10g, of which saturates 5g; Cholesterol 41mg; Calcium 57mg; Fibre 1g; Sodium 212mg.

Pumpkin: Energy 187kcal/785kJ; Protein 2g; Carbohydrate 29g, of which sugars 16g; Fat 8g, of which saturates 5g; Cholesterol 35mg; Calcium 53mg; Fibre 1g; Sodium 179mg.

Prune Muffins

MAKES 12

1 egg
250ml/8fl oz/1 cup milk
125ml/4fl oz/¹/₂ cup vegetable oil
50g/2oz/¹/₄ cup caster (superfine) sugar
25g/1oz/2 tbsp soft dark brown sugar
275g/10oz/2¹/₂ cups plain (all-purpose) flour
10ml/2 tsp baking powder
2.5ml/¹/₂ tsp salt
1.25ml/¹/₄ tsp grated nutmeg
115g/4oz/¹/₂ cup cooked pitted prunes, chopped

1 Preheat a 200°C/400°F/Gas 6 oven. Grease a 12-cup muffin tin (pan).

2 Break the egg into a mixing bowl and beat with a fork. Beat in the milk and oil.

3 ▼ Stir in the sugars. Set aside.

4 Sift the flour, baking powder, salt and nutmeg into a mixing bowl. Make a well in the centre, pour in the egg mixture and stir until moistened. Do not overmix; the batter should be slightly lumpy.

5 ▲ Fold in the prunes.

6 Fill the prepared cups two-thirds full. Bake until golden brown, about 20 minutes. Let stand 10 minutes before turning out. Serve warm or at room temperature.

Yogurt and Honey Muffins

MAKES 12

50g/2oz/¹/₄ cup butter
75ml/5 tbsp clear honey
250ml/8fl oz/1 cup natural (plain) yogurt
1 large (US extra large) egg
grated rind of 1 lemon
60ml/4 tbsp lemon juice
150g/5oz/1¹/₄ cups plain (all-purpose) flour
175g/6oz/1¹/₂ cups wholemeal (whole-wheat) flour
7.5ml/1¹/₂ tsp bicarbonate of soda (baking soda)
0.6ml/¹/₈ tsp grated nutmeg

~ VARIATION ~

For Walnut Yogurt Honey Muffins, add 50g/2oz/¹/₃ cup chopped walnuts, folded in with the flour.

1 Preheat a 190°C/375°F/Gas 5 oven. Grease a 12-cup muffin tin (pan) or use paper cases.

2 In a pan, melt the butter and honey. Remove from the heat and set aside to cool slightly.

3 ▲ In a bowl, whisk together the yogurt, egg, lemon rind and juice. Add the butter and honey mixture. Set aside.

4 ▲ In another bowl, sift together the dry ingredients.

5 Fold the dry ingredients into the yogurt mixture to blend.

6 Fill the prepared cups two-thirds full. Bake until the tops spring back when touched lightly, 20–25 minutes. Let cool in the tin for 5 minutes before turning out. Serve warm or at room temperature.

Prune: Energy 190kcal/801kJ; Protein 3.7g; Carbohydrate 28.1g, of which sugars 10.7g; Fat 7.8g, of which saturates 1.2g; Cholesterol 17mg; Calcium 66mg; Fibre 1.3g; Sodium 17mg.
Yogurt: Energy 155kcal/652kJ; Protein 4.7g; Carbohydrate 25.4g, of which sugars 6.9g; Fat 4.6g, of which saturates 2.5g; Cholesterol 25mg; Calcium 66mg; Fibre 1.7g; Sodium 50mg.

Banana Muffins

MAKES 10

250g/9oz/2¼ cups plain (all-purpose) flour

5ml/1 tsp baking powder

5ml/1 tsp bicarbonate of soda (baking soda)

1.25ml/¼ tsp salt

2.5ml/½ tsp ground cinnamon

1.25ml/¼ tsp grated nutmeg

3 large ripe bananas

1 egg

75g/3oz/6 tbsp soft dark brown sugar

45ml/3 tbsp vegetable oil

25g/1oz/2 tbsp raisins

1 ▼ Preheat the oven to 190°C/ 375°F/Gas 5. Lightly grease or line 10 deep muffin cups with paper cases.

2 Sift together the flour, baking powder, bicarbonate of soda, salt, cinnamon and nutmeg. Set aside.

3 ▲ With an electric mixer, beat the peeled bananas at moderate speed until mashed.

4 ▲ Beat in the egg, sugar and oil.

5 Add the dry ingredients and beat in gradually, on low speed. Mix just until blended. With a wooden spoon, stir in the raisins.

6 Fill the prepared cups two-thirds full. For even baking, half-fill any empty cups with water.

7 ▲ Bake until the tops spring back when touched lightly, 20–25 minutes. Transfer to a rack to cool.

Energy 208kcal/875kJ; Protein 4g; Carbohydrate 37g, of which sugars 17g; Fat 6g, of which saturates 1g; Cholesterol 23mg; Calcium 54mg; Fibre 2g; Sodium 220mg.

Maple Pecan Muffins

MAKES 20

175g/6oz/1 cup pecans
350g/12oz/3 cups plain (all-purpose) flour
5ml/1 tsp baking powder
5ml/1 tsp bicarbonate of soda (baking soda)
1.25ml/^{1}/$_4$ tsp salt
1.25ml/^{1}/$_4$ tsp ground cinnamon
90g/3^1/$_2$oz/^{1}/$_2$ cup caster (superfine) sugar
75g/3oz/6 tbsp soft light brown sugar
45ml/3 tbsp maple syrup
150g/5oz/10 tbsp butter, at room temperature
3 eggs, at room temperature
300ml/^{1}/$_2$ pint/1^1/$_4$ cups buttermilk
60 pecan halves, for decorating

1 Preheat the oven to 180°C/350°F/ Gas 4. Lightly grease 24 deep muffin cups or use paper cases.

2 ▲ Spread the pecans on a baking sheet and toast in the oven for 5 minutes. Keep a close eye on them as they can easily burn. When cool, chop coarsely and set aside.

3 In a bowl, sift together the flour, baking powder, bicarbonate of soda, salt and cinnamon. Set aside.

4 ▲ In a large mixing bowl, combine the caster sugar, light brown sugar, maple syrup and butter. Beat with an electric mixer until light and fluffy.

5 Add the eggs, one at a time, beating to incorporate thoroughly after each addition.

6 ▲ Pour half the buttermilk and half the dry ingredients into the butter mixture, then stir until blended. Repeat with the remaining buttermilk and dry ingredients.

7 Fold in the chopped pecans. Fill the prepared cups two-thirds full. Top with the pecan halves. For even baking, half-fill any empty cups with water.

8 Bake until puffed up and golden, 20–25 minutes. Let stand 5 minutes before unmoulding.

~ VARIATION ~

For Pecan Spice Muffins, substitute an equal quantity of golden (light corn) syrup for the maple syrup. Increase the cinnamon to 2.5ml/^{1}/$_2$ tsp, and add 5ml/1 tsp ground ginger and 2.5ml/^{1}/$_2$ tsp grated nutmeg, sifted with the dry ingredients.

Energy 301kcal/1253kJ; Protein 6g; Carbohydrate 26g, of which sugars 12g; Fat 20g, of which saturates 5g; Cholesterol 51mg; Calcium 73mg; Fibre 2g; Sodium 172mg.

Banana and Pecan Muffins

MAKES 8

150g/5oz/1¼ cups plain
(all-purpose) flour

7.5ml/1½ tsp baking powder

50g/2oz/¼ cup butter or margarine,
at room temperature

150g/5oz/¾ cup caster (superfine) sugar

1 egg

5ml/1 tsp vanilla extract

3 medium bananas, mashed

50g/2oz/⅓ cup pecans, chopped

75ml/5 tbsp milk

~ **VARIATION** ~

Use an equal quantity of walnuts
instead of the pecans.

1 Preheat the oven to 190°C/375°F/
Gas 5. Lightly grease eight deep muffin
tins (pans).

2 Sift the flour and baking powder
into a small bowl. Set aside.

3 ▲ With an electric mixer, cream
the butter or margarine and sugar
together. Add the egg and vanilla and
beat until fluffy. Mix in the banana.

4 ▼ Add the pecans. With the mixer
on low speed, beat in the flour
mixture alternately with the milk.

5 Spoon the mixture into the
prepared muffin tins, filling them
two-thirds full. Bake until golden
brown and a skewer inserted into the
centre of a muffin comes out clean,
20–25 minutes.

6 Let cool in the tin on a wire rack
for 10 minutes. To loosen, run a
knife gently around each muffin and
unmould on to the wire rack. Let cool
10 minutes longer before serving.

Blueberry and Cinnamon Muffins

MAKES 8

115g/4oz/1 cup plain (all-purpose) flour,

15ml/1 tbsp baking powder

pinch of salt

75g/3oz/6 tbsp soft light brown sugar

1 egg

175ml/6fl oz/¾ cup milk

45ml/3 tbsp vegetable oil

10ml/2 tsp ground cinnamon

115g/4oz/1 cup fresh or thawed
frozen blueberries

1 Preheat the oven to 190°C/375°F/
Gas 5. Lightly grease eight deep
muffin tins.

2 With an electric mixer, beat
the first eight ingredients together
until smooth.

3 ▲ Fold in the blueberries genly,
trying not to break them up.

4 ▲ Spoon the mixture into the
muffin cups, filling them two-thirds
full. Bake until a skewer inserted in
the centre of a muffin comes out
clean, about 25 minutes.

5 Let cool in the tins on a wire rack
for 10 minutes, then unmould the
muffins on to the wire rack and allow
to cool completely.

Banana: Energy 277kcal/1164kJ; Protein 4g; Carbohydrate 43.7g, of which sugars 28.5g; Fat 10.7g, of which saturates 4g; Cholesterol 38mg; Calcium 58mg; Fibre 1.3g; Sodium 53mg.
Blueberry: Energy 141kcal/593kJ; Protein 3.1g; Carbohydrate 21.4g, of which sugars 10.5g; Fat 5.4g, of which saturates 0.9g; Cholesterol 25mg; Calcium 60mg; Fibre 0.9g; Sodium 19mg.

Raspberry Muffins

MAKES 10–12

115g/4oz/1 cup self-raising (self-rising) flour

115g/4oz/1 cup wholemeal (whole-wheat) self-raising flour

45ml/3 tbsp caster (superfine) sugar

2.5ml/½ tsp salt

2 eggs, beaten

200ml/7fl oz/scant 1 cup milk

50g/2oz/¼ cup butter, melted

175g/6oz/1½ cups raspberries, fresh or frozen (defrosted for less than 30 minutes)

1 ▼ Preheat the oven to 190°C/ 375°F/Gas 5. Lightly grease the muffin tins (pans), or use paper cases. Sift the dry ingredients together, then tip back in the wholewheat flakes from the sieve (strainer).

2 ▲ Beat the eggs, milk and butter with the dry ingredients to give a thick batter. Add the raspberries.

3 ▲ Stir in the raspberries gently. (If you are using frozen raspberries, work quickly as the cold berries make the mixture solidify.) If you mix too much the raspberries begin to disintegrate and colour the dough. Spoon the mixture into the tins or paper cases.

4 Bake the muffins for 30 minutes, until well risen and just firm. Serve warm or cool.

Energy 165kcal/696kJ; Protein 3.6g; Carbohydrate 29.3g, of which sugars 11.9g; Fat 4.5g, of which saturates 0.7g; Cholesterol 17mg; Calcium 68mg; Fibre 1g; Sodium 17mg.

Cherry Marmalade Muffins

MAKES 12

225g/8oz/2 cups self-raising
  (self-rising) flour

5ml/1 tsp mixed (apple pie) spice

75g/3oz/6 tbsp caster (superfine) sugar

115g/4oz/^{1}/$_2$ cup glacé (candied)
  cherries, quartered

30ml/2 tbsp orange marmalade

150ml/^{1}/$_4$ pint/^{2}/$_3$ cup skimmed milk

50g/2oz/^{1}/$_4$ cup soft margarine

marmalade, to brush

1 ▲ Preheat the oven to 200°C/400°F/
Gas 6. Lightly grease 12 deep muffin
tins (pans) with oil.

2 ▲ Sift together the flour and spice
then stir in the sugar and cherries.

3 Mix the marmalade with the milk
and beat into the dry ingredients with
the margarine. Spoon into the greased
tins. Bake for 20–25 minutes, until
golden brown and firm.

4 ▼ Turn out on to a wire rack and
brush the tops with warmed
marmalade. Serve warm or cold.

~ VARIATION ~

To make Honey, Nut and Lemon
Muffins, substitute 30ml/2 tbsp
clear honey for the orange
marmalade, and the juice and finely
grated rind of a lemon, and 45ml/
3 tbsp toasted, chopped hazelnuts,
instead of the cherries.

Energy 162kcal/686kJ; Protein 2.3g; Carbohydrate 29.8g, of which sugars 15.5g; Fat 4.6g, of which saturates 0.7g; Cholesterol 1mg; Calcium 51mg; Fibre 0.7g; Sodium 9mg.

Blackberry and Almond Muffins

2 ▲ In another bowl, mix the eggs with the milk, then gradually add the butter, sloe gin and rosewater. Make a well in the centre of the bowl of dry ingredients and add the egg and milk mixture. Stir well.

3 Lightly grease 12 deep muffin tins (pans). Spoon in the mixture and bake for 20–25 minutes or until browned. Turn out the muffins on to a wire rack to cool. Serve with butter.

~ COOK'S TIP ~

Other berries can be substituted for the blackberries, such as elderberries or blueberries.

MAKES 12

300g/11oz/2²/₃ cups plain (all-purpose) flour

50g/2oz/4 tbsp soft light brown sugar

20ml/4 tsp baking powder

pinch of salt

50g/2oz/¹/₃ cup chopped blanched almonds

115g/4oz/1 cup fresh blackberries

2 eggs

200ml/7fl oz/scant 1 cup milk

60ml/4 tbsp melted butter, plus a little more to grease cups, if using

15ml/1 tbsp sloe gin

15ml/1 tbsp rosewater

1 ▼ Mix the flour, sugar, baking powder and salt in a bowl and stir in the almonds and blackberries, mixing them well to coat with the flour mixture. Preheat the oven to 200°C/400°F/Gas 6.

~ VARIATION ~

For Blackberry and Apple Muffins, substitute 2 eating apples, peeled, cored and diced for the almonds. Add 5ml/1 tsp ground coriander to the flour mixture, and instead of the sloe gin and rosewater, substitute 30ml/2 tbsp of Crème de Mûre.

Energy 183kcal/770kJ; Protein 4g; Carbohydrate 26g, of which sugars 6g; Fat 8g, of which saturates 3g; Cholesterol 13mg; Calcium 88mg; Fibre 2g; Sodium 198mg.

Bacon and Cornmeal Muffins

MAKES 14

8 bacon rashers (slices)

50g/2oz/¼ cup butter

50g/2oz/¼ cup margarine

115g/4oz/1 cup plain (all-purpose) flour,

15ml/1 tbsp baking powder

5ml/1 tsp sugar

1.25ml/¼ tsp salt

225g/8oz/2 cups cornmeal

125ml/4fl oz/½ cup milk

2 eggs

1 Preheat the oven to 200°C/400°F/ Gas 6. Lightly grease 14 deep muffin tins (pans) or use paper cases.

2 ▲ Fry the bacon until crisp. Drain on kitchen paper, then chop into small pieces. Set aside.

3 Gently melt the butter and margarine and set aside.

4 ▲ Sift the flour, baking powder, sugar, and salt into a large mixing bowl. Stir in the cornmeal, then make a well in the centre.

5 In a pan, heat the milk until lukewarm. In a small bowl, lightly whisk the eggs, then add to the milk. Stir in the melted fats.

6 ▼ Pour the milk mixture into the centre of the well and stir until smooth and well blended.

7 ▲ Stir the bacon into the mixture, then spoon the mixture into the prepared cups, filling them half-full.

8 Bake until risen and lightly coloured, about 20 minutes. Remove from the pans or paper cases and serve hot or warm.

Energy 476kcal/1968kJ; Protein 7g; Carbohydrate 20g, of which sugars 1g; Fat 41g, of which saturates 11g; Cholesterol 55mg; Calcium 41mg; Fibre 1g; Sodium 639mg.

Cheese Muffins

MAKES 9

50g/2oz/¼ cup butter
200g/7oz/1¾ cups plain (all-purpose) flour
10ml/2 tsp baking powder
30ml/2 tbsp sugar
1.25ml/¼ tsp salt
5ml/1 tsp paprika
2 eggs
125ml/4fl oz/½ cup milk
5ml/1 tsp dried thyme
50g/2oz mature (sharp) Cheddar cheese, cut into 1cm/½in dice

1 Preheat the oven to 190°C/375°F/ Gas 5. Thickly grease nine deep muffin tins (pans) or use paper cases.

2 Melt the butter and set aside.

3 ▼ In a mixing bowl, sift together the flour, baking powder, sugar, salt and paprika.

4 ▲ In another bowl, combine the eggs, milk, melted butter and thyme, and whisk to blend.

5 Add the milk mixture to the dry ingredients and stir just until moistened; do not mix until smooth.

6 ▲ Place a heaped spoonful of batter into the prepared cups. Drop a few pieces of cheese over each, then top with another spoonful of batter. For even baking, half-fill any empty muffin cups with water.

7 ▲ Bake until puffed and golden, about 25 minutes. Let stand 5 minutes before unmoulding on to a rack. Serve warm or at room temperature.

Energy 166kcal/698kJ; Protein 5.1g; Carbohydrate 19.3g, of which sugars 4.4g; Fat 8.1g, of which saturates 4.6g; Cholesterol 60mg; Calcium 93mg; Fibre 0.6g; Sodium 96mg.

Sweet Potato Scones

MAKES ABOUT 24

150g/5oz/1¼ cups plain (all-purpose) flour

20ml/4 tsp baking powder

5ml/1 tsp salt

15ml/1 tbsp soft light brown sugar

45ml/3 tbsp mashed cooked sweet potatoes

150ml/¼ pint/⅔ cup milk

50g/2oz/¼ cup butter or margarine, melted

1 Preheat the oven to 230°C/450°F/ Gas 8.

2 ▲ Sift the flour, baking powder and salt into a bowl. Add the sugar and stir to mix.

3 ▲ In a separate bowl, combine the sweet potatoes with the milk and melted butter or margarine. Mix well until evenly blended.

4 ▼ Stir the dry ingredients into the sweet potato mixture to make a dough. Turn on to a lightly floured surface and knead lightly, just to mix, for 1–2 minutes.

5 ▲ Roll or pat out the dough to 1cm/½in thickness. Stamp out rounds with a 4cm/1½in pastry cutter.

6 Arrange the rounds on a greased baking sheet. Bake until puffed and lightly golden, about 15 minutes. Serve the scones warm.

Energy 48kcal/200kJ; Protein 0.9g; Carbohydrate 7.1g, of which sugars 1.4g; Fat 1.9g, of which saturates 1.2g; Cholesterol 5mg; Calcium 18mg; Fibre 0.3g; Sodium 18mg.

Buttermilk Scones

MAKES 15

200g/7oz/1³/₄ cups plain (all-purpose) flour

5ml/1 tsp salt

5ml/1 tsp baking powder

2.5ml/¹/₂ tsp bicarbonate of soda (baking soda)

60ml/4 tbsp cold butter or margarine

175ml/6fl oz/³/₄ cup buttermilk

1 Preheat the oven to 220°C/425°F/ Gas 7. Grease a baking sheet.

2 Sift the dry ingredients into a bowl. Rub in the butter or margarine with your fingertips until the mixture resembles breadcrumbs.

3 ▼ Gradually pour in the buttermilk, stirring with a fork to form a soft dough.

4 ▲ Roll out the dough until it is about 1cm/¹/₂in thick. Stamp out rounds with a 5cm/2in pastry cutter.

5 Place the rounds on the prepared baking sheet and bake until golden, 12–15 minutes. Serve warm or at room temperature.

Traditional Sweet Scones

MAKES 8

175g/6oz/1¹/₂ cups plain (all-purpose) flour

30ml/2 tbsp sugar

15ml/1 tbsp baking powder

0.6ml/¹/₈ tsp salt

65g/2¹/₂oz/5 tbsp cold butter, cut in pieces

125ml/4fl oz/¹/₂ cup milk

1 Preheat the oven to 220°C/425°F/ Gas 7. Grease a baking sheet.

2 ▲ Sift the flour, sugar, baking powder, and salt into a bowl.

3 Cut in the butter with a pastry blender until the mixture resembles coarse crumbs.

4 Pour in the milk and stir with a fork to form a soft dough.

5 ▲ Roll out the dough about 5mm/ ¹/₄in thick. Stamp out rounds using a 6cm/2¹/₂in pastry cutter.

6 Place on the prepared sheet and bake until golden, about 12 minutes. Serve hot or warm, with butter and jam, to accompany tea or coffee.

~ VARIATION ~

To make a delicious and speedy dessert, split the scones in half while still warm. Butter one half, top with lightly sugared fresh strawberries, raspberries or blueberries, and sandwich with the other half. Serve at once with dollops of whipped cream.

Buttermilk: Energy 80kcal/336kJ; Protein 2g; Carbohydrate 11g, of which sugars 1g; Fat 4g, of which saturates 2g; Cholesterol 9mg; Calcium 36mg; Fibre 0g; Sodium 230mg.
Traditional: Energy 170kcal/711kJ; Protein 3g; Carbohydrate 22g, of which sugars 5g; Fat 9g, of which saturates 5g; Cholesterol 22mg; Calcium 67mg; Fibre 1g; Sodium 241mg.

Wholemeal Scones

MAKES 16

175g/6oz/³/4 cup cold butter

350g/12oz/3 cups wholemeal (whole-wheat) flour

150g/5oz/1¼ cups plain (all-purpose) flour

30ml/2 tbsp sugar

2.5ml/½ tsp salt

7.5ml/2½ tsp bicarbonate of soda (baking soda)

2 eggs

175ml/6fl oz/³/4 cup buttermilk

30ml/2 tbsp raisins

1 Preheat the oven to 200°C/400°F/ Gas 6. Grease and flour a baking sheet.

2 ▲ Cut the cold butter into small pieces with a knife.

3 Combine the dry ingredients in a large mixing bowl. Add the butter and rub in with your fingertips until the mixture resembles coarse breadcrumbs. Set aside.

4 In another bowl, whisk together the eggs and buttermilk. Set aside 30ml/2 tbsp for glazing.

5 Stir the remaining egg mixture into the dry ingredients until it just holds together. Stir in the raisins.

6 Roll out the dough about 2cm/³/4in thick. Stamp out circles with a pastry cutter. Place on the prepared sheet and brush with the glaze.

7 Bake until golden, 12–15 minutes. Allow to cool slightly before serving. Split in two with a fork while still warm and spread with butter and jam, if wished.

Orange and Raisin Scones

MAKES 16

275g/10oz/2½ cups plain (all-purpose) flour

7.5ml/1½ tsp baking powder

60ml/4 tbsp sugar

2.5ml/½ tsp salt

75g/3oz/6 tbsp butter, diced

75g/3oz/6 tbsp margarine, diced

grated rind of 1 large orange

50g/2oz/4 tbsp raisins

125ml/4fl oz/½ cup buttermilk

milk, for glazing

1 Preheat the oven to 220°C/425°F/ Gas 7. Grease and flour a large baking sheet.

2 Combine the dry ingredients in a large bowl. Add the butter and margarine and rub in with your fingertips until the mixture resembles coarse breadcrumbs.

3 ▲ Add the orange rind and raisins.

4 Gradually stir in the buttermilk to form a soft dough.

5 ▲ Roll out the dough about 2cm/ ³/4in thick. Stamp out circles with a pastry cutter.

6 ▲ Place on the prepared sheet and brush the tops with milk.

7 Bake until golden, 12–15 minutes. Serve hot or warm, with butter, or whipped or clotted cream, and jam.

~ COOK'S TIP ~

For light, tender scones, handle the dough as little as possible. If you wish, split the scones when cool and toast them under a preheated grill (broiler). Butter them while still hot.

Wholemeal: Energy 207kcal/869kJ; Protein 4.9g; Carbohydrate 25.3g, of which sugars 4.6g; Fat 10.3g, of which saturates 6g; Cholesterol 48mg; Calcium 42mg; Fibre 2.3g; Sodium 82mg.
Orange: Energy 145kcal/606kJ; Protein 2g; Carbohydrate 19.8g, of which sugars 6.7g; Fat 6.9g, of which saturates 2.2g; Cholesterol 9mg; Calcium 38mg; Fibre 0.6g; Sodium 63mg.

Sunflower Sultana Scones

MAKES 10–12

225g/8oz/2 cups

5ml/1 tsp baking powder

25g/1oz/2 tbsp soft sunflower margarine

30ml/2 tbsp caster (superfine) sugar

50g/2oz/4 tbsp sultanas (golden raisins)

30ml/2 tbsp sunflower seeds

150ml/¼ pint/⅔ cup natural (plain) yogurt

about 30–45ml/2–3 tbsp skimmed milk

1 Preheat the oven to 230°C/450°F/ Gas 8. Lightly oil a baking sheet. Sift the flour and baking powder into a bowl and rub in the margarine evenly.

2 Stir in the sugar, sultanas and half the sunflower seeds, then mix in the yogurt, with just enough milk to make a fairly soft, but not sticky dough.

3 ▼ Roll out on a lightly floured surface to about 2cm/¾in thickness. Cut into 6cm/2½in flower shapes or rounds with a pastry cutter and lift on to the baking sheet.

4 ▲ Brush with milk and sprinkle with the reserved sunflower seeds, then bake for 10–12 minutes, until well risen and golden brown.

5 Cool the scones on a wire rack. Serve split and spread with butter and jam.

Prune and Peel Rock Buns

MAKES 12

225g/8oz/2 cups plain (all-purpose) flour

10ml/2 tsp baking powder

75g/3oz/6 tbsp demerara (raw) sugar

50g/2oz/¼ cup chopped ready-to-eat dried prunes

50g/2oz/⅔ cup mixed chopped (candied) peel

finely grated rind of 1 lemon

45ml/3 tbsp sunflower oil

75ml/5 tbsp skimmed milk

~ VARIATION ~

For Spicy Rock Buns, substitute 50g/2oz/4 tbsp currants for the prunes, 50g/2oz/4 tbsp raisins for the peel, and add 5ml/1 tsp mixed (apple pie) spice, 1.25ml/¼ tsp ground ginger, and 1.25ml/¼ tsp ground cinnamon.

1 ▼ Preheat the oven to 200°C/ 400°F/Gas 6. Lightly oil a large baking sheet. Sift together the flour and baking powder, then stir in the sugar, prunes, peel and lemon rind.

2 Mix the oil and milk, then stir into the mixture, to make a dough which just binds together.

3 ▲ Spoon into rocky heaps on the baking sheet and bake for 20 minutes, until golden. Cool on a wire rack.

Sunflower: Energy 121kcal/513kJ; Protein 3g; Carbohydrate 21.2g, of which sugars 6.9g; Fat 3.3g, of which saturates 0.6g; Cholesterol 0mg; Calcium 99mg; Fibre 0.8g; Sodium 97mg.
Prune: Energy 132kcal/559kJ; Protein 2.1g; Carbohydrate 25.3g, of which sugars 11g; Fat 3.2g, of which saturates 0.4g; Cholesterol 0mg; Calcium 44mg; Fibre 1g; Sodium 16mg.

Cheese and Marjoram Scones

MAKES 18

115g/4oz/1 cup wholemeal
   (whole-wheat) flour

115g/4oz/1 cup self-raising
   (self-rising) flour

pinch of salt

50g/2oz/¼ cup butter

1.25ml/¼ tsp mustard powder

10ml/2 tsp dried marjoram

50–75g/2–3oz Cheddar cheese,
   finely grated

125ml/4fl oz/½ cup milk,
   or as required

5ml/1 tsp sunflower oil

50g/2oz/⅓ cup pecan or
   walnuts, chopped

1 ▼ Sift the two kinds of flour into a bowl and add the salt. Cut the butter into small pieces, and rub into the flour until the mixture resembles fine breadcrumbs.

2 ▲ Add the mustard, marjoram and grated cheese, and mix in sufficient milk to make a soft dough. Knead the dough lightly.

3 Preheat the oven to 220°C/425°F/ Gas 7. Roll out the dough on a lightly floured surface to about a 2cm/¾ in thickness and cut out about 18 scones using a 5cm/2in square cutter. Grease two baking sheets with a little sunflower oil, and place the scones on the trays.

4 Brush the scones with a little milk and sprinkle the chopped pecans or walnuts over the top. Bake for 12 minutes. Serve warm.

~ VARIATION ~

For Mixed Herb and Mustard Scones, use 30ml/2 tbsp chopped fresh parsley or chives instead of the dried marjoram and 5ml/1 tsp Dijon mustard instead of the mustard powder. Substitute 50g/2oz/⅓ cup chopped pistachio nuts for the pecans or walnuts.

Energy 121kcal/504kJ; Protein 3g; Carbohydrate 9.8g, of which sugars 0.9g; Fat 8g, of which saturates 2.4g; Cholesterol 8mg; Calcium 44mg; Fibre 1.1g; Sodium 39mg.

Cheese and Chive Scones

MAKES 9

115g/4oz/1 cup self-raising
  (self-rising) flour

150g/5oz/1¼ cups self-raising wholemeal
  (whole-wheat) flour

2.5ml/½ tsp salt

75g/3oz feta cheese

15ml/1 tbsp snipped fresh chives

150ml/¼ pint/⅔ cup skimmed milk, plus
  extra for glazing

1.25ml/¼ tsp cayenne pepper

1 ▲ Preheat the oven to 200°C/400°F/
Gas 6. Sift the flours and salt into a
mixing bowl, adding any bran left in
the sieve (strainer).

2 ▲ Crumble the feta cheese and rub
into the dry ingredients. Stir in the
chives, then add the milk and mix to
a soft dough.

3 ▼ Turn out the dough on to a
floured surface and lightly knead until
smooth. Roll out to 2cm/³⁄4 in thick
and stamp out nine scones with a
6cm/2¹⁄2in pastry cutter.

4 ▲ Transfer the scones to a
non-stick baking sheet. Brush with
skimmed milk, then sprinkle over the
cayenne pepper. Bake in the oven for
15 minutes, or until golden brown.
Serve warm or cold.

Energy 124kcal/524kJ; Protein 5.2g; Carbohydrate 21.5g, of which sugars 1.5g; Fat 2.5g, of which saturates 1.4g; Cholesterol 7mg; Calcium 74mg; Fibre 1.9g; Sodium 128mg.

Dill and Potato Cakes

MAKES 10

225g/8oz/2 cups self-raising
  (self-rising) flour

40g/1¹/₂oz/3 tbsp butter, softened

pinch of salt

15ml/1 tbsp finely chopped fresh dill

175g/6oz mashed potato, freshly made

30–45ml/3–4 tbsp milk, as required

1 ▼ Preheat the oven to 230°C/450°F/
Gas 8. Sift the flour into a bowl, and
add the butter, salt and dill. Mix in
the mashed potato and enough milk
to make a soft, pliable dough.

2 ▲ Roll out the dough on a well-
floured surface until it is fairly thin.
Cut into neat rounds using a
7.5cm/3in cutter.

3 ▲ Grease a baking sheet, place the
cakes on it, and bake for 20–25
minutes until risen and golden.

~ VARIATION ~

For Cheese and Herb Potato Cakes,
stir in about 50g/2oz crumbled blue
cheese, and substitute 15ml/1 tbsp
snipped fresh chives for the dill.
Mix in 45ml/3 tbsp sour cream
instead of the butter.

Energy 121kcal/508kJ; Protein 2.6g; Carbohydrate 20.6g, of which sugars 0.6g; Fat 3.7g, of which saturates 2.2g; Cholesterol 9mg; Calcium 37mg; Fibre 0.9g; Sodium 27mg.

Parmesan Popovers

MAKES 6

50g/2oz/¹/₃ cup grated Parmesan cheese

115g/4oz/1 cup plain (all-purpose) flour,

1.25ml/¹/₄ tsp salt

2 eggs

125ml/4fl oz/¹/₂ cup milk

15ml/1 tbsp melted butter or margarine

1 ▼ Preheat the oven to 230°C/
450°F/Gas 8. Grease six deep bun or
tartlet tins (pans). Sprinkle each with
15ml/1 tbsp of the grated Parmesan.
Alternatively, you can use ramekins;
heat them on a baking sheet in the
oven, then grease and sprinkle with
Parmesan just before filling.

2 Sift the flour and salt into a small
bowl. Set aside.

3 ▲ In a mixing bowl, beat together
the eggs, milk, and the butter or
margarine. Add the flour mixture and
stir until smoothly blended.

4 ▼ Divide the mixture evenly
among the tins, filling each one about
half full. Bake for 15 minutes, then
sprinkle the tops of the popovers
with the remaining grated Parmesan
cheese. Reduce the heat to 180°C/
350°F/Gas 4 and continue baking
until the popovers are firm and golden
brown, 20–25 minutes.

5 ▲ Remove the popovers from the
oven. To unmould, run a thin knife
around the inside of each tin to loosen
the popovers. Gently ease out, then
transfer to a wire rack to cool.

Energy 168kcal/706kJ; Protein 8g; Carbohydrate 17g, of which sugars 1g; Fat 8g, of which saturates 4g; Cholesterol 94mg; Calcium 159mg; Fibre 1g; Sodium 201mg.

Herb Popovers

MAKES 12

3 eggs

250ml/8fl oz/1 cup milk

25g/1oz/2 tbsp butter, melted

75g/3oz/²⁄₃ cup plain (all-purpose) flour

0.6ml/¹⁄₈ tsp salt

1 small sprig each mixed fresh herbs, such as chives, tarragon, dill and parsley

1 Preheat a 220°C/425°F/Gas 7 oven. Grease 12 small ramekins or individual baking cups.

2 With an electric mixer, beat the eggs until blended. Beat in the milk and melted butter.

3 Sift together the flour and salt, then beat into the egg mixture to combine thoroughly.

4 ▼ Strip the herb leaves from the stems and chop finely. Mix together and measure out 30ml/2 tbsp. Stir the herbs into the batter.

5 ▲ Fill the prepared cups half-full.

6 Bake until golden, 25–30 minutes. Do not open the oven door during baking time or the popovers may collapse. For drier popovers, pierce each one with a knife after the 30 minute baking time and bake for 5 minutes more. Serve hot.

Cheese Popovers

MAKES 12

3 eggs

250ml/8fl oz/1 cup milk

25g/1oz/2 tbsp butter, melted

75g/3oz/²⁄₃ cup plain (all-purpose) flour

1.25ml/¹⁄₄ tsp salt

1.25ml/¹⁄₄ tsp paprika

25g/1oz/¹⁄₃ cup freshly grated Parmesan cheese

~ VARIATION ~

For traditional Yorkshire Pudding, omit the cheese and paprika, and use 60–90ml/4–6 tbsp beef dripping to replace the butter. Put them into the oven in time to serve warm as an accompaniment for roast beef.

1 Preheat a 220°C/425°F/Gas 7 oven. Grease 12 small ramekins.

2 ▲ With an electric mixer, beat the eggs until blended. Beat in the milk and melted butter.

3 ▲ Sift together the flour, salt and paprika, then beat into the egg mixture. Add the cheese and stir.

4 Fill the prepared cups half-full and bake until golden, 25–30 minutes. Do not open the oven door or the popovers may collapse. For drier ones, pierce each popover with a knife after the 30 minute baking time and bake for 5 minutes more. Serve hot.

Herb: Energy 65kcal/272kJ; Protein 2.9g; Carbohydrate 5.9g, of which sugars 1.1g; Fat 3.5g, of which saturates 1.7g; Cholesterol 53mg; Calcium 41mg; Fibre 0.2g; Sodium 39mg.

Cheese: Energy 74kcal/311kJ; Protein 3.7g; Carbohydrate 5.9g, of which sugars 1.1g; Fat 4.2g, of which saturates 2.1g; Cholesterol 55mg; Calcium 66mg; Fibre 0.2g; Sodium 62mg.

Orange and Honey Teabread

Makes 1 loaf

400g/14oz/3¹/₂ cups plain (all-purpose) flour

12.5ml/2¹/₂ tsp baking powder

2.5ml/¹/₂ tsp bicarbonate of soda (baking soda)

2.5ml/¹/₂ tsp salt

25g/1oz/2 tbsp margarine

250ml/8fl oz/1 cup clear honey

1 egg, at room temperature, beaten

22.5ml/1¹/₂ tbsp grated orange rind

175ml/6fl oz/³/₄ cup freshly squeezed orange juice

115g/4oz/²/₃ cup, chopped

1 Preheat a 170°C/325°F/Gas 3 oven.

2 Sift together the flour, baking powder, bicarbonate of soda and salt.

3 Line the bottom and sides of a 23 × 13cm/9 × 5in loaf tin (pan) with baking parchment and grease.

4 ▲ With an electric mixer, cream the margarine until soft. Add the honey and beat until well blended, then stir in the egg with a wooden spoon. Add the orange rind and stir to combine thoroughly.

5 ▲ Fold the flour mixture into the honey and egg mixture in three batches, alternating with the orange juice. Stir in the walnuts.

6 Pour into the tin and bake until a skewer inserted in the centre comes out clean, 60–70 minutes. Let stand 10 minutes before turning out onto a rack to cool.

Apple Loaf

Makes 1 loaf

1 egg

250ml/8fl oz/1 cup bottled or home-made apple sauce

50g/2oz/¹/₄ cup butter or margarine, melted

115g/4oz/¹/₂ cup soft dark brown sugar

50g/2oz/¹/₄ cup caster (superfine) sugar

275g/10oz/2¹/₂ cups plain (all-purpose) flour

10ml/2 tsp baking powder

2.5ml/¹/₂ tsp bicarbonate of soda (baking soda)

2.5ml/¹/₂ tsp salt

5ml/1 tsp ground cinnamon

2.5ml/¹/₂ tsp grated nutmeg

75g/3oz/¹/₂ cup currants or raisins

50g/2oz/¹/₃ cup pecans or walnuts, chopped

1 Preheat a 180°C/350°F/Gas 4 oven. Line a 23 × 13cm/9 × 5in loaf tin (pan) with baking parchment; grease.

2 ▲ Break the egg into a bowl and beat lightly. Stir in the apple sauce, butter or margarine and both sugars. Set aside.

3 In another bowl, sift together the flour, baking powder, bicarbonate of soda, salt, cinnamon and nutmeg. Fold dry ingredients into the apple sauce mixture in three batches.

4 ▼ Stir in the currants or raisins, and nuts.

5 Pour into the prepared tin and bake until a skewer inserted in the centre comes out clean, about 1 hour. Let stand 10 minutes. Turn out onto a rack and cool completely.

Orange: Energy 3145kcal/13251kJ; Protein 61.3g; Carbohydrate 509.6g, of which sugars 215.4g; Fat 109.9g, of which saturates 8.8g; Cholesterol 190mg; Calcium 707mg; Fibre 16.1g; Sodium 335mg.

Apple: Energy 2558kcal/10777kJ; Protein 42.6g; Carbohydrate 432.4g, of which sugars 222.5g; Fat 85g, of which saturates 30.9g; Cholesterol 297mg; Calcium 586mg; Fibre 15.3g; Sodium 442mg.

Malt Loaf

MAKES 1 LOAF

150ml/¼ pint/⅔ cup warm skimmed milk
5ml/1 tsp dried yeast
pinch of caster (superfine) sugar
350g/12oz/3 cups plain (all-purpose) flour
2.5ml/½ tsp salt
30ml/2 tbsp light muscovado sugar
175g/6oz/1 cup sultanas (golden raisins)
15ml/1 tbsp sunflower oil
45ml/3 tbsp malt extract
FOR THE GLAZE
30ml/2 tbsp caster (superfine) sugar
30ml/2 tbsp water

1 ▲ Place the warm milk in a bowl. Sprinkle the yeast on top and add the sugar. Leave for 30 minutes until frothy. Stir the flour and salt into a mixing bowl, stir in the muscovado sugar and sultanas, and make a well.

2 ▲ Add the yeast mixture with the oil and malt extract. Gradually incorporate the flour and mix to a soft dough, adding a little extra milk if necessary.

3 ▲ Turn on to a floured surface and knead for about 5 minutes until smooth and elastic. Grease a 450g/1lb loaf tin (pan).

4 ▲ Shape the dough and place it in the prepared loaf tin. Cover with a damp dish towel and leave in a warm place for about 1–2 hours until the dough is well risen. Preheat the oven to 190°C/375°F/Gas 5.

5 ▲ Bake the loaf for 30–35 minutes, or until it sounds hollow when it is tapped underneath.

6 ▲ Meanwhile, prepare the glaze by dissolving the sugar in the water in a small pan. Bring to the boil, stirring, then lower the heat and simmer for 1 minute. Place the loaf on a wire rack and brush with the glaze while still hot. Leave the loaf to cool before serving.

> ### ~ COOK'S TIP ~
> This is a rich and sticky loaf. If it lasts long enough to go stale, try toasting it for a delicious tea-time treat.

> ### ~ VARIATION ~
> To make buns, divide the dough into 10 pieces, shape into rounds, leave to rise, then bake for about 15–20 minutes. Brush with the glaze while still hot.

Energy 259kcal/1101kJ; Protein 5.4g; Carbohydrate 58.4g, of which sugars 25g; Fat 2.1g, of which saturates 0.3g; Cholesterol 1mg; Calcium 101mg; Fibre 1.8g; Sodium 29mg.

Lemon and Walnut Teabread

MAKES 1 LOAF

115g/4oz/¹/₂ cup butter or margarine, at room temperature
90g/3¹/₂oz/¹/₂ cup sugar
2 eggs, at room temperature, separated
grated rind of 2 lemons
30ml/2 tbsp lemon juice
215g/7¹/₂ oz/scant 2 cups plain (all-purpose) flour
10ml/2 tsp baking powder
125ml/4fl oz/¹/₂ cup milk
50g/2oz/¹/₃ cup, chopped
0.6ml/¹/₈ tsp salt

1 Preheat a 180°C/350°F/Gas 4 oven. Line a 23 × 13cm/9 × 5in loaf tin (pan) with baking parchment; grease.

2 With an electric mixer, cream the butter or margarine with the sugar until light and fluffy.

3 ▲ Beat in the egg yolks until thoroughly combined.

4 Add the lemon rind and juice and stir until blended. Set aside.

5 ▲ In another bowl, sift together the flour and baking powder, three times. Fold into the butter mixture in three batches, alternating with the milk. Fold in the walnuts. Set aside.

6 ▲ Beat the egg whites and salt until stiff peaks form. Fold a large dollop of the egg whites into the walnut mixture to lighten it. Fold in the remaining egg whites carefully until just blended.

7 ▲ Pour the batter into the prepared tin and bake until a skewer inserted in the centre of the loaf comes out clean, 45–50 minutes. Let stand 5 minutes before turning out onto a rack to cool completely.

Energy 2490kcal/10413kJ; Protein 45.3g; Carbohydrate 269.1g, of which sugars 104.9g; Fat 144.7g, of which saturates 67.5g; Cholesterol 633mg; Calcium 617mg; Fibre 8.4g; Sodium 904mg.

Banana Bread

MAKES 1 LOAF

200g/7oz/1¾ cups plain (all-purpose) flour
12.5ml/2½ tsp baking powder
2.5ml/½ tsp salt
2.5ml/½ tsp ground cinnamon (optional)
60ml/4 tbsp wheat germ
65g/2½oz/5 tbsp butter or margarine, at room temperature
115g/4oz/scant ¾ cup caster (superfine) sugar
2.5ml/½ tsp grated lemon zest
3 ripe bananas, mashed
2 eggs, beaten to mix

1 Preheat a 180°C/350°F/Gas 4 oven. Grease and flour a 21 × 11cm/ 8½ × 4½in loaf tin (pan).

2 ▲ Sift the flour, baking powder, salt and cinnamon, if using, into a bowl. Stir in the wheat germ.

3 ▲ In another bowl, combine the butter or margarine with the sugar and lemon zest. Beat until the mixture is light and fluffy.

4 ▲ Add the mashed bananas and eggs and mix well.

5 Add the dry ingredients and blend quickly and evenly.

> ### ~ VARIATION ~
>
> For Banana Walnut Bread, add 50g/2oz/⅓ cup finely chopped walnuts with the dry ingredients.

6 ▼ Spoon into the prepared loaf tin. Bake for 50–60 minutes or until a wooden skewer inserted in the centre comes out clean.

7 Let cool in the pan for about 5 minutes, then turn out on to a wire rack to cool completely.

Energy 2265kcal/9548kJ; Protein 51.9g; Carbohydrate 372.4g, of which sugars 195.9g; Fat 73.6g, of which saturates 38.4g; Cholesterol 519mg; Calcium 461mg; Fibre 18.9g; Sodium 553mg.

Pineapple and Apricot Cake

SERVES 10–12

175g/6oz/³/₄ cup unsalted butter

150g/5oz/³/₄ cup caster (superfine) sugar

3 eggs, beaten

few drops of vanilla extract

225g/8oz/2 cups plain (all-purpose) flour

2.5ml/½ tsp salt

7.5ml/2½ tsp baking powder

225g/8oz/1 cup ready-to-eat dried
   apricots, chopped

115g/4oz/½ cup each chopped
   crystallized(candied) ginger
   and crystallized pineapple

grated rind and juice of ½ orange

grated rind and juice of ½ lemon

a little milk

1 ▲ Preheat the oven to 180°C/
350°F/180°C/Gas 4. Double line a
20cm/8in round or 18cm/7in square
cake tin (pan). Cream the butter and
sugar together until light and fluffy.

2 Gradually beat the eggs into the
creamed mixture with the vanilla
extract, beating well after each
addition. Sift together the flour, salt
and baking powder, and add a little
with the last of the egg, then fold in
the rest.

3 ▲ Fold in the fruit, crystallized
fruit and fruit rinds gently, then add
sufficient fruit juice and milk to give
a fairly soft dropping consistency.

4 ▲ Spoon into the prepared tin
(pan) and smooth the top with a wet
spoon. Bake for 20 minutes, then
reduce the heat to 160°C/325°F/Gas 3
for a further 1½–2 hours, or until firm
to the touch and a skewer comes out
of the centre clean. Leave the cake
to cool in the tin, turn out and wrap
in fresh paper before storing in an
airtight tin.

~ COOK'S TIP ~

This is not a long-keeping cake, but
it does freeze, well-wrapped in baking
parchment and then foil.

Energy 3400kcal/14276kJ; Protein 52.3g; Carbohydrate 455.1g, of which sugars 283.7g; Fat 165.6g, of which saturates 96.3g; Cholesterol 944mg; Calcium 748mg; Fibre 25.9g; Sodium 1326mg.

Date and Nut Malt Loaf

MAKES 2 LOAVES

300g/11oz/2²/₃ cups strong white bread flour
275g/10oz/2¹/₂ cups strong wholemeal (whole-wheat) bread flour
5ml/1 tsp salt
75g/3oz/6 tbsp soft light brown sugar
5ml/1 tsp easy-blend (rapid-rise) dried yeast
50g/2oz/¹/₄ cup butter or margarine
15ml/1 tbsp black treacle (molasses)
60ml/4 tbsp malt extract
250ml/8fl oz/1 cup tepid milk
115g/4oz/1 cup chopped dates
75g/3oz/¹/₂ cup sultanas (golden raisins)
75g/3oz/¹/₂ cup raisins
50g/2oz/¹/₃ cup chopped nuts
30ml/2 tbsp clear honey, to glaze

1 Sift the flours and salt into a large bowl, adding any bran from the sieve (strainer). Stir in the sugar and yeast.

2 ▲ Mix the butter or margarine with the treacle and malt extract. Stir over a low heat until melted. Leave to cool, then combine with the milk.

3 Stir the liquid into the dry ingredients and knead for 15 minutes until the dough is elastic. (If you have a dough blade on your food processor, follow the manufacturer's instructions for timings.)

4 ▲ Knead in the fruits and nuts. Transfer the dough to an oiled bowl, cover with clear film (plastic wrap), and leave in a warm place for about 1½ hours, until the dough has doubled in size.

5 ▲ Grease two 450g/1lb loaf tins (pans). Knock back the dough and knead lightly. Divide in half, form into loaves and place in the tins. Cover and leave in a warm place for about 30 minutes, until risen. Meanwhile, preheat the oven to 190°C/375°F/Gas 5.

6 Bake for 35–40 minutes, until well risen and sounding hollow when tapped underneath. Cool on a wire rack. Brush with honey while warm.

~ COOK'S TIP ~

This moist loaf is perfect for picnics or packed lunches.

Energy 2083kcal/8806kJ; Protein 50g; Carbohydrate 395g, of which sugars 187g; Fat 45g, of which saturates 19g; Cholesterol 71mg; Calcium 667mg; Fibre 29g; Sodium 1354mg.

Banana Orange Loaf

3 ▲ Sift the flours with the baking powder and spice, adding any bran that is caught in the sieve (strainer). Stir in the toasted hazelnuts.

3 ▲ Peel and mash the bananas. Beat together with the egg, oil, honey and the orange rind and juice. Stir evenly into the dry ingredients.

5 Spoon into the prepared baking tin and smooth the top. Bake for 40–45 minutes, or until firm and golden brown. Turn out and cool on a wire rack.

6 Sprinkle the orange slices with the icing sugar and grill until golden brown. Use to decorate the cake.

MAKES 1 LOAF

30ml/2 tbsp sunflower oil

90g/3¹/₂oz/³/₄ cup wholemeal (whole-wheat) flour

90g/3¹/₂oz/³/₄ cup plain (all-purpose) flour

5ml/1 tsp baking powder

5ml/1 tsp mixed (apple pie) spice

45ml/3 tbsp flaked (sliced) hazelnuts, toasted

2 large ripe bananas

1 egg

30ml/2 tbsp clear honey

finely grated rind and juice of 1 small orange

4 orange slices, halved

10ml/2 tsp icing (confectioners') sugar

1 Preheat the oven to 180°C/350°F/ Gas 4.

2 ▲ Brush a 1 litre/1¾ pint loaf tin (pan) with sunflower oil and line the base with baking parchment.

~ COOK'S TIP ~

If you plan to keep the loaf for more than two or three days, omit the orange slices. Instead, brush with honey and sprinkle with flaked hazelnuts.

Energy 1483kcal/6238kJ; Protein 35.3g; Carbohydrate 214.3g, of which sugars 84.6g; Fat 59.9g, of which saturates 7g; Cholesterol 190mg; Calcium 276mg; Fibre 16.1g; Sodium 89mg.

Apple, Apricot and Walnut Loaf

MAKES 1 LOAF

225g/8oz/2 cups wholemeal
  (whole-wheat) flour

5ml/1 tsp baking powder

pinch of salt

115g/4oz/¹/₂ cup sunflower margarine

175g/6oz/scant 1 cup soft light
  brown sugar

2 large (US extra large) eggs,
  lightly beaten

grated rind and juice of 1 orange

50g/2oz/¹/₃ cup chopped walnuts

50g/2oz/¹/₄ cup ready-to-eat dried
  apricots, chopped

1 large cooking apple

1 ▲ Preheat the oven to 180°C/
350°F/Gas 4. Line and grease a
900g/2lb loaf tin (pan).

2 ▲ Sift the flour, baking powder and
salt into a large mixing bowl, then
tip the bran remaining in the sieve
(strainer) into the mixture.

3 Add the margarine, sugar, eggs,
orange rind and juice. Stir, then
beat with a hand-held electric beater
until smooth. Stir in the walnuts
and apricots.

4 ▲ Peel, quarter, and core the apple,
chop it roughly and add it to the
mixture. Stir, then spoon into
the prepared tin and level the top.

5 Bake for 1 hour, or until a skewer
inserted into the centre comes out
clean. Cool in the tin for 5 minutes,
then turn the loaf out on to a wire
rack and peel off the lining paper.

~ COOK'S TIP ~

This cake is delicious served
warm. Store any leftovers in an
airtight container.

Energy 2850kcal/11954kJ; Protein 54g; Carbohydrate 356g, of which sugars 215g; Fat 148g, of which saturates 27g; Cholesterol 466mg; Calcium 395mg; Fibre 35g; Sodium 1892mg.

Banana and Ginger Teabread

MAKES 1 LOAF

175g/6oz/1½ cups self-raising (self-rising) flour

5ml/1 tsp baking powder

40g/1½oz/3 tbsp soft margarine

50g/2oz/4 tbsp dark muscovado (molasses) sugar

50g/2oz drained preserved stem ginger, chopped

60ml/4 tbsp skimmed milk

2 ripe bananas, mashed

1 ▲ Preheat the oven to 180°C/ 350°F/Gas 4. Grease and line a 450g/1lb loaf tin (pan). Sift the flour and baking powder into a large mixing bowl.

2 ▲ Rub in the margarine until the mixture resembles breadcrumbs.

3 ▲ Stir in the sugar. Add the ginger, milk and bananas and mix.

4 ▲ Spoon into the prepared tin and bake for 40–45 minutes, or until an inserted skewer comes out clean. Run a metal spatula around the edges to loosen, then turn the teabread on to a wire rack and leave to cool.

Energy 162kcal/685kJ; Protein 2.7g; Carbohydrate 29.7g, of which sugars 12.5g; Fat 4.5g, of which saturates 0.1g; Cholesterol 0mg; Calcium 45mg; Fibre 1g; Sodium 45mg.

Pear and Sultana Teabread

MAKES 1 LOAF

25g/1oz/2 tbsp rolled oats
50g/2oz/4 tbsp light muscovado sugar
30ml/2 tbsp pear or apple juice
30ml/2 tbsp sunflower oil
1 large or 2 small pears
115g/4oz/1 cup self-raising (self-rising) flour
115g/4oz/8 tbsp sultanas (golden raisins)
2.5ml/½ tsp baking powder
10ml/2 tsp mixed (apple pie) spice
1 egg

1 ▲ Preheat the oven to 180°C/ 350°F/Gas 4. Grease and line a 450g/1lb loaf tin (pan) with baking parchment. Mix the oats with the sugar, pour over the pear or apple juice and oil, mix well and leave for 15 minutes.

2 ▲ Quarter, core and coarsely grate the pears. Add the fruit to the oat mixture with the flour, sultanas, baking powder, mixed spice and egg, then mix together thoroughly until well combined.

3 ▲ Spoon the mixture into the prepared loaf tin and level the top. Bake for 50–60 minutes or until a skewer inserted into the centre comes out clean.

4 ▲ Transfer the teabread on to a wire rack and peel off the lining paper. Leave to cool completely.

~ COOK'S TIP ~

Health food shops sell concentrated pear and apple juice, ready for diluting as required.

Energy 184kcal/780kJ; Protein 3.1g; Carbohydrate 36.3g, of which sugars 23.1g; Fat 4g, of which saturates 0.6g; Cholesterol 24mg; Calcium 43mg; Fibre 1.8g; Sodium 16mg.

Cardamom and Saffron Tealoaf

3 ▲ Beat the remaining milk with the honey and egg, then mix this into the flour with the saffron milk and strands, stirring well until a firm dough is formed. You may not need all the milk; it depends on the flour.

4 ▲ Turn out the dough and knead it on a lightly floured board for about 5 minutes until smooth.

5 Return the dough to the mixing bowl, cover with oiled clear film (plastic wrap) and leave in a warm place until doubled in size. This could take between 1–3 hours. Grease a 1kg/2lb loaf tin (pan). Turn the dough out on to a floured board again, punch it down, knead for 3 minutes, then shape it into a fat roll and fit it into the greased loaf tin.

6 Cover with a sheet of lightly oiled clear film and stand in a warm place until the dough begins to rise again. Preheat the oven to 200°C/400°F/ Gas 6. Bake the loaf for 25 minutes until golden brown and firm on top. Turn out of the tin and as it cools, brush the top with honey.

MAKES 1 LOAF

good pinch of saffron strands

750ml/1¼ pints/3 cups lukewarm milk

25g/1oz/2 tbsp butter

900g/2lb/8 cups strong white bread flour

10ml/2 tsp easy-blend (rapid-rise) dried yeast

30ml/2 tbsp caster (superfine) sugar

6 cardamom pods, split open and seeds extracted

115g/4oz/8 tbsp raisins

30ml/2 tbsp clear honey, plus extra for brushing

1 egg, beaten

~ COOK'S TIP ~

Slice this loaf when cold and spread with butter. It is also good lightly toasted.

1 ▲ Crush the saffron into a cup containing a little of the warm milk and leave to infuse for 5 minutes.

2 Rub the butter into the flour, then mix in the yeast, sugar and cardamom seeds (these may need rubbing to separate them). Stir in the raisins.

Energy 4423kcal/18733kJ; Protein 139g; Carbohydrate 853g, of which sugars 188g; Fat 73g, of which saturates 38g; Cholesterol 401mg; Calcium 2242mg; Fibre 40g; Sodium 694mg.

Bilberry Teabread

MAKES 8 PIECES

50g/2oz/¹/₄ cup butter or margarine,
   at room temperature

175g/6oz/scant 1 cup caster (superfine) sugar

1 egg, at room temperature

125ml/4fl oz/¹/₂ cup milk

225g/8oz/2 cups plain (all-purpose) flour

10ml/2 tsp baking powder

2.5ml/¹/₂ tsp salt

275g/10oz/2¹/₂ cups fresh bilberries

FOR THE TOPPING

115g/4oz/scant ³/₄ cup sugar

45ml/3 tbsp plain (all-purpose) flour

2.5ml/¹/₂ tsp ground cinnamon

50g/2oz/¹/₄ cup butter, cut in pieces

1 Preheat a 190°C/375°F/Gas 5 oven.
Grease a 23cm/9in baking dish.

2 With an electric mixer, cream the
butter or margarine with the sugar
until light and fluffy. Add the egg,
beat to combine, then mix in the milk
until blended.

3 ▼ Sift over the flour, baking
powder and salt and stir just enough
to blend the ingredients, without
overmixing the batter.

4 ▲ Add the berries and stir.

5 Transfer to the baking dish.

6 ▲ For the topping, place the sugar,
flour, cinnamon and butter in a
mixing bowl. Cut in with a pastry
blender until the mixture resembles
coarse breadcrumbs.

7 ▲ Sprinkle the topping over the
mixture in the baking dish.

8 Place in the oven and bake until a
skewer inserted in the centre comes
out clean, about 45 minutes. Serve
warm or cold.

Energy 374kcal/1575kJ; Protein 5g; Carbohydrate 66.2g, of which sugars 40.9g; Fat 11.7g, of which saturates 6.9g; Cholesterol 51mg; Calcium 104mg; Fibre 2.1g; Sodium 95mg.

Glazed Banana Spice Loaf

4 Sift together the flour, salt, bicarbonate of soda, nutmeg, allspice and cloves. Add to the butter mixture and stir to combine well.

5 ▲ Add the sour cream, banana, and vanilla and mix just enough to blend. Pour into the prepared tin.

6 ▲ Bake until the top springs back when touched lightly, 45–50 minutes. Let cool in the pan for 10 minutes. Turn out onto a wire rack to cool.

MAKES 1 LOAF

1 large ripe banana

115g/4oz/¹/₂ cup butter, at room temperature

150g/5oz/³/₄ cup caster (superfine) sugar

2 eggs, at room temperature

215g/7¹/₂ oz/scant 2 cups plain (all-purpose) flour

5ml/1 tsp salt

5ml/1 tsp bicarbonate of soda (baking soda)

2.5ml/¹/₂ tsp grated nutmeg

2.5ml/¹/₂ tsp ground allspice

1.25ml/¹/₄ tsp ground cloves

175ml/6fl oz/³/₄ cup sour cream

5ml/1 tsp vanilla extract

FOR THE GLAZE

115g/4oz/1 cup icing (confectioners') sugar

15–30ml/1–2 tbsp lemon juice

1 Preheat a 180°C/350°F/Gas 4 oven. Line a 21.5 × 11.5cm/8¹/₂ × 4¹/₂in loaf tin (pan) with baking parchment; grease.

2 ▼ With a fork, mash the banana in a bowl. Set aside.

3 With an electric mixer, cream the butter and sugar together until light and fluffy. Add the eggs, one at a time, beating to blend well after each addition.

7 ▲ For the glaze, combine the icing sugar and lemon juice in a bowl, then stir until smooth.

8 To glaze, place the cooled loaf on a rack set over a baking sheet. Pour the glaze over the top of the loaf and allow to set.

Energy 2520kcal/10659kJ; Protein 50g; Carbohydrate 480g, of which sugars 312g; Fat 58g, of which saturates 28g; Cholesterol 800mg; Calcium 599mg; Fibre 11g; Sodium 3417mg.

Chocolate Chip Walnut Loaf

MAKES 1 LOAF

90g/3¹/₂oz/¹/₂ cup caster (superfine) sugar

90g/3¹/₂oz/³/₄ cup plain (all-purpose) flour

5ml/1 tsp baking powder

60ml/4 tbsp cornflour (cornstarch)

130g/4¹/₂oz/generous ¹/₂ cup butter, at room temperature

2 eggs, at room temperature

5ml/1 tsp vanilla extract

30ml/2 tbsp currants or raisins

30ml/2 tbsp walnuts, finely chopped

grated rind of ¹/₂ lemon

45ml/3 tbsp plain (semisweet) chocolate chips

icing (confectioners') sugar, for dusting

1 Preheat the oven to 180°C/350°F/ Gas 4. Grease and line a 22 × 12cm/ 8¹/₂ × 4¹/₂in loaf tin (pan).

2 ▲ Sprinkle 22.5ml/1¹/₂ tbsp of the caster sugar into the pan and tilt to distribute the sugar in an even layer over the bottom and sides. Shake out any excess.

> ### ~ COOK'S TIP ~
>
> For the best results, the eggs should be at room temperature. If they are too cold when folded into the creamed butter mixture, they may separate. If this happens, add a spoonful of the flour to help stabilize the mixture.

3 ▼ Sift together the flour, baking powder and cornflour into a mixing bowl three times. Set aside.

4 With an electric mixer, cream the butter until soft. Add the remaining sugar and continue beating until light and fluffy. Add the eggs, one at a time, beating to incorporate thoroughly after each addition.

5 Gently fold the dry ingredients into the butter mixture, in three batches; do not overmix.

6 ▲ Fold in the vanilla, currants or raisins, walnuts, lemon rind, and chocolate chips until just blended.

7 Pour the mixture into the prepared tin and bake until a cake tester inserted in the centre comes out clean, 45–50 minutes.

8 Let the loaf cool in the tin for 5 minutes before transferring to a wire rack to cool completely. Dust over an even layer of icing sugar before serving.

Energy 3759kcal/15650kJ; Protein 60.1g; Carbohydrate 294g, of which sugars 149.5g; Fat 268.6g, of which saturates 76.5g; Cholesterol 626mg; Calcium 543mg; Fibre 12.5g; Sodium 913mg.

Fruity Teabread

MAKES 1 LOAF

225g/8oz/2 cups plain (all-purpose) flour

115g/4oz/scant ¾ cup caster (superfine) sugar

15ml/1 tbsp baking powder

2.5ml/½ tsp salt

grated rind of 1 large orange

175ml/6fl oz/¾ cup fresh orange juice

2 eggs, lightly beaten

75g/3oz/6 tbsp butter or margarine, melted

115g/4oz/1 cup fresh cranberries, or bilberries

50g/2oz/⅓ cup chopped walnuts

1 Preheat a 180°C/350°F/Gas 4 oven. Line a 23 × 13cm/9 × 5in loaf tin (pan) with baking parchment; grease.

2 Sift the flour, sugar, baking powder and salt into a mixing bowl.

3 ▼ Stir in the orange rind.

4 ▲ Make a well in the centre and add the orange juice, eggs and melted butter or margarine. Stir from the centre until the ingredients are blended; do not overmix.

5 ▲ Add the berries and walnuts and stir until blended.

6 Transfer the mixture to the prepared tin and bake until a skewer inserted in the centre comes out clean, 45–50 minutes.

7 ▲ Let cool in the tin for 10 minutes before transferring to a rack to cool completely. Serve thinly sliced, toasted or plain, with butter or cream cheese and jam.

Energy 2356kcal/9885kJ; Protein 43.9g; Carbohydrate 317g, of which sugars 145.2g; Fat 110.3g, of which saturates 45.4g; Cholesterol 540mg; Calcium 557mg; Fibre 12.4g; Sodium 630mg.

Dried Fruit Loaf

MAKES 1 LOAF

450g/1lb/2¹/₂ cups mixed dried fruit, such as currants, raisins, chopped dried apricots and dried cherries
300ml/¹/₂ pint/1¹/₄ cups cold strong tea
200g/7oz/scant 1 cup soft dark brown sugar
grated rind and juice of 1 small orange
grated rind and juice of 1 lemon
1 egg, lightly beaten
200g/7oz/1³/₄ cups plain (all-purpose) flour
15ml/1 tbsp baking powder
0.6ml/¹/₈ tsp salt

1 ▲ In a bowl, mix the dried fruit with the tea and soak overnight.

2 Preheat a 180°C/350°F/Gas 4 oven. Line the bottom and sides of a 23 × 13cm/9 × 5in loaf tin (pan) with baking parchment and grease the paper.

3 ▲ Strain the fruit, reserving the liquid. In a bowl, combine the brown sugar, grated orange and lemon rind, and fruit.

4 ▼ Pour the orange and lemon juice into a measuring jug; if the quantity is less than 250ml/8fl oz/1 cup, top up with the soaking liquid.

5 Stir the citrus juices and egg into the dried fruit mixture.

6 In another bowl, sift together the flour, baking powder and salt. Stir into the fruit mixture until blended.

7 Transfer to the prepared tin and bake until a skewer inserted in the centre comes out clean, about 1¹/₄ hours. Let stand 10 minutes before unmoulding.

Energy 2763kcal/11770kJ; Protein 36.6g; Carbohydrate 673.9g, of which sugars 521.5g; Fat 10g, of which saturates 2g; Cholesterol 190mg; Calcium 838mg; Fibre 14.8g; Sodium 156mg.

Mango Teabread

MAKES 2 LOAVES

275g/10oz/2¹/₂ cups plain (all-purpose) flour
10ml/2 tsp bicarbonate of soda (baking soda)
10ml/2 tsp ground cinnamon
2.5ml/¹/₂ tsp salt
115g/4oz/¹/₂ cup margarine
3 eggs, at room temperature
300g/10oz/1¹/₂ cups sugar
125ml/4fl oz/¹/₂ cup vegetable oil
1 large ripe mango, peeled and chopped
90ml/6 tbsp desiccated (dry unsweetened shredded) coconut
75g/3oz/¹/₂ cup raisins

1 Preheat the oven to 180°C/350°F/ Gas 4. Line the bottom and sides of two 23 × 13cm/9 × 5in loaf tins (pans) with baking parchment and grease.

2 Sift together the flour, bicarbonate of soda, cinnamon and salt. Set aside.

3 With an electric mixer, cream the margarine until soft.

4 ▼ Beat in the eggs and sugar until light and fluffy. Beat in the oil.

5 Fold the dry ingredients into the creamed ingredients in three batches.

6 Fold in the mangoes, two-thirds of the coconut and the raisins.

7 ▲ Spoon the batter into the pans.

8 Sprinkle over the remaining coconut. Bake until a skewer inserted in the centre comes out clean, 50–60 minutes. Let stand for about 10 minutes before turning out onto a rack to cool completely.

Courgette Teabread

MAKES 1 LOAF

50g/2oz/¹/₄ cup butter
3 eggs
250ml/8fl oz/1 cup vegetable oil
300g/10oz/1¹/₂ cups sugar
2 medium unpeeled courgettes (zucchini), grated
275g/10oz/2¹/₂ cups plain (all-purpose) flour
10ml/2 tsp bicarbonate of soda (baking soda)
5ml/1 tsp baking powder
5ml/1 tsp salt
5ml/1 tsp ground cinnamon
5ml/1 tsp grated nutmeg
1.25ml/¹/₄ tsp ground cloves
115g/4oz/²/₃ cup walnuts, chopped

1 Preheat the oven to 180°C/350°F/ Gas 4.

2 Line the bottom and sides of a 23 × 13cm/9 × 5in loaf tin (pan) with baking parchment and grease.

3 ▲ In a pan, melt the butter over low heat. Set aside.

4 With an electric mixer, beat the eggs and oil together until thick. Beat in the sugar. Stir in the melted butter and courgettes. Set aside.

5 ▲ In another bowl, sift all the dry ingredients together three times. Carefully fold into the courgette mixture. Fold in the walnuts.

6 Pour into the tin and bake until a skewer inserted in the centre comes out clean, 60–70 minutes. Let stand 10 minutes before turning out onto wire rack to cool completely.

Mango: Energy 2291kcal/9601kJ; Protein 26.7g; Carbohydrate 292.2g, of which sugars 187.2g; Fat 121.2g, of which saturates 29.8g; Cholesterol 285mg; Calcium 347mg; Fibre 12.7g; Sodium 611mg.
Courgette: Energy 5135kcal/21437kJ; Protein 70.4g; Carbohydrate 522.8g, of which sugars 312g; Fat 321.5g, of which saturates 59.1g; Cholesterol 677mg; Calcium 839mg; Fibre 16.1g; Sodium 2515mg.

PIES & TARTS

HERE IS EVERY SORT OF FILLING –
FROM ORCHARD FRUITS TO AUTUMN
NUTS, TANGY CITRUS TO LUSCIOUS
CHOCOLATE – FOR THE MOST
MEMORABLE PIES AND TARTS. SOME
ARE PLAIN AND SOME ARE FANCY,
BUT ALL ARE DELICIOUS.

Traditional Apple Pie

SERVES 8

about 900g/2lb tart eating apples

15ml/1 tbsp fresh lemon juice

5ml/1 tsp vanilla extract

115g/4oz/scant ¾ cup caster (superfine) sugar

2.5ml/½ tsp ground cinnamon

50g/2oz/¼ cup butter or margarine

1 egg yolk

10ml/2 tsp whipping cream

FOR THE PASTRY

225g/8oz/2 cups plain (all-purpose) flour

5ml/1 tsp salt

175g/6oz/¾ cup lard or white cooking fat

60–75ml/4–5 tbsp iced water

15ml/1 tbsp quick-cooking tapioca

1 Preheat a 230°C/450°F/Gas 8 oven.

2 For the pastry, sift the flour and salt into a bowl. Using a pastry blender, cut in the fat until the mixture resembles coarse breadcrumbs.

3 ▲ Sprinkle in the water, 15ml/ 1 tbsp at a time, tossing lightly with your fingertips or with a fork until the pastry forms a ball.

4 ▲ Divide the pastry in half and shape each half into a ball. On a lightly floured surface, roll out one of the balls to a circle about 30cm/12in in diameter.

5 ▲ Use it to line a 23cm/9in pie tin (pan), easing the dough in and being careful not to stretch it. Trim off the excess pastry and use the trimmings for decorating. Sprinkle the tapioca over the bottom of the pie shell.

6 ▲ Roll out the remaining pastry to 3mm/⅛in thickness. With a sharp knife, cut out eight large leaf-shapes. Cut the trimmings into small leaf shapes. Score the leaves with the back of the knife to mark veins.

7 ▲ In a bowl, toss the apples with the lemon juice, vanilla, sugar and cinnamon. Fill the pastry case with the apple mixture and dot with the butter or margarine.

8 ▲ Arrange the large pastry leaves in a decorative pattern on top. Decorate the edge with small leaves.

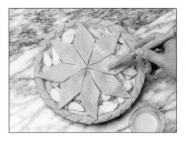

9 ▲ Mix together the egg yolk and cream and brush over the leaves to glaze them.

10 Bake 10 minutes, then reduce the heat to 180°C/350°F/Gas 4 and continue baking until the pastry is golden brown, 35–45 minutes. Let the pie cool in the tin, set on a wire rack.

Energy 447kcal/1868kJ; Protein 3g; Carbohydrate 49g, of which sugars 26g; Fat 28g, of which saturates 12g; Cholesterol 60mg; Calcium 51mg; Fibre 3g; Sodium 40mg.

Apple and Cranberry Lattice Pie

3 ▲ Put the orange rind and juice into a mixing bowl. Peel and core the apples and grate into the bowl. Stir in the cranberries, raisins, walnuts, all except 15ml/1 tbsp of the caster sugar, the brown sugar and flour.

4 Place a baking sheet in the oven and preheat to 200°C/400°F/Gas 6.

5 On a lightly floured surface, roll out one ball of dough about 3mm/¹/₈in thick. Transfer to a 23cm/9in pie plate and trim. Spoon the cranberry and apple mixture into the shell.

6 ▲ Roll out the remaining dough to a circle about 28cm/11in in diameter. With a serrated pastry wheel, cut the dough into ten strips, 2cm/³/₄in wide. Place five strips horizontally across the top of the tart at 2.5cm/1in intervals. Weave in five vertical strips and trim. Sprinkle the top with the remaining sugar.

7 Bake the pie for 20 minutes. Reduce the heat to 180°C/350°F/Gas 4 and bake for about 15 minutes more, until the crust is golden and the filling is bubbling.

SERVES 8

grated rind of 1 orange

45ml/3 tbsp fresh orange juice

2 large, tart cooking apples

175g/6oz/1¹/₂ cups cranberries

75g/3oz/¹/₂ cup raisins

30ml/2 tbsp walnuts, chopped

215g/7¹/₂oz/generous 1 cup caster (superfine) sugar

115g/4oz/¹/₂ cup soft dark brown sugar

30ml/2 tbsp plain (all-purpose) flour

FOR THE CRUST

275g/10oz/2¹/₂ cups plain (all-purpose) flour

2.5ml/¹/₂ tsp salt

75g/3oz/6 tbsp cold butter, cut into pieces

75g/3oz/6 tbsp cold lard or white cooking fat, cut into pieces

60–120ml/4–8 tbsp iced water

1 ▼ For the crust, sift the flour and salt into a bowl. Add the butter and fat and rub in with your fingertips until the mixture resembles coarse breadcrumbs. With a fork, stir in just enough water to bind the dough.

2 Gather the dough into two equal balls, wrap in clear film (plastic wrap), and refrigerate for at least 20 minutes.

Energy 528kcal/2223kJ; Protein 4.6g; Carbohydrate 83.3g, of which sugars 54.7g; Fat 22g, of which saturates 10.1g; Cholesterol 33mg; Calcium 86mg; Fibre 2.2g; Sodium 75mg.

Rhubarb and Cherry Pie

SERVES 8

450g/1lb rhubarb, cut into
2.5cm/1in pieces

450g/1lb canned pitted tart red or black
cherries, drained

300g/10oz/1½ cups caster (superfine) sugar

30ml/2 tbsp quick-cooking tapioca

FOR THE PASTRY

275g/10oz/2½ cups plain (all-purpose) flour

5ml/1 tsp salt

75g/3oz/6 tbsp cold butter, cut in pieces

50g/2oz/¼ cup cold lard or white
cooking fat

60–120ml/4–8 tbsp iced water

milk, for glazing

1 ▲ For the pastry, sift the flour and salt into a bowl. Add the butter and fat to the dry ingredients and cut in with a pastry blender until the mixture resembles coarse breadcrumbs.

2 With a fork, stir in just enough water to bind the pastry. Gather into two balls, one slightly larger than the other. Wrap the pastry in clear film (plastic wrap) and refrigerate for at least 20 minutes.

3 Preheat a baking sheet in the centre of a 200°C/400°F/Gas 6 oven.

4 On a lightly floured surface, roll out the larger pastry ball to a thickness of about 3mm/⅛in.

5 ▼ Roll the pastry around the rolling pin and transfer to a 23cm/9in pie dish. Trim the edge to leave a 1cm/½in overhang.

6 Refrigerate the pastry case while making the filling.

7 In a mixing bowl, combine the rhubarb, cherries, sugar and tapioca and spoon into the pie shell.

8 ▲ Roll out the remaining pastry and cut out leaf shapes.

9 Transfer the pastry lid to the pie and trim to leave a 2cm/¾in overhang. Fold the top edge under the bottom and flute. Roll small balls from the scraps. Mark veins in the pastry leaves and place on top with the balls.

10 Glaze the top and bake until golden, 40–50 minutes.

Energy 442kcal/1868kJ; Protein 4.3g; Carbohydrate 78.9g, of which sugars 47.4g; Fat 14.4g, of which saturates 7.5g; Cholesterol 26mg; Calcium 129mg; Fibre 2.2g; Sodium 312mg.

Rhubarb Pie

SERVES 6

175g/6oz/1½ cups plain (all-purpose) flour

2.5ml/½ tsp salt

10ml/2 tsp caster (superfine) sugar

75g/3oz/6 tbsp butter or white cooking fat

45ml/3 tbsp or more iced water

30ml/2 tbsp whipping cream

FOR THE FILLING

900g/2lb rhubarb, cut in 1–2.5cm/
  ½–1in pieces

30ml/2 tbsp cornflour (cornstarch)

1 egg

300g/10oz/1½ cups caster (superfine) sugar

15ml/1 tbsp grated orange rind

1 ▲ For the pastry, sift the flour, salt, and sugar into a bowl. Using a pastry blender or two knives, cut the butter or fat into the dry ingredients as quickly as possible until the mixture resembles coarse breadcrumbs.

2 Sprinkle with the iced water and mix until the dough holds together. If the dough is too crumbly, add a little more water, a little at a time.

~ COOK'S TIP ~

Be sure to cut off and discard the green rhubarb leaves from the pink stalks as they are toxic and not edible.

3 ▲ Gather the dough into a ball, flatten into a disc, wrap in clear film (plastic wrap), and chill for 20 minutes.

4 ▲ Roll out the dough between two sheets of greaseproof (waxed) paper to a thickness of about 3mm/⅛in. Use to line a 23cm/9in pie dish. Trim all round, leaving a 1cm/½in overhang. Fold the overhang under the edge and flute. Refrigerate the pie shell and dough trimmings for 30 minutes.

5 ▲ For the filling, place the rhubarb in a bowl and sprinkle with the cornflour. Toss to coat.

6 Preheat oven to 220°C/425°F/Gas 7.

7 In a small bowl, beat the egg with the sugar. Mix in the orange rind.

8 ▲ Stir the sugar mixture into the rhubarb and mix well. Spoon the fruit into the pie shell.

9 ▲ Roll out the dough trimmings. Stamp out decorative shapes with a biscuit cutter or cut shapes with a small knife, using a template made out of card as a guide, if wished.

10 Arrange the shapes on top of the pie. Brush the trimmings and the rim of the pie with cream.

11 Bake for 30 minutes. Reduce the heat to 160°C/325°F/Gas 3 and continue baking until the pastry is golden brown and the rhubarb is tender, about 15–20 minutes more.

Energy 286kcal/1201kJ; Protein 6g; Carbohydrate 32g, of which sugars 4g; Fat 16g, of which saturates 9g; Cholesterol 76mg; Calcium 196mg; Fibre 5g; Sodium 265mg.

Plum Pie

SERVES 8

900g/2lb red or purple plums	
grated rind of 1 lemon	
15ml/1 tbsp fresh lemon juice	
150g/5oz/³/4 cup caster (superfine) sugar	
45ml/3 tbsp quick-cooking tapioca	
2.5ml/¹/2 tsp salt	
2.5ml/¹/2 tsp ground cinnamon	
1.25ml/¹/4 tsp grated nutmeg	

FOR THE PASTRY

275g/10oz/2¹/2 cups plain (all-purpose) flour	
2.5ml/¹/2 tsp salt	
75g/3oz/6 tbsp cold butter, cut into pieces	
75g/3oz/6 tbsp cold lard or white cooking fat, cut into pieces	
60–120ml/4–8 tbsp iced water	
milk, for glazing	

1 ▼ For the pastry, sift the flour and salt into a large bowl. Add the butter and fat and cut in with a pastry blender until the mixture resembles coarse breadcrumbs.

2 Stir in just enough water to bind the pastry. Gather into two balls, one slightly larger than the other. Wrap and refrigerate for 20 minutes.

3 Preheat a baking sheet in the centre of a 220°C/425°F/Gas 7 oven.

4 On a lightly floured surface, roll out the larger pastry ball to about 3mm/¹/8in thick. Transfer to a 23cm/9in pie dish and trim the edge.

5 ▲ Halve the plums, discard the stones (pits), and cut into pieces. Mix all the filling ingredients together (if the plums are very tart, use extra sugar). Transfer to the pastry case.

6 ▲ Roll out the remaining pastry and place on a baking tray lined with greaseproof paper. With a cutter, stamp out four hearts. Transfer the pastry lid to the pie using the paper.

7 Trim to leave a 2cm/³/4in overhang. Fold the top edge under the bottom and pinch to seal. Arrange the hearts on top. Brush with the milk. Bake for 15 minutes. Reduce the heat to 180°C/350°F/Gas 4 and bake 30–35 minutes more. If the crust browns too quickly, protect with a sheet of foil.

Energy 360kcal/1516kJ; Protein 4.1g; Carbohydrate 57g, of which sugars 25.5g; Fat 14.5g, of which saturates 7.5g; Cholesterol 26mg; Calcium 73mg; Fibre 2.9g; Sodium 61mg.

Lattice Berry Pie

SERVES 8

450g/1lb berries, such as bilberries, blueberries, blackcurrants etc

115g/4oz/scant ³/₄ cup caster (superfine) sugar

45ml/3 tbsp cornflour (cornstarch)

30ml/2 tbsp fresh lemon juice

25g/1oz/2 tbsp butter, diced

FOR THE PASTRY

275g/10oz/2¹/₂ cups plain (all-purpose) flour

2.5ml/¹/₂ tsp salt

115g/4oz/¹/₂ cup cold butter, cut in pieces

40g/1¹/₂oz/3 tbsp cold lard or white cooking fat, cut in pieces

75–90ml/5–6 tbsp iced water

1 egg beaten with 15ml/1 tbsp water, for glazing

1 For the pastry, sift the flour and salt into a bowl. Add the butter and fat and cut in until it resembles breadcrumbs. Stir in enough water to bind. Form into two balls and wrap in clear film (plastic wrap). Chill for 20 minutes.

2 On a lightly floured surface, roll out one ball about 3mm/¹/₈in thick. Transfer to a 23cm/9in pie dish and trim to leave a 1cm/¹/₂in overhang. Brush the bottom with egg glaze.

3 ▲ Mix all the filling ingredients together, except the butter (reserve a few berries for decoration). Spoon into the pastry case and dot with the butter. Brush the egg glaze around the rim of the pastry case.

4 Preheat a baking sheet in the centre of a 220°C/425°F/Gas 7 oven.

5 ▼ Roll out the remaining pastry on a baking tray lined with grease-proof (waxed) paper. With a serrated pastry wheel, cut out 24 thin pastry strips. Roll out the scraps and cut out leaf shapes. Mark veins in the leaves with the point of a knife.

6 ▲ Weave the strips in a close lattice, then transfer to the pie using the paper. Press the edges to seal and trim. Arrange the pastry leaves around the rim. Brush with egg glaze.

7 Bake for 10 minutes. Reduce the heat to 180°C/350°F/Gas 4 and bake until the pastry is golden, 40–45 minutes more. Decorate with berries.

Energy 384kcal/1607kJ; Protein 3.9g; Carbohydrate 50.4g, of which sugars 19g; Fat 19.9g, of which saturates 11.2g; Cholesterol 42mg; Calcium 69mg; Fibre 1.7g; Sodium 114mg.

Cherry Pie

SERVES 8

900g/2lb fresh Morello cherries, pitted, or 2 × 450g/1lb cans or jars, drained and pitted

75g/3oz/6 tbsp caster (superfine) sugar

25g/1oz/¼ cup plain (all-purpose) flour

22.5ml/1½ tbsp fresh lemon juice

7.25ml/¼ tsp almond extract

25g/1oz/2 tbsp butter or margarine

FOR THE PASTRY

225g/8oz/2 cups plain (all-purpose) flour

5ml/1 tsp salt

175g/6oz/¾ cup lard or white cooking fat

60–75ml/4–5 tbsp iced water

1 For the pastry, sift the flour and salt into a mixing bowl. Using a pastry blender, cut in the fat until the mixture resembles coarse breadcrumbs.

2 ▲ Sprinkle in the water, 15ml/ 1 tbsp at a time, tossing lightly with your fingertips or a fork until the pastry forms a ball.

3 Divide the pastry in half and shape each half into a ball. On a lightly floured surface, roll out one of the balls to a circle about 30cm/12in in diameter.

4 ▲ Use it to line a 23cm/9in pie tin (pan), easing the pastry in and being careful not to stretch it. With scissors, trim off excess pastry, leaving a 1cm/ ½in overhang around the pie rim.

5 ▲ Roll out the remaining pastry to 3mm/⅛in thickness. Cut out 11 strips 1cm/½in wide.

6 ▲ In a mixing bowl, combine the cherries, sugar, flour, lemon juice and almond extract. Spoon the mixture into the pastry case and dot with the butter or margarine.

7 ▲ To make the lattice, place five of the pastry strips evenly across the filling. Fold every other strip back. Lay the first strip across in the opposite direction. Continue in this pattern, folding back every other strip each time you add a cross strip.

8 ▲ Trim the ends of the lattice strips even with the case overhang. Press together so that the edge rests on the pie tin rim. With your thumbs, flute the edge. Refrigerate 15 minutes.

9 Preheat the oven to 220°C/425°F/ Gas 7.

10 Bake the pie 30 minutes, covering the edge of the pastry case with foil, if necessary, to prevent over-browning. Let cool, in the tin, on a wire rack.

Energy 420kcal/1754kJ; Protein 4g; Carbohydrate 47g, of which sugars 23g; Fat 25g, of which saturates 11g; Cholesterol 28mg; Calcium 61mg; Fibre 3g; Sodium 271mg.

Peach Leaf Pie

SERVES 8

1.2kg/2½lb ripe peaches
juice of 1 lemon
90g/3½oz/½ cup sugar
45ml/3 tbsp cornflour (cornstarch)
1.25ml/¼ tsp grated nutmeg
2.5ml/½ tsp ground cinnamon
25g/1oz/2 tbsp butter, diced

FOR THE CRUST

275g/10oz/2½ cups plain (all-purpose) flour
2.5ml/½ tsp salt
115g/4oz/½ cup cold butter, cut into pieces
65g/2½oz/5 tbsp lard or white cooking fat, cut into pieces
75–90ml/5–6 tbsp iced water
1 egg beaten with 15ml/1 tbsp water, for glazing

1 For the pastry, sift the flour and salt into a large bowl. Add the butter and lard or fat and rub in with your fingertips until the mixture resembles coarse breadcrumbs.

2 ▲ With a fork, stir in just enough water to bind the dough. Gather into two balls, one slightly larger than the other. Wrap in clear film (plastic wrap) and refrigerate for at least 20 minutes.

3 Place a baking sheet in the oven and preheat to 220°C/425°F/Gas 7.

4 ▲ Drop a few peaches at a time into boiling water for 20 seconds, then transfer to a bowl of cold water. When cool, peel off the skins.

5 Slice the peaches and combine with the lemon juice, sugar, cornstarch and spices. Set aside.

6 ▲ On a lightly floured surface, roll out the larger dough ball abou 3mm/⅛in thick. Transfer to a 23cm/9in pie tin (pan) and trim. Refrigerate.

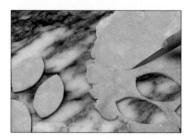

7 ▲ Roll out the remaining dough 5mm/¼in thick. Cut out leaf shapes 7.5m/3in long, using a template if needed. Mark veins with a knife. With the scraps, roll a few balls.

8 ▲ Brush the bottom of the pastry shell with egg glaze. Add the peaches, piling them higher in the centre. Dot with the butter.

9 ▲ To assemble, start from the outside edge and cover the peaches with a ring of leaves. Place a second ring of leaves above, staggering the positions. Continue with rows of leaves until covered. Place the balls in the centre. Brush with glaze.

10 Bake for 10 minutes. Lower the heat to 180°C/350°F/Gas 4 and bake for 35–40 minutes more.

~ COOK'S TIP ~

Baking the pie on a preheated baking sheet helps to make the bottom crust crisp. The moisture from the filling keeps the bottom crust more humid than the top, but this baking method helps compensate for the top crust being better exposed to the heat source.

Energy 424kcal/1778kJ; Protein 4.8g; Carbohydrate 54.2g, of which sugars 22.8g; Fat 22.4g, of which saturates 12.2g; Cholesterol 44mg; Calcium 68mg; Fibre 3.1g; Sodium 112mg.

Maryland Peach and Blueberry Pie

SERVES 8

225g/8oz/2 cups plain
(all-purpose) flour

2.5ml/¹/₂ tsp salt

10ml/2 tsp sugar

150g/5oz/10 tbsp butter or margarine

1 egg yolk

45ml/3 tbsp or more iced water

30ml/2 tbsp milk, for glazing

FOR THE FILLING

7 fresh peaches, peeled and sliced

225g/8oz fresh blueberries

150g/5oz/³/₄ cup sugar

30ml/2 tbsp fresh lemon juice

40g/1¹/₂oz/¹/₃ cup plain
(all-purpose) flour

2.5ml/¹/₂ tsp grated nutmeg

25g/1oz/2 tbsp butter or margarine,
cut in pea-size pieces

1 For the pastry, sift the flour, salt, and sugar into a bowl. Using a pastry blender or two knives, cut the butter or margarine into the dry ingredients as quickly as possible until the mixture resembles coarse breadcrumbs.

2 Mix the egg yolk with the iced water and sprinkle over the flour mixture. Combine with a fork until the dough holds together. If the dough is too crumbly, add a little more water, 15ml/1 tbsp at a time. Gather the dough into a ball and flatten into a disk. Wrap in greaseproof (waxed) paper and refrigerate for at least 20 minutes.

3 Roll out two-thirds of the dough between two sheets of greaseproof paper to a thickness of about 3mm/¹/₈in. Use to line a 23cm/9in pie dish. Trim the edge, leaving a 1cm/¹/₂in overhang. Fold the overhang under to form the edge. Using a fork, press the edge to the rim of the pie dish.

4 ▲ Gather the trimmings and remaining dough into a ball, and roll out to a thickness of about 5mm/¹/₄in. Using a serrated pastry wheel or sharp knife, cut strips 1cm/¹/₂in wide. Refrigerate both the pastry case and the strips of dough for 20 minutes.

5 Preheat a 200°C/400°F/Gas 6 oven.

6 ▲ Line the pastry case with greaseproof paper and fill with baking beans. Bake until the case is just set, 7–10 minutes. Remove from the oven and carefully lift out the paper with the beans. Prick the bottom of the pastry case all over with a fork, then return to the oven and bake for 5 minutes more. Let the pastry case cool slightly before filling. Leave the oven on.

7 ▲ In a mixing bowl, combine the peach slices with the blueberries, sugar, lemon juice, flour and nutmeg. Spoon the fruit mixture evenly into the pastry case. Dot with the pieces of butter or margarine.

8 ▲ Weave a lattice top with the chilled pastry strips, pressing the ends to the baked pastry case edge. Brush the strips with the milk.

9 Bake the pie for 15 minutes. Reduce the heat to 180°C/350°F/Gas 4, and continue baking until the filling is tender and bubbling and the pastry lattice is golden, about 30 minutes more. If the pastry gets too brown, cover loosely with a piece of foil. Serve the pie warm or at room temperature.

Energy 391kcal/1640kJ; Protein 4.7g; Carbohydrate 53g, of which sugars 27.7g; Fat 19.3g, of which saturates 11.7g; Cholesterol 72mg; Calcium 86mg; Fibre 2.9g; Sodium 139mg.

Blueberry Pie

Serves 6–8

basic or rich shortcrust for a two-crust pie (page 222, shortcrust variations)
500g/1¼lb/4 cups blueberries
150g/5oz/¾ cup caster (superfine) sugar
45ml/3 tbsp plain (all-purpose) flour
5ml/1 tsp grated orange zest
1.25ml/¼ tsp grated nutmeg
30ml/2 tbsp orange juice
5ml/1 tsp lemon juice

1 Preheat a 190°C/375°F/Gas 5 oven.

2 ▲ Roll out half of the pastry and use to line a 23cm/9in pie tin (pan) that is about 5cm/2in deep.

3 ▲ Combine the blueberries, 150g/5oz/¾ cup of the sugar, the flour, orange zest and nutmeg in a bowl. Toss the mixture gently to coat the fruit evenly with the dry ingredients.

4 ▼ Pour the blueberry mixture into the pastry case and spread it evenly. Sprinkle over the citrus juices.

5 ▲ Roll out the remaining pastry and cover the pie. Cut out small decorative shapes or cut two or three slits for steam vents. Finish the edge.

6 ▲ Brush the top lightly with water and sprinkle evenly with the remaining caster sugar.

7 Bake the pie in the preheated oven for about 45 minutes or until the pastry is golden brown. Serve warm or at room temperature.

Energy 371kcal/1559kJ; Protein 4.4g; Carbohydrate 55.8g, of which sugars 25.7g; Fat 16g, of which saturates 4.9g; Cholesterol 8mg; Calcium 93mg; Fibre 3.2g; Sodium 228mg.

Walnut and Pear Lattice Pie

SERVES 6–8

nut shortcrust for a two-crust pie (page 18, pastry variations), using walnuts

900g/2lb pears, peeled, cored and thinly sliced

50g/2oz/¼ cup caster (superfine) sugar

25g/1oz/¼ cup plain (all-purpose) flour

2.5ml/½ tsp grated lemon zest

30ml/2 tbsp raisins or sultanas (golden raisins)

30ml/2 tbsp walnuts, chopped

2.5ml/½ tsp ground cinnamon

50g/2oz/½ icing (confectioners') sugar

15ml/1 tbsp lemon juice

about 10ml/2 tsp cold water

1 Preheat a 190°C/375°F/Gas 5 oven.

2 Roll out half of the pastry dough and use to line a 23cm/9in tin (pan) that is about 5cm/2in deep.

3 ▲ Combine the pears, caster sugar, flour and lemon zest in a bowl. Toss gently until the fruit is evenly coated with the dry ingredients. Mix in the raisins, nuts and cinnamon.

> **~ COOK'S TIP ~**
>
> For a simple cutout lattice top, roll out the dough for the top into a circle. Using a small pastry cutter, cut out shapes in a pattern, spacing them evenly and not too close together.

4 ▲ Put the pear filling into the pastry case and spread it evenly.

5 Roll out the remaining pastry dough and use to make a lattice top.

6 Put the pie in the oven and bake for 55 minutes or until the pastry is golden brown.

7 Combine the icing sugar, lemon juice and water in a bowl and stir until smoothly blended.

8 ▼ Remove the pie from the oven. Drizzle the icing sugar glaze evenly over the top of the pie, on pastry and filling. Leave the pie to cool, set on a wire rack, before serving.

Energy 366kcal/1536kJ; Protein 4.3g; Carbohydrate 49.7g, of which sugars 21.5g; Fat 18.1g, of which saturates 5.1g; Cholesterol 8mg; Calcium 70mg; Fibre 2.6g; Sodium 228mg.

Mince Pies

MAKES 36

175g/6oz/1 cup blanched almonds, chopped

150g/5oz/generous 1/2 cup dried apricots, finely chopped

175g/6oz/1 cup raisins

150g/5oz/1 cup currants

150g/5oz/generous 1/2 cup glacé (candied) cherries, chopped

150g/5oz/1²/3 cups mixed chopped (candied) peel

115g/4oz/scant 1 cup suet (US chilled, grated shortening)

grated rind and juice of 2 lemons

grated rind and juice of 1 orange

200g/7oz/scant 1 cup soft dark brown sugar

4 apples, peeled, cored and chopped

10ml/2 tsp ground cinnamon

5ml/1 tsp grated nutmeg

2.5ml/1/2 tsp ground cloves

250ml/8fl oz/1 cup brandy

225g/8oz/1 cup cream cheese

30ml/2 tbsp caster (superfine) sugar

icing (confectioners') sugar (optional)

FOR THE PASTRY

425g/15oz/3³/4 cups plain (all-purpose) flour

150g/5oz/3³/4 cups icing (confectioners') sugar

350g/12oz/1¹/2 cups cold butter, cubed

grated rind and juice of 1 orange

milk, for glazing

1 ▲ Mix the chopped nuts, dried and preserved fruit, suet, citrus rind and juice, sugar, apples, spices and brandy. Cover and leave for 2 days.

2 For the pastry, sift the flour and icing sugar into a bowl. Cut in the butter until the mixture resembles coarse breadcrumbs.

3 ▲ Add the orange rind. Stir in just enough orange juice to bind. Gather into a ball, wrap in clear film (plastic wrap), and chill for at least 20 minutes.

4 Preheat a 220°C/425°F/Gas 7 oven. Grease two or three bun trays. Beat together the cream cheese and sugar.

5 ▲ Roll out the pastry 5mm/¹/4 in thick. With a fluted pastry cutter, stamp out 36 8cm/3in rounds.

~ COOK'S TIP ~

The mincemeat mixture may be packed into sterilized jars and sealed. It will keep refrigerated for several months. Add a few tablespoonfuls to give apple pies a lift, or make small mincemeat-filled parcels using filo pastry.

6 ▲ Transfer the rounds to the bun tray. Fill halfway with mincemeat. Top with a teaspoonful of the cream cheese mixture.

7 ▲ Roll out the remaining pastry and stamp out 36 5cm/2in rounds with a fluted cutter. Brush the edges of the pies with milk, then set the rounds on top. Cut a small steam vent in the top of each pie.

8 ▲ Brush lightly with milk. Bake until golden, 15–20 minutes. Let cool for 10 minutes before unmoulding. Dust with icing sugar, if wished.

Energy 236kcal/993kJ; Protein 2.5g; Carbohydrate 36.7g, of which sugars 22.4g; Fat 9.8g, of which saturates 5.2g; Cholesterol 37mg; Calcium 43mg; Fibre 1g; Sodium 70mg.

Pear and Apple Crumble Pie

SERVES 8

3 firm pears
4 cooking apples
175g/6oz/scant 1 cup caster (superfine) sugar
30ml/2 tbsp cornflour (cornstarch)
0.6ml/⅛ tsp salt
grated rind of 1 lemon
30ml/2 tbsp fresh lemon juice
75g/3oz/½ cup raisins
75g/3oz/⅔ cup plain (all-purpose) flour
5ml/1 tsp ground cinnamon
75g/3oz/6 tbsp butter

FOR THE PASTRY

150g/5oz/1¼ cups plain (all-purpose) flour
2.5ml/½ tsp salt
75g/3oz/6 tbsp lard or white cooking fat, cut in pieces
30ml/2 tbsp iced water

1 For the pastry, combine the flour and salt in a bowl. Add the fat and cut in with a pastry blender until the mixture resembles breadcrumbs. Stir in just enough water to bind the pastry. Gather into a ball and transfer to a lightly floured surface. Roll out 3mm/⅛in thick.

2 ▲ Transfer to a shallow 23cm/9in pie dish and trim to leave a 1cm/½in overhang. Fold the overhang under for double thickness. Flute the edge. Refrigerate for 30 minutes.

3 Preheat a baking sheet in the centre of a 230°C/450°F/Gas 8 oven.

4 ▲ Peel and core the pears. Slice them into a bowl. Peel, core and slice the apples. Add to the pears. Stir in one-third of the sugar, the cornflour, salt and lemon rind. Add the lemon juice and raisins and stir to blend.

5 For the crumble topping, combine the remaining sugar, flour, cinnamon, and butter in a bowl. Blend with your fingertips until the mixture resembles coarse breadcrumbs. Set aside.

6 ▲ Spoon the fruit filling into the pastry case. Sprinkle the crumbs lightly and evenly over the top.

7 Bake the pie for 10 minutes, then reduce the heat to 180°C/350°F/Gas 4. Cover the top of the pie loosely with a sheet of foil and continue baking until lightly browned, 35–40 minutes more.

Energy 390kcal/1639kJ; Protein 3.3g; Carbohydrate 61.3g, of which sugars 39.9g; Fat 16.3g, of which saturates 8.2g; Cholesterol 28mg; Calcium 65mg; Fibre 3.1g; Sodium 190mg.

Open Apple Pie

SERVES 8

1.3kg/3lb sweet-tart firm eating or cooking apples
50g/2oz/¼ cup sugar
10ml/2 tsp ground cinnamon
grated rind and juice of 1 lemon
25g/1oz/2 tbsp butter, diced
30–45ml/2–3 tbsp honey
FOR THE CRUST
275g/10oz/2½ cups plain (all-purpose) flour
2.3ml/½ tsp salt
65g/2½oz/5 tbsp cold butter, cut into pieces
65g/2½oz/5 tbsp cold lard or white cooking fat, cut into pieces
75–90ml/5–6 tbsp iced water

1 For the crust, sift the flour and salt into a large bowl. Add the butter and fat and rub in with your fingertips or cut in until the mixture resembles coarse breadcrumbs.

2 ▲ With a fork, stir in just enough water to bind the dough. Gather into a ball, wrap in clear film (plastic wrap), and refrigerate for at least 20 minutes.

3 Place a baking sheet in the centre of the oven and preheat to 200°C/400°F/Gas 6.

4 ▼ Peel, core, and slice the apples. Combine the sugar and cinnamon in a bowl. Add the apples, lemon rind and juice and stir.

5 On a lightly floured surface, roll out the dough to a circle about 30cm/12in in diameter. Transfer to a 23cm/9in diameter deep pie dish; leave the dough hanging over the edge. Fill with the apple slices.

6 ▲ Fold in the edges and crimp loosely for a decorative border. Dot the apples with diced butter.

7 Bake on the hot sheet until the pastry is golden and the apples are tender, about 45 minutes.

8 Melt the honey in a pan and brush over the apples to glaze. Serve warm or at room temperature.

Energy 422kcal/1722kJ; Protein 4g; Carbohydrate 54g, of which sugars 26g; Fat 23g, of which saturates 13g; Cholesterol 46mg; Calcium 72mg; Fibre 5g; Sodium 115mg.

Brethren's Cider Pie

SERVES 6

175g/6oz/1¹/₂ cups plain (all-purpose) flour
2.5ml/¹/₄ tsp salt
10ml/2 tsp sugar
115g/4oz/¹/₂ cup cold butter or margarine
45ml/3 tbsp or more iced water
FOR THE FILLING
600ml/1 pint/2¹/₂ cups unfiltered apple juice
15ml/1 tbsp butter
250ml/8fl oz/1 cup maple syrup
45ml/3 tbsp water
2.5ml/¹/₄ tsp salt
2 eggs, at room temperature, separated
5ml/1 tsp grated nutmeg

1 ▲ For the pastry, sift the flour, salt, and sugar into a bowl. Using a pastry blender or two knives, cut the butter or margarine into the dry ingredients as quickly as possible until the mixture resembles coarse breadcrumbs.

2 Sprinkle the iced water over the flour mixture. Combine with a fork until the dough holds together. If the dough is too crumbly, add a little more water, 15ml/1 tbsp at a time. Gather the dough into a ball and flatten into a disc. Wrap in greaseproof (waxed) paper and refrigerate for at least 20 minutes.

3 ▲ Meanwhile, place the apple juice in a heavy pan. Boil until only 175ml/6fl oz/³/₄ cup remains. Leave to cool.

4 ▲ Roll out the dough between two sheets of greaseproof paper to a thickness of about 3mm/¹/₈in. Use to line a 23cm/9in pie dish.

5 ▲ Trim the edge, leaving a 1cm/¹/₂in overhang. Fold the overhang under to form the edge. Using a fork, press the edge to the rim of the dish and press up from under with your fingers at intervals for a ruffle effect. Refrigerate for 20 minutes.

6 Preheat a 180°C/350°F/Gas 4 oven.

7 ▲ For the filling, add the butter, maple syrup, water and salt to the juice and simmer gently for 5–6 minutes. Remove the pan from the heat and leave to cool slightly. Beat the egg yolks and whisk them into the pan.

8 ▲ In a large bowl, beat the egg whites until they form stiff peaks. Add the juice mixture and fold gently together until evenly blended.

9 ▲ Pour into the prepared pastry case. Dust with the grated nutmeg.

10 Bake until the pastry is golden brown and the filling is well set, 30–35 minutes. Serve warm.

Energy 444kcal/1858kJ; Protein 6g; Carbohydrate 62g, of which sugars 38g; Fat 21g, of which saturates 12g; Cholesterol 123mg; Calcium 92mg; Fibre 1g; Sodium 324mg.

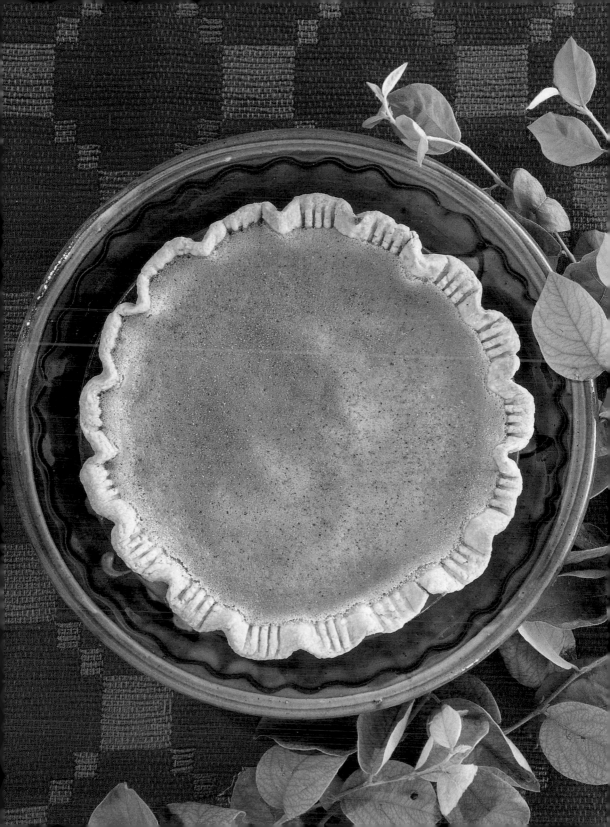

Caramelized Upside-Down Pear Pie

SERVES 8

5–6 firm, ripe pears
175g/6oz/scant 1 cup sugar
115g/4oz/¹/₂ cup unsalted butter
whipped cream, for serving
FOR THE PASTRY
115g/4oz/1 cup plain (all-purpose) flour
1.25ml/¹/₄ tsp salt
130g/4¹/₂oz/generous ¹/₂ cup cold butter, cut into pieces
40g/1¹/₂oz/3 tbsp cold white cooking fat, cut into pieces
60ml/4 tbsp iced water

1 ▲ For the pastry, combine the flour and salt in a large bowl. Add the butter and vegetable fat and cut in with a pastry blender until the mixture resembles coarse crumbs. With a fork, stir in enough iced water to bind the dough. Gather into a ball, wrap in clear film (plastic wrap) and refrigerate for at least 20 minutes. Preheat the oven to 200°C/400°F/ Gas 6.

~ VARIATION ~

For Caramelized Upside-Down Apple Pie, replace the pears with 8–9 firm, tart apples. There may seem to be too many apples, but they shrink slightly as they cook.

2 ▲ Quarter, peel and core the pears. Place in a bowl and toss with a few tablespoons of the sugar.

3 ▲ In a 27cm/10¹/₂in ovenproof frying pan, melt the butter over moderately high heat. Add the remaining sugar. When it starts to colour, arrange the pears evenly around the edge and in the centre.

4 ▲ Continue cooking, uncovered, until the sugar has caramelized, about 20 minutes.

5 ▲ Let the fruit cool. Roll out a circle of dough slightly larger than the diameter of the pan. Place the dough on top of the pears, tucking it around the edges. Transfer the pan to the oven and bake for 15 minutes, then reduce the heat to 180°C/350°F/ Gas 4. Bake until golden, about 15 minutes more.

6 ▲ Let the pie cool in the pan for about 3–4 minutes. Run a knife around the edge of the pan to loosen the pie, ensuring that the knife reaches down to the bottom of the pan. Invert a plate on top and, protecting your hands with oven gloves, hold plate and pan firmly, and turn them both over quickly.

7 Lift off the pan. If any pears stick to the pan, remove them gently with a metal spatula and replace them carefully on the pie. Serve the pie warm, with the whipped cream passed separately.

Energy 447kcal/1874kJ; Protein 2g; Carbohydrate 44g, of which sugars 33g; Fat 31g, of which saturates 18g; Cholesterol 72mg; Calcium 38mg; Fibre 3g; Sodium 101mg.

Lemon Meringue Pie

SERVES 8

grated rind and juice of 1 large lemon

250ml/8fl oz/1 cup plus 15ml/1 tbsp cold water

115g/4oz/scant ³/4 cup plus 90ml/6 tbsp caster (superfine) sugar

25g/1oz/2 tbsp butter

45ml/3 tbsp cornflour (cornstarch)

3 eggs, separated

0.6ml/¹/8 tsp salt

0.6ml/¹/8 tsp cream of tartar

FOR THE PASTRY

150g/5oz/1¹/4 cups plain (all-purpose) flour

2.5ml/¹/2 tsp salt

65g/2¹/2oz/5 tbsp lard or white cooking fat, cut in pieces

30ml/2 tbsp iced water

1 For the pastry, sift the flour and salt into a bowl. Add the fat and cut in with a pastry blender until the mixture resembles coarse breadcrumbs. With a fork, stir in enough water to bind the mixture. Gather the pastry into a ball.

2 ▲ On a lightly floured surface, roll out the pastry about 3mm/¹/8in thick. Transfer to a 23cm/9in pie dish and trim the edge to leave a 2cm/¹/2in overhang.

3 ▲ Fold the overhang under and crimp the edge. Refrigerate the pastry case for at least 20 minutes.

4 Preheat a 200°C/400°F/Gas 6 oven.

5 ▲ Prick the case all over with a fork. Line with crumpled baking parchment and fill with baking beans. Bake for 12 minutes. Remove the paper and beans and continue baking until golden, 6–8 minutes more.

6 In a pan, combine the lemon rind and juice, 250ml/8fl oz/1 cup of the water, 115g/4oz/scant ³/4 cup of the sugar, and butter. Bring the mixture to a boil.

7 Meanwhile, in a mixing bowl, dissolve the cornflour in the remaining water. Add the egg yolks.

8 ▲ Add the egg yolks to the lemon mixture and return to the boil, whisking continuously until the mixture thickens, about 5 minutes.

9 Cover the surface with baking parchment and let cool.

10 ▲ For the meringue, using an electric mixer beat the egg whites with the salt and cream of tartar until they hold stiff peaks. Add the remaining sugar and beat until glossy.

11 ▲ Spoon the lemon mixture into the pastry case and level. Spoon the meringue on top, smoothing it up to the pastry rim to seal. Bake until golden, 12–15 minutes.

Energy 357kcal/1497kJ; Protein 6.8g; Carbohydrate 42.8g, of which sugars 25.1g; Fat 18.9g, of which saturates 9g; Cholesterol 129mg; Calcium 108mg; Fibre 0.7g; Sodium 137mg.

Lime Meringue Pie

SERVES 8

3 egg yolks

350ml/12fl oz/1½ cups sweetened
condensed milk

finely grated rind and juice of 4 limes

7 egg whites

0.6ml/⅛ tsp salt

squeeze of fresh lemon juice

115g/4oz/scant ¾ cup sugar

2.5ml/½ tsp vanilla extract

FOR THE PASTRY

165g/5½oz/generous ¼ cup plain (all-
purpose) flour

2.5ml/½ tsp salt

115g/4oz/½ cup lard or white cooking fat

30–45ml/2–3 tbsp iced water

1 Preheat a 220°C/425°F/Gas 7 oven.

2 ▲ For the pastry, sift the flour and salt into a mixing bowl. Using a pastry blender or two knives, cut in the fat until the mixture resembles coarse breadcrumbs. Sprinkle in the water, 15ml/1 tbsp at a time, tossing lightly with a fork until the mixture comes together to form a ball.

~ COOK'S TIP ~

When beating egg whites with an electric mixer, start slowly, and increase speed after they become frothy. Turn the bowl constantly.

3 ▲ On a lightly floured surface, roll out the pastry. Use it to line a 23cm/9in pie tin (pan), easing in the pastry. Make a fluted edge.

4 Using a fork, prick the bottom and sides of the pastry case all over. Bake until lightly browned, 10–15 minutes. Let cool in the tin on a wire rack. Reduce oven temperature to 180°C/ 350°F/Gas 4.

5 ▲ With an electric mixer on high speed, beat the yolks and condensed milk. Stir in the lime rind and juice.

6 ▲ In another clean bowl, beat 3 of the egg whites until stiff. Fold into the lime mixture.

7 ▲ Spread the lime filling in the pastry case. Bake 10 minutes.

8 ▲ Meanwhile, beat the remaining egg whites with the salt and lemon juice until soft peaks form. Beat in the sugar, 15ml/1 tbsp at a time, until stiff peaks form. Add the vanilla.

9 ▲ Remove the pie from the oven. Using a metal spatula, spread the meringue over the lime filling, making a swirled design and covering the surface completely.

10 Bake until the meringue is lightly browned and the pastry is golden brown, about 12 minutes longer. Let cool, in the tin, on a wire rack.

Energy 267kcal/1117kJ; Protein 6g; Carbohydrate 31g, of which sugars 15g; Fat 15g, of which saturates 6g; Cholesterol 78mg; Calcium 41mg; Fibre 1g; Sodium 231mg.

Glacé Fruit Pie

SERVES 10

15ml/1 tbsp rum
50g/2oz/²/₃ cup mixed glacé (candied) fruit, chopped
450ml/³/₄ pint/scant 2 cups milk
10ml/4 tsp gelatin
90g/3¹/₂oz/¹/₂ cup sugar
2.5ml/¹/₂ tsp salt
3 eggs, separated
250ml/8fl oz/1 cup whipping cream
chocolate curls, for decorating

FOR THE CRUST

175g/6oz/3 cups broken digestive biscuits (graham crackers)
65g/2¹/₂oz/5 tbsp butter, melted
15ml/1 tbsp sugar

1 For the crust, mix the crushed digestive biscuits, butter and sugar. Press evenly and firmly over the bottom and side of a 23cm/9in pie plate. Refrigerate until firm.

2 ▲ In a bowl, stir together the rum and glacé fruit. Set aside.

3 Pour 120ml/4fl oz/¹/₂ cup of the milk into a small bowl. Sprinkle over the gelatin and let stand 5 minutes.

4 ▲ In the top of a double boiler, combine 45ml/3 tbsp of the sugar, the remaining milk and salt. Stir in the gelatin mixture. Cook over hot water, stirring, until gelatin dissolves.

5 Whisk in the egg yolks and cook, stirring, until thick enough to coat a spoon. Do not boil. Pour the custard over the glacé fruit mixture. Set in a bowl of ice water to cool.

6 Whip the cream lightly. Set aside.

7 With an electric mixer, beat the egg whites until they hold soft peaks. Add the remaining sugar and beat just enough to blend. Fold in a large dollop of the egg whites into the cooled gelatin mixture. Pour into the remaining egg whites and carefully fold together. Fold in the cream.

8 ▲ Pour into the pie shell and chill until firm. Decorate the top with chocolate curls.

Energy 334kcal/1392kJ; Protein 5.2g; Carbohydrate 29.3g, of which sugars 19.6g; Fat 22.3g, of which saturates 12.8g; Cholesterol 109mg; Calcium 106mg; Fibre 0.4g; Sodium 200mg.

Pumpkin Pie

SERVES 8

450g/1lb cooked or canned pumpkin

250ml/8fl oz/1 cup whipping cream

2 eggs

115g/4oz/½ cup soft dark brown sugar

60ml/4 tbsp golden (light corn) syrup

7.5ml/1½ tsp ground cinnamon

5ml/1 tsp ground ginger

1.25ml/¼ tsp ground cloves

2.5ml/½ tsp salt

FOR THE PASTRY

175g/6oz/1½ cups plain (all-purpose) flour

2.5ml/½ tsp salt

75g/3oz/6 tbsp cold butter, cut into pieces

40g/1½oz/3 tbsp cold white cooking fat, cut into pieces

45–60ml/3–4 tbsp iced water

1 For the pastry, sift the flour and salt into a bowl. Cut in the butter and fat until it resembles coarse crumbs. Bind with iced water. Wrap in clear film (plastic wrap) and chill for 20 minutes.

2 Roll out the dough and line a 23cm/9in pie tin (pan). Trim off the overhang. Roll out the trimmings and cut out leaf shapes. Wet the rim of the case with a brush dipped in water.

3 ▲ Place the dough leaves around the rim of the pastry case. Chill for about 20 minutes. Preheat the oven to 200°C/400°F/Gas 6.

4 ▲ Line the pastry case with baking parchment. Fill with baking beans and bake for 12 minutes. Remove paper and beans and bake until golden, 6–8 minutes more. Reduce the heat to 190°C/375°F/Gas 5.

5 ▼ Beat together the pumpkin, cream, eggs, sugar, golden syrup, spices and salt. Pour into the pastry case and bake until set, 40 minutes.

Energy 434kcal/1809kJ; Protein 6.2g; Carbohydrate 35.3g, of which sugars 19.4g; Fat 30.8g, of which saturates 13.8g; Cholesterol 94mg; Calcium 108mg; Fibre 1.2g; Sodium 60mg.

Chess Pie

SERVES 8

2 eggs
45ml/3 tbsp whipping cream
115g/4oz/¹/² cup soft dark brown sugar
30ml/2 tbsp sugar
30ml/2 tbsp plain (all-purpose) flour
15ml/1 tbsp whisky
40g/1¹/²oz/3 tbsp butter, melted
50g/2oz/¹/³ cup walnuts chopped walnuts
75g/3oz/generous ¹/² cup stoned (pitted) dates
whipped cream, for serving
FOR THE PASTRY
75g/3oz/6 tbsp cold butter
40g/1¹/²oz/3 tbsp cold white cooking fat, cut into pieces
175g/6oz/1¹/² cups plain (all-purpose) flour
2.5ml/¹/² tsp salt
45–60ml/3–4 tbsp iced water

1 ▲ For the pastry, cut the butter and fat into small pieces.

2 Sift the flour and salt into a bowl. With a pastry blender, cut in the butter and fat until the mixture resembles coarse crumbs. Stir in just enough water to bind. Gather into a ball, wrap in baking parchment and refrigerate for at least 20 minutes.

3 Place a baking sheet in the oven and preheat it to 190°C/375°F/Gas 5.

4 Roll out the dough thinly and line a 23cm/9in pie tin (pan). Trim the edge. Roll out the trimmings, cut thin strips and plait them. Brush the edge of the pastry case with water and fit the pastry plaits around the rim.

5 ▲ In a mixing bowl, whisk together the eggs and cream.

6 Add both sugars and beat until well combined. Sift over 15ml/1 tbsp of the flour and stir in. Add the whisky, the melted butter and the walnuts. Stir to combine.

7 ▲ Mix the dates with the remaining 15ml/1 tbsp of flour and stir into the walnut mixture.

8 Pour into the pastry case and bake until the pastry is golden and the filling puffed up, about 35 minutes. Serve at room temperature, with whipped cream, if liked.

Energy 450kcal/1880kJ; Protein 6g; Carbohydrate 47g, of which sugars 27g; Fat 28g, of which saturates 14g; Cholesterol 101mg; Calcium 73mg; Fibre 2g; Sodium 162mg.

Shoofly Pie

SERVES 8

115g/4oz/1 cup plain (all-purpose) flour
115g/4oz/½ cup soft dark brown sugar
1.25ml/¼ tsp each salt, ground ginger, cinnamon, mace and grated nutmeg
75g/3oz/6 tbsp cold butter, cut into pieces
2 eggs
120ml/4fl oz/½ cup molasses
120ml/4fl oz/½ cup boiling water
2.5ml/½ tsp bicarbonate of soda (baking soda)

FOR THE PASTRY

115g/4oz/½ cup cream cheese, at room temperature, cut into pieces
115g/4oz/½ cup cold butter, at room temperature, cut into pieces
115g/4oz/1 cup plain (all-purpose) flour,

1 For the pastry, put the cream cheese and butter in a mixing bowl. Sift over the flour.

2 ▲ Cut in with a pastry blender until the dough just holds together. Wrap in clear film (plastic wrap) and refrigerate for at least 30 minutes.

3 Put a baking sheet in the centre of the oven and preheat the oven to 190°C/375°F/Gas 5.

4 In a bowl, mix the flour, sugar, salt and spices. Rub in the butter with your fingertips until the mixture resembles coarse crumbs. Set aside.

5 On a lightly floured surface, roll out the dough and line a 23cm/9in pie tin (pan). Trim the overhanging pastry and flute the rim.

6 ▲ Spoon a third of the crumbed mixture into the pastry case.

7 ▲ To complete the filling, whisk the eggs with the molasses in a large bowl until combined.

8 Pour the boiling water into a small bowl. Stir in the bicarbonate of soda; the mixture will foam. Immediately whisk into the egg mixture. Pour carefully into the pastry case and sprinkle the remaining crumbed mixture evenly over the top.

9 Stand on the hot baking sheet and bake until browned, about 35 minutes. Leave to cool to room temperature, then serve.

Energy 441kcal/1838kJ; Protein 3g; Carbohydrate 48g, of which sugars 24g; Fat 28g, of which saturates 17g; Cholesterol 67mg; Calcium 100mg; Fibre 1g; Sodium 274mg.

Rich Chocolate Pie

SERVES 8

75g/3oz plain (semisweet) chocolate

50g/2oz/¼ cup butter or margarine

45ml/3 tbsp golden (light corn) syrup

3 eggs, beaten

150g/5oz/¾ cup caster (superfine) sugar

5ml/1 tsp vanilla extract

115g/4oz milk chocolate

475ml/16fl oz/2 cups whipping cream

FOR THE PASTRY

175g/6oz/1½ cups plain (all-purpose) flour

2.5ml/½ tsp salt

115g/4oz/½ cup lard or white
   cooking fat

30–45ml/2–3 tbsp iced water

1 Preheat a 220°C/425°F/Gas 7 oven.

2 For the pastry, sift the flour and salt into a mixing bowl. Using a pastry blender, cut in the fat until the mixture resembles coarse breadcrumbs. Sprinkle in the water, 15ml/1 tbsp at a time. Toss lightly with a fork until the pastry forms a ball.

3 On a lightly floured surface, roll out the pastry. Use to line an 20cm (8in) or 23cm (9in) pie tin (pan), easing in the pastry and being careful not to stretch it. Make a fluted edge.

4 Using a fork, prick the bottom and sides of the pastry case all over. Bake until lightly browned, 10–15 minutes. Let cool, in the tin, on a wire rack.

5 ▲ In a heatproof bowl set over a pan of simmering water, or in a double boiler, melt the plain chocolate, the butter or margarine and golden syrup. Remove the bowl from the heat and stir in the eggs, sugar and vanilla.

6 Reduce the oven temperature to 180°C/350°F/Gas 4. Pour the chocolate mixture into the case. Bake until the filling is set, 35–40 minutes. Let cool in the tin, set on a rack.

7 ▲ For the decoration, use the heat of your hands to soften the chocolate bar slightly. Draw the blade of a swivel-headed vegetable peeler along the side of the chocolate bar to shave off short, wide curls. Chill the chocolate curls until needed.

8 Before serving, lightly whip the cream until soft peaks form. Using a rubber spatula, spread the cream over the surface of the chocolate filling. Decorate with the chocolate curls.

Energy 712kcal/2962kJ; Protein 7.2g; Carbohydrate 55.8g, of which sugars 40g; Fat 52.7g, of which saturates 28.9g; Cholesterol 164mg; Calcium 121mg; Fibre 1g; Sodium 109mg.

Chocolate Chiffon Pie

SERVES 8

200g/7oz plain (semisweet) chocolate

250ml/8fl oz/1 cup milk

15ml/1 tbsp gelatin

90g/3¹/₂oz/¹/₂ cup sugar

2 large (US extra large) eggs, separated

5ml/1 tsp vanilla extract

350ml/12fl oz/1¹/₂ cups whipping cream

0.6ml/¹/₈ tsp salt

whipped cream and chocolate curls,
   for decorating

FOR THE CRUST

200g/7oz/3¹/₂ cups crushed digestive
   biscuits (graham crackers)

75g/3oz/6 tbsp butter, melted

1 Place a baking sheet in the oven and preheat to 180°C/350°F/Gas 4.

2 For the crust, mix the crushed digestive biscuits and butter in a bowl. Press evenly over the bottom and side of a 23cm/9in pie plate. Bake for 8 minutes. Let cool.

3 Chop the chocolate, then grate in a food processor or blender. Set aside.

4 Place the milk in the top of a double boiler. Sprinkle over the gelatin. Let stand 5 minutes to soften.

5 ▲ Set the top of a double boiler over hot water. Add 45ml/3 tbsp sugar, the chocolate and the egg yolks. Stir until dissolved. Add the vanilla extract.

6 ▲ Set the top of the double boiler in a bowl of ice and stir until the mixture reaches room temperature. Remove the pan from the ice and set aside.

7 Whip the cream lightly. Set aside. With an electric mixer, beat the egg whites and salt until they hold soft peaks. Add the remaining sugar and beat only enough to blend.

8 Fold a dollop of egg whites into the chocolate mixture, then pour back into the whites and fold in.

9 ▲ Fold in the whipped cream and pour into the pie shell. Put in the freezer until just set, about 5 minutes. If the centre sinks, fill with any remaining mixture. Refrigerate for 3–4 hours. Decorate with whipped cream and chocolate curls. Serve cold.

Energy 557kcal/2323kJ; Protein 6.4g; Carbohydrate 47.5g, of which sugars 33.5g; Fat 39.3g, of which saturates 23.1g; Cholesterol 127mg; Calcium 109mg; Fibre 1.2g; Sodium 251mg.

Black Bottom Pie

SERVES 8

10ml/2 tsp gelatin
45ml/3 tbsp cold water
2 eggs, separated
150g/5oz/³⁄4 cup caster (superfine) sugar
15ml/1 tbsp cornflour (cornstarch)
2.5ml/¹⁄2 tsp salt
475ml/16fl oz/2 cups milk
50g/2oz plain (semisweet) chocolate, finely chopped
30ml/2 tbsp rum
1.25ml/¹⁄4 tsp cream of tartar
chocolate curls, for decorating
FOR THE CRUST
175g/6oz/3 cups ginger nut biscuits (gingersnaps), crushed
65g/2¹⁄2oz/5 tbsp butter, melted

1 Preheat a 180°C/350°F/Gas 4 oven.

2 For the crust, mix the crushed ginger nut biscuits and melted butter.

3 ▲ Press the mixture evenly over the bottom and side of a 23cm/9in pie plate. Bake for 6 minutes.

4 Sprinkle the gelatin over the water and let stand to soften.

5 Beat the egg yolks in a large mixing bowl and set aside.

6 In a pan, combine half the sugar, the cornflour and salt. Gradually stir in the milk. Boil for 1 minute, stirring constantly.

7 ▲ Whisk the hot milk mixture into the yolks, then pour all back into the saucepan and return to the boil, whisking. Cook for 1 minute, still whisking. Remove from the heat.

8 ▲ Measure out 225g/8oz of the hot custard mixture and pour into a bowl. Add the chopped chocolate to the custard mixture, and stir until melted. Stir in half the rum and pour into the pie shell.

9 ▲ Whisk the softened gelatin into the plain custard until it has dissolved, then stir in the remaining rum. Position the pan in a bowl of cold water and leave until it reaches room temperature.

10 ▲ With an electric mixer, beat the egg whites and cream of tartar until they hold stiff peaks. Add the remaining sugar gradually, beating or whisking thoroughly at each addition.

11 ▲ Fold the custard into the egg whites, then spoon over the chocolate mixture in the pie shell. Refrigerate until set, about 2 hours.

12 Decorate the top with chocolate curls. Keep the pie refrigerated until ready to serve.

> ### ~ COOK'S TIP ~
>
> To make chocolate curls, melt 225g/8oz plain (semisweet) chocolate over hot water, stir in 15ml/1 tbsp of white cooking fat and mould in a small foil-lined loaf tin (pan). For large curls, soften the bar between your hands and scrape off curls from the wide side with a peeler; for small curls, grate from the narrow side using a box grater.

Energy 545kcal/2276kJ; Protein 9.3g; Carbohydrate 51.3g, of which sugars 25.1g; Fat 34.2g, of which saturates 20g; Cholesterol 189mg; Calcium 148mg; Fibre 1.4g; Sodium 173mg.

Brown Sugar Pie

SERVES 8

175g/6oz/1½ cups plain (all-purpose) flour

2.5ml/½ tsp salt

10ml/2 tsp sugar

75g/3oz/6 tbsp cold butter

45ml/3 tbsp or more iced water

FOR THE FILLING

25g/1oz/¼ cup plain (all-purpose)
flour, sifted

225g/8oz/1 cup soft light brown sugar

2.5ml/½ tsp vanilla extract

350ml/12fl oz/1½ cups whipping cream

40g/1½oz/3 tbsp butter, cut in tiny pieces

0.6ml/⅛ tsp grated nutmeg

1 Sift the flour, salt, and sugar into
a bowl. Using a pastry blender or
two knives, cut in the butter until
it resembles coarse breadcrumbs.

2 ▲ Sprinkle with the water and
mix until the dough holds together.
If it is too crumbly, add more water,
15ml/1 tbsp at a time. Gather into
a ball and flatten. Wrap in baking
parchment and chill for 20 minutes.

3 Roll out the dough about 3mm/⅛ in
thick and line a 23cm/9in pie dish.
Trim the edge, leaving a 1cm/½in
overhang. Fold it under and flute the
edge. Refrigerate for 30 minutes.

4 Preheat a 220°C/425°F/Gas 7 oven.

5 Line the pastry case with a piece of
baking parchment that is 5cm/2in
larger all around than the diameter of
the pan. Fill the case with dried beans.
Bake until the pastry has just set, 8–10
minutes. Remove from the oven and
lift out the paper and beans. Prick the
bottom of the pastry case all over with
a fork. Return to the oven and bake
for 5 minutes more. Let the pastry case
cool slightly before filling. Turn the
oven down to 190°C/375°F/Gas 5.

6 ▲ In a small bowl, mix together the
flour and sugar using a fork. Spread
this mixture in an even layer on the
bottom of the pastry case.

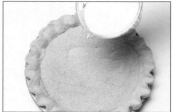

7 ▲ Stir the vanilla into the cream.
Pour the flavoured cream over the
flour and sugar mixture and gently
swirl with a fork to mix. Dot with the
butter. Sprinkle the nutmeg on top.

8 Cover the edge of the pie with foil
strips to prevent overbrowning. Set
on a baking sheet and bake until
the filling is golden brown and firm
to the touch, about 45 minutes.
Serve the pie at room temperature.

Energy 475kcal/1982kJ; Protein 3g; Carbohydrate 51g, of which sugars 32g; Fat 30g, of which saturates 19g; Cholesterol 77mg; Calcium 71mg; Fibre 1g; Sodium 223mg.

Creamy Banana Pie

SERVES 6

200g/7oz/3¹/2 cups crushed ginger nut
    biscuits (gingersnaps)

65g/2¹/2oz/5 tbsp butter, melted

2.5ml/¹/2 tsp grated nutmeg or
    ground cinnamon

175g/6oz ripe bananas, mashed

350g/12oz/1¹/2 cups cream cheese,
    at room temperature

60ml/4 tbsp thick plain (natural) yogurt
    or sour cream

45ml/3 tbsp dark rum or 5ml/1 tsp
    vanilla extract

FOR THE TOPPING

250ml/8fl oz/1 cup whipping cream

3–4 bananas

1   Preheat a 190°C/375°F/Gas 5 oven.

2 ▲ In a bowl, combine the crushed biscuits, butter and spice. Mix thoroughly with a wooden spoon.

3 ▲ Press the biscuit mixture into a 23cm/9in pie dish, building up thick sides with a neat edge. Bake for 5 minutes. Let cool, in the dish.

4 ▼ With an electric mixer, beat the mashed bananas with the cream cheese. Fold in the yogurt or sour cream and rum or vanilla. Spread the filling in the biscuit base. Refrigerate at least 4 hours or overnight.

5 ▲ For the topping, whip the cream until soft peaks form. Spread on the pie filling. Slice the bananas and arrange on top in a decorative pattern.

Energy 753kcal/3128kJ; Protein 6.2g; Carbohydrate 50.4g, of which sugars 33.8g; Fat 58.1g, of which saturates 35.6g; Cholesterol 122mg; Calcium 148mg; Fibre 1.5g; Sodium 369mg.

Georgia Peanut Butter Pie

SERVES 8

115g/4oz/2 cups finely crushed digestive
biscuits (graham crackers)

50g/2oz/4 tbsp soft light brown sugar,
firmly packed

75g/3oz/6 tbsp butter or margarine, melted

whipped cream or ice cream,
for serving

FOR THE FILLING

3 egg yolks

90g/3¹/₂oz/¹/₂ cup granulated sugar

50g/2oz/4 tbsp soft light brown sugar,
firmly packed

50g/2oz/¹/₂ cup cornflour (cornstarch)

0.6ml/¹/₈ tsp salt

600ml/1 pint/2¹/₂ cups evaporated milk

25g/1oz/2 tbsp unsalted butter

7.5ml/1¹/₂ tsp vanilla extract

115g/4oz/¹/₂ cup chunky peanut butter,
preferably made from freshly
ground peanuts

75g/3oz/²/₃ cup icing (confectioners') sugar

1 Preheat a 180°C/350°F/Gas 4 oven.

2 ▲ Combine the crumbs, sugar, and butter or margarine in a bowl and blend well. Spread the mixture in a well-greased 23cm/9in pie dish, pressing evenly over the bottom and sides with your fingertips.

3 Bake the crust for 10 minutes. Remove from the oven and leave to cool. Leave the oven on.

4 ▲ For the filling, combine the egg yolks, granulated and brown sugars, cornflour and salt in a heavy pan.

5 Slowly whisk in the milk. Cook over a medium heat, stirring constantly, until the mixture thickens, about 8–10 minutes. Reduce the heat to very low and cook until very thick, 3–4 minutes more.

6 ▲ Beat in the butter. Stir in the vanilla. Remove from the heat. Cover the surface closely with clear film (plastic wrap) and leave to cool.

> ### ~ VARIATIONS ~
> If preferred, use an equal amount of finely crushed ginger nut biscuits (gingersnaps) in place of digestives (graham crackers). Or make the pie with a ready-made biscuit (cookie) crust.

7 ▲ In a small bowl, combine the peanut butter with the icing sugar, working with your fingers to blend the ingredients to the consistency of fine crumbs.

8 ▲ Sprinkle all but 45ml/3 tbsp of the peanut butter crumbs evenly over the bottom of the crumb crust.

9 ▲ Pour in the filling, spreading it in an even layer. Sprinkle with the remaining crumbs. Bake for 15 minutes.

10 Let the pie cool for 1 hour. Serve with whipped cream or ice cream.

Energy 532kcal/2225kJ; Protein 12g; Carbohydrate 57g, of which sugars 43g; Fat 30g, of which saturates 14g; Cholesterol 134mg; Calcium 258mg; Fibre 2g; Sodium 392mg.

Lime Tart

SERVES 8

3 large (US extra large) egg yolks

1 × 400g/14oz can sweetened condensed milk

15g/1 tbsp grated lime zest

120ml/4fl oz/$\frac{1}{2}$ cup fresh lime juice

green food colouring (optional)

120ml/4fl oz/$\frac{1}{2}$ cup whipping cream

FOR THE BASE

115g/4oz/2 cups crushed digestive biscuits (graham crackers)

65g/2$\frac{1}{2}$oz/5 tbsp butter or margarine, melted

1 Preheat a 180°C/350°F/Gas 4 oven.

2 ▲ For the base, place the crushed biscuits in a bowl and add the butter or margarine. Mix to combine.

> ~ **VARIATION** ~
>
> Use lemons instead of limes, with yellow food colouring.

3 Press the mixture evenly over the bottom and sides of a 23cm/9in pie dish. Bake for 8 minutes. Let cool.

4 ▲ Beat the yolks until thick. Beat in the milk, lime rind and juice and colouring, if using. Pour into the pastry case and refrigerate until set, about 4 hours. To serve, whip the cream. Pipe a lattice pattern on top.

Fruit Tartlets

MAKES 8

175ml/6fl oz/$\frac{3}{4}$ cup red currant jelly

15ml/1 tbsp fresh lemon juice

175ml/6fl oz/$\frac{3}{4}$ cup whipping cream

675g/1$\frac{1}{2}$lb fresh fruit, such as strawberries, raspberries, kiwi fruit, peaches, grapes or currants, peeled and sliced as necessary

FOR THE PASTRY

175ml/6fl oz/$\frac{3}{4}$ cup cold butter, cubed

75g/3oz/6 tbsp soft dark brown sugar

45ml/3 tbsp unsweetened cocoa powder

200g/7oz/1$\frac{3}{4}$ cups plain (all-purpose) flour

1 egg white

1 For the pastry, combine the butter, brown sugar and cocoa over low heat. When the butter is melted, remove from the heat and sift over the flour. Stir, then add just enough egg white to bind the mixture. Gather into a ball, wrap in greaseproof (waxed) paper and chill for 30 minutes.

2 ▲ Grease eight 8cm/3in tins (pans). Roll out the pastry between sheets of greaseproof paper. Stamp out eight 10cm/4in rounds with a fluted cutter.

3 Line the tartlet tins. Prick the bottoms. Refrigerate for 15 minutes. Preheat a 180°C/350°F/Gas 4 oven.

4 Bake until firm, 20–25 minutes. Cool, then remove from the tins.

5 ▲ Melt the jelly with the lemon juice. Brush a thin layer in the bottom of the tartlets. Whip the cream and spread a thin layer in the tartlet cases. Arrange the fruit on top. Brush with the glaze and serve.

Lime: Energy 373kcal/1558kJ; Protein 6.6g; Carbohydrate 38.1g, of which sugars 30.2g; Fat 22.6g, of which saturates 13g; Cholesterol 133mg; Calcium 178mg; Fibre 0.3g; Sodium 215mg.
Fruit: Energy 437kcal/1828kJ; Protein 5.2g; Carbohydrate 49.5g, of which sugars 29.8g; Fat 25.6g, of which saturates 15.9g; Cholesterol 63mg; Calcium 80mg; Fibre 2.4g; Sodium 196mg.

Chocolate Lemon Tart

SERVES 8–10

250g/9oz/1¼ cups caster (superfine) sugar

6 eggs

grated rind of 2 lemons

175ml/6fl oz/¾ cup fresh lemon juice

175ml/6fl oz/¾ cup whipping cream

chocolate curls, for decorating

FOR THE CRUST

175g/6oz/1½ cups plain (all-purpose) flour

30ml/2 tbsp unsweetened cocoa powder

25g/1oz/¼ cup icing (confectioners') sugar

2.5ml/½ tsp salt

115g/4oz/½ cup butter or margarine

15ml/1 tbsp water

1 ▲ Liberally grease a 25cm/10in tart tin (pan).

2 For the crust, sift the flour, cocoa powder, sugar and salt into a bowl.

3 ▲ Melt the butter and water over a low heat. Pour over the flour mixture and stir with a wooden spoon until the dough is smooth and the flour has absorbed all the liquid.

4 Press the dough evenly over the base and side of the prepared tart tin. Refrigerate the tart shell while preparing the filling.

5 Preheat a baking sheet in a 190°C/ 375°F/ Gas 5 oven.

6 ▲ Whisk the sugar and eggs until the sugar is dissolved. Add the lemon rind and juice and mix well. Add the cream. Taste the mixture and add more lemon juice or sugar if needed. It should taste tart but also sweet.

7 Pour the filling into the tart shell and bake on the hot sheet until the filling is set, 20–25 minutes. Cool on a wire rack. When cool, decorate with the chocolate curls.

Energy 379kcal/1585kJ; Protein 6.1g; Carbohydrate 40.5g, of which sugars 27g; Fat 22.6g, of which saturates 12.9g; Cholesterol 163mg; Calcium 68mg; Fibre 0.7g; Sodium 127mg.

Lemon Almond Tart

SERVES 8

150g/5oz/scant 1 cup blanched almonds

90g/3¹/₂oz/¹/₂ cup sugar

2 eggs

grated rind and juice of 1¹/₂ lemons

115g/4oz/¹/₂ cup butter, melted

strips of lemon rind, for decorating

FOR THE CRUST

175g/6oz/1¹/₂ cups plain (all-purpose) flour

15ml/1 tbsp sugar

2.5ml/¹/₂ tsp salt

2.5ml/¹/₂ tsp baking powder

75g/3oz/6 tbsp cold unsalted butter,
    cut into pieces

45–60ml/3–4 tbsp whipping cream

1 For the crust, sift the flour, sugar, salt and baking powder into a bowl. Add the butter and rub in with your fingertips until the mixture resembles coarse breadcrumbs.

2 ▲ With a fork, stir in just enough cream to bind the dough.

3 Gather into a ball and transfer to a lightly floured surface. Roll out the dough about 3mm/¹/₈in thick and carefully transfer to a 23cm/9in tart tin (pan). Trim and prick the base all over with a fork. Refrigerate for at least 20 minutes.

4 Preheat a baking sheet in a 200°C/400°F/Gas 6 oven.

5 Line the tart shell with crumpled baking parchment and fill with baking beans. Bake for 12 minutes. Remove the paper and beans and continue baking until golden, 6–8 minutes more. Reduce the oven temperature to 180°C/350°F/Gas 4.

6 ▲ Grind the almonds finely with 15ml/1 tbsp of the sugar in a food processor, blender, or coffee grinder.

7 ▲ Set a mixing bowl over a pan of hot water. Add the eggs and the remaining sugar, and beat with an electric mixer until the mixture is thick enough to leave a ribbon trail when the beaters are lifted.

8 Stir in the lemon rind and juice, butter and ground almonds.

9 Pour into the prebaked shell. Bake until the filling is golden and set, about 35 minutes. Decorate with lemon rind.

Energy 504kcal/2102kJ; Protein 8g; Carbohydrate 34g, of which sugars 17g; Fat 38g, of which saturates 18g; Cholesterol 126mg; Calcium 101mg; Fibre 3g; Sodium 367mg.

Orange Tart

4 ▲ Cut the oranges into 5mm/¹/₄in slices. Do not peel. Add to the syrup. Simmer gently for 10 minutes, or until glazed. Transfer to a wire rack to dry. When cool, cut in half. Reserve the syrup. Place a baking sheet in the oven and heat to 200°C/400°F/Gas 6.

5 Grind the almonds finely in a food processor, blender or coffee grinder. With an electric mixer, cream the butter and remaining sugar until light and fluffy. Beat in the egg and 30ml/ 2 tbsp of the orange syrup. Stir in the almonds and flour.

6 Melt the jam over low heat, then brush over the tart shell. Pour in the almond mixture. Bake until set, about 20 minutes. Let cool.

SERVES 8

200g/7oz/1 cup sugar
250ml/8fl oz/1 cup fresh orange juice, strained
2 large navel oranges
175g/6oz/1 cup whole blanched almonds
50g/2oz/¹/₄ cup butter
1 egg
15ml/1 tbsp plain (all-purpose) flour
45ml/3 tbsp apricot jam
FOR THE CRUST
215g/7¹/₂oz/scant 2 cups plain (all-purpose) flour
2.5ml/¹/₂ tsp salt
50g/2oz/¹/₄ cup cold butter, cut into pieces
40g/1¹/₂oz/3 tbsp cold margarine, cubed
45–60ml/3–4 tbsp iced water

1 For the crust, sift the flour and salt into a bowl. Add the butter and margarine and rub in with your fingertips until the mixture resembles coarse breadcrumbs. Stir in just enough water to bind the dough. Gather into a ball, wrap in clear film (plastic wrap), and refrigerate for at least 20 minutes.

2 On a lightly floured surface, roll out the dough 5mm/¹/₄in thick and transfer to a 20cm/8in tart tin (pan). Trim off the overhang. Refrigerate until needed.

3 In a pan, combine 150g/5oz/³/₄ cup of the sugar and the strained orange juice and boil until thick and syrupy, about 10 minutes.

7 ▲ Arrange overlapping orange slices on top of the set almond mixture. Boil the remaining syrup until thick. Brush on top of the oranges to glaze.

Energy 500kcal/2093kJ; Protein 8.6g; Carbohydrate 59.4g, of which sugars 37.4g; Fat 27g, of which saturates 7.7g; Cholesterol 50mg; Calcium 130mg; Fibre 3.1g; Sodium 137mg.

Rich Orange Cheesecake

SERVES 8

675g/1½lb full-fat soft cheese, at
room temperature

200g/7oz/1 cup caster (superfine) sugar

30ml/2 tbsp plain (all-purpose) flour

3 eggs

115g/4oz/½ cup butter, melted

5ml/1 tsp vanilla extract

15ml/1 tbsp grated orange zest

20cm/8in biscuit (cookie) case, made
with digestive biscuits (graham
crackers) and orange zest, chilled

4 sweet oranges, peeled and segmented

squeeze of lemon juice

15–30ml/1–2 tbsp orange liqueur
(optional)

1 Preheat a 150°C/300°F/Gas 2 oven.

2 ▲ Combine the soft cheese, sugar
and flour in a bowl. Beat until the
mixture is light and fluffy.

3 ▲ Add the eggs, butter, vanilla
extract and orange zest and beat until
smoothly blended.

4 ▲ Pour the filling into the biscuit
case. Set the springform tin on a
baking sheet.

5 Bake for 1–1¼ hours or until the
filling is gently set (it will continue to
firm up as it cools). If the top browns
too quickly, cover with foil. Turn off
the oven and open the door.

6 Leave the cheesecake to cool in
the oven. When it is cold, cover and
refrigerate overnight.

7 Mix together the orange segments,
lemon juice and liqueur, if using.
Serve with the cheesecake.

~ VARIATIONS ~

For Lemon Cheesecake, use
7.5ml/1½ tsp lemon zest instead of
orange in the filling. For a lighter
cheesecake, use a mixture of
ricotta or curd (farmer's) cheese
and full-fat soft cheese, worked in
a food processor until smooth.

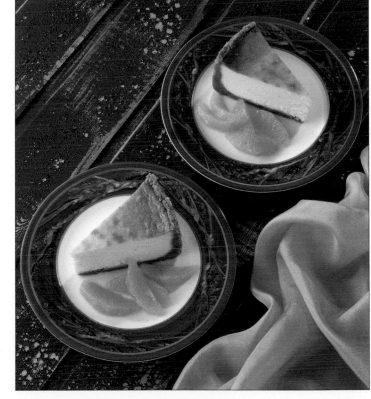

Energy 905kcal/3760kJ; Protein 9g; Carbohydrate 56g, of which sugars 36g; Fat 73g, of which saturates 44g; Cholesterol 243mg; Calcium 174mg; Fibre 3g; Sodium 367mg.

Blueberry-Hazelnut Cheesecake

SERVES 6–8

350g/12oz/3 cups blueberries

15ml/1 tbsp honey

75g/3oz/6 tbsp sugar

5ml/1 tsp plus 15ml/1 tbsp fresh
 lemon juice

175g/6oz/¾ cup cream cheese,
 at room temperature

1 egg

5ml/1 tsp hazelnut liqueur (optional)

120ml/4fl oz/½ cup whipping cream

FOR THE BASE

175g/6oz/1½ cups ground hazelnuts

75g/3oz/⅔ cup plain (all-purpose) flour

0.6ml/⅛ tsp salt

50g/2oz/¼ cup butter, at room temperature

75g/3oz/6 tbsp soft light brown sugar,
 firmly packed

1 egg yolk

1 ▲ For the base, put the hazelnuts in
a large bowl. Sift in the flour and salt,
and stir to mix. Set aside.

~ COOK'S TIP ~

The cheesecake can be prepared a
day in advance, but add the fruit
shortly before serving. Instead of
covering the top completely, leave
spaces to make a design, if wished.

---

2 Beat the butter with the brown
sugar until light and fluffy. Beat in
the egg yolk. Gradually fold in the
nut mixture, in three batches.

3 ▲ Press the mixture into a greased
23cm/9in pie dish, spreading it evenly
against the sides. Form a rim around
the top edge that is slightly thicker
than the sides. Cover and refrigerate
for at least 30 minutes.

4 Preheat a 180°C/350°F/Gas 4 oven.

5 ▲ Meanwhile, for the topping,
combine the blueberries, honey,
15ml/1 tbsp of the sugar, and 5ml/
1 tsp lemon juice in a heavy pan.
Cook the mixture over a low heat,
stirring occasionally, until the berries
have given off some liquid but still
retain their shape, 5–7 minutes.
Remove from the heat and set aside.

6 Place the base in the oven and bake
15 minutes. Remove and leave to cool
while making the filling.

7 ▲ Beat together the cream cheese
and remaining granulated sugar until
light and fluffy. Add the egg,
remaining lemon juice, the liqueur,
if using, and the cream and beat until
thoroughly incorporated.

8 ▲ Pour the cheese mixture into the
base and spread evenly. Bake until
just set, 20–25 minutes.

9 Let the cheesecake cool completely
on a wire rack, then cover and
refrigerate for at least 1 hour.

10 Spread the blueberry mixture
evenly over the top of the cheesecake.
Serve the cheesecake at a cool room
temperature.

Energy 446kcal/1852kJ; Protein 7g; Carbohydrate 24g, of which sugars 17g; Fat 37g, of which saturates 15g; Cholesterol 104mg; Calcium 92mg; Fibre 3g; Sodium 153mg.

Chocolate Cheesecake Tart

SERVES 8

350g/12oz/1¹/₂ cups cream cheese

60ml/4 tbsp whipping cream

225g/8oz/generous 1 cup caster (superfine) sugar

50g/2oz/¹/₂ cup unsweetened cocoa powder

2.5ml/¹/₂ tsp ground cinnamon

3 eggs

whipped cream, for decorating

chocolate curls, for decorating

FOR THE BASE

75g/3oz/1¹/₂ cups digestive biscuits (graham crackers), crushed

50g/2oz/1 cup crushed amaretti biscuits (if unavailable, use extra crushed digestive biscuits)

75g/3oz/6 tbsp butter, melted

1 Preheat a baking sheet in the centre of a 180°C/350°F/Gas 4 oven.

2 For the base, mix the crushed biscuits and butter in a bowl.

3 ▲ With a spoon, press the mixture over the bottom and sides of a 23cm/9in pie dish. Bake for 8 minutes. Let cool. Keep the oven on.

4 With an electric mixer, beat the cheese and cream together until smooth. Beat in the sugar, cocoa and cinnamon until blended.

5 ▼ Add the eggs, one at a time, beating just enough to blend.

6 Pour into the biscuit base and bake on the hot sheet for 25–30 minutes. The filling will sink down as it cools. Decorate with whipped cream and chocolate curls.

Frozen Strawberry Tart

SERVES 8

225g/8oz/1 cup cream cheese

250ml/8fl oz/1 cup sour cream

575g/1lb 4oz frozen strawberries, thawed and sliced

FOR THE BASE

115g/4oz/2 cups crushed digestive biscuits (graham crackers)

15ml/1 tbsp caster (superfine) sugar

65g/2¹/₂oz/5 tbsp butter, melted

~ **VARIATION** ~

For Frozen Raspberry Tart, use raspberries in place of the strawberries and prepare the same way, or try other frozen fruit.

1 ▲ For the base, mix together the biscuits, sugar and butter.

2 Press the mixture evenly and firmly over the bottom and sides of a 23cm/9in pie dish. Freeze until firm.

3 ▼ Blend together the cream cheese and sour cream. Reserve 90ml/6 tbsp of the strawberries. Add the rest to the cream cheese mixture.

4 Pour the filling into the biscuit base and freeze 6–8 hours until firm. To serve, spoon some of the reserved berries and juice on top.

Chocolate: Energy 569kcal/2366kJ; Protein 7g; Carbohydrate 42g, of which sugars 35g; Fat 43g, of which saturates 25g; Cholesterol 171mg; Calcium 94mg; Fibre 1g; Sodium 365mg.
Strawberry: Energy 415kcal/1722kJ; Protein 4g; Carbohydrate 28g, of which sugars 13g; Fat 33g, of which saturates 19g; Cholesterol 76mg; Calcium 98mg; Fibre 3g; Sodium 320mg.

Kiwi Ricotta Cheese Tart

Serves 8

75g/3oz/1/2 cup blanched almonds, ground

90g/31/2oz/1/2 cup sugar

900g/2lb ricotta cheese

250ml/8fl oz/1 cup whipping cream

1 egg and 3 egg yolks

15ml/1 tbsp plain (all-purpose) flour

pinch of salt

30ml/2 tbsp rum

grated rind of 1 lemon

37.5ml/21/2 tbsp lemon juice

30ml/2 tbsp honey

5 kiwi fruit

For the pastry

150g/5oz/11/4 cups plain (all-purpose) flour

15ml/1 tbsp sugar

2.5ml/1/2 tsp salt

2.5ml/1/2 tsp baking powder

75g/3oz/6 tbsp butter

1 egg yolk

45–60ml/3–4 tbsp whipping cream

1 For the pastry, mix together the flour, sugar, salt and baking powder in a large bowl. Cut the butter into cubes and gradually rub it into the pastry mixture. Mix in the egg yolk and cream. Stir in just enough to bind the pastry.

2 ▲ Transfer to a lightly floured surface, flatten slightly, wrap and refrigerate for 30 minutes. Preheat the oven to 220°C/ 425°F/Gas 7.

3 ▲ On a lightly floured surface, roll out the dough to a 3mm/1/8in thickness. Transfer to a 23cm/9in springform tin (pan). Crimp the edge.

4 ▲ Prick the pastry with a fork. Line with baking parchment and fill with dried beans. Bake for 10 minutes. Remove the paper and beans and bake for 6–8 minutes more until golden. Leave to cool. Reduce the temperature to 180°C/350°F/Gas 4.

5 ▲ Mix the almonds with 15ml/ 1 tbsp of the sugar in a food processor or blender.

6 Beat the ricotta until creamy. Add the cream, egg, yolks, remaining sugar, flour, salt, rum, lemon rind and 30ml/2 tbsp of lemon juice. Combine.

7 ▲ Stir in the ground almonds until well blended.

8 Pour into a pastry case and bake for 1 hour. Chill, loosely covered for 2–3 hours. Unmould and put on a plate.

9 Combine the honey and remaining lemon juice for the glaze.

10 ▲ Peel the kiwis. Halve them lengthwise, then slice. Arrange the slices in rows across the top of the tart. Just before serving, brush with the honey glaze.

Energy 688kcal/2865kJ; Protein 17.8g; Carbohydrate 47g, of which sugars 30.9g; Fat 48g, of which saturates 25.9g; Cholesterol 231mg; Calcium 109mg; Fibre 2.1g; Sodium 84mg.

Raspberry Tart

SERVES 8

4 egg yolks

75g/3oz/6 tbsp caster (superfine) sugar

45ml/3 tbsp plain (all-purpose) flour

300ml/¹/₂ pint/1¹/₄ cups milk

0.6ml/¹/₈ tsp salt

2.5ml/¹/₂ tsp vanilla extract

450g/1lb fresh raspberries

75ml/5 tbsp red currant jelly

15ml/1 tbsp fresh orange juice

FOR THE PASTRY

190g/6¹/₂oz/1²/₃ cups plain (all-purpose) flour

2.5ml/¹/₂ tsp baking powder

1.25ml/¹/₄ tsp salt

15ml/1 tbsp sugar

grated rind of ¹/₂ orange

75g/3oz/6 tbsp cold butter, cut into pieces

1 egg yolk

45–60ml/3–4 tbsp whipping cream

1 For the pastry, sift the flour, baking powder and salt into a bowl. Stir in the sugar and orange rind. Add the butter and cut in with a pastry blender until the mixture resembles coarse breadcrumbs. Stir in the egg yolk and just enough cream to bind the dough. Gather into a ball, wrap in baking parchment and refrigerate.

2 For the custard filling, beat the egg yolks and sugar until thick and lemon coloured. Gradually stir in the flour.

3 In a pan, bring the milk and salt just to the boil, then remove from the heat. Whisk into the egg yolk mixture, return to the pan and continue whisking over moderately high heat until just bubbling. Cook for 3 minutes to thicken. Transfer immediately to a bowl. Add the vanilla and stir to blend.

4 ▲ Cover with baking parchment to prevent a skin from forming.

5 ▲ Preheat a 200°C/400°F/Gas 6 oven. On a floured surface, roll out the pastry 3mm/¹/₈in thick, transfer to a 25cm/10in pie dish and trim. Prick the bottom with a fork and line with crumpled baking parchment. Fill with baking beans and bake for 15 minutes. Remove the paper and beans. Continue baking until golden, 6–8 minutes more. Let cool.

6 ▲ Spread an even layer of the pastry cream filling in the pastry case and arrange the raspberries on top. Melt the jelly and orange juice in a pan and brush on top to glaze.

Energy 323kcal/1359kJ; Protein 6.9g; Carbohydrate 44g, of which sugars 22.1g; Fat 14.6g, of which saturates 7.8g; Cholesterol 154mg; Calcium 126mg; Fibre 2.3g; Sodium 86mg.

Treacle Tart

SERVES 4–6

175ml/6fl oz/³/4 cup golden (light corn) syrup
75g/3oz fresh white breadcrumbs
grated rind of 1 lemon
30ml/2 tbsp fresh lemon juice
FOR THE PASTRY
175g/6oz/1¹/2 cups plain (all-purpose) flour
2.5ml/¹/2 tsp salt
75g/3oz/6 tbsp cold butter, cut in pieces
40g/1¹/2oz/3 tbsp cold margarine, cubed
45–60ml/3–4 tbsp iced water

1 For the pastry, combine the flour and salt in a bowl. Add the butter and margarine and cut in with a pastry blender until the mixture resembles coarse breadcrumbs.

2 ▲ With a fork, stir in just enough water to bind the pastry. Gather into a ball, wrap in baking parchment, and refrigerate for at least 20 minutes.

3 On a lightly floured surface, roll out the pastry to a thickness of 3mm/¹/8in. Transfer to a 20cm/8in pie dish and trim off the overhang. Refrigerate for at least 20 minutes. Reserve the trimmings for the lattice top.

4 Preheat a baking sheet at the top of a 200°C/400°F/Gas 6 oven.

5 In a pan, warm the syrup until thin and runny.

6 ▲ Remove from the heat and stir in the breadcrumbs and lemon rind. Let sit for 10 minutes so the bread can absorb the syrup. Add more breadcrumbs if the mixture is thin. Stir in the lemon juice and spread evenly in the pastry case.

7 Roll out the pastry trimmings and cut into 10–12 thin strips.

8 ▼ Lay half the strips on the filling, then lay the remaining strips at an angle over them to form a lattice.

9 Place the tart on the hot sheet and bake for 10 minutes. Lower the heat to 190°C/375°F/Gas 5. Bake until the top of the tart is golden, about 15 minutes more. Leave to cool slightly in the tin. Serve warm or cold.

Energy 373kcal/1567kJ; Protein 4.4g; Carbohydrate 55.5g, of which sugars 24g; Fat 16.3g, of which saturates 7.7g; Cholesterol 27mg; Calcium 64mg; Fibre 1.2g; Sodium 304mg.

Coconut Cream Tart

SERVES 8

150g/5oz/1½ cups desiccated (dry unsweetened shredded) coconut

150g/5oz/¾ cup caster (superfine) sugar

60ml/4 tbsp cornflour (cornstarch)

0.6ml/⅛ tsp salt

600ml/1 pint/2½ cups milk

60ml/4 tbsp whipping cream

2 egg yolks

25g/1oz/2 tbsp unsalted butter

10ml/2 tsp vanilla extract

FOR THE PASTRY

150g/5oz/1¼ cups plain (all-purpose) flour

1.25ml/¼ tsp salt

40g/1½oz/3 tbsp cold butter, cut in pieces

25g/1oz/2 tbsp lard or white cooking fat

30–45ml/2–3 tbsp iced water

1 For the pastry, sift the flour and salt into a bowl. Add the butter and fat and cut in with a pastry blender until the mixture resembles coarse breadcrumbs.

2 ▲ With a fork, stir in just enough water to bind the pastry. Gather into a ball, wrap in baking parchment and refrigerate for 20 minutes.

3 Preheat a 220°C/425°F/Gas 7 oven. Roll out the pastry 3mm/⅛in thick. Line a 23cm/9in pie dish. Trim and flute the edges. Prick the bottom. Line with crumpled baking parchment and fill with baking beans. Bake 10–12 minutes. Remove paper and beans, reduce heat to 180°C/350°F/Gas 4 and bake until brown, 10–15 minutes.

4 ▲ Spread 50g/2oz/3 tbsp of the coconut on a baking sheet and toast in the oven until golden, 6–8 minutes, stirring often. Set aside for decorating.

5 Put the sugar, cornflour and salt in a pan. In a bowl, whisk the milk, cream and egg yolks. Add the egg mixture to the pan.

6 ▼ Cook over a low heat, stirring, until the mixture comes to the boil. Boil for 1 minute, then remove from the heat. Add the butter, vanilla and remaining coconut.

7 Pour into the prebaked pastry case. When cool, sprinkle toasted coconut in a ring in the centre.

Energy 400kcal/1671kJ; Protein 6.2g; Carbohydrate 39.6g, of which sugars 23.4g; Fat 25.2g, of which saturates 17g; Cholesterol 78mg; Calcium 140mg; Fibre 2.9g; Sodium 101mg.

Brandy Alexander Tart

SERVES 8

120ml/4fl oz/^{1}/$_2$ cup cold water
15ml/1 tbsp powdered gelatine
115g/4oz/scant ^{3}/$_4$ cup caster (superfine) sugar
3 eggs, separated
60ml/4 tbsp brandy
60ml/4 tbsp crème de cacao
pinch of salt
300ml/^{1}/$_2$ pint/1^1/$_4$ cups whipping cream
chocolate curls, for decorating
FOR THE CASE
225g/8oz/4 cups crushed digestive biscuits (graham crackers)
65g/2^1/$_2$oz/5 tbsp butter, melted
15ml/1 tbsp sugar

1 Preheat the oven to 375°F/190°C/ Gas 5. For the case, mix the biscuit with the butter and sugar in a bowl.

3 ▲ Press the crumbs evenly on to the bottom and sides of a 23cm/9in tart tin (pan). Bake until just brown, about 10 minutes. Cool on a rack.

4 Place the water in the top of a double boiler set over hot water. Sprinkle over the powdered gelatine and leave to stand for 5 minutes to soften. Add half the sugar and the egg yolks. Whisk constantly over a very low heat until the gelatine dissolves and the mixture has thickened slightly. Do not allow the mixture to boil.

5 ▲ Remove from the heat and stir in the brandy and crème de cacao.

6 Set the pan over iced water and stir occasionally until it cools and thickens; it should not set firmly.

7 With an electric mixer, beat the egg whites and salt until they hold stiff peaks. Beat in the remaining sugar. Spoon a dollop of whites into the yolk mixture and fold in to lighten.

8 ▼ Pour the egg yolk mixture over the remaining whites and fold together.

9 Whip the cream until soft peaks form, then gently fold into the filling. Spoon into the baked biscuit case and chill until set, 3–4 hours. Decorate the top with chocolate curls before serving.

Energy 457kcal/1905kJ; Protein 6g; Carbohydrate 40g, of which sugars 24g; Fat 30g, of which saturates 17g; Cholesterol 156mg; Calcium 65mg; Fibre 1g; Sodium 314mg.

Velvety Mocha Tart

SERVES 8

10ml/2 tsp instant espresso coffee
30ml/2 tbsp hot water
350ml/12fl oz/1½ cups whipping cream
175g/6oz plain (semisweet) chocolate
25g/1oz dark (bittersweet) chocolate
120ml/4fl oz/½ cup whipped cream, for decorating
chocolate-covered coffee beans, for decorating
FOR THE BASE
150g/5oz chocolate wafers, crushed
30ml/2 tbsp caster (superfine) sugar
65g/2½oz/5 tbsp butter, melted

1 ▲ For the base, mix the crushed chocolate wafers and sugar together, then stir in the melted butter.

2 Press the mixture evenly over the bottom and sides of a 23cm/9in pie dish. Refrigerate until firm.

3 In a bowl, dissolve the coffee in the water and set aside.

4 Pour the cream into a mixing bowl. Set the bowl in hot water to warm the cream, bringing it closer to the temperature of the chocolate.

5 Melt both the chocolates in the top of a double boiler, or in a heatproof bowl set over a pan of hot water. Remove from the heat when nearly melted and stir to continue melting. Set the bottom of the pan in cool water to reduce the temperature. Be careful not to splash any water on the chocolate or it will become grainy.

6 ▲ With an electric mixer, whip the cream until it is lightly fluffy. Add the dissolved coffee and whip until the cream just holds its shape.

7 ▲ When the chocolate is at room temperature, fold it gently into the cream with a large metal spoon.

8 Pour into the chilled base and refrigerate until firm. To serve, pipe a ring of whipped cream rosettes around the edge, then place a chocolate-covered coffee bean in the centre of each rosette.

Energy 507kcal/2103kJ; Protein 3.6g; Carbohydrate 30.3g, of which sugars 27g; Fat 42.1g, of which saturates 26.2g; Cholesterol 83mg; Calcium 71mg; Fibre 0.8g; Sodium 83mg.

Chocolate Pear Tart

SERVES 8

115g/4oz plain (semisweet) chocolate, grated
3 large firm, ripe pears
1 egg
1 egg yolk
120ml/4fl oz/¹/₂ cup single (light) cream
2.5ml/¹/₂ tsp vanilla extract
45ml/3 tbsp caster (superfine) sugar
FOR THE PASTRY
150g/5oz/1¹/₄ cups plain (all-purpose) flour
0.6ml/¹/₈ tsp salt
30ml/2 tbsp sugar
115g/4oz/¹/₂ cup cold unsalted butter, cut into pieces
1 egg yolk
15ml/1 tbsp fresh lemon juice

1 For the pastry, sift the flour and salt into a bowl. Add the sugar and butter. Cut in with a pastry blender until the mixture resembles coarse breadcrumbs. Stir in the egg yolk and lemon juice until the mixture forms a ball. Wrap in baking parchment, and refrigerate for at least 20 minutes.

2 Preheat a baking sheet in the centre of a 200°C/400°F/Gas 6 oven.

3 On a lightly floured surface, roll out the pastry 3mm/¹/₈in thick. Transfer to a 25cm/10in tart dish and trim.

4 ▲ Sprinkle the bottom of the case with the grated chocolate.

5 ▲ Peel, halve and core the pears. Cut in thin slices crosswise, then fan them out slightly.

6 Carefully transfer the pear halves to the tart, maintaining the fan shape, with the help of a metal spatula. Arrange on top of the chocolate like the spokes of a wheel.

7 ▼ Whisk together the egg and egg yolk, cream and vanilla. Ladle over the pears, then sprinkle with sugar.

8 Bake for 10 minutes. Reduce the heat to 180°C/350°F/Gas 4 and cook until the custard is set and the pears begin to caramelize, about 20 minutes more. Serve warm.

Energy 357kcal/1493kJ; Protein 4.8g; Carbohydrate 39.5g, of which sugars 25.1g; Fat 21.1g, of which saturates 12.4g; Cholesterol 114mg; Calcium 68mg; Fibre 2.2g; Sodium 106mg.

Maple Walnut Tart

SERVES 8

3 eggs

0.6ml/¹/₈ tsp salt

50g/2oz/¹/₄ cup caster (superfine) sugar

50g/2oz/¹/₄ cup butter or margarine, melted

250ml/8fl oz/1 cup pure maple syrup

115g/4oz/²/₃ cup chopped walnuts

whipped cream, for decorating

FOR THE PASTRY

65g/2¹/₂oz/9 tbsp plain (all-purpose) flour

65g/2¹/₂oz/9 tbsp wholemeal
(whole-wheat) flour

0.6ml/¹/₈ tsp salt

50g/2oz/¹/₄ cup cold butter, cut in pieces

40g/1¹/₂oz/3 tbsp cold lard or white cooking
fat, cut in pieces

1 egg yolk

30–45ml/2–3 tbsp iced water

1 ▼ For the pastry, mix the flours and salt in a bowl. Add the butter and fat and cut in with a pastry blender until the mixture resembles coarse breadcrumbs. With a fork, stir in the egg yolk and just enough water to bind the pastry. Form into a ball.

2 Wrap the pastry in clear film (plastic wrap) or baking parchment and refrigerate for 20 minutes.

3 Preheat a 220°C/425°F/Gas 7 oven.

4 On a lightly floured surface, roll out the pastry about 3mm/¹/₈in thick and transfer to a 23cm/9in pie dish. Trim the edge. To decorate, roll out the trimmings. With a small heart-shaped cutter, stamp out enough hearts to go around the rim of the pie. Brush the edge with water, then arrange the pastry hearts all around.

5 ▲ Prick the bottom with a fork. Line with crumpled baking parchment and fill with baking beans. Bake for 10 minutes. Remove the paper and beans and continue baking until golden brown, 3–6 minutes more.

6 In a bowl, whisk the eggs, salt and sugar together. Stir in the butter and maple syrup.

7 ▲ Set the pastry case on a baking sheet. Pour in the filling, then sprinkle the nuts over the top.

8 Bake until just set, for about 35 minutes. Cool on a rack. Decorate with whipped cream, if wished.

Energy 442kcal/1846kJ; Protein 6.8g; Carbohydrate 43.3g, of which sugars 32g; Fat 28.1g, of which saturates 10.2g; Cholesterol 128mg; Calcium 52mg; Fibre 1.5g; Sodium 190mg.

Pecan Tart

SERVES 8

3 eggs
0.6ml/¹/₈ tsp salt
200g/7oz/scant 1 cup soft dark brown sugar
120ml/4fl oz/¹/₂ cup golden (light corn) syrup
30ml/2 tbsp fresh lemon juice
75g/3oz/6 tbsp butter, melted
150g/5oz/scant 1 cup chopped pecan nuts
50g/2oz/¹/₂ cup pecan halves
FOR THE PASTRY
175g/6oz/1¹/₂ cups plain (all-purpose) flour
15ml/1 tbsp caster (superfine) sugar
5ml/1 tsp baking powder
2.5ml/¹/₂ tsp salt
75g/3oz/6 tbsp cold unsalted butter, cut in pieces
1 egg yolk
45–60ml/3–4 tbsp whipping cream

1 For the pastry, sift the flour, sugar, baking powder and salt into a bowl. Add the butter and cut in with a pastry blender until the mixture resembles coarse breadcrumbs.

2 ▼ In a bowl, beat together the egg yolk and cream until blended.

~ COOK'S TIP ~

Serve this tart warm, accompanied by ice cream or whipped cream, if wished.

3 ▲ Pour the cream mixture into the flour mixture and stir with a fork.

4 Gather the pastry into a ball. On a lightly floured surface, roll out 3mm/¹/₈in thick and transfer to a 23cm/9in pie dish. Trim the overhang and flute the edge with your fingers. Refrigerate for at least 20 minutes.

5 Preheat a baking sheet in the middle of a 200°C/400°F/Gas 6 oven.

6 In a bowl, lightly whisk the eggs and salt. Add the sugar, syrup, lemon juice and butter. Mix well and stir in the chopped nuts.

7 ▲ Pour into the pastry case and arrange the pecan halves in concentric circles on top.

8 Bake for 10 minutes. Reduce the heat to 170°C/325°F/Gas 3 and continue baking for 25 minutes.

Energy 587kcal/2449kJ; Protein 7.5g; Carbohydrate 56.7g, of which sugars 39.6g; Fat 38.3g, of which saturates 13.4g; Cholesterol 142mg; Calcium 82mg; Fibre 1.9g; Sodium 185mg.

Peach Tart with Almond Cream

SERVES 8–10

4 large ripe peaches

115g/4oz/²/₃ cup blanched almonds

30ml/2 tbsp plain (all-purpose) flour

90g/3¹/₂oz/7 tbsp unsalted butter,
at room temperature

115g/4oz/scant ³/₄ cup plus 30ml/2 tbsp
caster (superfine) sugar

1 egg plus 1 yolk

2.5ml/¹/₂ tsp vanilla extract,
or 10ml/2 tsp rum

FOR THE PASTRY

190g/6¹/₂oz/1²/₃ cups plain
(all-purpose) flour

3.75ml/³/₄ tsp salt

90g/3¹/₂oz/7 tbsp cold unsalted butter,
cut in pieces

1 egg yolk

30–45ml/2–3 tbsp iced water

1 ▲ For the pastry, sift the flour and salt into a bowl.

2 Add the butter and cut in with a pastry blender until the mixture resembles coarse breadcrumbs. Stir in the egg yolk and just enough water to bind the pastry. Gather into a ball, wrap in baking parchment, and refrigerate for at least 20 minutes.

3 Preheat a baking sheet in the centre of a 200°C/400°F/Gas 6 oven.

4 ▲ On a floured surface, roll out the pastry 3mm/¹/₈in thick. Transfer to a 25cm/10in pie dish. Trim the edge, prick the bottom and refrigerate.

5 ▲ Score the bottoms of the peaches. Drop the peaches, one at a time, into boiling water. Boil for 20 seconds, then dip in cold water. Peel off the skins using a sharp knife.

6 ▲ Grind the almonds finely with the flour in a food processor, blender or grinder. With an electric mixer, cream the butter and 90g/3¹/₂oz/¹/₂ cup of the sugar until light and fluffy. Gradually beat in the egg and yolk. Stir in the almonds and vanilla or rum. Spread in the pastry case.

7 ▲ Halve the peaches and remove the stones (pits). Cut crosswise in thin slices and arrange on top of the almond cream like the spokes of a wheel; keep the slices of each peach-half together. Fan out by pressing down gently at a slight angle.

8 ▲ Bake until the pastry begins to brown, 10–15 minutes. Lower the heat to 180°C/350°F/Gas 4 and continue baking until the almond cream sets, about 15 minutes more. 10 minutes before the end of the cooking time, sprinkle with the remaining sugar.

~ VARIATION ~

For a Nectarine and Apricot Tart with Almond Cream, replace the peaches with nectarines, prepared and arranged the same way. Peel and chop 3 fresh apricots. Fill the spaces between the fanned-out nectarines with 15ml/1 tbsp chopped apricots. Bake as above.

Energy 376kcal/1569kJ; Protein 6.3g; Carbohydrate 33.4g, of which sugars 17.5g; Fat 24.8g, of which saturates 11.4g; Cholesterol 102mg; Calcium 78mg; Fibre 2.4g; Sodium 134mg.

Almond Syrup Tart

SERVES 6

75g/3oz/1½ cups fresh white breadcrumbs

250ml/8fl oz/1 cup golden
  (light corn) syrup

finely grated zest of ½ lemon

10ml/2 tsp lemon juice

23cm/9in pastry case, made with
  basic, nut or rich shortcrust pastry

30ml/2 tbsp flaked (sliced) almonds

1 Preheat a 200°C/400°F/Gas 6 oven.

2 ▲ In a mixing bowl, combine the
breadcrumbs with the golden syrup
and the lemon zest and juice.

3 Spoon into the pastry case and
spread out evenly.

4 ▲ Sprinkle the flaked almonds
evenly over the top.

5 ▼ Brush the pastry with milk to
glaze, if you like. Bake for 25–30
minutes or until the pastry and filling
are golden brown.

6 Remove to a wire rack to cool.
Serve warm or cold, with cream,
custard or ice cream.

~ VARIATIONS ~

For Walnut Syrup Tart, replace
the almonds with chopped walnuts.
For Ginger Syrup Tart, mix 5ml/1 tsp
ground ginger with the breadcrumbs
before adding the syrup and lemon
zest and juice. Omit the nuts if liked.
For Coconut Syrup Tart, replace
30ml/2 tbsp of the breadcrumbs
with 45ml/3 tbsp desiccated (dry
unsweetened shredded) coconut.

Energy 407kcal/1712kJ; Protein 5.3g; Carbohydrate 63g, of which sugars 30.6g; Fat 16.6g, of which saturates 4.6g; Cholesterol 7mg; Calcium 75mg; Fibre 1.5g; Sodium 397mg.

Apple Maple Dumplings

SERVES 8

475g/1lb 2oz/4½ cups plain (all-purpose) flour
10ml/2 tsp salt
350g/12oz/1½ cups white cooking fat
175–250ml/6–8fl oz/¾–1 cup iced water
8 firm eating apples
1 egg white
130g/4½oz/scant ¾ cup caster (superfine) sugar
45ml/3 tbsp whipping cream
2.5ml/½ tsp vanilla extract
250ml/8fl oz/1 cup maple syrup
whipped cream, for serving

1 Sift the flour and salt into a large bowl. Using a pastry blender or two knives, cut in the fat until the mixture resembles breadcrumbs. Sprinkle with 175ml/6fl oz/¾ cup water and mix until the dough holds together. If it is too crumbly, add a little more water. Gather into a ball. Wrap and refrigerate for 20 minutes.

2 Preheat a 220°C/425°F/Gas 7 oven.

3 Peel the apples. Remove the cores, without cutting through the base.

4 ▲ Roll out the dough thinly. Cut squares almost large enough to enclose the apples. Brush with egg white. Set an apple in the centre of each square.

5 Combine the sugar, cream and vanilla in a small bowl. Spoon some into the hollow in each apple.

6 ▼ Pull the points of the dough squares up around the apples and moisten the edges where they overlap. Mould the dough round the apples, pleating the top. Do not cover the centre hollows. Crimp the edges tightly to seal.

7 Set the apples in a large greased baking dish, at least 2cm/¾in apart. Bake for 30 minutes.

8 Lower the oven temperature to 180°C/350°F/Gas 4 and continue baking until the pastry is golden brown and the apples are tender, about 20 minutes more.

9 Transfer the dumplings to a serving dish. Mix the maple syrup with the juices in the baking dish and drizzle over the dumplings.

10 Serve the dumplings hot with whipped cream.

Apple Strudel

SERVES 10–12

75g/3oz/¹/₂ cup raisins

30ml/2 tbsp brandy

5 eating apples

3 large cooking apples

100g/3³/₄oz/scant ¹/₂ cup soft dark
    brown sugar

5ml/1 tsp ground cinnamon

grated rind and juice of 1 lemon

30ml/2 tbsp dry breadcrumbs

50g/2oz/¹/₃ cup chopped pecans or walnuts

12 sheets frozen filo pastry, thawed

175g/6oz/³/₄ cup butter, melted

icing (confectioners') sugar,
    for dusting

1 Soak the raisins in the brandy for at least 15 minutes.

2 ▼ Peel, core and thinly slice the apples. In a bowl, combine the sugar, cinnamon and lemon rind. Stir in the apples and half the breadcrumbs.

3 Add the raisins, nuts and lemon juice and stir until blended.

4 Preheat a 190°C/375°F/Gas 5 oven. Grease two baking sheets.

5 ▲ Carefully unfold the filo sheets. Keep the unused sheets covered with greaseproof (waxed) paper. Lift off one sheet, place on a clean surface and brush with melted butter. Lay a second sheet on top and brush with butter. Continue until you have a stack of 6 buttered sheets.

6 Sprinkle a few tablespoons of breadcrumbs over the last sheet and spoon half the apple mixture at the bottom edge of the strip.

7 ▲ Starting at the apple-filled end, roll up the pastry, as for a Swiss roll (jelly roll). Place on a baking sheet, seam-side down, and carefully fold under the ends to seal. Repeat the procedure to make a second strudel. Brush both with butter.

8 Bake the strudels for 45 minutes. Let cool slightly. Using a small sieve (strainer), dust with a fine layer of icing sugar. Serve warm.

Energy 231kcal/966kJ; Protein 2.3g; Carbohydrate 21.3g, of which sugars 8.6g; Fat 15.2g, of which saturates 7.9g; Cholesterol 31mg; Calcium 33mg; Fibre 1.5g; Sodium 109mg.

Cherry Strudel

SERVES 8

75ml/5 tbsp fresh breadcrumbs
175g/6oz/³⁄₄ cup butter, melted
200g/7oz/1 cup sugar
15ml/1 tbsp ground cinnamon
5ml/1 tsp grated lemon rind
450g/1lb sour cherries, pitted
8 sheets filo pastry
icing (confectioners') sugar, for dusting

1 In a frying pan, lightly fry the fresh breadcrumbs in 75g/3oz/6 tbsp of the melted butter until golden. Set aside to cool.

2 ▲ In a large mixing bowl, toss together the sugar, cinnamon and lemon rind. Stir in the cherries.

3 Preheat the oven to 190°C/375°F/ Gas 5. Grease a baking sheet.

4 Carefully unfold the filo sheets. Keep the unused sheets covered with damp kitchen paper. Lift off one sheet, place on a flat surface lined with baking parchment. Brush the pastry with melted butter. Sprinkle about an eighth of the breadcrumbs evenly over the surface.

5 ▲ Lay a second sheet of filo on top, brush with butter and sprinkle with crumbs. Continue until you have a stack of eight sheets.

6 Spoon the cherry mixture on to the bottom edge of the strip. Starting at that end, roll up the pastry as for a Swiss roll (jelly roll). Flip the strudel onto the baking sheet, seam-side down.

7 ▼ Carefully fold under the ends to seal in the fruit. Brush the top with any remaining butter.

8 Bake the strudel for 45 minutes. Let cool slightly. Using a small sieve (strainer), dust with a fine layer of icing sugar.

Energy 370kcal/1553kJ; Protein 3.2g; Carbohydrate 51.2g, of which sugars 33.2g; Fat 18.4g, of which saturates 11.4g; Cholesterol 47mg; Calcium 57mg; Fibre 1.2g; Sodium 197mg.

Chicken-Mushroom Pie

SERVES 6

15ml/1 tbsp dried porcini mushrooms

25g/1oz/2 tbsp butter

15ml/1 tbsp plain (all-purpose) flour

250ml/8fl oz/1 cup hot chicken stock

45ml/3 tbsp whipping cream or milk

salt and pepper

1 onion, roughly chopped

2 carrots, sliced

2 celery sticks, roughly chopped

50g/2oz fresh mushrooms, quartered

450g/1lb cooked chicken meat, cubed

50g/2oz shelled fresh or frozen peas

beaten egg, for glazing

FOR THE CRUST

225g/8oz/2 cups plain (all-purpose) flour

1.25ml/¼ tsp salt

115g/4oz/½ cup cold butter, cut
   into pieces

75g/3oz/6 tbsp white cooking fat

90–120ml/6–8 tbsp iced water

1 ▲ For the crust, sift the flour and salt into a bowl. With a pastry blender or two knives, cut in the butter and fat until the mixture resembles coarse breadcrumbs. Sprinkle with 90ml/ 6 tbsp iced water and mix until the dough holds together. If the dough is too crumbly, add a little more water, 15ml/1 tbsp at a time. Gather the dough into a ball and flatten into a disk. Wrap in baking parchment and refrigerate for at least 30 minutes.

2 Place the porcini mushrooms in a small bowl. Add hot water to cover and soak until soft, about 30 minutes. Lift out of the water with a slotted spoon to leave any grit behind and drain. Discard the soaking water.

3 Preheat a 190°C/375°F/Gas 5 oven.

4 ▲ Melt 25g/1oz/2 tbsp of the butter in a heavy pan. Whisk in the flour and cook until bubbling, whisking constantly. Add the stock and cook over a moderate heat, whisking, until the mixture boils. Cook for 2–3 minutes more. Whisk in the cream or milk. Season with salt and pepper. Set aside.

5 ▲ Heat the remaining butter in a large non-stick frying pan until foamy. Add the onion and carrots and cook until softened, about 5 minutes. Add the celery and fresh mushrooms and cook for 5 minutes more. Stir in the chicken, peas, and drained porcini mushrooms.

6 Add the chicken mixture to the cream sauce and stir to mix. Taste for seasoning. Transfer to a 2.8 litre (3¾ pint) rectangular pie dish.

7 ▲ Roll out the dough to about 3mm/⅛in thickness. Cut out a rectangle about 2.5cm/1in larger all round than the dish. Lay the rectangle of dough over the filling. Make a decorative edge, crimping the dough by pushing the index finger of one hand between the thumb and index finger of the other.

8 Cut several vents to allow steam to escape. Brush with the egg glaze.

9 ▲ Press together the dough trimmings, then roll out again. Cut into strips and lay them over the top. Glaze again. If desired, roll small balls of dough and set them in the 'windows' in the lattice.

10 Bake until the pastry top is browned, about 30 minutes.

Energy 674kcal/2807kJ; Protein 32g; Carbohydrate 38g, of which sugars 5g; Fat 45g, of which saturates 24g; Cholesterol 187mg; Calcium 117mg; Fibre 9g; Sodium 478mg.

Ricotta and Basil Tart

3 Preheat a baking sheet in a 190°C/375°F/Gas 5 oven.

4 Roll out the dough 3mm/¹/₈in thick and transfer to a 25cm/10in tart tin (pan). Prick the base with a fork and line with baking parchment. Fill with dried beans and bake for 12 minutes. Remove the paper and beans and bake until golden, 3–5 minutes more. Lower the heat to 180°C/350°F/Gas 4.

5 ▲ In a food processor, combine the basil, parsley and olive oil. Season well with salt and pepper and process until finely chopped.

6 In a bowl, whisk the eggs and yolk to blend. Gently fold in the ricotta.

SERVES 8–10

45ml/3 tbsp basil leaves
15ml/1 tbsp flat leaf parsley
120ml/4fl oz/¹/₂ cup extra-virgin olive oil
salt and pepper
2 eggs
1 egg yolk
800g/1³/₄lb/3¹/₂ cups ricotta cheese
90g/3¹/₂oz/scant 1 cup black olives, pitted
65g/2¹/₂oz/³/₄ cup Parmesan cheese, freshly grated
FOR THE CRUST
175g/6oz/1¹/₂ cups plain (all-purpose) flour
2.5ml/¹/₂ tsp salt
75g/3oz/6 tbsp cold butter, cut into pieces
40g/1¹/₂oz/3 tbsp cold margarine, cut into pieces
45–60ml/3–4 tablespoon iced water

1 ▲ For the crust, combine the flour and salt in a bowl. Add the butter and margarine.

2 Rub in with your fingertips until the mixture resembles breadcrumbs. With a fork, stir in just enough water to bind the dough. Wrap in clear film (plastic wrap), and chill for 20 minutes.

7 ▲ Fold in the basil mixture and olives until well combined. Stir in the Parmesan and adjust the seasoning.

8 Pour the fillin mixture into the prebaked shell and bake until set, 30–35 minutes.

Energy 333kcal/1380kJ; Protein 6g; Carbohydrate 14g, of which sugars 0g; Fat 28g, of which saturates 10g; Cholesterol 91mg; Calcium 124mg; Fibre 1g; Sodium 368mg.

Onion and Anchovy Tart

SERVES 8

60ml/4 tbsp olive oil
900g/2lb onions, sliced
5ml/1 tsp dried thyme
salt and pepper
2–3 tomatoes, sliced
24 small black olives, pitted
1 × 50g/2oz can anchovy fillets, drained and sliced
6 sun-dried tomatoes, cut into slivers

FOR THE CRUST

175g/6oz/1¹/₂ cups plain (all-purpose) flour
2.5ml/¹/₂ tsp salt
115g/4oz/¹/₂ cup cold butter, cubed
1 egg yolk
30–45ml/2–3 tbsp iced water

1 ▲ For the crust, sift the flour and salt into a bowl. Rub in the butter with your fingertips until the mixture resembles coarse breadcrumbs. Stir in the yolk and enough water to bind.

2 ▲ Roll out the dough to a thickness of about 3mm/¹/₈in. Transfer to a 23cm/9in tart tin (pan) and trim the edge. Chill until needed.

3 ▲ Heat the oil in a frying pan. Add the onions, thyme and seasoning. Cook over low heat, covered, for 25 minutes. Uncover and continue cooking until soft. Let cool. Preheat the oven to 200°C/400°F/Gas 6.

4 ▼ Spoon the onions into the tart shell and top with the tomato slices. Arrange the olives in rows. Make a lattice pattern, alternating lines of anchovies and sun-dried tomatoes. Bake until golden, 20–25 minutes.

Energy 334kcal/1391kJ; Protein 6g; Carbohydrate 29g, of which sugars 10g; Fat 22g, of which saturates 9g; Cholesterol 58mg; Calcium 92mg; Fibre 4g; Sodium 623mg.

Mushroom Quiche

SERVES 8

450g/1lb mushrooms

30ml/2 tbsp olive oil

15ml/1 tbsp butter

1 clove garlic, finely chopped

15ml/1 tbsp lemon juice

salt and pepper

30ml/2 tbsp finely chopped parsley

3 eggs

350ml/12fl oz/1¹/₂ cups whipping cream

65g/2¹/₂oz/³/₄ cup Parmesan cheese, grated

FOR THE CRUST

175g/6oz/1¹/₂ cups plain (all-purpose) flour

2.5ml/¹/₂ tsp salt

75g/3oz/6 tbsp cold butter, cut into pieces

40g/1¹/₂oz/3 tbsp cold margarine,
   cut into pieces

45–60ml/3–4 tbsp iced water

1 For the crust, sift the flour and salt into a bowl. Rub in the butter and margarine until the mixture resembles coarse breadcrumbs. Stir in just enough water to bind.

2 Gather into a ball. Wrap in clear film (plastic wrap). Chill for 20 minutes.

3 Preheat a baking sheet in a 190°C/375°F/Gas 5 oven.

4 Roll out the dough 3mm/¹/₈in thick. Transfer to a 23cm/9in tart tin (pan) and trim. Prick the base all over with a fork. Line with baking parchment and fill with dried beans. Bake for 12 minutes. Remove the paper and beans and continue baking until golden, about 5 minutes more.

5 ▲ Wipe the mushrooms with damp kitchen paper to remove any dirt. Trim the ends of the stalks, place on a cutting board, and slice thinly.

6 Heat the oil and butter in a frying pan. Stir in the mushrooms, garlic and lemon juice. Season with salt and pepper. Cook until the mushrooms render their liquid, then raise the heat and cook until dry.

7 ▼ Stir in the parsley and add more salt and pepper if necessary.

8 Whisk the eggs and cream together, then stir in the mushrooms. Sprinkle the cheese over the bottom of the prebaked shell and pour the mushroom filling over the top.

9 Bake the quiche until puffed and brown, about 30 minutes. Serve the quiche warm.

Bacon and Cheese Quiche

SERVES 8

115g/4oz medium-thick bacon slices

3 eggs

350ml/12fl oz/1¹/₂ cups whipping cream

90g/3¹/₂oz/1 cup Gruyère cheese, grated

0.6ml/¹/₈ tsp grated nutmeg

salt and pepper

FOR THE CRUST

175g/6oz/1¹/₂ cups plain (all-purpose) flour

2.5ml/¹/₂ tsp salt

75g/3oz/6 tbsp cold butter, cubed

40g/1¹/₂oz/3 tbsp cold margarine, cubed

45–60ml/3–4 tbsp iced water

1 Make the crust as directed in steps 1–4 above. Maintain the oven temperature at 190°C/375°F/Gas 5.

2 ▲ Fry the bacon until crisp. Drain, then crumble. Sprinkle in the shell.

3 ▲ Beat together the eggs, cream, cheese, nutmeg, salt and pepper. Pour over the bacon and bake until puffed and brown, about 30 minutes. Serve the quiche warm.

Mushroom: Energy 461kcal/1909kJ; Protein 10g; Carbohydrate 19g, of which sugars 2g; Fat 39g, of which saturates 21g; Cholesterol 161mg; Calcium 150mg; Fibre 2g; Sodium 211mg.
Bacon: Energy 449kcal/1858kJ; Protein 9g; Carbohydrate 19g, of which sugars 2g; Fat 38g, of which saturates 22g; Cholesterol 89mg; Calcium 178mg; Fibre 1g; Sodium 531mg.

Asparagus, Corn and Red Pepper Quiche

SERVES 6

225g/8oz fresh asparagus, woody
  stalks removed

25g/1oz/2 tbsp butter or margarine

1 small onion, finely chopped

1 red (bell) pepper, seeded and
  finely chopped

115g/4oz drained canned corn,
  or frozen corn, thawed

2 eggs

250ml/8fl oz/1 cup single (light) cream

50g/2oz/½ cup Cheddar cheese, grated

salt and pepper

FOR THE PASTRY

190g/6½oz/1⅔ cups plain
  (all-purpose) flour

2.5ml/½ tsp salt

115g/4oz/½ cup lard or white cooking fat

30–45ml/2–3 tbsp iced water

1 Preheat a 200°C/400°F/Gas 6 oven.

2 For the pastry, sift the flour and salt into a mixing bowl. Using a pastry blender or two knives, cut in the fat until the mixture resembles coarse breadcrumbs. Sprinkle in the water, 15ml/1 tbsp at a time, tossing lightly with your fingertips or a fork until the dough forms a ball.

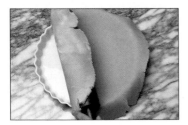

3 ▲ On a lightly floured surface, roll out the dough. Use it to line a 25cm/10in quiche dish or loose-bottomed tart tin (pan), easing the pastry in and being careful not to stretch it. Trim off excess pastry.

4 ▲ Line the pastry case with baking parchment and weigh it down with pastry weights or dried beans. Bake 10 minutes. Remove the paper and weight or beans and bake until the pastry is set and beige in colour, about 5 minutes longer. Let cool.

5 Trim the stem ends of eight of the asparagus spears to make them 10cm/4in in length. Set aside.

6 ▲ Finely chop the asparagus trimmings and any remaining spears. Place in the bottom of the case.

7 ▲ Melt the butter or margarine in a frying pan. Add the onion and red pepper and cook until softened, about 5 minutes. Stir in the corn and cook for 2 minutes longer.

8 Spoon the corn mixture over the chopped asparagus.

9 ▲ In a small bowl, beat the eggs with the cream. Stir in the cheese and salt and pepper to taste. Pour into the pastry case.

10 ▲ Arrange the reserved asparagus spears like the spokes of a wheel on top of the filling.

11 Bake until the filling is set, about 25–30 minutes.

~ VARIATION ~

To make individual tarts, roll out the pastry and use to line a 12-cup bun tray. For the filling, cut off and reserve the asparagus tips and chop the tender part of the stalks. Mix the asparagus and the cooked vegetables into the egg mixture with the cheese. Spoon the filling into the pastry cases and bake as directed, decreasing baking time by about 8–10 minutes.

Energy 471kcal/1960kJ; Protein 9g; Carbohydrate 34g, of which sugars 6g; Fat 34g, of which saturates 16g; Cholesterol 129mg; Calcium 110mg; Fibre 3g; Sodium 289mg.

Cheesy Tomato Quiche

SERVES 6–8

10 medium tomatoes

1 × 50g/2oz can anchovy fillets, drained and finely chopped

120ml/4fl oz/¹⁄₂ cup whipping cream

200g/7oz/scant 2 cups mature (sharp) Cheddar cheese, grated

30ml/2 tbsp wholemeal (whole-wheat) breadcrumbs

2.5ml/¹⁄₂ tsp dried thyme

salt and pepper

FOR THE CRUST

215g/7¹⁄₂ oz/scant 2 cups plain (all-purpose) flour

115g/4oz/¹⁄₂ cup cold butter, cut into pieces

1 egg yolk

30–45ml/2–3 tbsp iced water

1 Preheat the oven to 200°C/400°F/ Gas 6.

2 For the crust, sift the flour into a bowl. Rub in the butter with your fingertips until the mixture resembles coarse breadcrumbs.

3 ▲ With a fork, stir in the egg yolk and enough water to bind the dough.

4 Roll out the dough about 3mm/¹⁄₈in thick and transfer to a 23cm/9in (tart tin (pan). Refrigerate until needed.

5 ▲ Score the bottoms of the tomatoes. Plunge in boiling water for 1 minute. Remove and peel off the skin with a knife. Cut in quarters and remove the seeds with a spoon.

6 ▲ In a bowl, mix the anchovies and cream. Stir in the cheese.

7 Sprinkle the breadcrumbs in the tart. Arrange the tomatoes on top. Season with thyme, salt and pepper.

8 ▲ Spoon the cheese mixture on top. Bake until golden, 25–30 minutes.

Energy 406kcal/1869kJ; Protein 12g; Carbohydrate 26g, of which sugars 4g; Fat 29g, of which saturates 17g; Cholesterol 100mg; Calcium 263mg; Fibre 3g; Sodium 498mg.

Quiche Lorraine

SERVES 6

225g/8oz smoked streaky (fatty) bacon
  rashers, chopped

23cm/9in flan case, partially baked
  blind

3 eggs

2 egg yolks

350ml/12fl oz/1½ cups whipping cream

120ml/4fl oz/½ cup milk

salt and pepper

1 Preheat a 200°C/400°F/Gas 6 oven.

2 ▲ Fry the bacon in a frying pan
until it is crisp and golden brown.
Drain the bacon on kitchen paper.

3 ▲ Scatter the bacon in the
partially baked flan case.

4 Whisk the eggs, egg yolks, cream
and milk. Season with salt and pepper.

5 ▼ Pour the egg mixture into the
flan case.

6 Bake for 35–40 minutes or until
the filling is set and golden brown
and the pastry is golden.

~ VARIATIONS ~

Add 75g/3oz/¾ cup grated Gruyère
cheese with the bacon. Replace the
bacon with diced cooked ham, if
desired. For a vegetarian quiche, omit
the bacon. Slice 450g/1lb courgettes
(zucchini) and fry in a little oil until
lightly browned on both sides. Drain
on kitchen paper, then arrange in
the flan case. Scatter 50g/2oz/½ cup
grated cheese on top. Make the egg
mixture with 4 eggs, 250ml/8fl oz/
1 cup cream, 60ml/4 tbsp milk,
0.6ml/⅛ tsp grated nutmeg, salt
and pepper.

Energy 670kcal/2775kJ; Protein 13g; Carbohydrate 23.7g, of which sugars 1.4g; Fat 58.9g, of which saturates 32.9g; Cholesterol 302mg; Calcium 94mg; Fibre 0.9g; Sodium 611mg.

Pizza

MAKES 2

500g/1¼lb/4⅔ cups plain (all-purpose) flour

5ml/1 tsp salt

10ml/2 tsp active dried yeast

300ml/½ pint/1¼ cups lukewarm water

60–120ml/4–8 tbsp extra-virgin olive oil

120ml/4fl oz/½ cup fresh tomatoes,
  skinned, cooked and sieved,
  115g/4oz/½ cup grated cheese,
  10 pitted olives and herbs, for topping

1 Combine the flour and salt in a bowl. Make a well and add the yeast, water and 30ml/2 tbsp of the oil. Leave for 15 minutes to dissolve the yeast.

2 With your hands, stir until the dough just holds together. Transfer to a floured surface and knead until smooth and elastic. Avoid adding too much flour while kneading.

3 ▲ Brush the inside of a clean bowl with 15ml/1 tbsp of the oil. Place the dough in the bowl and roll around to coat with the oil. Cover with a plastic bag and leave to rise in a warm place until more than doubled in volume, about 45 minutes.

4 Divide the dough into two balls. Preheat a 200°C/400°F/Gas 6 oven.

5 ▲ Roll each ball into a 25cm/10in circle. Set each circle on the work surface and rotate, stretching the dough as you turn, until it is about 30cm/12in in diameter.

6 ▲ Brush two pizza pans with oil. Place the dough circles in the pans and neaten the edges. Brush with oil.

7 ▲ Cover with the toppings and bake until golden, 10–12 minutes.

Energy 1457kcal/2174kJ; Protein 12g; Carbohydrate 44g, of which sugars 7g; Fat 34g, of which saturates 5g; Cholesterol 13mg; Calcium 135mg; Fibre 5g; Sodium 993mg.

Onion, Olive and Anchovy Pizza

SERVES 4

90ml/6 tbsp olive oil
450g/1lb onions, thinly sliced
3 garlic cloves, crushed
1 bay leaf
10ml/2 tsp dried thyme
salt and pepper
2 cans anchovy fillets, drained and blotted dry on kitchen paper
12 olives, mixed black and green
FOR THE PIZZA DOUGH
115g/4oz/1 cup wholemeal (whole-wheat) flour
75g/3oz/²/₃ cup plain (all-purpose) flour
6.25ml/1¼ tsp active dried yeast
0.6ml/⅛ tsp sugar
150ml/¼ pint/²/₃ cup tepid water
30ml/2 tbsp olive oil
2.5g/½ tsp salt

1 For the pizza dough, in a food processor combine the flours, yeast and sugar. With the motor running, pour in the water. Add the oil and salt. Process until a ball is formed.

2 Put the dough in an oiled bowl and turn it to coat with oil. Cover and let rise until doubled in size.

3 ▲ Heat 45ml/3 tbsp of the oil in a frying pan. Add the onions, garlic and herbs. Cook over a low heat until the onions are very soft and the moisture has evaporated, about 45 minutes. Season with salt and pepper to taste.

4 Preheat the oven to the highest setting. Oil a 33 × 23cm/13 × 9in baking tray.

5 ▼ Transfer the risen dough onto a lightly floured surface. Punch down the dough and knead it briefly. Roll it into a rectangle to fit the baking tray. Lay the dough on the tray and press it up the edges of the tray.

6 Brush the dough with 15ml/1 tbsp olive oil. Discard the bay leaf, and spoon the onion mixture onto the dough. Spread it out evenly, leaving a 1cm/½in border around the edge.

7 ▲ Arrange the anchovies and olives on top. Drizzle the remaining 30ml/2 tbsp olive oil over the top.

8 Bake the pizza until the edges are puffed and browned, 15–20 minutes.

Energy 522kcal/2174kJ; Protein 12g; Carbohydrate 44g, of which sugars 7g; Fat 34g, of which saturates 5g; Cholesterol 13mg; Calcium 135mg; Fibre 5g; Sodium 993mg.

Broccoli and Goat's Cheese Pizza

SERVES 2–3

225g/8oz broccoli florets

30ml/2 tbsp cornmeal, or polenta

120ml/4fl oz/½ cup fresh tomatoes,
skinned, cooked and sieved

6 cherry tomatoes, halved

12 black olives, pitted

115g/4oz/½ cup goat's cheese, cubed

45ml/3 tbsp Parmesan cheese, grated

15ml/1 tbsp olive oil

FOR THE PIZZA DOUGH

225–250g/8–9oz/2–2¼ cups plain
(all-purpose) flour

10g/¼oz active dried yeast

0.6ml/⅛ tsp sugar

150ml/¼ pint/⅔ cup tepid water

30ml/2 tbsp olive oil

2.5ml/½ tsp salt

1 For the pizza dough, combine
75g/3oz/⅔ cup of the flour, the yeast
and sugar in a food processor. With the
motor running, add the water. Turn
the motor off. Add the oil, 150g/5oz/
1¾ cups of the remaining flour and
the salt.

2 ▲ Process until a ball of dough is
formed, adding more water, 5ml/1 tsp
at a time, if the dough is too dry, or the
remaining flour, 15ml/1 tbsp at a time,
if it is too wet.

3 ▲ Put the dough in an oiled bowl
and turn it so the ball of dough is oiled
all over. Cover the bowl and let the
dough rise in a warm place until
doubled in size, about 1 hour.

4 ▲ Meanwhile, cook the broccoli
florets in boiling salted water or steam
them until just tender, about 5 minutes.
Drain well and set aside.

5 Preheat the oven to the highest
setting. Oil a 30cm/12in round pizza
pan and sprinkle with the cornmeal.

6 When the dough has risen, turn out
onto a lightly floured surface. Punch
down the dough to deflate it, and
knead it briefly.

~ COOK'S TIP~

If it is more convenient, the pizza
dough can be used as soon as it is
made, without any rising.

7 ▲ Roll out the dough to a 30cm/
12in round. Lay the dough on the pizza
pan and press it down evenly.

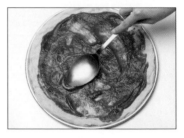

8 ▲ Spread the tomato sauce evenly
onto the pizza base, leaving a rim of
dough uncovered around the edge
about 1cm/½in wide.

9 ▲ Arrange the broccoli florets,
tomatoes, and olives on the tomato
sauce and sprinkle with the cheeses.
Drizzle the olive oil over the top.

10 Bake until the cheese melts and
the edge of the pizza base is puffed and
browned, 10–15 minutes.

Energy 530kcal/2222kJ; Protein 17g; Carbohydrate 67g, of which sugars 3g; Fat 23g, of which saturates 6g; Cholesterol 14mg; Calcium 312mg; Fibre 4g; Sodium 723mg.

CAKES & GATEAUX

AS DELICIOUS AS THEY ARE
BEAUTIFUL, THESE CAKES AND
GÂTEAUX ARE PERFECT TO SERVE
AT TEATIME OR FOR DESSERT.
DELIGHTFUL PARTY CAKES MAKE
SPECIAL OCCASIONS MEMORABLE.

Apple Ring Cake

SERVES 12

7 eating apples

350ml/12fl oz/1¹/₂ cups vegetable oil

450g/1lb/2¹/₂ cups caster (superfine) sugar

3 eggs

425g/15oz/3²/₃ cups plain (all-purpose) flour

5ml/1 tsp salt

5ml/1 tsp bicarbonate of soda
   (baking soda)

5ml/1 tsp ground cinnamon

5ml/1 tsp vanilla extract

115g/4oz/²/₃ cup chopped walnuts

175g/6oz/1 cup raisins

icing (confectioners') sugar, for dusting

1 Preheat a 180°C/350°F/Gas 4 oven.
Grease a 34cm/9in ring mould.

2 ▲ Quarter, peel, core and slice the
apples into a bowl. Set aside.

3 With an electric mixer, beat the
oil and sugar together until blended.
Add the eggs and continue beating
until the mixture is creamy.

4 Sift together the flour, salt,
bicarbonate of soda and cinnamon.

5 ▼ Fold the flour mixture into the
egg mixture with the vanilla. Stir in
the apples, walnuts and raisins.

6 Pour into the tin and bake until
the cake springs back when touched
lightly, about 1¹/₄ hours. Let stand for
15 minutes, then unmould and
transfer to a cooling rack. Dust with
a layer of icing sugar before serving.

Orange Cake

SERVES 6

175g/6oz/1¹/₂ cups plain (all-purpose) flour

7.5ml/1¹/₂ tsp baking powder

0.6ml/¹/₈ tsp salt

115g/4oz/¹/₂ cup butter or margarine

115g/4oz/scant ³/₄ cup caster
   (superfine) sugar

grated rind of 1 large orange

2 eggs, at room temperature

30ml/2 tbsp milk

FOR THE SYRUP AND DECORATION

115g/4oz/scant ³/₄ cup caster
   (superfine) sugar

250ml/8fl oz/1 cup fresh orange
   juice, strained

3 orange slices, for decorating

1 Preheat the oven to 180°C/350°F/
Gas 4. Line a 20cm/8in cake tin (pan)
with baking parchment and grease
the parchment.

2 ▲ Sift the flour, salt and baking
powder onto baking parchment.

3 With an electric mixer, cream the
butter or margarine until soft. Add the
sugar and orange rind and continue
beating until light and fluffy. Beat in
the eggs, one at a time. Fold in the flour
in three batches, then add the milk.

4 Spoon into the tin and bake until
the cake pulls away from the sides,
about 30 minutes. Remove from the
oven but leave in the tin.

5 Meanwhile, for the syrup, dissolve
the sugar in the orange juice over a
low heat. Add the orange slices and
simmer for 10 minutes. Remove and
drain. Let the syrup cool.

6 ▲ Prick the cake all over with a
fine skewer. Pour the syrup over the
hot cake. It may seem at first that
there is too much syrup for the cake
to absorb, but it will soak it all up.
Unmould when completely cooled
and decorate with small triangles of
the orange slices arranged on top.

Apple: Energy 408kcal/1726kJ; Protein 5g; Carbohydrate 86g, of which sugars 57g; Fat 7g, of which saturates 1g; Cholesterol 0mg; Calcium 77mg; Fibre 4g; Sodium 269mg.
Orange: Energy 440kcal/1850kJ; Protein 6g; Carbohydrate 67g, of which sugars 45g; Fat 19g, of which saturates 11g; Cholesterol 119mg; Calcium 80mg; Fibre 1g; Sodium 311mg.

Angel Cake

SERVES 12–14

125g/4¹/₂oz/1¹/₄ cups plain (all-purpose) flour

30ml/2 tbsp cornflour (cornstarch)

300g/10oz/1¹/₂ cups caster (superfine) sugar

300–325ml/10–11fl oz/1¹/₄–1³/₈ cups egg white (about 10–11 eggs)

7.5ml/1¹/₂ tsp cream of tartar

1.25ml/¹/₄ tsp salt

5ml/1 tsp vanilla extract

1.25ml/¹/₄ tsp almond extract

icing (confectioners') sugar, for dusting

1 Preheat the oven to 170°C/325°F/ Gas 3.

2 ▼ Sift the flours before measuring, then sift them four times with 90g/3¹/₂oz/¹/₂ cup of the sugar.

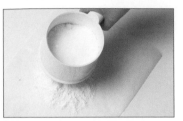

3 With an electric mixer, beat the egg whites until foamy. Sift over the cream of tartar and salt and continue to beat until the whites hold soft peaks when the beaters are lifted.

4 ▲ Add the remaining sugar in three batches, beating well after each addition. Stir in the vanilla and almond extracts.

5 ▲ Add the flour mixture, in two batches, and fold in with a large metal spoon after each addition.

6 Transfer to an ungreased 25cm/10in tube tin (pan) and bake until just browned on top, about 1 hour.

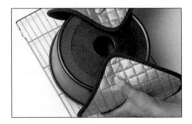

7 ▲ Turn the tin upside down onto a cake rack and let cool for 1 hour. If the cake does not turn out, run a knife around the edge to loosen it. Invert on a serving plate.

8 When cool, lay a star-shaped template on top of the cake, sift over icing sugar and remove template.

Energy 1788kcal/7618kJ; Protein 42.6g; Carbohydrate 426.4g, of which sugars 299.8g; Fat 1.9g, of which saturates 0.3g; Cholesterol 0mg; Calcium 354mg; Fibre 4.1g; Sodium 645mg.

Marbled Ring Cake

SERVES 16

115g/4oz plain (semisweet) chocolate
350g/12oz/3 cups plain (all-purpose) flour
5ml/1 tsp baking powder
450g/1lb/2 cups butter, at room temperature
740g/1lb 10oz/3¼ cups caster (superfine) sugar
15ml/1 tbsp vanilla extract
10 eggs, at room temperature
icing (confectioners') sugar, for dusting

1 ▲ Preheat a 180°C/350°F/Gas 4 oven. Line a 25 × 10cm/10 × 4in ring mould with baking parchment and grease the paper. Dust with flour.

2 ▲ Melt the chocolate in the top of a double boiler, or in a heatproof bowl set over a pan of hot water. Stir occasionally. Set aside.

3 In a bowl, sift together the flour and baking powder. In another bowl, cream the butter, sugar and vanilla with an electric mixer until light and fluffy. Add the eggs, two at a time, then gradually incorporate the flour mixture on low speed.

4 ▲ Spoon half of the mixture into the prepared mould.

5 ▲ Stir the chocolate into the remaining mixture, then spoon into the tin. With a metal spatula, swirl the mixtures for a marbled effect.

6 Bake until a skewer inserted in the centre comes out clean, about 1 hour 45 minutes. Cover with foil halfway through baking. Let stand for 15 minutes, then unmould and transfer to a cooling rack. To serve, dust with icing sugar.

Energy 8720kcal/36545kJ; Protein 107.5g; Carbohydrate 1105.3g, of which sugars 837.6g; Fat 462.1g, of which saturates 269.9g; Cholesterol 2869mg; Calcium 1278mg; Fibre 13.7g; Sodium 3488mg.

Carrot Cake

SERVES 10

450g/1lb/2½ cups caster (superfine) sugar

250ml/8fl oz/1 cup vegetable oil

4 eggs

about 225g/8oz carrots, finely grated

225g/8oz/2 cups plain (all-purpose) flour

7.5ml/1½ tsp bicarbonate of soda
(baking soda)

7.5ml/1½ tsp baking powder

5ml/1 tsp ground allspice

5ml/1 tsp ground cinnamon

FOR THE ICING

225g/8oz/2 cups icing
(confectioners') sugar

225g/8oz/1 cup cream cheese,
at room temperature

50g/2oz/¼ cup butter, at room temperature

10ml/2 tsp vanilla extract

175g/6oz/1 cup chopped walnuts or pecans

1 Preheat a 190°C/375°F/Gas 5 oven.

2 Butter and flour two 23cm/9in round cake tins (pans).

3 ▲ In a mixing bowl, combine the caster sugar, vegetable oil, eggs, and carrots. Beat for 2 minutes with a wooden spoon.

4 Sift the dry ingredients into another bowl. Add in four equal batches to the carrot mixture, mixing well after each addition.

5 ▲ Divide the cake mixture evenly between the prepared cake tins and place in the oven. Bake until a skewer inserted in the centre of the cake comes out clean, 35–45 minutes.

6 Let cool in the tins on wire racks for 10 minutes, then unmould the cakes from the tins onto the wire racks and let cool completely.

7 For the icing, combine everything except the chopped nuts in a bowl and beat until smooth.

8 ▲ To assemble, set one cake layer on a serving plate and spread with one-third of the icing. Place the second cake layer on top. Spread the remaining icing all over the top and sides of the cake, swirling it to make a decorative finish. Sprinkle the nuts around the top edge.

Energy 835kcal/3488kJ; Protein 6g; Carbohydrate 91g, of which sugars 73g; Fat 53g, of which saturates 14g; Cholesterol 33mg; Calcium 89mg; Fibre 2g; Sodium 278mg.

Madeira Cake

SERVES 12

225g/8oz/2 cups plain (all-purpose) flour

15ml/1 tsp baking powder

225g/8oz/1 cup butter or margarine, at room temperature

225g/8oz/generous 1 cup caster (superfine) sugar

grated rind of 1 lemon

5ml/1 tsp vanilla extract

4 eggs

1 Preheat a 170°C/325°F/Gas 3 oven. Grease a 23 × 13cm/9 × 5in loaf tin (pan).

2 Sift the flour and baking powder into a small bowl. Set aside.

3 ▲ With an electric mixer, cream the butter or margarine, adding the sugar a little at a time, until light and fluffy. Stir in the lemon rind and vanilla.

5 ▼ Add the flour mixture and stir until just combined.

6 ▲ Pour the cake mixture into the tin and tap lightly. Bake until a metal skewer inserted in the centre comes out clean, about 1¼ hours.

7 Let cool in the tin on a wire rack for 10 minutes, then unmould the cake from the tin onto the wire rack and let cool completely.

4 ▲ Add the eggs to the mixture one at a time, beating after each addition.

Energy 453kcal/1894kJ; Protein 6.1g; Carbohydrate 51.4g, of which sugars 30g; Fat 26.3g, of which saturates 15.5g; Cholesterol 155mg; Calcium 74mg; Fibre 0.9g; Sodium 208mg.

Lemon Yogurt Ring

SERVES 12

225g/8oz/2 cups butter,
  at room temperature

300g/10oz/1½ cups caster (superfine) sugar

4 eggs, at room temperature, separated

10ml/2 tsp grated lemon rind

90ml/6 tbsp lemon juice

250ml/8fl oz/1 cup natural
  (plain) yogurt

275g/10oz/2½ cups plain
  (all-purpose) flour

10ml/2 tsp baking powder

5ml/1 tsp bicarbonate of soda
  (baking soda)

0.5ml/⅛ tsp salt

FOR THE GLAZE

115g/4oz/1 cup icing (confectioners') sugar

30ml/2 tbsp lemon juice

45–60ml/3–4 tbsp plain (natural) yogurt

1 Preheat a 180°C/350°F/Gas 4 oven. Grease a 3 litre/5¼ pint/12 cup bundt or fluted tube tin (pan) and dust with flour.

2 With an electric mixer, cream the butter and sugar until light and fluffy. Add the egg yolks, one at a time, beating well after each addition.

3 ▲ Add the lemon rind, juice and yogurt and stir to blend.

4 Sift together the flour, baking powder and bicarbonate of soda. In another bowl, beat the egg whites and salt until they hold stiff peaks.

5 ▲ Fold the dry ingredients into the butter mixture, then fold in a dollop of egg whites. Fold in the remaining whites until blended.

6 Pour into the tin and bake until a skewer inserted in the centre comes out clean, about 50 minutes. Let stand 15 minutes, then turn out and cool on a wire rack.

7 For the glaze, sift the icing sugar into a bowl. Stir in the lemon juice and just enough yogurt to make a smooth glaze.

8 ▲ Set the cooled cake on the rack over a sheet of baking parchment or a baking sheet. Pour over the glaze and let it drip down the sides. Allow the glaze to set before serving.

Energy 387kcal/1626kJ; Protein 5.8g; Carbohydrate 54.6g, of which sugars 37.1g; Fat 17.8g, of which saturates 10.5g; Cholesterol 104mg; Calcium 109mg; Fibre 0.7g; Sodium 160mg.

Banana Lemon Layer Cake

SERVES 8–10

250g/9oz/2¼ cups plain (all-purpose) flour

7.5ml/1½ tsp baking powder

2.5ml/½ tsp salt

115g/4oz/½ cup butter butter,
    at room temperature

200g/7oz/1 cup sugar

115g/4oz/½ cup soft light brown sugar,
    firmly packed

2 eggs

2.5ml/½ tsp grated lemon rind

3 medium very ripe bananas, mashed

5ml/1 tsp vanilla extract

45ml/3 tbsp milk

75ml/5 tbsp chopped walnuts

FOR THE FROSTING

115g/4oz/½ cup butter, at room temperature

475g/1lb 2oz/4½ cups icing
    (confectioners') sugar

2.5ml/½ tsp grated lemon rind

45–75ml/3–5 tbsp fresh lemon juice

1 Preheat the oven to 180°C/350°F/ Gas 4. Grease two 23cm/9in round cake tins (pans), and line the bottoms with buttered baking parchment.

2 Sift the flour with the baking powder and salt.

3 ▲ In a large mixing bowl, cream the butter with the sugars until light and fluffy. Beat in the eggs, one at a time. Stir in the lemon rind.

4 ▲ In a small bowl, mix the bananas with the vanilla and milk. Add the banana mixture and the dry ingredients to the butter mixture alternately in two or three batches and stir until just blended. Fold in the nuts.

5 Divide the batter between the cake tins and spread it out evenly. Bake until a skewer inserted in the centre comes out clean, 30–35 minutes. Leave to stand for 5 minutes before unmoulding on to a wire rack. Peel off the baking parchment.

6 For the frosting, cream the butter until smooth, then gradually beat in the sugar. Stir in the lemon rind and enough lemon juice to make a spreadable consistency.

7 ▼ Set one of the cake layers on a serving plate. Cover with about one-third of the frosting. Top with the second cake layer. Spread the remaining frosting evenly over the top and sides of the cake.

Energy 666kcal/2,804kJ; Protein 6g; Carbohydrate 110g, of which sugars 89g; Fat 26g, of which saturates 13g; Cholesterol 96mg; Calcium 77mg; Fibre 2g; Sodium 230mg.

Light Fruit Cake

MAKES 2 LOAVES

225g/8oz/1 cup prunes

225g/8oz/1 cup dates

225g/8oz/1 cup currants

225g/8oz/1 cup sultanas (golden raisins)

250ml/8fl oz/1 cup dry white wine

250ml/8fl oz/1 cup rum

350g/12oz/3 cups plain (all-purpose) flour

10ml/2 tsp baking powder

5ml/1 tsp ground cinnamon

2.5ml/½ tsp grated nutmeg

225g/8oz/1 cup butter, at room temperature

225g/8oz/generous 1 cup caster (superfine) sugar

4 eggs, at room temperature, lightly beaten

5ml/1 tsp vanilla extract

1 Remove the pits (stones) from the prunes and dates and chop finely. Put in a bowl with the currants and sultanas.

2 ▲ Stir in the wine and rum and leave to stand, covered with clear film (plastic wrap), for 48 hours. Stir occasionally.

3 Preheat a 150°C/300°F/Gas 2 oven with a tray of hot water in the bottom. Line two 23 × 13cm/9 × 5in tins (pans) with baking parchment and grease.

4 Sift together the flour, baking powder, cinnamon, and nutmeg.

5 ▲ With an electric mixer, cream the butter and sugar together until light and fluffy.

6 Gradually add the eggs and vanilla. Fold in the flour mixture in three batches. Fold in the dried fruit mixture and its soaking liquid.

7 ▲ Divide the mixture between the tins and bake until a skewer inserted in the centre comes out clean, about 1½ hours.

8 Let stand 20 minutes, then unmould and transfer to a cooling rack. Wrap in foil and store in an airtight container. If possible, leave for at least 1 week before serving to allow the flavours to mellow.

Energy 5719kcal/24077kJ; Protein 75.8g; Carbohydrate 918.1g, of which sugars 689.5g; Fat 218.7g, of which saturates 8.5g; Cholesterol 951mg; Calcium 1232mg; Fibre 28.3g; Sodium 2664mg.

Rich Fruit Cake

SERVES 12

150g/5oz/scant 1 cup currants

175g/6oz/1 cup raisins

50g/2oz/4 tbsp sultanas (golden raisins)

50g/2oz/4 tbsp glacé (candied)
  cherries, halved

45ml/3 tbsp sweet sherry

175g/6oz/³/4 cup butter

200g/7oz/scant 1 cup soft dark brown sugar

2 large (US extra large) eggs, at
  room temperature

200g/7oz/1³/4 cups plain (all-purpose) flour

10ml/2 tsp baking powder

10ml/2 tsp each ground ginger, allspice,
  and cinnamon

15ml/1 tbsp golden (light corn) syrup

15ml/1 tbsp milk

45ml/3 tbsp mixed chopped (candied) peel

115g/4oz/²/3 cup chopped walnuts

For the decoration

225g/8oz/generous 1 cup caster
  (superfine) sugar

120ml/4fl oz/¹/2 cup water

1 lemon, thinly sliced

¹/2 orange, thinly sliced

120ml/4fl oz/¹/2 cup orange marmalade

glacé (candied) cherries

1 One day before preparing, combine the currants, raisins, sultanas and cherries in a bowl. Stir in the sherry. Cover and let stand overnight to soak.

2 Preheat a 150°C/300°F/Gas 2 oven. Line a 23 × 8cm/9 × 3in springform tin (pan) with baking parchment and grease. Place a tray of hot water on the bottom of the oven.

3 With an electric mixer, cream the butter and sugar until light and fluffy. Beat in the eggs, one at a time.

4 ▲ Sift the flour, baking powder and spices together three times. Fold into the butter mixture in three batches. Fold in the syrup, milk, dried fruit and liquid, mixed peel and nuts.

5 ▲ Spoon into the tin, spreading out so there is a slight depression in the centre of the mixture.

6 Bake until a skewer inserted in the centre comes out clean, 2¹/2–3 hours. Cover with foil when the top is golden to prevent over-browning. Cool in the tin on a rack.

7 ▲ For the decoration, combine the sugar and water in a pan and bring to the boil. Add the lemon and orange slices and cook until crystallized, about 20 minutes. Work in batches, if necessary. Remove the fruit with a slotted spoon. Pour the remaining syrup over the cake and let cool. Melt the marmalade over low heat, then brush over the top of the cake. Decorate with the crystallized citrus slices and cherries.

Energy 7388kcal/31049kJ; Protein 123.7g; Carbohydrate 1047.9g, of which sugars 850.7g; Fat 320.2g, of which saturates 124.8g; Cholesterol 1378mg; Calcium 1781mg; Fibre 39.1g; Sodium 2041mg.

Ginger Cake with Spiced Whipped Cream

SERVES 9

175g/6oz/1½ cups plain (all-purpose) flour

10ml/2 tsp baking powder

2.5ml/½ tsp salt

10ml/2 tsp ground ginger

10ml/2 tsp ground cinnamon

5ml/1 tsp ground cloves

1.25ml/¼ tsp grated nutmeg

2 eggs

225g/8oz/generous 1 cup caster
    (superfine) sugar

250ml/8fl oz/1 cup whipping cream

5ml/1 tsp vanilla extract

icing (confectioners') sugar, for sprinkling

FOR THE SPICED WHIPPED CREAM

175ml/6fl oz/¾ cup whipping cream

5ml/1 tsp icing (confectioners') sugar

1.25ml/¼ tsp ground cinnamon

1.25ml/¼ tsp ground ginger

1.25ml/¼ tsp grated nutmeg

1 Preheat a 180°C/350°F/Gas 4 oven. Grease a 23cm/9in square baking tin (pan).

2 Sift the flour, baking powder, salt and spices into a bowl. Set aside.

3 ▲ With an electric mixer, beat the eggs on high speed until very thick, about 5 minutes. Gradually beat in the caster sugar.

4 ▲ With the mixer on low speed, beat in the flour mixture alternately with the whipping cream, beginning and ending with the flour. Stir in the vanilla extract.

5 ▲ Pour the cake mixture into the tin and bake until the top springs back when touched lightly, 35–40 minutes. Let cool in the tin on a wire rack for 10 minutes.

6 ▲ Meanwhile, to make the spiced whipped cream, combine the ingredients in a bowl and whip until the cream will hold soft peaks.

7 Sprinkle icing sugar over the hot cake, cut in nine squares, and serve with spiced whipped cream.

Energy 365kcal/1527kJ; Protein 5g; Carbohydrate 43g, of which sugars 28g; Fat 21g, of which saturates 12g; Cholesterol 101mg; Calcium 84mg; Fibre 1g; Sodium 247mg.

Rich Sticky Gingerbread

MAKES A 20CM/8IN SQUARE CAKE

225g/8oz/2 cups plain (all-purpose) flour

pinch of salt

5ml/1 tsp bicarbonate of soda (baking soda)

10ml/2 tsp ground ginger

5ml/1 tsp mixed (apple pie) spice

115g/4oz/¹/₂ cup butter or margarine

120ml/4fl oz/¹/₂ cup golden
(light corn) syrup

120ml/4fl oz/¹/₂ cup black
treacle (molsasses)

50g/2oz/4 tbsp soft dark brown sugar

2 eggs, beaten

120ml/4fl oz/¹/₂ cup

115g/4oz/8 tbsp sultanas (golden raisins)
or chopped preserved stem ginger

FOR THE ICING (OPTIONAL)

115g/4oz/1 cup icing sugar

about 20ml/4 tsp water

1 ▲ Preheat a 180°C/350°F/Gas 4 oven. Grease and line a 20cm/8in square cake tin (pan).

2 ▲ Sift the flour, salt, bicarbonate of soda and spices into a bowl.

3 Put the butter or margarine, golden syrup, treacle and brown sugar in a large, heavy pan and warm over a gentle heat, stirring occasionally, until the fat has melted and the mixture is smooth. Remove from the heat and leave to cool slightly.

4 ▼ Make a well in the centre of the dry ingredients and add the melted mixture, the beaten eggs and milk. Beat with a wooden spoon until the mixture is smooth. Add the sultanas or ginger.

5 Turn the cake mixture into the prepared tin. Bake for about 1 hour. To test if the gingerbread is done, press it lightly in the centre; it should spring back. Allow to cool in the tin for 5 minutes before turning out on to a wire rack to cool completely.

6 ▲ If icing the gingerbread, sift the icing sugar into a bowl and add 15ml/1 tbsp of the water. Stir to mix, then add more water 5ml/1 tsp at a time until the icing is smooth and has a pouring consistency. Pour the icing over the gingerbread and leave to set before serving.

Energy 3501kcal/14763kJ; Protein 47g; Carbohydrate 609g, of which sugars 433g; Fat 116g, of which saturates 67g; Cholesterol 726mg; Calcium 1312mg; Fibre 15g; Sodium

Walnut Layer Cake

SERVES 8

225g/8oz/2 cups plain (all-purpose) flour
15ml/1 tbsp baking powder
2.5ml/¹/₂ tsp salt
115g/4oz/¹/₂ cup butter or margarine, at room temperature
200g/7oz/1 cup sugar
2 eggs
5ml/1 tsp grated orange rind
5ml/1 tsp vanilla extract
115g/4oz/1 cup ground walnuts
175ml/6fl oz/³/₄ cup milk
black walnut halves, for decoration
FOR THE FROSTING
115g/4oz/¹/₂ cup butter
175g/6oz/scant 1 cup soft light brown sugar, firmly packed
45ml/3 tbsp maple syrup
45ml/3 tbsp milk
175–225g/6–8oz/1¹/₂–2 cups icing (confectioners') sugar, sifted

1 ▲ Grease two 20 × 5cm/8 × 2in tins (pans), line the bottoms and grease. Preheat a 190°C/375°F/Gas 5 oven.

2 Sift together the flour, baking powder and salt.

~ VARIATION ~

If black walnuts are not available, substitute ordinary walnuts, or use pecan nuts instead.

3 ▲ Beat the butter or margarine to soften, then gradually beat in the granulated sugar until light and fluffy. Beat in the eggs, one at a time. Add the orange rind and vanilla and beat to mix well.

4 ▲ Stir in the ground walnuts. Add the flour alternately with the milk, stirring only enough to blend after each addition.

5 ▲ Divide the mixture between the prepared cake tins. Bake in the preheated oven until a skewer inserted in the centre comes out clean, about 25 minutes. Cool in the cake tins for 5 minutes before unmoulding on to a wire rack.

6 ▲ For the frosting, melt the butter in a medium pan. Add the brown sugar and maple syrup and boil for 2 minutes, stirring constantly.

7 ▲ Add the milk. Bring back to the boil and stir in 25g/1oz/¹/₄ cup of the icing sugar. Remove from the heat and allow to cool until lukewarm. Gradually beat in the remaining icing sugar. Set the pan in a bowl of iced water and stir until the frosting is thick enough to spread.

8 ▲ Spread some of the frosting on one of the cake layers. Set the other layer on top. Spread the remaining frosting over the top and sides of the cake. Decorate with walnut halves.

Energy 815kcal/3430kJ; Protein 9g; Carbohydrate 103g, of which sugars 80g; Fat 44g, of which saturates 17g; Cholesterol 120mg; Calcium 123mg; Fibre 3g; Sodium 513mg.

Coffee-Iced Ring

SERVES 16

275g/10oz/2¹/₂ cups plain (all-purpose) flour

15ml/1 tbsp baking powder

5ml/1 tsp salt

350g/12oz/1³/₄ cups caster (superfine) sugar

120ml/4fl oz/¹/₂ cup vegetable oil

7 eggs, at room temperature, separated

175ml/6fl oz/³/₄ cup cold water

10ml/2 tsp vanilla extract

10ml/2 tsp grated lemon rind

2.5ml/¹/₂ tsp cream of tartar

FOR THE ICING

65g/5¹/₂oz/11 tbsp unsalted butter,
    at room temperature

575g/1lb 4oz/5 cups icing
    (confectioners') sugar

20ml/4 tsp instant coffee dissolved in
    60ml/4 tbsp hot water

1 Preheat a 170°C/325°F/Gas 3 oven.

2 ▼ Sift the flour, baking powder and salt into a large bowl. Stir in 225g/8oz/generous 1 cup of the sugar. Make a well in the centre and add in the following order: oil, egg yolks, water, vanilla and lemon rind. Beat with a whisk or metal spoon until smooth and well combined.

3 With an electric mixer, beat the egg whites with the cream of tartar until they hold soft peaks. Add the remaining sugar and beat until they hold stiff peaks.

4 ▲ Pour the flour mixture over the whites in three batches, folding well after each addition.

5 Transfer the mixture to a 25 × 10cm/ 10 × 4in ring mould and bake until the top springs back when touched lightly, about 1 hour.

6 ▲ When baked, remove from the oven and immediately hang the cake upside-down over the neck of a funnel or a narrow bottle. Let cool. To remove the cake, run a knife around the inside to loosen, then turn the mould over and tap the sides sharply. Invert the cake onto a serving plate.

7 For the icing, beat together the butter and icing sugar with an electric mixer until smooth. Add the coffee and beat until fluffy. With a metal spatula, spread over the sides and top of the cake.

Energy 562kcal/2368kJ; Protein 5g; Carbohydrate 98g, of which sugars 84g; Fat 19g, of which saturates 7g; Cholesterol 123mg; Calcium 51mg; Fibre 1g; Sodium 260mg.

Forgotten Gâteau

SERVES 6

6 egg whites, at room temperature
2.5ml/¹/₂ tsp cream of tartar
2.5ml/¹/₂ tsp salt
300g/10oz/1¹/₂ cups caster (superfine) sugar
5ml/1 tsp vanilla extract
175ml/6fl oz/³/₄ cup whipping cream
FOR THE SAUCE
350g/12oz fresh or thawed frozen raspberries
45ml/3 tbsp icing (confectioners') sugar

1 Preheat a 230°C/450°F/Gas 8 oven. Grease a 1.5 litre/2¹/₂ pint/6¹/₃ cup ring mould.

2 ▲ With an electric mixer, beat the egg whites, cream of tartar and salt until they hold soft peaks. Gradually add the sugar and beat until glossy and stiff. Fold in the vanilla.

4 Place in the oven, then turn the oven off. Leave overnight; do not open the oven door at any time.

5 ▼ To serve, gently loosen the edge with a sharp knife and turn out onto a serving plate. Whip the cream until firm. Spread it over the top and upper sides of the meringue and decorate with any meringue crumbs.

3 ▲ Spoon into the prepared mould and smooth the top level.

6 ▲ For the sauce, purée the fruit, then strain. Sweeten to taste.

~ COOK'S TIP ~

This recipe is not suitable for fan assisted and solid fuel ovens.

Energy 545kcal/2308kJ; Protein 4g; Carbohydrate 112g, of which sugars 111g; Fat 12g, of which saturates 7g; Cholesterol 31mg; Calcium 39mg; Fibre 4g; Sodium 79mg.

Nut and Apple Gâteau

SERVES 8

115g/4oz/²/₃ cup pecan nuts or walnuts
50g/2oz/¹/₂ cup plain (all-purpose) flour
10ml/2 tsp baking powder
1.25ml/¹/₄ tsp salt
2 large cooking apples
3 eggs
225g/8oz/generous 1 cup caster (superfine) sugar
5ml/1 tsp vanilla extract
175ml/6fl oz/³/₄ cup whipping cream

1 Preheat a 170°C/325°F/Gas 3 oven. Line two 23cm/9in cake tins (pans) with baking parchment and grease the paper. Spread the nuts on a baking sheet and bake for 10 minutes.

2 Finely chop the nuts. Reserve 22.5ml/1¹/₂ tbsp and place the rest in a mixing bowl. Sift over the flour, baking powder and salt and stir to combine thoroughly.

3 ▲ Quarter, core and peel the apples. Cut into 3mm/¹/₈in dice, then stir them into the nut-flour mixture.

4 ▲ With an electric mixer, beat the eggs until frothy. Gradually add the sugar and vanilla and beat until a ribbon forms, about 8 minutes. Gently fold in the flour mixture.

5 Pour into the tins and level the tops. Bake until a skewer inserted in the centre comes out clean, about 35 minutes. Let stand 10 minutes.

6 ▲ To loosen, run a knife around the inside edge of each layer. Let cool.

7 ▲ Whip the cream until firm. Spread half over the cake. Top with the second cake. Pipe whipped cream rosettes on top and sprinkle over the reserved nuts before serving.

Energy 2807kcal/11741kJ; Protein 39.3g; Carbohydrate 303.2g, of which sugars 263.3g; Fat 168.6g, of which saturates 55.5g; Cholesterol 755mg; Calcium 454mg; Fibre 10.2g; Sodium 274mg.

Almond Cake

SERVES 4–6

225g/8oz/1½ cups blanched whole almonds, plus more for decorating
25g/1oz/2 tbsp butter
75g/3oz/⅔ cup icing (confectioners') sugar
3 eggs
2.5ml/½ tsp almond extract
25g/1oz/¼ cup plain (all-purpose) flour
3 egg whites
15ml/1 tbsp caster (superfine) sugar

1 ▲ Preheat a 170°C/325°F/Gas 3 oven. Line a 23cm/9in round tin (pan) with baking parchment and grease.

2 ▲ Spread the almonds in a baking tray and toast for 10 minutes. Cool, then coarsely chop all but 30ml/2 tbsp of the almonds.

3 Melt the butter and set aside. Preheat a 200°C/400°F/Gas 6 oven.

5 Grind the chopped toasted almonds with half the icing sugar in a food processor, blender or grinder. Transfer to a mixing bowl.

6 ▲ Add the whole eggs and remaining icing sugar. With an electric mixer, beat until the mixture forms a ribbon when the beaters are lifted. Mix in the butter and almond extract. Sift over the flour and fold in gently.

7 With an electric mixer, beat the egg whites until they hold soft peaks. Add the caster sugar and beat until stiff and glossy.

8 ▲ Fold the egg whites into the almond mixture in four batches.

9 Spoon the mixture into the prepared tin and bake in the centre of the oven until golden brown, about 15–20 minutes. Decorate the top with the remaining toasted whole almonds. Serve warm.

Energy 2258kcal/9407kJ; Protein 77.8g; Carbohydrate 129.2g, of which sugars 104g; Fat 163.1g, of which saturates 27.7g; Cholesterol 624mg; Calcium 718mg; Fibre 17.4g; Sodium 582mg.

Walnut Coffee Gâteau

SERVES 8–10

150g/5oz/scant 1 cup walnuts
150g/5oz/³/4 cup sugar
5 eggs, separated
60ml/4 tbsp dry breadcrumbs
15ml/1 tbsp unsweetened cocoa powder
15ml/1 tbsp instant coffee powder
30ml/2 tbsp rum or lemon juice
0.6ml/¹/8 tsp salt
90ml/6 tbsp redcurrant jelly
chopped walnuts, for decorating
FOR THE FROSTING
225g/8oz plain (semisweet) chocolate
750ml/1¹/4 pints/3 cups whipping cream

1 ▲ For the frosting, combine the chocolate and cream in the top of a double boiler, or in a heatproof bowl set over simmering water. Stir until the chocolate melts. Let cool, then cover and refrigerate overnight or until the mixture is firm.

2 Preheat the oven to 180°C/350°F/ Gas 4. Line a 23 × 5cm/9 × 2in cake tin (pan) with baking parchment and grease.

3 ▲ Grind the nuts with 45ml/3 tbsp of the sugar in a food processor, blender or coffee grinder.

4 With an electric mixer, beat the egg yolks and remaining sugar until thick and lemon-coloured.

5 ▲ Fold in the walnuts. Stir in the breadcrumbs, cocoa, coffee and rum or lemon juice.

6 ▲ In another bowl, beat the egg whites with the salt until they hold stiff peaks. Fold carefully into the walnut mixture with a rubber scraper.

7 Pour the meringue batter into the prepared tin and bake until the top of the cake springs back when touched lightly, about 45 minutes. Let the cake stand for 5 minutes, then turn out and cool on a rack.

8 ▲ When cool, slice the cake in half horizontally.

9 With an electric mixer, beat the chocolate frosting mixture on low speed until it becomes lighter, about 30 seconds. Do not overbeat or it may become grainy.

10 ▲ Warm the jelly in a pan until melted, then brush over the cut cake layer. Spread with some of the chocolate frosting, then sandwich with the remaining cake layer. Brush the top of the cake with jelly, then cover the side and top with the remaining chocolate frosting. Make a starburst pattern by pressing gently with a table knife in lines radiating from the centre. Sprinkle the chopped walnuts around the edge.

Energy 651kcal/2707kJ; Protein 9.5g; Carbohydrate 43.5g, of which sugars 38.5g; Fat 50.1g, of which saturates 24.9g; Cholesterol 175mg; Calcium 101mg; Fibre 1.8g; Sodium 149mg.

Coconut Cake

SERVES 10

175g/6oz/1½ cups icing
(confectioners') sugar

115g/4oz/1 cup plain (all-purpose) flour,

350ml/12fl oz/1½ cups egg whites
(about 12 eggs)

7.5ml/1½ tsp cream of tartar

225g/8oz/generous 1 cup caster
(superfine) sugar

1.25ml/¼ tsp salt

10ml/2 tsp almond extract

90g/3½oz/1 cup desiccated (dry
unsweetened shredded) coconut

FOR THE ICING

2 egg whites

115g/4oz/scant ¾ cup caster
(superfine) sugar

1.25ml/¼ tsp salt

30ml/2 tbsp cold water

10ml/2 tsp almond extract

200g/7oz/2 cups desiccated (dry
unsweetened shredded) coconut, toasted

1 ▲ Preheat a 180°C/350°F/Gas 4
oven. Sift the icing sugar and flour
into a bowl. Set aside.

2 With an electric mixer, beat the
egg whites with the cream of tartar on
medium speed until very thick. Turn
the mixer to high speed and beat in
the caster sugar, 30ml/2 tbsp at a time,
reserving 30ml/2 tbsp.

3 ▲ Continue beating until stiff and
glossy. Swiftly beat in the reserved
30ml/2 tbsp of sugar, with the salt and
almond extract.

4 ▲ One heaped teaspoon at a time,
sprinkle the flour mixture over the
meringue, quickly folding until just
combined. Fold in the desiccated
coconut in two batches.

5 ▲ Transfer the cake mixture to an
ungreased 25cm/10in non-stick tube
tin (pan), and cut gently through the
mixture with a metal spatula.

6 Bake until the top of the cake
springs back when touched lightly,
30–35 minutes.

7 ▲ As soon as the cake is cooked,
turn the tin upside down and suspend
its funnel over the neck of a funnel or
bottle. Let cool, about 1 hour.

8 ▲ For the icing, combine the egg
whites, sugar, salt and water in a
heatproof bowl. Beat with an electric
mixer until blended. Set the bowl
over a pan of boiling water and
continue beating on medium speed
until the icing is stiff, about 3 minutes.
Remove the pan from the heat and stir
in the almond extract.

9 ▲ Unmould the cake onto a
serving plate. Spread the icing gently
over the top and sides of the cake.
Sprinkle with the toasted coconut.

Energy 2205kcal/9244kJ; Protein 30.4g; Carbohydrate 277.5g, of which sugars 220.5g; Fat 116.3g, of which saturates 82.4g; Cholesterol 611mg; Calcium 313mg; Fibre 16.2g; Sodium 506mg.

Lemon Coconut Layer Cake

SERVES 8–10

175g/6oz/1½ cups plain (all-purpose) flour
1.25ml/¼ tsp salt
7 eggs
350g/12oz/1¾ cups caster (superfine) sugar
15ml/1 tbsp grated orange rind
grated rind of 1½ lemons
juice of 1 lemon
60ml/4 tbsp desiccated (dry unsweetened shredded) coconut
15ml/1 tbsp cornflour (cornstarch)
120ml/4fl oz/½ cup water
40g/1½oz/3 tbsp
FOR THE ICING
75g/3oz/6 tbsp unsalted butter
175g/6oz/1½ cups icing (confectioners') sugar
grated rind of 1½ lemon
30ml/2 tbsp lemon juice
200g/7oz/2 cups desiccated (dry unsweetened shredded) coconut

1 Preheat the oven to 180°C/350°F/ Gas 4. Line three 20cm/8in cake tins (pans) with baking parchment and grease. In a bowl, sift together the flour and salt and set aside.

2 ▲ Place 6 eggs in a large heatproof bowl set over hot water. With an electric mixer, beat until frothy. Gradually beat in 225g/8oz/generous 1 cup sugar until the mixture doubles in volume and leaves a ribbon trail when the beaters are lifted, about 10 minutes.

3 ▲ Remove the bowl from the hot water. Fold in the orange rind, half the grated lemon rind and 15ml/1 tbsp of the lemon juice until blended. Fold in the coconut.

4 Sift over the flour mixture in three batches, gently folding in thoroughly after each addition.

5 ▲ Divide the mixture between the prepared tins.

6 Bake until the cakes pull away from the sides of the tins, 20–25 minutes. Leave to stand for 5 minutes, then turn out to cool on a wire rack.

7 In a bowl, blend the cornflour with a little cold water to dissolve. Whisk in the remaining egg until just blended. Set aside.

8 ▲ In a pan, combine the remaining lemon rind and juice, the water, remaining sugar and butter.

9 Over a medium heat, bring the mixture to the boil. Whisk in the eggs and cornflour mixture, and return to the boil. Whisk continuously until thick, about 5 minutes. Remove from the heat and pour into a bowl. Cover and set aside to cool.

10 ▲ For the icing, cream the butter and icing sugar in a large bowl until smooth. Stir in the lemon rind and enough lemon juice to obtain a thick, spreadable consistency.

11 Sandwich the three cake layers with the lemon custard mixture. Spread the icing over the top and sides. Cover the cake with the coconut, pressing it in gently.

Energy 5225kcal/21906kJ; Protein 74.3g; Carbohydrate 659.5g, of which sugars 517.6g; Fat 274g, of which saturates 173.1g; Cholesterol 1927mg; Calcium 760mg; Fibre 20.4g; Sodium 1793mg.

Coconut Lime Gâteau

SERVES 8 OR MORE

225g/8oz/2 cups plain (all-purpose) flour

12.5ml/2½ tsp baking powder

1.25ml/¼ tsp salt

225g/8oz/1 cup butter, at room temperature

225g/8oz/generous 1 cup caster (superfine) sugar

grated zest of 2 limes

4 eggs

60ml/4 tbsp fresh lime juice (from about 2 limes)

90ml/6 tbsp desiccated (dry unsweetened shredded) coconut

1 recipe quantity American frosting (page 29)

1 Preheat a 180°C/350°F/Gas 4 oven. Grease two 23cm/9in sandwich tins (pans) and line the bottoms with greased baking parchment.

2 Sift together the flour, baking powder and salt.

3 In a large bowl, beat the butter until it is soft and pliable. Add the sugar and lime zest and beat until the mixture is pale and fluffy. Beat in the eggs, one at a time.

4 ▲ Using a wooden spoon fold in the sifted dry ingredients in small portions, alternating with the lime juice. When the mixture is smooth, stir in two-thirds of the coconut.

5 ▲ Divide the mixture between the prepared tins and spread it evenly to the sides. Bake for 30–35 minutes (test with a skewer).

6 ▲ Remove the cakes from the oven and set them, in their tins, on a wire rack. Cool for 10 minutes. Then turn out and peel off the lining paper. Cool completely on the rack.

7 ▲ Spread the remaining coconut in another cake tin. Bake until golden brown, stirring occasionally. Watch carefully so that the coconut does not get too dark. Cool.

8 ▲ Put one of the cakes, base up, on a serving plate. Spread a layer of frosting evenly over the cake.

9 ▲ Set the second layer on top, base down. Spread the remaining frosting all over the top and round the sides of the cake.

10 ▲ Scatter the toasted coconut over the top of the cake and leave to set before serving.

Energy 5859kcal/24634kJ; Protein 58g; Carbohydrate 886.4g, of which sugars 714.9g; Fat 256.6g, of which saturates 163.9g; Cholesterol 1241mg; Calcium 846mg; Fibre 17.3g; Sodium 1773mg.

Cranberry Upside-Down Cake

SERVES 8

350–400g/12–14oz/3–3¹/₂ cups
   fresh cranberries

50g/2oz/¹/₄ cup butter

150g/5oz/³/₄ cup sugar

FOR THE CAKE MIXTURE

65g/2¹/₂oz/9 tbsp plain (all-purpose) flour

5ml/1 tsp baking powder

3 eggs

115g/4oz/scant ³/₄ cup sugar

grated rind of 1 orange

40g/1¹/₂oz/3 tbsp butter, melted

1 Preheat the oven to 180°C/350°F/
Gas 4. Place a baking sheet on the
middle shelf of the oven.

2 Wash the cranberries and pat dry.
Thickly smear the butter on the
bottom and sides of a 23 × 5cm/9 × 2in
round cake tin (pan). Add the sugar
and swirl the tin to coat evenly.

3 ▲ Add the cranberries and spread
in an even layer over the bottom of
the tin.

4 For the cake mixture, sift the flour
and baking powder twice. Set aside.

5 ▲ Combine the eggs, sugar and
orange rind in a heatproof bowl set
over a pan of hot but not boiling
water. With an electric mixer, beat
until the eggs leave a ribbon trail
when the beaters are lifted.

6 Add the flour mixture in three
batches, folding in well after each
addition. Gently fold in the melted
butter, then pour over the cranberries.

7 Bake for 40 minutes. Leave to
cool for 5 minutes, then run a knife
around the inside edge to loosen.

8 ▲ While the cake is still warm,
invert a plate on top of the tin.
Protecting your hands with oven
gloves, hold both the plate and tin
firmly and turn them both over
quickly. Lift off the tin carefully,
leaving the cake on the plate.

Energy 305kcal/1283kJ; Protein 4g; Carbohydrate 46g, of which sugars 39g; Fat 13g, of which saturates 7g; Cholesterol 114mg; Calcium 43mg; Fibre 1g; Sodium 169mg.

Pineapple Upside-Down Cake

SERVES 8

115g/4oz/¹/₂ cup butter

200g/7oz/scant 1 cup soft dark brown sugar

450g/1lb canned pineapple slices, drained

4 eggs, separated

grated rind of 1 lemon

0.6ml/¹/₈ tsp salt

115g/4oz/scant ³/₄ cup caster (superfine) sugar

75g/3oz/²/₃ cup plain (all-purpose) flour

5ml/1 tsp baking powder

1 Preheat a 180°C/350°F/Gas 4 oven.

2 Melt the butter in a 25cm/10in ovenproof cast-iron frying pan. Remove 15ml/1 tbsp of the melted butter and set aside.

3 ▲ Add the brown sugar to the pan and stir until blended. Place the drained pineapple slices on top in one layer. Set aside.

4 In a bowl, whisk together the egg yolks, reserved butter and lemon rind until well blended. Set aside.

5 ▼ With an electric mixer, beat the egg whites with the salt until stiff. Gently fold in the caster sugar, 30ml/2 tbsp at a time. Fold in the egg yolk mixture.

7 ▲ Pour the mixture over the pineapple and smooth level.

8 Bake until a skewer inserted in the centre comes out clean, about 30 minutes.

9 While still hot, place a serving plate on top of the pan, bottom-side up. Holding them tightly together with oven gloves, quickly flip over so the cake is inverted on to the plate. Serve hot or cold.

6 Sift the flour and baking powder together. Carefully fold into the egg mixture in three batches.

~ VARIATION ~

For Dried Apricot Upside-Down Cake, replace the pineapple slices with 225g/8oz/1 cup of dried apricots. If they need softening, simmer the apricots in about 120ml/4fl oz/¹/₂ cup orange juice until plump and soft. Drain the apricots and discard any remaining cooking liquid.

Energy 2858kcal/12025kJ; Protein 35.7g; Carbohydrate 443g, of which sugars 385.9g; Fat 117.7g, of which saturates 66.3g; Cholesterol 1006mg; Calcium 443mg; Fibre 4.6g; Sodium 1003mg.

Spice Cake with Cream Cheese Frosting

SERVES 10–12

300ml/¹/₂ pint/1¹/₄ cups milk
30ml/2 tbsp golden (light corn) syrup
10ml/2 tsp vanilla extract
75g/3oz/¹/₂ cup walnuts, chopped
175g/6oz/³/₄ cup butter, at room temperature
300g/10oz/1¹/₂ cups caster (superfine) sugar
1 egg, at room temperature
3 egg yolks, at room temperature
275g/10oz/2¹/₂ cups plain (all-purpose) flour
15ml/1 tbsp baking powder
5ml/1 tsp grated nutmeg
5ml/1 tsp ground cinnamon
2.ml/¹/₂ tsp ground cloves
1.25ml/¹/₄ tsp ground ginger
1.25ml/¹/₄ tsp ground allspice
FOR THE FROSTING
175g/6oz/³/₄ cup cream cheese
25g/1oz/2 tbsp unsalted butter
200g/7oz/1³/₄ cups icing (confectioners') sugar
30ml/2 tbsp finely chopped stem ginger
30ml/2 tbsp syrup from stem ginger
stem ginger pieces, for decorating

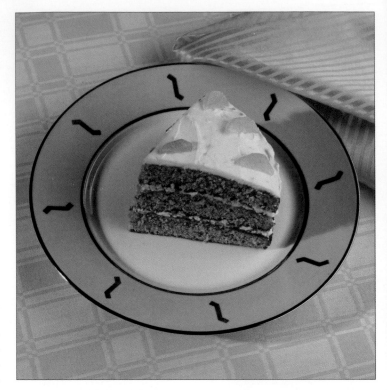

1 Preheat a 180°C/350°F/Gas 4 oven. Line three 20cm/8in cake tins (pans) with baking parchment and grease. In a bowl, combine the milk, golden syrup, vanilla and walnuts.

2 ▼ With an electric mixer, cream the butter and sugar until light and fluffy. Beat in the egg and egg yolks. Add the milk mixture and stir well.

3 Sift together the flour, baking powder and spices three times.

4 ▲ Add the flour mixture in four batches, and fold in carefully after each addition.

5 Divide the cake mixture between the tins. Bake until the cakes spring back when touched lightly, about 25 minutes. Let stand 5 minutes, then turn out and cool on a rack.

6 ▼ For the frosting, combine all the ingredients and beat with an electric mixer. Spread the frosting between the layers and over the top. Decorate with pieces of stem ginger.

Energy 460kcal/1922kJ; Protein 4g; Carbohydrate 51g, of which sugars 50g; Fat 28g, of which saturates 14g; Cholesterol 122mg; Calcium 92mg; Fibre 0g; Sodium 211mg.

Sour Cream Crumble Cake

SERVES 12–14

115g/4oz/¹/₂ cup butter, at room temperature

130g/4¹/₂oz/scant ³/₄ cup caster (superfine) sugar

3 eggs, at room temperature

215g/7¹/₂ oz/scant 2 cups plain (all-purpose) flour

5ml/1 tsp bicarbonate of soda (baking soda)

5ml/1 tsp baking powder

250ml/8fl oz/1 cup sour cream

FOR THE TOPPING

225g/8oz/1 cup soft dark brown sugar

10ml/2 tsp ground cinnamon

115g/4oz/²/₃ cup walnuts, finely chopped

50g/2oz/¹/₄ cup cold butter, cut into pieces

1 Preheat a 180°C/350°F/Gas 4 oven. Line the bottom of a 23cm/9in square cake tin (pan) with baking parchment and grease.

2 ▲ For the topping, place the brown sugar, cinnamon and walnuts in a bowl. Mix with your fingertips, then add the butter and continue working with your fingertips until the mixture resembles breadcrumbs.

3 To make the cake, cream the butter with an electric mixer until soft. Add the sugar and continue beating until the mixture is light and fluffy.

4 Add the eggs, one at a time, beating well after each addition.

5 In another bowl, sift the flour, bicarbonate of soda and baking powder together three times.

6 ▲ Fold the dry ingredients into the butter mixture in three batches, alternating with the sour cream. Fold until blended after each addition.

7 ▲ Pour half of the batter into the prepared tin and sprinkle over half of the walnut crumb topping mixture.

8 Pour the remaining batter on top and sprinkle over the remaining walnut crumb mixture.

9 Bake until browned, 60–70 minutes. Let stand 5 minutes, then turn out and cool on a rack.

Energy 4867kcal/20353kJ; Protein 65.4g; Carbohydrate 548.4g, of which sugars 387.6g; Fat 283.5g, of which saturates 128.7g; Cholesterol 1073mg; Calcium 938mg; Fibre 10.5g; Sodium 1348mg.

Carrot Cake with Maple Butter Icing

SERVES 12

450g/1lb carrots, peeled
175g/6oz/1½ cups plain (all-purpose) flour
10ml/2 tsp baking powder
2.5ml/½ tsp bicarbonate of soda (baking soda)
5ml/1 tsp salt
10ml/2 tsp ground cinnamon
4 eggs
10ml/2 tsp vanilla extract
115g/4oz/½ cup soft dark brown sugar
50g/2oz/¼ cup caster (superfine) sugar
300ml/½ pint/1¼ cups sunflower oil
115g/4oz/1 cup finely chopped walnuts
75g/3oz/½ cup raisins
walnut halves, for decorating (optional)

FOR THE ICING

75g/3oz/6 tbsp unsalted butter, at room temperature
350g/12oz/3 cups icing (confectioners') sugar
60ml/4 tbsp maple syrup

1 Preheat a 180°C/350°F/Gas 4 oven. Line a 28 × 20cm/11 × 8in tin (pan) with baking parchment and grease.

2 ▲ Grate the carrots and set aside. Sift the flour, baking powder, bicarbonate of soda, salt and cinnamon into a bowl. Set aside.

3 With an electric mixer, beat the eggs until blended. Add the vanilla, sugars and oil. Add the dry ingredients, in three batches, folding in well.

4 ▲ Add the carrots, walnuts and raisins and fold in thoroughly.

5 Pour the mixture into the prepared cake tin and bake until the cake springs back when touched lightly, 40–45 minutes. Leave the cake to stand in the tin for 10 minutes, then unmould it and transfer to a wire rack to cool completely.

6 ▼ For the icing, cream the butter with half the icing sugar until soft. Add the syrup, then beat in the remaining sugar until blended.

7 Spread the icing over the top of the cake. Using the tip of a palette knife or metal spatula, make ridges in the icing. Cut into squares. Decorate with walnut halves, if wished.

Energy 835kcal/3488kJ; Protein 6g; Carbohydrate 91g, of which sugars 73g; Fat 53g, of which saturates 14g; Cholesterol 33mg; Calcium 89mg; Fibre 2g; Sodium 278mg.

Peach Torte

SERVES 8

115g/4oz/1 cup plain (all-purpose) flour,

5ml/1 tsp baking powder

pinch of salt

115g/4oz/½ cup unsalted butter,
  at room temperature

175g/6oz/scant 1 cup sugar

2 eggs, at room temperature

6–7 peaches

sugar and lemon juice, for sprinkling

whipped cream, for serving (optional)

1 Preheat the oven to 180°C/350°F/
Gas 4. Grease a 25cm/10in springform
tin (pan).

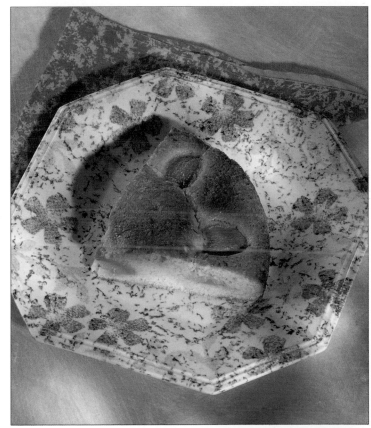

2 ▲ Sift together the flour, baking
powder and salt. Set aside.

3 With an electric mixer, cream the
butter and sugar until light and fluffy.
Beat in the eggs, then fold in the dry
ingredients until blended.

4 ▲ Spoon the mixture into the tin
and smooth it to make an even layer
over the bottom.

5 ▼ To skin the peaches, drop
several at a time into a pan of gently
boiling water. Boil for 10 seconds,
then remove with a slotted spoon.
Peel off the skin with the aid of a
sharp knife. Cut the peaches in half
and discard the stones (pits).

6 ▲ Arrange the peach halves on
top of the mixture. Sprinkle lightly
with sugar and lemon juice.

7 Bake until golden brown and set,
50–60 minutes. Serve warm, with
whipped cream, if liked.

Energy 292kcal/1236kJ; Protein 4g; Carbohydrate 40g, of which sugars 29g; Fat 14g, of which saturates 8g; Cholesterol 91mg; Calcium 45mg; Fibre 3g; Sodium 133mg.

Plum Crumble Cake

6 In a bowl, sift together the flour and baking powder, then fold into the butter mixture in three batches.

7 ▲ Pour the mixture into the tin. Arrange the plums on top.

8 ▲ Sprinkle the topping over the plums in an even layer.

9 Bake until a skewer inserted in the centre comes out clean, about 45 minutes. Let cool in the tin.

10 To serve, run a knife around the inside edge and invert onto a plate. Invert again onto a serving plate so the topping is right-side up.

SERVES 8–10

150g/5oz/10 tbsp butter,
   at room temperature

150g/5oz/³⁄4 cup caster (superfine) sugar

4 eggs, at room temperature

7.5ml/1¹⁄2 tsp vanilla extract

150g/5oz/1¹⁄4 cups plain (all-purpose) flour

5ml/1 tsp baking powder

700g/1¹⁄2lb red plums, halved and
   stoned (pitted)

FOR THE TOPPING

115g/4oz/1 cup plain (all-purpose) flour,

130g/4¹⁄2oz/generous ¹⁄2 cup soft light
   brown sugar

7.5ml/1¹⁄2 tsp ground cinnamon

75g/3oz/6 tbsp butter, cut in pieces

1 Preheat a 180°C/350°F/Gas 4 oven.

2 For the topping, combine the flour, light brown sugar and cinnamon in a bowl. Add the butter and work the mixture lightly with your fingertips until it resembles coarse breadcrumbs. Set aside.

3 ▲ Line a 25 × 5cm/10 × 2in tin (pan) with baking parchment; grease.

4 Cream the butter and sugar until light and fluffy.

5 ▲ Beat in the eggs, one at a time. Stir in the vanilla.

~ **VARIATION** ~

This cake can also be made with the same quantity of apricots, peeled if preferred, or pitted cherries, or use a mixture of fruit, such as red or yellow plums, greengages and apricots.

Energy 426kcal/1787kJ; Protein 5.7g; Carbohydrate 57g, of which sugars 36.8g; Fat 21.1g, of which saturates 12.4g; Cholesterol 124mg; Calcium 77mg; Fibre 1.9g; Sodium 168mg.

Yule Log Cake

SERVES 8 OR MORE

4 eggs, separated

150g/5oz/³/₄ cup caster (superfine) sugar

5ml/1 tsp vanilla extract

pinch of cream of tartar (if needed)

115g/4oz/1 cup plain (all-purpose)
flour, sifted

250ml/8fl oz/1 cup whipping cream

300g/10oz plain (semisweet) or dark
(bittersweet) chocolate, chopped

30ml/2 tbsp rum or Cognac

1 Preheat a 190°C/375°F/Gas 5 oven.
Grease, line and flour a 40 × 28cm/
16 × 11in Swiss roll tin (jelly roll pan).

2 Put the egg yolks in a large bowl.
Reserve 30ml/2 tbsp sugar; add the
remainder to the egg yolks. Whisk
until pale and thick. Add the vanilla.

3 In another bowl, scrupulously clean
and grease-free, whisk the egg whites
(with the cream of tartar if not using
a copper bowl) until they will hold
soft peaks. Add the reserved sugar and
continue whisking until the whites are
glossy and will hold stiff peaks.

4 Gently fold half the flour into the
egg yolk mixture. Add one-quarter of
the egg whites and fold in to lighten the
mixture. Fold in the remaining flour,
then the remaining egg whites.

5 ▲ Spread the mixture in the
prepared tin. Bake for 15 minutes.

6 Turn on to paper sprinkled with
caster sugar. Roll up and cool.

7 Bring the cream to the boil in a
small pan. Put the chocolate in a
bowl, add the cream and stir until the
chocolate has melted.

8 ▲ Beat the chocolate mixture until
it is fluffy and has thickened to a
spreading consistency. Spoon one-
third of the chocolate mixture into
another bowl. Mix in rum or Cognac.

9 Unroll the cake. Spread the rum
and chocolate mixture evenly over the
surface. Roll up the cake again.

10 Cut off about one-quarter of the
cake, at an angle. Place it against
the side of the larger piece of cake, to
resemble a branch from a tree trunk.

11 ▼ Spread the remaining
chocolate mixture all over the cake.
Mark with the prongs of a fork to
resemble bark. Before serving, add
small Christmas decorations and sprigs
of holly if liked, and dust with a little
icing sugar 'snow'.

Energy 479kcal/2006kJ; Protein 8g; Carbohydrate 55g, of which sugars 44g; Fat 26g, of which saturates 15g; Cholesterol 150mg; Calcium 70mg; Fibre 1g; Sodium 54mg.

Orange and Walnut Swiss Roll

SERVES 8

4 eggs, separated

115g/4oz/scant ³/₄ cup caster (superfine) sugar

115g/4oz/1 cup finely chopped walnuts

0.6ml/¹/₈ tsp cream of tartar

0.6ml/¹/₈ tsp salt

icing (confectioners') sugar, for dusting

FOR THE FILLING

300ml/¹/₂ pint/1¹/₄ cups whipping cream

15ml/1 tbsp caster (superfine) sugar

grated rind of 1 orange

15ml/1 tbsp orange liqueur, such as Grand Marnier

1 Preheat a 180°C/350°F/Gas 4 oven. Line a 30 × 24cm/12 × 9¹/₂in Swiss roll tin (jelly roll pan) with baking parchment and grease the paper.

2 With an electric mixer, beat the egg yolks and sugar until thick.

3 ▲ Stir in the walnuts.

4 In another bowl, beat the egg whites with the cream of tartar and salt until they hold stiff peaks. Fold gently but thoroughly into the walnut mixture.

5 Pour the mixture into the prepared tin and spread level with a spatula. Bake for 15 minutes.

6 Run a knife along the inside edge to loosen, then invert the cake onto a sheet of baking parchment dusted with icing sugar.

7 ▲ Peel off the baking paper. Roll up the cake while it is still warm with the help of the sugared paper. Set aside to cool.

8 For the filling, whip the cream until it holds soft peaks. Stir together the caster sugar and orange rind, then fold into the whipped cream. Add the liqueur.

9 ▲ Gently unroll the cake. Spread the inside with a layer of orange whipped cream, then re-roll. Keep refrigerated until ready to serve. Dust the top with icing sugar just before serving.

Energy 2788kcal/11573kJ; Protein 48.6g; Carbohydrate 151.4g, of which sugars 150.6g; Fat 221.9g, of which saturates 88.3g; Cholesterol 1076mg; Calcium 465mg; Fibre 4g; Sodium 372mg.

Chocolate Swiss Roll

SERVES 10

225g/8oz plain (semisweet) chocolate

45ml/3 tbsp water

30ml/2 tbsp rum, brandy or strong coffee

7 eggs, separated

175g/6oz/scant 1 cup caster (superfine) sugar

0.6ml/^{1}/$_8$ tsp salt

350ml/12fl oz/1^1/$_2$ cups whipping cream

icing (confectioners') sugar, for dusting

1 Preheat a 180°C/350°F/Gas 4 oven. Line a 38 × 33cm/15 × 13in Swiss roll tin (jelly roll pan) with baking parchment and grease the parchment.

2 ▲ Combine the chocolate, water and rum or other flavouring in the top of a double boiler, or in a heatproof bowl set over hot water. Heat until melted. Set aside.

3 With an electric mixer, beat the egg yolks and sugar until thick.

4 ▲ Stir in the melted chocolate.

5 In another bowl, beat the egg whites and salt until they hold stiff peaks. Fold a large dollop of egg whites into the yolk mixture to lighten it, then carefully fold in the rest of the whites.

6 ▼ Pour the mixture into the pan; smooth evenly with a metal spatula.

7 Bake for 15 minutes. Remove from the oven, cover with baking parchment and a damp cloth. Let stand for 1–2 hours.

8 With an electric mixer, whip the cream until stiff. Set aside.

9 Run a knife along the inside edge to loosen, then invert the cake onto a sheet of baking parchment that has been dusted with icing sugar.

10 Peel off the baking paper. Spread with an even layer of whipped cream, then roll up the cake with the help of the sugared paper.

11 Refrigerate for several hours. Before serving, dust with an even layer of icing sugar.

Energy 3732kcal/15572kJ; Protein 62.9g; Carbohydrate 330g, of which sugars 327.9g; Fat 242.9g, of which saturates 137g; Cholesterol 1713mg; Calcium 567mg; Fibre 5.6g; Sodium 601mg.

Traditional Chocolate Cake

SERVES 10

115g/4oz plain (semisweet) chocolate

275ml/9fl oz/generous 1 cup milk

200g/7oz/scant 1 cup soft light brown sugar

1 egg yolk

250g/9oz/2¼ cups plain (all-purpose) flour

5ml/1 tsp bicarbonate of soda
    (baking soda)

2.5ml/½ tsp salt

150g/5oz/10 tbsp butter or margarine,
    at room temperature

250g/9oz/1¼ cups caster (superfine) sugar

3 eggs

5ml/1 tsp vanilla extract

FOR THE ICING

225g/8oz plain (semisweet) chocolate

1.25ml/¼ tsp salt

175ml/6fl oz/¾ cup sour cream

1 Preheat a 180°C/350°F/Gas 4 oven.
Line two 20–23cm/8–9in round cake
tins (pans) with baking parchment.

2 ▲ In a heatproof bowl set over a
pan of simmering water, or in a double
boiler, combine the chocolate, one-
third of the milk, the brown sugar and
egg yolk. Cook, stirring, until smooth
and thickened. Let cool.

3 ▲ Sift the flour, bicarbonate of
soda and salt into a bowl. Set aside.

4 ▲ With an electric mixer, cream
the butter or margarine with the caster
sugar until light and fluffy. Beat in the
whole eggs, one at a time, then mix in
the vanilla.

5 On low speed, beat the flour
mixture into the butter mixture
alternately with the remaining milk,
beginning and ending with flour.

6 ▲ Pour in the chocolate mixture
and mix until just combined.

7 Divide the cake mixture evenly
between the cake tins. Bake until a
skewer inserted in the centre comes
out clean, 35–40 minutes.

8 Let cool in the tins on wire racks
for 10 minutes, then unmould the
cakes from the tins onto the wire racks
and let cool completely.

9 ▲ For the icing, melt the
chocolate in a heatproof bowl set over
a pan of hot, not boiling, water, or in
the top of a double boiler. Remove the
bowl from the heat and stir in the salt
and sour cream. Let cool slightly.

10 ▲ Set one cake layer on a serving
plate and spread with one-third of the
icing. Place the second cake layer on
top. Spread the remaining icing all
over the top and sides of the cake,
swirling it to make a decorative finish.

Energy 506kcal/2135kJ; Protein 7g; Carbohydrate 90g, of which sugars 70g; Fat 16g, of which saturates 9g; Cholesterol 102mg; Calcium 91mg; Fibre 1g; Sodium 142mg.

Chocolate Frosted Layer Cake

5 In another bowl, beat the egg whites with the salt until they hold stiff peaks. Set aside.

6 ▲ Gently fold the dry ingredients into the butter mixture in three batches, alternating with the milk.

7 Add a large dollop of the whites and fold in to lighten the mixture. Carefully fold in the remaining whites until just blended.

8 Divide the batter between the tins and bake until the cakes pull away from the sides of the tins, for about 30 minutes. Let stand 5 minutes. Turn out and cool on a rack.

SERVES 8

225g/8oz/1 cup butter or margarine, at room temperature

300g/10oz/1¹/2 cups caster (superfine) sugar

4 eggs, at room temperature, separated

10ml/2 tsp vanilla extract

375g/13oz/3¹/4 cups plain (all-purpose) flour

10ml/2 tsp baking powder

0.6ml/¹/8 tsp salt

250ml/8fl oz/1 cup milk

FOR THE FROSTING

150g/5oz plain (semisweet) chocolate

120ml/4fl oz/¹/2 cup sour cream

0.6ml/¹/8 tsp salt

1 Preheat a 180°C/350°F/Gas 4 oven. Line two 20cm/8in round cake tins (pans) with baking parchment and grease. Dust the tins with flour. Tap to dislodge excess flour.

2 With an electric mixer, cream the butter or margarine until soft. Gradually add the sugar and continue beating until light and fluffy.

3 ▲ Lightly beat the egg yolks, then mix into the creamed butter and sugar with the vanilla.

4 Sift the flour with the baking powder three times. Set aside.

9 ▲ For the frosting, melt the chocolate in the top of a double boiler or a bowl set over hot water. When cool, stir in the sour cream and salt.

10 Sandwich the layers with frosting, then spread on the top and side.

Energy 5530kcal/23187kJ; Protein 83.4g; Carbohydrate 709.9g, of which sugars 415.2g; Fat 282.3g, of which saturates 167g; Cholesterol 1337mg; Calcium 1306mg; Fibre 15.7g; Sodium 1838mg.

Devil's Food Cake with Orange Frosting

SERVES 8–10

50g/2oz/¹/₂ cup unsweetened cocoa powder

175ml/6fl oz/³/₄ cup boiling water

175g/6oz/³/₄ cup butter, at
  room temperature

350g/12oz/1¹/₂ cups soft dark brown sugar

3 eggs, at room temperature

275g/10oz/2¹/₂ cups plain (all-purpose) flour

7.5ml/1¹/₂ tsp bicarbonate of soda
  (baking soda)

1.25ml/¹/₄ tsp baking powder

120ml/4fl oz/¹/₂ cup sour cream

orange rind strips, for decoration

FOR THE FROSTING

300g/10oz/1¹/₂ cups caster (superfine) sugar

2 egg whites

60ml/4 tbsp frozen orange juice concentrate

15ml/1 tbsp lemon juice

grated rind of 1 orange

1 Preheat a 180°C/350°F/Gas 4 oven.
Line two 23cm/9in cake tins (pans)
with baking parchment and grease. In
a bowl, mix the cocoa and water until
smooth. Set aside.

2 With an electric mixer, cream the
butter and sugar until light and fluffy.
Add the eggs, one at a time, beating
well after each addition.

3 ▲ When the cocoa mixture has
cooled to lukewarm, add to the
butter mixture.

4 ▼ Sift together the flour, soda and
baking powder twice. Fold into the
cocoa mixture in three batches,
alternating with the sour cream.

5 Pour into the tins and bake until
the cakes pull away from the sides of
the tins, 30–35 minutes. Let stand for
15 minutes. Turn out onto a rack.

6 Thinly slice the orange rind strips.
Blanch in boiling water for 1 minute.

7 ▲ For the frosting, place all the
ingredients in the top of a double
boiler or in a bowl set over hot water.
With an electric mixer, beat until the
mixture holds soft peaks. Continue
beating off the heat until thick
enough to spread.

8 Sandwich the cake layers with
frosting, then spread over the top and
side. Arrange the blanched orange
rind strips on top of the cake.

Energy 589kcal/2463kJ; Protein 5g; Carbohydrate 71g, of which sugars 70g; Fat 34g, of which saturates 21g; Cholesterol 152mg; Calcium 62mg; Fibre 0g; Sodium 496mg.

Best-Ever Chocolate Sandwich

SERVES 12–14

115g/4oz/½ cup unsalted butter
115g/4oz/1 cup plain (all-purpose) flour,
50g/2oz/½ cup unsweetened cocoa powder
5ml/1 tsp baking powder
0.6ml/⅛ tsp salt
6 eggs
225g/8oz/generous 1 cup caster (superfine) sugar
10ml/2 tsp vanilla extract

FOR THE ICING

225g/8oz plain (semisweet) chocolate, chopped
75g/3oz/6 tbsp unsalted butter
3 eggs, separated
250ml/8fl oz/1 cup whipping cream
45ml/3 tbsp caster (superfine) sugar

1 Preheat a 180°C/350°F/Gas 4 oven. Line three 20 × 3cm/8 × 1½in round tins (pans) with baking parchment; and grease.

2 ▲ Dust evenly with flour and spread with a brush. Set aside.

~ VARIATION ~

For a simpler icing, combine 250ml/8fl oz/1 cup whipping cream with 225g/8oz finely chopped plain (semisweet) chocolate in a pan. Stir over a low heat until the chocolate has melted. Cool and whisk to spreading consistency.

3 ▲ Melt the butter over a low heat. With a spoon, skim off any foam that rises to the surface. Set aside.

4 ▲ Sift the flour, cocoa, baking powder and salt together three times and set aside.

5 Place the eggs and sugar in a large heatproof bowl set over a pan of hot water. With an electric mixer, beat until the mixture doubles in volume and is thick enough to leave a ribbon trail when the beaters are lifted, about 10 minutes. Add the vanilla.

6 ▲ Sift over the dry ingredients in three batches, folding in carefully after each addition. Fold in the butter.

7 Divide the mixture between the tins and bake until the cakes pull away from the sides of the tin, about 25 minutes. Transfer to a rack.

8 For the icing, melt the chopped chocolate in the top of a double boiler, or in a heatproof bowl set over hot water.

9 ▲ Off the heat, stir in the butter and egg yolks. Return to a low heat and stir until thick. Remove from the heat and set aside.

10 Whip the cream until firm; set aside. In another bowl, beat the egg whites until stiff. Add the sugar and beat until glossy.

11 Fold the cream into the chocolate mixture, then carefully fold in the egg whites. Refrigerate for 20 minutes to thicken the icing.

12 ▲ Sandwich the cake layers with icing, stacking them carefully on a serving plate. Spread the remaining icing evenly over the top and sides of the cake.

Energy 5787kcal/24151kJ; Protein 95g; Carbohydrate 528g, of which sugars 432.6g; Fat 382.2g, of which saturates 220.4g; Cholesterol 2393mg; Calcium 879mg; Fibre 15.2g; Sodium 2352mg.

Mississippi Mud Cake

4 ▲ Pour the chocolate mixture into a large bowl. Using an electric mixer on low speed, gradually beat in the sugar. Continue beating until the sugar has dissolved.

5 Increase the speed to medium and add the sifted dry ingredients. Mix well, then beat in the eggs and vanilla until thoroughly blended.

6 Pour the batter into a well-greased 3 litre/5 pint/12½ cup ring mould that has been dusted lightly with cocoa powder. Bake until a skewer inserted in the cake comes out clean, about 1 hour 20 minutes.

7 ▲ Leave to cool in the mould for 15 minutes, then unmould on to a wire rack. Leave to cool completely.

8 When the cake is cold, dust it lightly with cocoa powder. Serve with sweetened whipped cream or ice cream, if desired.

SERVES 8–10

225g/8oz/2 cups plain (all-purpose) flour

0.6ml/⅛ tsp salt

5ml/1 tsp baking powder

300ml/½ pint/1¼ cups strong brewed coffee

45ml/3 tbsp bourbon or brandy

150g/5oz unsweetened chocolate

225g/8oz/1 cup butter or margarine

400g/14oz/2 cups caster (superfine) sugar

2 eggs, at room temperature

7.5ml/1½ tsp vanilla extract

unsweetened cocoa powder

sweetened whipped cream or ice cream, for serving

1 Preheat the oven to 275°F/140°C/ Gas 1.

2 Sift the flour, salt and baking powder together.

3 ▼ Combine the coffee, bourbon or brandy, chocolate, and butter or margarine in the top of a double boiler. Heat until the chocolate and butter have melted and the mixture is smooth, stirring occasionally.

Energy 534kcal/2227kJ; Protein 6.3g; Carbohydrate 49.5g, of which sugars 38.5g; Fat 35.2g, of which saturates 19.6g; Cholesterol 87mg; Calcium 110mg; Fibre 2.1g; Sodium 142mg.

Blueberry Cake

SERVES 10

225g/8oz/2 cups plain (all-purpose) flour
15ml/1 tbsp baking powder
5ml/1 tsp salt
175g/6oz/³/4 cup butter or margarine, at room temperature
150g/5oz/³/4 cup sugar
1 egg
250ml/8fl oz/1 cup milk
2.5ml/¹/2 tsp grated lemon rind
225g/8oz/2 cups fresh or frozen blueberries, well drained
115g/4oz/1 cup icing (confectioners') sugar
30ml/2 tbsp fresh lemon juice

1 Preheat a 180°C/350°F/Gas 4 oven.

2 ▲ Sift the flour with the baking powder and salt.

3 ▲ In a large bowl, beat the butter or margarine with the granulated sugar until light and fluffy. Beat in the egg and milk. Fold in the flour mixture, mixing well until evenly blended to a batter. Mix in the lemon rind.

4 ▼ Spread half the batter in a greased 33 × 23 × 5cm/13 × 9 × 2in ovenproof dish. Sprinkle with 115g/4oz/¹/2 cup of the berries. Top with the remaining batter and sprinkle with the rest of the berries. Bake until brown and a skewer inserted in the centre comes out clean, 35–45 minutes.

5 ▲ Mix the icing sugar gradually into the lemon juice with a wooden spoon to make a smooth glaze with a pourable consistency. Add a little more icing sugar or lemon juice as required. Drizzle the glaze over the top of the cake and allow it to set before serving, still warm or cooled.

Energy 167kcal/698kJ; Protein 2.3g; Carbohydrate 19g, of which sugars 11.3g; Fat 9.6g, of which saturates 2g; Cholesterol 39mg; Calcium 29mg; Fibre 0.7g; Sodium 115mg.

Chocolate Cinnamon Cake with Banana Sauce

SERVES 6

115g/4oz plain (semisweet) chocolate, chopped

115g/4oz/½ cup unsalted butter, at room temperature

15ml/1 tbsp instant coffee powder

5 eggs, separated

200g/7oz/1 cup sugar

115g/4oz/1 cup plain (all-purpose) flour,

10ml/2 tsp ground cinnamon

FOR THE SAUCE

4 ripe bananas

50g/2oz/4 tbsp soft light brown sugar, firmly packed

15ml/1 tbsp fresh lemon juice

175ml/6fl oz/¾ cup whipping cream

15ml/1 tbsp rum (optional)

1 Preheat the oven to 180°C/350°F/ Gas 4. Grease a 20cm/8in round cake tin (pan).

2 ▲ Combine the chocolate and butter in the top of a double boiler or in a heatproof bowl set over hot water. Stir until melted. Remove from the heat and stir in the coffee. Set aside.

3 Beat the egg yolks with the granulated sugar until thick and lemon-coloured. Add the chocolate mixture and beat just to blend the mixtures evenly.

4 Sift together the flour and cinnamon into a bowl.

5 ▲ In another bowl, beat the egg whites until they hold stiff peaks.

6 ▲ Fold a dollop of whites into the chocolate mixture to lighten it. Fold in the remaining whites in three batches, alternating with the sifted flour.

7 ▲ Pour the mixture into the prepared tin. Bake until a skewer inserted in the centre comes out clean, 40–50 minutes. Unmould the cake on to a wire rack.

8 Preheat the grill (broiler).

9 ▲ For the sauce, slice the bananas into a shallow, heatproof dish. Add the brown sugar and lemon juice and stir to blend. Place under the grill and cook, stirring occasionally, until the sugar is caramelized and bubbling, about 8 minutes.

10 ▲ Transfer the bananas to a bowl and mash with a fork until almost smooth. Stir in the cream and rum, if using. Serve the cake and sauce warm.

~ VARIATION ~

For a special occasion, top the cake slices with a scoop of ice cream (rum-raisin, chocolate, or vanilla) before adding the banana sauce. With this addition, the dessert will make at least eight portions.

Energy 642kcal/2691kJ; Protein 8.9g; Carbohydrate 80.9g, of which sugars 64.8g; Fat 33.8g, of which saturates 19.4g; Cholesterol 230mg; Calcium 100mg; Fibre 1.4g; Sodium 186mg.

Rich Chocolate Nut Cake

4 Fold in three-quarters of the nuts, then pour the mixture into the prepared tin.

5 ▲ Set the tin inside a large tin and pour 2.5cm/1in hot water into the outer tin. Bake until the cake is firm to the touch, about 45 minutes. Let stand 15 minutes, then unmould and transfer to a cooling rack.

6 Wrap the cake in baking parchment and refrigerate for 6 hours.

7 For the glaze, combine the butter, chocolate, milk and vanilla in the top of a double boiler or in a heatproof bowl set over hot water, until melted.

8 Place a piece of baking parchment under the cake, then drizzle spoonfuls of glaze along the edge to drip down and coat the sides. Pour the remaining glaze on top of the cake.

SERVES 10

225g/8oz/1 cup butter

225g/8oz plain (semisweet) chocolate

115g/4oz/1 cup unsweetened cocoa powder

350g/12oz/1¾ cups caster (superfine) sugar

6 eggs

90ml/6 tbsp brandy or cognac

225g/8oz/2 cups finely chopped hazelnuts

FOR THE GLAZE

50g/2oz/¼ cup butter

150g/5oz dark (bittersweet) chocolate

30ml/2 tbsp milk

5ml/1 tsp vanilla extract

1 Preheat a 180°C/350°F/Gas 4 oven. Line a 23 × 5 cm/9 × 2in round tin (pan) with baking parchment and grease.

2 Melt the butter and chocolate together in the top of a double boiler, or in a heatproof bowl set over hot water. Set aside to cool.

3 ▼ Sift the cocoa into a bowl. Add the sugar and eggs and stir until just combined. Pour in the melted chocolate mixture and brandy.

9 ▲ Cover the sides of the cake with the remaining nuts, gently pressing them on with the palm of your hand.

Energy 7802kcal/32523kJ; Protein 113.7g; Carbohydrate 633.7g, of which sugars 612.6g; Fat 532.7g, of which saturates 241.2g; Cholesterol 1752mg; Calcium 1030mg; Fibre 37.9g; Sodium 3249mg.

Chocolate Layer Cake

SERVES 8–10

115g/4oz plain (semisweet) chocolate
175g/6oz/³/4 cup butter
450g/1lb/2¹/2 cups caster (superfine) sugar
3 eggs
5ml/1 tsp vanilla extract
175g/6oz/1¹/2 cups plain (all-purpose) flour
5ml/1 tsp baking powder
115g/4oz/1 cup chopped walnuts

FOR THE TOPPING

350ml/12fl oz/1¹/2 cups whipping cream
225g/8oz plain (semisweet) chocolate
15ml/1 tbsp vegetable oil

1 Preheat a 180°C/350°F/Gas 4 oven. Line two 20cm/8in cake tins (pans), at least 4.5cm/1³/4in deep, with baking parchment and grease.

2 Melt the chocolate and butter together in the top of a double boiler, or in a heatproof bowl set over a pan of hot water.

3 ▲ Transfer the chocolate to a mixing bowl if necessary and stir in the sugar. Add the eggs and vanilla and mix until well blended.

~ VARIATION ~

To make Chocolate Ice Cream Layer Cake, sandwich the cake layers with softened vanilla ice cream. Freeze before serving.

4 ▲ Sift over the flour and baking powder. Stir in the walnuts.

5 Divide the mixture between the prepared tins and spread level.

6 Bake until a skewer inserted in the centre comes out clean, for about 30 minutes. Let stand 10 minutes, then unmould and transfer to a rack.

7 When the cakes are cool, whip the cream until it is firm. With a long serrated knife, carefully slice each cake in half horizontally.

8 Sandwich the layers with some of the whipped cream and spread the remainder over the top and sides of the cake. Refrigerate until needed.

9 ▼ For the chocolate curls, melt the chocolate and oil in the top of a double boiler or a bowl set over hot water. Transfer to a non-porous surface. Spread to a 1cm/¹/2in thick rectangle. Just before the chocolate sets, hold the blade of a straight knife at an angle to the chocolate and scrape across the surface to make curls. Place on top of the cake.

Energy 9521kcal/39888kJ; Protein 94.2g; Carbohydrate 1196.3g, of which sugars 972.4g; Fat 518.1g, of which saturates 312.1g; Cholesterol 1472mg; Calcium 1419mg; Fibre 27.5g; Sodium 1382mg.

Sachertorte

SERVES 8–10

115g/4oz plain (semisweet) chocolate
75g/3oz/6 tbsp unsalted butter, at room temperature
50g/2oz/¼ cup caster (superfine) sugar
4 eggs, separated
1 extra egg white
1.25ml/¼ tsp salt
75g/3oz/⅔ cup plain (all-purpose) flour, sifted

FOR THE TOPPING

75ml/5 tbsp apricot jam
250ml/8fl oz/1 cup plus 15ml/1 tbsp water
15ml/1 tbsp unsalted butter
175g/6oz plain (semisweet) chocolate
75g/3oz/6 tbsp caster (superfine) sugar
ready-made chocolate icing (optional)

1 Preheat the oven to 170°C/ 325°F/ Gas 3. Line a 23 × 5cm/9 × 2in cake tin (pan) with baking parchment and grease.

2 ▲ Melt the chocolate in the top of a double boiler, or in a heatproof bowl set over hot water. Set aside.

3 With an electric mixer, cream the butter and sugar until light and fluffy. Stir in the chocolate.

4 ▲ Beat in the yolks, one at a time.

5 In another bowl, beat the egg whites with the salt until stiff.

6 ▲ Fold a dollop of whites into the chocolate mixture to lighten it. Fold in the remaining whites in three batches, alternating with the flour.

7 ▲ Pour into the tin and bake until a cake tester comes out clean, about 45 minutes. Turn out onto a rack.

8 ▲ Meanwhile, melt the jam with 15ml/1 tbsp of the water over low heat, then strain for a smooth consistency.

9 For the frosting, melt the butter and chocolate in the top of a double boiler or a bowl set over hot water.

10 ▲ In a heavy pan, dissolve the sugar in the remaining water over low heat. Raise the heat and boil until it reaches 107°C/225°F/ (thread stage) on a sugar thermometer. Immediately plunge the bottom of the pan into cold water for 1 minute. Pour into the chocolate mixture and stir to blend. Let cool for a few minutes.

11 To assemble, brush the warm jam over the cake. Starting in the centre, pour over the frosting and work outward in a circular movement. Tilt the rack to spread; use a palette knife to smooth the side of the cake. Leave to set overnight. If wished, decorate with chocolate icing.

Energy 625kcal/2618kJ; Protein 7.6g; Carbohydrate 73.1g, of which sugars 65.5g; Fat 35.8g, of which saturates 20.8g; Cholesterol 184mg; Calcium 73mg; Fibre 1.2g; Sodium 143mg.

Boston Cream Pie

SERVES 8

225g/8oz/2 cups plain (all-purpose) flour

15ml/1 tbsp baking powder

2.5ml/½ tsp salt

115g/4oz/½ cup butter, at room temperature

200g/7oz/1 cup sugar

2 eggs

5ml/1 tsp vanilla extract

175ml/6fl oz/¾ cup milk

FOR THE FILLING

250ml/8fl oz/1 cup milk

3 egg yolks

90g/3½oz/½ cup sugar

25g/1oz/¼ cup plain (all-purpose) flour

15ml/1 tbsp butter

15ml/1 tbsp brandy or 5ml/1 tsp vanilla extract

FOR THE CHOCOLATE GLAZE

25g/1oz plain (semisweet) chocolate

25g/1oz/2 tbsp butter or margarine

50g/2oz/½ cup icing (confectioners') sugar, plus extra for dusting

2.5ml/½ tsp vanilla extract

about 15ml/1 tbsp hot water

1 Preheat the oven to 190°C/375°F/ Gas 5.

2 Grease two 20 × 5cm/8 × 2in round cake tins (pans), and line the bottoms with rounds of buttered baking parchment.

3 Sift the flour with the baking powder and salt.

4 Beat the butter and granulated sugar together until light and fluffy. Add the eggs one at a time, beating well after each addition. Stir in the vanilla. Add the milk and dry ingredients alternately, mixing only enough to blend thoroughly each time. Do not over-beat the mixture.

5 Divide the cake mixture between the prepared tins and spread it out evenly. Bake until a skewer inserted in the centre comes out clean, about 25 minutes.

6 Meanwhile, make the filling. Heat the milk in a small pan to boiling point. Remove from the heat.

7 ▲ In a heatproof mixing bowl, beat the egg yolks until smooth. Gradually add the granulated sugar and continue beating until pale yellow. Beat in the flour.

8 ▲ Pour the hot milk into the egg yolk mixture in a steady stream, beating constantly. When all the milk has been added, place the bowl over a pan of boiling water, or pour the mixture into the top of a double boiler. Heat, stirring constantly, until thickened. Cook 2 minutes more, then remove from the heat. Stir in the butter and brandy or vanilla. Allow to cool.

9 ▲ When the cakes have cooled, use a large sharp knife to slice off the domed top to make a flat surface. Place one cake on a serving plate and spread on the filling in a thick layer. Set the other cake on top, cut side down. Smooth the edge of the filling layer so it is flush with the sides of the cake layers.

10 ▲ For the glaze, melt the chocolate with the butter or margarine in the top of a double boiler. When smooth, remove from the heat and beat in the sugar to make a thick paste. Add the vanilla. Beat in a little of the hot water. If the glaze does not have a spreadable consistency, add more water, 5ml/1 tsp at a time.

11 Spread the glaze evenly over the top of the cake, using a palette knife. Dust the top with icing sugar. Because of the custard filling, refrigerate any leftover cake.

Energy 499kcal/2099kJ; Protein 6g; Carbohydrate 77g, of which sugars 53.1g; Fat 20.3g, of which saturates 12.1g; Cholesterol 146mg; Calcium 112mg; Fibre 1g; Sodium 296mg.

Caramel Layer Cake

SERVES 8–10

275g/10oz/2¹/₂ cups plain (all-purpose) flour

7.5ml/1¹/₂ tsp baking powder

175g/6oz/³/₄ cup butter, at room temperature

150g/5oz/³/₄ cup caster (superfine) sugar

4 eggs, at room temperature, beaten

5ml/1 tsp vanilla extract

120ml/4fl oz/¹/₂ cup milk

whipped cream, for decorating

caramel threads, for decorating
(optional, see below)

FOR THE FROSTING

300g/10oz/1¹/₂ cups soft dark
brown sugar

250ml/8fl oz/1 cup milk

25g/1oz/2 tbsp unsalted butter

45–75ml/3–5 tbsp whipping cream

1 Preheat a 180°C/350°F/Gas 4 oven. Line two 20cm/8in cake tins (pans) with baking parchment and grease lightly.

2 ▲ Sift the flour and baking powder together three times. Set aside.

~ COOK'S TIP ~

To make caramel threads, combine 75ml/5 tbsp sugar and 60ml/4 tbsp water in a heavy pan. Boil until light brown. Dip the pan in cold water to halt cooking. Trail from a spoon on an oiled baking sheet.

3 With an electric mixer, cream the butter and caster sugar until light and fluffy.

4 ▲ Slowly mix in the beaten eggs. Add the vanilla. Fold in the flour mixture, alternating with the milk.

5 ▲ Divide the batter between the prepared tins and spread evenly, hollowing out the centres slightly.

6 Bake until the cakes pull away from the sides of the tin, about 30 minutes. Let stand 5 minutes, then turn out and cool on a wire rack.

7 ▲ For the frosting, combine the brown sugar and milk in a pan.

8 Bring to the boil, cover and cook for 3 minutes. Remove lid and continue to boil, without stirring, until the mixture reaches 119°C/238°F (soft ball stage) on a sugar thermometer.

9 ▲ Immediately remove the pan from the heat and add the butter, but do not stir it in. Let cool until lukewarm, then beat until the mixture is smooth and creamy.

10 Stir in enough cream to obtain a spreadable consistency. If necessary, refrigerate to thicken more.

11 ▲ Spread a layer of frosting on top of one cake. Sandwich with the second cake, then spread the top and sides with the rest of the frosting and smooth the surface.

12 To decorate, pipe whipped cream rosettes around the edge. If using, place a mound of caramel threads in the centre before serving.

Energy 5236kcal/21969kJ; Protein 66.1g; Carbohydrate 701.3g, of which sugars 491.8g; Fat 260.9g, of which saturates 155.2g; Cholesterol 1375mg; Calcium 1169mg; Fibre 8.5g; Sodium 1676mg.

Whiskey Cake

MAKES 1 LOAF

175g/6oz/1 cup chopped walnuts

75g/3oz/¹/2 cup raisins, chopped

75g/3oz/¹/2 cup currants

115g/4oz/1 cup plain (all-purpose) flour

5ml/1 tsp baking powder

1.25ml/¹/4 tsp salt

115g/4oz/¹/2 cup butter

225g/8oz/generous 1 cup caster (superfine) sugar

3 eggs, at room temperature, separated

5ml/1 tsp grated nutmeg

2.5ml/¹/2 tsp ground cinnamon

90ml/6 tbsp Irish whiskey or bourbon

icing (confectioners') sugar, for dusting

1 ▼ Preheat a 170°C/325°F/Gas 3 oven. Line a 23 × 13cm/9 × 5in loaf tin (pan) with baking parchment. Grease the paper and sides of the pan.

2 ▲ Place the walnuts, raisins, and currants in a bowl. Sprinkle over 30ml/2 tbsp of the flour, mix and set aside. Sift together the remaining flour, baking powder and salt.

3 ▲ Cream the butter and sugar until light and fluffy. Beat in the egg yolks.

4 Mix the nutmeg, cinnamon and whiskey. Fold into the butter mixture, alternating with the flour mixture.

5 ▲ In another bowl, beat the egg whites until stiff. Fold into the whiskey mixture until just blended. Fold in the walnut mixture.

6 Bake until a skewer inserted in the centre comes out clean, about 1 hour. Let cool in the pan. Dust with icing sugar over a template.

Energy 4093kcal/17119kJ; Protein 69g; Carbohydrate 448g, of which sugars 360g; Fat 238g, of which saturates 77g; Cholesterol 1100mg; Calcium 620mg; Fibre 24g; Sodium 1573mg.

American Berry Shortcake

SERVES 8

300ml/¹/₂ pint/1¹/₄ cups whipping cream

25g/1oz/¹/₄ cup icing (confectioners') sugar, sifted

675g/1¹/₂lb strawberries or mixed berries, halved or sliced if large

50g/2oz/¹/₄ cup caster (superfine) sugar, or to taste

FOR THE SHORTCAKE

275g/10oz/2¹/₂ cups plain (all-purpose) flour

10ml/2 tsp baking powder

75g/3oz/6 tbsp caster (superfine) sugar

115g/4oz/¹/₂ cup butter

75ml/5 tbsp milk

1 large (US extra large) egg

1 Preheat a 230°C/450°F/Gas 8 oven. Grease a 20cm/8in round cake tin (pan).

2 For the shortcake, sift the flour, baking powder and sugar into a bowl. Add the butter and rub in until the mixture resembles fine crumbs. Combine the milk and egg. Add to the crumb mixture and stir just until evenly mixed to a soft dough.

3 Put the dough in the prepared tin and pat out to an even layer. Bake for 15–20 minutes or until a wooden skewer inserted in the centre comes out clean. Leave to cool slightly.

5 Put the berries in a bowl. Sprinkle with the caster sugar and toss together lightly. Cover and set aside for the berries to give up some juice.

6 ▼ Remove the cooled shortcake from the tin. With a long, serrated knife, split the shortcake horizontally into two equal layers.

4 ▲ Whip the cream until it starts to thicken. Add the icing sugar. Continue whipping until it holds soft peaks.

7 ▲ Put the bottom layer on a serving plate. Top with half of the berries and most of the cream. Set the second layer of shortcake on top and press down gently. Spoon the remaining berries over the top layer (or serve them separately) and add the remaining cream in small, decorative dollops, if you like.

Energy 500kcal/2090kJ; Protein 6g; Carbohydrate 57g, of which sugars 28g; Fat 29g, of which saturates 18g; Cholesterol 103mg; Calcium 120mg; Fibre 3g; Sodium 238mg.

Lady Baltimore Cake

SERVES 8–10

275g/10oz/2¹/2 cups plain (all-purpose) flour
12.5ml/2¹/2 tsp baking powder
2.5ml/¹/2 tsp salt
4 eggs
350g/12oz/1³/4 cups sugar
grated rind of l large orange
250ml/8fl oz/1 cup fresh orange juice
250ml/8fl oz/1 cup vegetable oil
18 pecan halves, for decorating
FOR THE FROSTING
2 egg whites
350g/12oz/1³/4 cups caster (superfine) sugar
75ml/5 tbsp cold water
1.25ml/¹/4 tsp cream of tartar
5ml/1 tsp vanilla extract
50g/2oz/¹/3 cup pecans, finely chopped
75g/3oz/¹/2 cup raisins, chopped
3 dried figs, finely chopped

1 Preheat the oven to 180°C/350°F/ Gas 4. Grease two 23cm/9in round cake tins (pans) and line with baking parchment. Grease the paper. In a bowl, sift together the flour, baking powder and salt. Set aside.

2 ▲ With an electric mixer, beat the eggs and sugar until thick and lemon-coloured. Beat in the orange rind and juice, then the oil.

3 On low speed, beat in the flour mixture in three batches. Divide the cake mixture between the tins.

4 ▲ Bake until a skewer inserted in the centre comes out clean, about 30 minutes. Leave to stand for 15 minutes, then run a knife around the inside of the cakes and transfer them to racks to cool completely.

5 ▲ For the frosting, combine the egg whites, sugar, water and cream of tartar in the top of a double boiler, or in a heatproof bowl set over boiling water. With an electric mixer, beat until glossy and thick. Off the heat, add the vanilla extract and continue beating until thick. Fold in the pecans, raisins and figs.

6 Spread a layer of frosting on top of one cake. Sandwich with the second cake, then spread the top and sides with the rest of the frosting. Arrange the pecan halves on top.

Energy 529kcal/2229kJ; Protein 5.9g; Carbohydrate 90.2g, of which sugars 74.3g; Fat 18.6g, of which saturates 2.2g; Cholesterol 63mg; Calcium 107mg; Fibre 1.9g; Sodium 51mg.

Raspberry-Hazelnut Meringue Cake

SERVES 8

150g/5oz/scant 1 cup hazelnuts
4 egg whites
0.6ml/¹/₈ tsp salt
200g/7oz/1 cup sugar
2.5ml/¹/₂ tsp vanilla extract
FOR THE FILLING
300ml/¹/₂ pint/1¹/₄ cups whipping cream
675g/1¹/₂lb/4 cups raspberries

1 Preheat a 180°C/350°F/Gas 4 oven. Line two 20cm/8in cake tins (pans) with baking parchment and grease.

2 Spread the hazelnuts on a baking sheet and bake until lightly toasted, about 8 minutes. Let cool slightly.

3 ▲ Rub the hazelnuts vigorously in a clean tea towel to remove most of the skins.

4 Grind the nuts in a food processor, blender, or coffee grinder until they are the consistency of coarse sand. Reduce the oven temperature to 150°C/300°F/Gas 2.

5 With an electric mixer, beat the egg whites and salt until they hold stiff peaks. Beat in 30ml/2 tbsp of the sugar, then fold in the remaining sugar, a few tablespoons at a time, with a rubber scraper. Fold in the vanilla and the hazelnuts.

6 ▲ Divide the batter between the prepared tins and spread level.

7 Bake for 1¹/₄ hours. If the meringues brown too quickly, protect with a sheet of foil. Let stand 5 minutes, then carefully run a knife around the inside edge of the tins to loosen. Turn out onto a rack to cool.

8 For the filling, whip the cream just until firm.

9 ▲ Spread half the cream in an even layer on one meringue round and top with half the raspberries.

10 Top with the other meringue round. Spread the remaining cream on top and arrange the remaining raspberries over the cream. Refrigerate for 1 hour to facilitate cutting.

Energy 383kcal/1598kJ; Protein 6g; Carbohydrate 32g, of which sugars 32g; Fat 26g, of which saturates 10g; Cholesterol 39mg; Calcium 71mg; Fibre 7g; Sodium 74mg.

Classic Cheesecake

SERVES 8

50g/2oz/1 cup crushed digestive biscuits (graham crackers)

900g/2lb/4 cups cream cheese, at room temperature

250g/9oz/1¼ cups sugar

grated rind of 1 lemon

45ml/3 tbsp lemon juice

5ml/1 tsp vanilla extract

4 eggs, at room temperature

1 Preheat the oven to 170°C/325°F/ Gas 3. Grease a 20cm/8in springform tin (pan). Place on a round of foil 10–12.5cm/4–5in larger than the diameter of the tin. Press it up the sides to seal tightly.

2 Sprinkle the biscuits in the base of the tin. Press to form an even layer.

3 With an electric mixer, beat the cream cheese until smooth. Add the sugar, lemon rind and juice, and vanilla, and beat until blended. Beat in the eggs, one at a time. Beat just enough to blend thoroughly.

4 ▲ Pour into the prepared tin. Set the tin in a larger baking tray and place in the oven. Pour enough hot water in the outer tray to come 2.5cm/1in up the side of the tin.

5 Bake until the top of the cake is golden brown, about 1¹/₂ hours. Let cool in the tin.

6 ▼ Run a knife around the edge to loosen, then remove the rim of the tin. Refrigerate for at least 4 hours before serving.

Chocolate Cheesecake

SERVES 10–12

275g/10oz plain (semisweet) chocolate

1.2kg/2¹/₂lb/5 cups cream cheese, at room temperature

200g/7oz/1 cup sugar

10ml/2 tsp vanilla extract

4 eggs, at room temperature

175ml/6fl oz/³/₄ cup sour cream

15ml/1 tbsp unsweetened cocoa powder

FOR THE BASE

200g/7oz/4 cups crushed chocolate biscuits (cookies)

75g/3oz/6 tbsp butter, melted

2.5ml/¹/₂ tsp ground cinnamon

1 Preheat a 180°C/350°F/Gas 4 oven. Grease a 23 × 7.5cm/9 × 3in spring-form tin (pan).

2 ▲ For the base, mix the crushed biscuits with the butter and cinnamon. Press evenly onto the bottom of the tin.

3 Melt the chocolate in the top of a double boiler, or in a heatproof bowl set over hot water. Set aside.

4 Beat the cream cheese until smooth, then beat in the sugar and vanilla. Add the eggs, one at a time.

5 Stir the sour cream into the cocoa powder to form a paste. Add to the cream cheese mixture. Stir in the melted chocolate.

6 ▼ Pour into the crust. Bake for 1 hour. Let cool in the tin; remove rim. Refrigerate before serving.

Classic: Energy 680kcal/2823kJ; Protein 7.2g; Carbohydrate 36.3g, of which sugars 32.9g; Fat 57.5g, of which saturates 34.8g; Cholesterol 205mg; Calcium 147mg; Fibre 0.1g; Sodium 412mg.
Chocolate: Energy 772kcal/3204kJ; Protein 8g; Carbohydrate 43.8g, of which sugars 37.1g; Fat 64.1g, of which saturates 38.9g; Cholesterol 182mg; Calcium 146mg; Fibre 1.1g; Sodium 431mg.

Lemon Mousse Cheesecake

4 In another bowl, beat the egg whites until they hold soft peaks. Add the remaining sugar and beat until stiff and glossy.

5 ▲ Add the egg whites to the cheese mixture and gently fold in.

6 Pour the mixture into the prepared tin, then place the tin in a larger baking tin. Place in the oven and pour hot water in the outer tin to come 2.5cm/1in up the side.

7 Bake until golden, 60–65 minutes. Let cool in the pan on a rack. Cover and refrigerate for at least 4 hours.

8 To unmould, run a knife around the inside edge. Place a flat plate, bottom-side up, over the pan and invert onto the plate. Smooth the top with a metal spatula.

9 ▲ Sprinkle the biscuits over the top in an even layer, pressing down slightly to make a top crust.

10 To serve, cut slices with a sharp knife dipped in hot water.

SERVES 10–12

1.2kg/2¹/₂lb/5 cups cream cheese, at room temperature

350g/12oz/1³/₄ cups caster (superfine) sugar

40g/1¹/₂oz/¹/₃ cup plain (all-purpose) flour

4 eggs, at room temperature, separated

120ml/4fl oz/¹/₂ cup fresh lemon juice

grated rind of 2 lemons

115g/4oz/2 cups crushed digestive biscuits (graham crackers)

1 Preheat a 170°C/325°F/Gas 3 oven. Line a 25 × 5cm/10 × 2in round cake tin (pan) with baking parchment and grease the paper.

2 With an electric mixer, beat the cream cheese until smooth. Gradually add 300g/10oz/1¹/₂ cups of the sugar, and beat until light. Beat in the flour.

3 ▲ Add the egg yolks, and lemon juice and rind, and beat until smooth and well blended.

Energy 629kcal/2612kJ; Protein 6g; Carbohydrate 37g, of which sugars 32g; Fat 52g, of which saturates 31g; Cholesterol 176mg; Calcium 122mg; Fibre 0g; Sodium 388mg.

Marbled Cheesecake

SERVES 10

50g/2oz/¹/2 cup unsweetened cocoa powder

75ml/5 tbsp hot water

900g/2lb/4 cups cream cheese,
  at room temperature

200g/7oz/1 cup sugar

4 eggs

5ml/1 tsp vanilla extract

75g/3oz/1¹/2 cups crushed digestive
  biscuits (graham crackers)

1 Preheat a 180°C/350°F/Gas 4 oven. Line a 20 × 8cm/8 × 3in cake tin (pan) with baking parchment; grease.

2 Sift the cocoa powder into a bowl. Pour over the hot water and stir to dissolve. Set aside.

3 With an electric mixer, beat the cheese until smooth and creamy. Add the sugar and beat to incorporate. Beat in the eggs, one at a time. Do not overmix.

4 Divide the mixture evenly between two bowls. Stir the chocolate mixture into one, then add the vanilla to the remaining mixture.

5 ▲ Pour a cupful of the plain mixture into the centre of the tin; it will spread out into an even layer. Slowly pour over a cupful of chocolate mixture in the centre.

6 ▲ Repeat alternating cupfuls of the batters in a circular pattern until both are used up.

7 Set the tin in a larger baking tray and pour in hot water to come 4cm/1¹/2in up the sides of the cake tin.

8 Bake until the top of the cake is golden, about 1¹/2 hours. It will rise during baking but will sink later. Let cool in the tin on a rack.

9 To turn out, run a knife around the inside edge. Place a flat plate, bottom-side up, over the tin and invert onto the plate.

10 ▼ Sprinkle the crushed biscuits evenly over the base, gently place another plate over them, and invert again. Cover and refrigerate for at least 3 hours, or overnight. To serve, cut slices with a sharp knife dipped in hot water.

Energy 552kcal/2287kJ; Protein 6.8g; Carbohydrate 26.3g, of which sugars 21.9g; Fat 47.5g, of which saturates 28.6g; Cholesterol 164mg; Calcium 123mg; Fibre 0.8g; Sodium 389mg.

Chocolate Fairy Cakes

MAKES 24

115g/4oz good-quality plain (semisweet)
   chocolate, cut into small pieces

15ml/1 tbsp water

275g/10oz/2¹/₂ cups plain (all-purpose) flour

5ml/1 tsp baking powder

2.5ml/¹/₂ tsp bicarbonate of soda
   (baking soda)

pinch of salt

300g/10oz/1¹/₂ cups caster (superfine) sugar

175g/6oz/³/₄ cup butter or margarine,
   at room temperature

150ml/¹/₄ pint/²/₃ cup milk

5ml/1 tsp vanilla extract

3 eggs

1 recipe quantity buttercream,
   flavoured to taste

1 Preheat a 180°C/350°F/Gas 4 oven.
Grease and flour 24 deep bun tins
(pans), about 6cm/2¹/₂in in diameter,
or use paper cases in the tins.

2 ▲ Put the chocolate and water
in a bowl set over a pan of almost
simmering water. Heat until melted
and smooth, stirring. Remove from
the heat and leave to cool.

3 Sift the flour, baking powder,
bicarbonate of soda, salt and sugar
into a large bowl. Add the cooled
chocolate mixture, butter, milk and
vanilla extract.

4 ▲ With an electric mixer on
medium-low speed, beat everything
together until smoothly blended.
Increase the speed to high and beat
for 2 minutes. Add the eggs and beat
again for 2 minutes.

5 Divide the mixture evenly among
the prepared bun tins.

6 Bake for 20–25 minutes or until a
skewer inserted into the centre of a
cake comes out clean. Cool in the tins
for 10 minutes, then turn out to cool
completely on a wire rack.

7 ▼ Ice the top of each cake with
buttercream, swirling it into a peak in
the centre.

Energy 228kcal/957kJ; Protein 2.5g; Carbohydrate 30.6g, of which sugars 21g; Fat 11.5g, of which saturates 3.3g; Cholesterol 33mg; Calcium 40mg; Fibre 0.5g; Sodium 95mg.

Chocolate Orange Sponge Drops

MAKES ABOUT 14

2 eggs

50g/2oz/¼ cup caster (superfine) sugar

2.5ml/½ tsp grated orange zest

50g/2oz/½ cup plain (all-purpose) flour

60ml/4 tbsp fine shred orange marmalade

40g/1½oz plain chocolate, cut into small pieces

1 Preheat a 200°C/400°F/Gas 6 oven. Line three large baking sheets with baking parchment.

2 ▲ Put the eggs and sugar in a large bowl and set over a pan of just simmering water. Whisk until the mixture is thick and pale.

3 ▲ Remove the bowl from the pan of water and continue whisking until the mixture is cool. Whisk in the grated orange zest.

4 Sift the flour over the whisked mixture and fold it in gently with a rubber spatula.

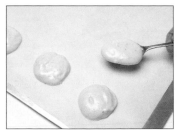

5 ▲ Using a dessertspoon, put spoonfuls of the mixture on the prepared baking sheets, leaving space around each spoonful to allow for spreading. The mixture will make 28–30 drops.

6 Bake for about 8 minutes or until golden. Cool for a few minutes on the baking sheets, then transfer to a wire rack to cool completely.

7 Sandwich pairs of sponge drops together with the orange marmalade.

8 ▼ Melt the chocolate in a double pan over simmering water until smooth. Using a small spoon, drizzle chocolate over the tops of the sponge drops, or pipe it in fine lines using a small greaseproof paper piping bag. Leave to set before serving.

Energy 73kcal/309kJ; Protein 2g; Carbohydrate 13g, of which sugars 10g; Fat 2g, of which saturates 1g; Cholesterol 33mg; Calcium 14mg; Fibre 0g; Sodium 16mg.

Iced Fancies

MAKES 16

115g/4oz/¹/₂ cup butter, at room temperature

225g/8oz/1 cup caster (superfine) sugar

2 eggs, at room temperature

175g/6oz/1¹/₂ cups plain (all-purpose) flour

1.25ml/¹/₄ tsp salt

7.5ml/1¹/₂ tsp baking powder

120ml/4fl oz/¹/₂ cup plus 15ml/1 tbsp milk

5ml/1 tsp vanilla extract

FOR ICING AND DECORATING

2 large egg whites

400g/14oz/3¹/₂ cups sifted icing (confectioners') sugar

1–2 drops glycerine

juice of 1 lemon

food colourings

hundreds and thousands, for decorating

crystallized (candied) lemon and orange slices, for decorating

1 Preheat a 190°C/375°F/Gas 5 oven.

2 ▲ Line 16 bun-tray cups with fluted paper baking cases, or grease.

~ COOK'S TIP ~

Ready-made cake decorating products are widely available, and may be used, if preferred, instead of the recipes given for icing and decorating. Coloured icing in ready-to-pipe tubes is useful.

---

3 With an electric mixer, cream the butter and sugar until light and fluffy. Add the eggs, one at a time, beating well after each addition.

4 Sift together the flour, salt and baking powder. Stir into the butter mixture, alternating with the milk. Stir in the vanilla.

5 ▲ Fill the cups half-full and bake until the tops spring back when touched lightly, about 20 minutes. Let the cakes stand in the tray for 5 minutes, then unmould and transfer to a rack to cool completely.

6 For the icing, beat the egg whites until stiff but not dry. Gradually add the sugar, glycerine and lemon juice, and continue beating for 1 minute. The consistency should be spreadable. If necessary, thin with a little water or add more sifted icing sugar.

7 ▲ Divide the icing between several bowls and tint with food colourings. Spread different coloured icings over the cooled cakes.

8 ▲ Decorate the cakes as wished, with sugar decorations such as hundreds and thousands.

9 ▲ Other decorations include crystallized orange and lemon slices. Cut into small pieces and arrange on top of the cakes. Alternatively, use other suitable sweets.

10 ▲ To make freehand iced decorations, fill paper piping bags with different colour icings. Pipe on faces, or make other designs.

Energy 259kcal/1094kJ; Protein 2.7g; Carbohydrate 49.7g, of which sugars 41.4g; Fat 6.9g, of which saturates 4g; Cholesterol 40mg; Calcium 50mg; Fibre 0.3g; Sodium 66mg.

Heart Cake

MAKES 1 CAKE

225g/8oz/1 cup butter or margarine,
   at room temperature

225g/8oz/generous 1 cup caster
   (superfine) sugar

4 eggs, at room temperature

175g/6oz/1½ cups plain (all-purpose) flour

5ml/1 tsp baking powder

2.5ml/½ tsp bicarbonate of soda
   (baking soda)

30ml/2 tbsp milk

5ml/1 tsp vanilla extract

FOR ICING AND DECORATING

3 egg whites

350g/12oz/1¾ cups caster (superfine) sugar

30ml/2 tbsp cold water

30ml/2 tbsp fresh lemon juice

1.25ml/¼ tsp cream of tartar

pink food colouring

75–120ml/5–8 tbsp icing
   (confectioners') sugar

1 Preheat a 180°C/350°F/Gas 4 oven. Line a 20cm/8in heart-shaped tin (pan) with baking parchment; grease.

2 ▲ With an electric mixer, cream the butter or margarine and sugar until light and fluffy. Add the eggs, one at a time, beating thoroughly.

3 Sift the flour, baking powder and baking soda. Fold into the butter mixture in three batches, alternating with the milk. Stir in the vanilla.

4 ▲ Spoon the mixture into the prepared tin and bake until a skewer inserted in the centre comes out clean, 35–40 minutes. Let the cake stand in the tin for 5 minutes, then unmould and transfer to a rack to cool completely.

5 For the icing, combine 2 of the egg whites, the caster sugar, water, lemon juice and cream of tartar in the top of a double boiler or in a bowl set over simmering water. With an electric mixer, beat until thick and holding soft peaks, about 7 minutes. Remove from the heat and continue beating until the mixture is thick enough to spread. Tint the icing with the pink food colouring.

6 ▲ Put the cake on a board, about 30cm/12in square, covered in foil or in paper suitable for contact with food. Spread the icing evenly on the cake. Smooth the top and sides. Leave to set for 3–4 hours, or overnight.

7 ▲ For the paper piping bags, fold a 28 × 20cm/11 × 8in sheet of grease-proof (waxed) paper in half diagonally, then cut into two pieces along the fold mark. Roll over the short side, so that it meets the right-angled corner and forms a cone. To form the piping bag, hold the cone in place with one hand, wrap the point of the long side of the triangle around the cone, and tuck inside, folding over twice to secure. Snip a hole in the pointed end and slip in a small metal piping nozzle to extend about 5mm/¼in.

8 For the piped decorations, place 15ml/1 tbsp of the remaining egg white in a bowl and whisk until frothy. Gradually beat in enough icing sugar to make a stiff mixture suitable for piping.

9 ▲ Spoon into a paper piping bag to half fill. Fold over the top and squeeze to pipe decorations on the top and sides of the cake.

Energy 3638kcal/15233kJ; Protein 53.2g; Carbohydrate 455.6g, of which sugars 301.6g; Fat 190.4g, of which saturates 40.6g; Cholesterol 783mg; Calcium 533mg; Fibre 6.3g; Sodium 2470mg.

Snake Cake

SERVES 10–12

225g/8oz/1 cup butter or margarine, at room temperature

grated rind and juice of 1 small orange

225g/8oz/generous 1 cup sugar

4 eggs, at room temperature, separated

175g/6oz/1½ cups plain (all-purpose) flour

5ml/1 tsp baking powder

pinch of salt

FOR THE ICING AND DECORATING

25g/1oz/2 tbsp butter, at room temperature

350g/12oz/3 cups icing (confectioners') sugar

150g/5oz plain (semisweet) chocolate

pinch of salt

120ml/4fl oz/½ cup sour cream

1 egg white

green and blue food colourings

1 Preheat the oven to 190°C/375°F/ Gas 5. Grease two 21cm/8½in ring tins (pans) and dust them with flour.

2 Cream the butter or margarine, orange rind and sugar until light. Beat in the egg yolks, one at a time.

3 Sift the flour and baking powder. Fold into the butter mixture, alternating with the orange juice.

4 ▲ In another bowl, beat the egg whites and salt until stiff.

5 Fold a large dollop of the egg whites into the creamed butter mixture to lighten it, then gently fold in the remaining whites.

6 Divide the mixture between the prepared tins and bake until a skewer inserted in the centre comes out clean, about 25 minutes. Leave to stand for 5 minutes, then turn out on to a wire rack to cool.

7 Prepare a board, 60 × 20cm/ 24 × 8in, covered in paper suitable for contact with food, or in foil.

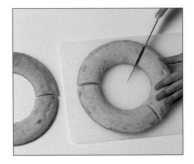

8 ▲ Cut the cakes into three even pieces. Trim to level the flat side, if necessary, and shape the head by cutting off wedges from the front. Shape the tail in the same way.

9 ▲ For the buttercream, mix the butter with 45ml/3 tbsp of the icing sugar in a small bowl until smooth. Use to join the cake sections and arrange on the board.

10 ▲ For the chocolate icing, melt the chocolate. Stir in the salt and sour cream. When cool, spread over the cake and smooth the surface.

11 ▲ For the decoration, beat the egg white until frothy. Add enough of the remaining icing sugar to obtain a thick mixture. Divide among several bowls and add food colourings.

12 ▲ Fill paper piping bags with icing and pipe decorations along the top of the cake.

Energy 478kcal/2006kJ; Protein 2g; Carbohydrate 70g, of which sugars 58g; Fat 23g, of which saturates 14g; Cholesterol 52mg; Calcium 44mg; Fibre 1g; Sodium 211mg.

Sun Cake

Serves 10–12

115g/4oz/¹/₂ cup unsalted butter
6 eggs
225g/8oz/generous 1 cup caster (superfine) sugar
115g/4oz/1 cup plain (all-purpose) flour,
2.5ml/¹/₂ tsp salt
5ml/1 tsp vanilla extract
For icing and decorating
25g/1oz/2 tbsp unsalted butter, at room temperature
450g/1lb/4 cups icing (confectioners') sugar, sifted
120ml/4fl oz/¹/₂ cup apricot jam
30ml/2 tbsp water
2 large egg whites
1–2 drops glycerine
juice of 1 lemon
yellow and orange food colourings

1 Preheat a 180°C/350°F/Gas 4 oven. Line 20 × 5cm/28 × 2in round cake tins (pans), then grease and flour.

2 Melt the butter in a pan. Skim off any foam that rises to the surface.

3 ▲ Place a heatproof bowl over a pan of hot water. Add the eggs and sugar. Beat with an electric mixer until the mixture doubles in volume and is thick enough to leave a ribbon trail when the beaters are lifted, 8–10 minutes.

4 Sift the flour and salt together three times. Sift over the egg mixture in three batches, folding in well after each addition. Fold in the melted butter and vanilla.

5 Divide the mixture between the tins. Level the surfaces and bake until the cakes shrink slightly from the sides of the tins, 25–30 minutes. Let stand 5 minutes, then unmould and transfer to a cooling rack.

6 Prepare a board, 40cm/16in square, covered in paper suitable for contact with food, or in foil.

7 ▲ For the sunbeams, cut one of the cakes into eight equal wedges. Cut away a rounded piece from the base of each so that they fit nearly up against the sides of the whole cake.

8 ▲ For the butter icing, mix the butter and 30ml/2 tbsp of the icing sugar. Use to attach the sunbeams to the central circle of cake.

9 ▲ Melt the jam with the water and brush over the cake. Place on the board and straighten, if necessary.

10 ▲ For the icing, beat the egg whites until stiff but not dry. Gradually add 400g/14oz/3¹/₂ cups icing sugar, the glycerine and lemon juice, and continue beating for 1 minute. If necessary, thin with water or thicken with a little more sugar. Tint with yellow food colouring and spread over the cake.

11 ▲ Divide the remaining icing in half and tint with more food colouring to obtain bright yellow and orange. Pipe decorative zigzags on the sunbeams and a face in the middle.

Energy 7899kcal/33176kJ; Protein 84.5g; Carbohydrate 1182g, of which sugars 918g; Fat 346.9g, of which saturates 82.6g; Cholesterol 1396mg; Calcium 1089mg; Fibre 10.8g; Sodium 4247mg.

Jack-O'-Lantern Cake

SERVES 8–10

175g/6oz/1¹/₂ cups plain (all-purpose) flour

12.5ml/2¹/₂ tsp baking powder

pinch of salt

115g/4oz/¹/₂ cup butter, at room temperature

225g/8oz/generous 1 cup caster (superfine) sugar

3 egg yolks, at room temperature, well beaten

15ml/1 tbsp grated lemon rind

175ml/6fl oz/³/₄ cup milk

FOR THE CAKE COVERING

500–700g/1¹/₄–1¹/₂lb/4²/₃–6 cups icing (confectioners') sugar

2 egg whites

30ml/2 tbsp liquid glucose

orange and black food colourings

1 Preheat the oven to 190°C/375°F/ Gas 5. Line a 20cm/8in round cake tin with baking parchment and grease.

2 Sift together the flour, baking powder and salt. Set aside.

3 With an electric mixer, cream the butter and sugar until light and fluffy. Gradually beat in the egg yolks, then add the lemon rind. Fold in the flour mixture in three batches, alternating with the milk.

4 Spoon the mixture into the prepared cake tin. Bake until a skewer inserted in the centre of the cake comes out clean, about 35 minutes. Leave to stand for 10 minutes, then turn out on to a rack.

~ COOK'S TIP ~

If preferred, use ready-made roll-out cake covering, available at cake decorating supply stores. Knead in food colouring, if required.

---

5 For the icing, sift 500g/1¹/₄lb/ 4²/₃ cups of the icing sugar into a bowl. Make a well, add 1 egg white, the glucose and orange food colouring. Stir until a dough forms.

6 ▲ Transfer to a clean work surface dusted with icing sugar and knead briefly.

7 ▲ Carefully roll out the orange cake covering to a thin sheet.

8 ▲ Place the sheet on top of the cooled cake and smooth the sides. Trim the excess icing and reserve.

9 ▲ From the trimmings, cut shapes for the top. Tint the remaining cake covering trimmings with black food colouring. Roll out thinly and cut shapes for the face.

10 ▲ Brush the undersides with water and arrange the face on top of the cake.

11 ▲ Place 15ml/1 tbsp of the remaining egg white in a bowl and stir in enough icing sugar to make a thick icing. Tint with black food colouring, fill a paper piping bag and complete the decoration.

Energy 432kcal/1828kJ; Protein 4g; Carbohydrate 83g, of which sugars 67g; Fat 12g, of which saturates 7g; Cholesterol 87mg; Calcium 67mg; Fibre 1g; Sodium 223mg.

Stars and Stripes Cake

SERVES 20

225g/8oz/1 cup butter or margarine, at room temperature

225g/8oz/generous 1 cup soft dark brown sugar

225g/8oz/generous 1 cup sugar

5 eggs, at room temperature

275g/10oz/2¹/₂ cups plain (all-purpose) flour

10ml/2 tsp baking powder

5ml/1 tsp bicarbonate of soda (baking soda)

5ml/1 tsp ground cinnamon

5ml/1 tsp ground ginger

2.5ml/¹/₂ tsp ground allspice

1.25ml/¹/₄ tsp ground cloves

1.25ml/¹/₄ tsp salt

350ml/12fl oz/1¹/₂ cups buttermilk

75g/3oz/¹/₂ cup raisins

FOR THE CAKE COVERING

25g/1oz/2 tbsp butter

1–1.3 kg/2¹/₄–3lb/9–12 cups icing (confectioners') sugar

3 egg whites

60ml/4 tbsp liquid glucose

red and blue food colourings

1 Preheat the oven to 180°C/350°F/ Gas 4. Line a 30 × 23cm/12 × 9in baking tin (pan) with baking parchment and lightly grease.

2 With an electric mixer, cream the butter or margarine and sugars until light and fluffy. Gradually beat in the eggs, one at a time, beating well after each addition.

3 Sift together the flour, baking powder, bicarbonate of soda, spices and salt. Fold into the butter mixture in three batches, alternating with the buttermilk. Stir in the raisins.

4 Pour the mixture into the tin and bake until the cake springs back when touched lightly, about 35 minutes. Leave to stand for 10 minutes, then turn out on to a wire rack.

5 Make buttercream for assembling the cake by mixing the butter with 40g/1¹/₂oz/²/₃ cup of the icing sugar.

6 ▲ When the cake is cool, cut a curved shape from the top.

7 ▲ Attach it to the bottom of the cake with the buttercream.

8 Prepare a board, about 40 × 30cm/ 16 × 12in, covered in paper suitable for contact with food, or in foil. Transfer the cake to the board.

9 For the cake covering, sift 1kg/ 2¹/₄lb/9 cups of the icing sugar into a bowl. Add 2 of the egg whites and the liquid glucose. Stir until the mixture forms a dough.

10 Cover and set aside half of the covering. On a clean work surface lightly dusted with icing sugar, roll out the remaining covering to a sheet. Carefully transfer to the cake. Smooth the sides and trim any excess from the bottom edges.

11 ▲ Tint one quarter of the remaining covering blue and tint the rest red. Roll out the blue to a thin sheet and cut out the background for the stars. Place on the cake.

12 ▲ Roll out the red covering, cut out stripes and place on the cake.

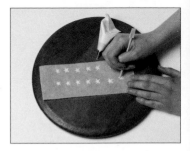

13 ▲ For the stars, mix 15ml/ 1 tbsp of the egg white with just enough icing sugar to thicken. Pipe small stars on to a sheet of greaseproof (waxed) paper and leave to set. When dry, peel them off and place on the blue background.

Energy 517kcal/2190kJ; Protein 5g; Carbohydrate 104g, of which sugars 91g; Fat 12g, of which saturates 7g; Cholesterol 85mg; Calcium 68mg; Fibre 1g; Sodium 262mg.

LOW-FAT CAKES & BAKES

ALL THE CAKES AND BAKES IN THIS
CHAPTER ARE LOW IN FAT, IN MANY
CASES CONTAIN LITTLE OR NO
EGGS, AND OFTEN SUGAR IS
REDUCED BY USING FRUITS TO
SWEETEN THE MIXTURE.
EVERYONE WILL LOVE THESE
BAKED GOODS – THEY'RE BURSTING
WITH FLAVOUR AND SUITED TO
ALL OCCASIONS.

Spiced Apple Cake

SERVES 8

225g/8oz/2 cups wholemeal self-raising (whole-wheat self-rising) flour

5ml/1 tsp baking powder

10ml/2 tsp ground cinnamon

175g/6oz/1 cup chopped dates

75g/3oz/6 tbsp light muscovado sugar

15ml/1 tbsp pear and apple spread

120ml/4fl oz/¹/₂ cup apple juice

2 eggs

90ml/6 tbsp sunflower oil

2 eating apples, cored and grated

15ml/1 tbsp chopped walnuts

1 ▲ Preheat the oven to 180°C/350°F/ Gas 4. Grease and line a deep round 20cm/8in cake tin (pan). Sift the flour, baking powder and cinnamon into a mixing bowl, then mix in the dates and make a well in the centre.

2 ▲ Mix the sugar with the pear and apple spread. Stir in the juice. Add to the dry ingredients with the eggs, oil and apples. Mix thoroughly.

3 ▲ Spoon the mixture into the prepared cake tin, sprinkle liberally with the walnuts and bake for 60–65 minutes or until a skewer inserted into the centre of the cake comes out clean. Transfer to a wire rack, remove the lining paper and leave to cool.

Energy 282kcal/1186kJ; Protein 4.9g; Carbohydrate 42.8g, of which sugars 21.3g; Fat 11.3g, of which saturates 1.5g; Cholesterol 48mg; Calcium 60mg; Fibre 1.6g; Sodium 22mg.

Spiced Date and Walnut Cake

SERVES 10

300g/11oz/2²/₃ cups wholemeal self-raising (whole-wheat self-rising) flour

10ml/2 tsp mixed (apple pie) spice

150g/5oz/scant 1 cup chopped dates

50g/2oz/¹/₃ cup chopped walnuts

60ml/4 tbsp sunflower oil

115g/4oz/¹/₂ cup muscovado (molasses) sugar

300ml/¹/₂ pint/1¹/₄ cups skimmed milk

walnut halves, to decorate

1 Preheat the oven to 180°C/350°F/ Gas 4. Grease and line a 900g/2lb loaf tin (pan) with baking parchment.

2 ▲ Sift together the flour and spice, adding back any bran from the sieve (strainer). Stir in the dates and walnuts.

~ VARIATION ~

Pecan nuts can be used in place of the walnuts in this cake.

4 ▲ Mix the oil, sugar and milk together in a jug (pitcher) or small bowl, then stir evenly into the dry ingredients. Spoon the mixture into the prepared tin.

5 ▲ Arrange the walnut halves on top. Bake the cake for about 45–50 minutes, or until golden brown and firm. Turn out the cake, remove the lining paper and leave to cool.

Energy 294kcal/1235kJ; Protein 7g; Carbohydrate 43g, of which sugars 24g; Fat 12g, of which saturates 1g; Cholesterol 1mg; Calcium 76mg; Fibre 4g; Sodium 20mg.

Greek Honey and Lemon Cake

MAKES 16 SLICES

40g/1¹/₂oz/3 tbsp sunflower margarine

60ml/4 tbsp clear honey

finely grated rind and juice of 1 lemon

150ml/¹/₄ pint/²/₃ cup skimmed milk

150g/5oz/1¹/₄ cups plain (all-purpose) flour

7.5ml/1¹/₂ tsp baking powder

2.5 ml/¹/₂ tsp grated nutmeg

50g/2oz/¹/₂ cup semolina

2 egg whites

10ml/2 tsp sesame seeds

1 Preheat the oven to 200°C/400°F/Gas 6.

1 Lightly oil a 19cm/7½in square deep cake tin (pan) and line the base with baking parchment.

2 ▲ Gently melt the margarine and 45ml/3 tbsp of the honey. Reserve 15ml/1 tbsp lemon juice, then stir in the rest with the rind and milk. Transfer to a bowl.

3 ▲ Add the flour, baking powder and nutmeg, and stir through. Gradually beat the semolina into the mixture. Whisk the egg whites until soft peaks form, then fold them in.

4 ▲ Spoon into the tin and sprinkle with sesame seeds. Bake the cake for 25–30 minutes, until golden brown. Mix together the reserved honey and lemon juice and drizzle over the cake while warm. Cool in the tin, then cut into fingers to serve.

Energy 1307kcal/5510kJ; Protein 32.4g; Carbohydrate 208.7g, of which sugars 55.6g; Fat 43.8g, of which saturates 9.2g; Cholesterol 12mg; Calcium 474mg; Fibre 6.5g; Sodium 525mg.

Cranberry and Apple Ring

SERVES 8

225g/8oz/2 cups self-raising (self-rising) flour

5ml/1 tsp ground cinnamon

75g/3oz/6 tbsp light muscovado sugar

1 crisp eating apple, cored and diced

75g/3oz/³/₄ cup fresh or frozen cranberries

60ml/4 tbsp sunflower oil

150ml/¹/₄ pint/²/₃ cup apple juice

cranberry jelly and apple slices, to decorate

1 ▲ Preheat the oven to 180°C/ 350°F/Gas 4. Lightly grease a 1 litre/ 1¾ pint/4 cup ring mould with oil.

2 Sift together the flour and ground cinnamon, then stir in the sugar.

3 ▲ Toss together the diced apple and cranberries in a large bowl. Stir into the dry ingredients, then add the oil and apple juice and beat well.

4 ▲ Spoon the mixture into the prepared ring mould and bake for about 35–40 minutes, or until the cake is firm to the touch. Turn out and leave to cool completely.

5 To serve, drizzle warmed cranberry jelly over the cake and decorate with apple slices.

Energy 1565kcal/6610kJ; Protein 22.1g; Carbohydrate 280.7g, of which sugars 109.2g; Fat 47.2g, of which saturates 5.7g; Cholesterol 0mg; Calcium 371mg; Fibre 9.2g; Sodium 17mg.

Lemon Chiffon Cake

SERVES 8

2 eggs

75g/3oz/6 tbsp caster (superfine) sugar

grated rind of 1 lemon

50g/2oz/¹/₂ cup plain (all-purpose) flour, sifted

lemon shreds, to decorate

FOR THE FILLING

2 eggs, separated

75g/3oz/6 tbsp caster (superfine) sugar

grated rind and juice of 1 lemon

30ml/2 tbsp water

15ml/1 tbsp gelatine

125ml/4fl oz/¹/₂ cup low fat fromage frais or ricotta cheese

FOR THE ICING

15ml/1 tbsp lemon juice

115g/4oz/scant 1 cup icing (confectioners') sugar, sifted

1 ▲ Preheat the oven to 180°C/350°F/Gas 4. Grease and line a 20cm/8in loose-bottomed cake tin (pan). Whisk the eggs, sugar and lemon rind together until mousse-like. Gently fold in the flour, then turn the mixture into the tin.

2 Bake for 20–25 minutes until the cake springs back when lightly pressed in the centre. Turn on to a wire rack.

3 ▲ Once cold, split the cake in half horizontally and return the lower half to the clean cake tin.

4 ▲ Make the filling. Put the egg yolks, sugar, lemon rind and juice in a bowl. Beat with a hand-held electric whisk until thick, pale and creamy.

5 ▲ Pour the water into a heatproof bowl and sprinkle the gelatine on top. Leave until spongy, then stir over simmering water until dissolved. Cool, then whisk into the yolk mixture. Fold in the fromage frais. When the mixture begins to set, whisk the egg whites to soft peaks. Carefully the egg whites into the mousse mixture.

6 ▲ Pour the lemon mousse over the sponge in the cake tin, spreading it to the edges. Set the second layer of sponge on top and chill until set.

7 Slide a palette knife or metal spatula dipped in hot water between the tin and the cake to loosen it. Transfer to a plate.

8 ▲ To make icing, add enough lemon juice to the icing sugar to make a mixture thick enough to coat the back of a wooden spoon. Pour over the cake. Decorate with lemon shreds.

~ COOK'S TIP ~

The mousse should be just setting when the egg whites are added. Speed up this process by placing the bowl of mousse in iced water.

Energy 356kcal/1491kJ; Protein 6.7g; Carbohydrate 43.6g, of which sugars 29.8g; Fat 18.4g, of which saturates 4g; Cholesterol 118mg; Calcium 68mg; Fibre 0.6g; Sodium 227mg.

Strawberry Gâteau

SERVES 6

2 eggs

75g/3oz/6 tbsp caster (superfine) sugar

grated rind of ¹/₂ orange

50g/2oz/¹/₂ cup plain (all-purpose) flour

strawberry leaves, to decorate (optional)

icing (confectioners') sugar,
    for dusting

FOR THE FILLING

275g/10oz/1¹/₃ cups low-fat soft cheese

grated rind of ¹/₂ orange

30ml/2 tbsp caster (superfine) sugar

60ml/4 tbsp low-fat fromage frais

225g/8oz strawberries, halved

25g/1oz/¹/₄ cup chopped
    almonds, toasted

1 ▲ Preheat the oven to 190°C/
375°F/Gas 5. Grease a 30 × 20cm/
12 × 8in Swiss roll tin (jelly roll
pan) and line the tin with
baking parchment.

2 ▲ In a bowl, whisk the eggs, sugar
and orange rind together with a
hand-held electric whisk until thick
and mousse-like (when the whisk is
lifted, a trail should remain on the
surface of the mixture for 15 seconds).

3 ▲ Fold in the flour. Turn into the
prepared tin. Bake for 15–20 minutes,
or until the cake springs back when
lightly pressed. Turn on to a wire rack,
remove the paper and leave to cool.

4 ▲ Make the filling. Mix the soft
cheese with the orange rind, sugar
and fromage frais until smooth.

5 Divide the icing between two
bowls. Chop half of the strawberry
halves and add to one bowl of filling.

6 ▲ Cut the sponge widthways into
three equal pieces and sandwich
them together with the strawberry
filling. Spread two-thirds of the
plain filling over the sides of the
cake and press on the almonds.

7 ▲ Spread the rest of the filling
over the top of the cake and decorate
with strawberry halves, and strawberry
leaves, if liked. Dust with icing sugar
and transfer to a serving plate.

~ VARIATION ~
Use other soft fruits in season,
such as currants, raspberries,
blackberries or blueberries, or try
a mixture of different berries.

Energy 305kcal/1288kJ; Protein 25.6g; Carbohydrate 35.7g, of which sugars 22.4g; Fat 7.6g, of which saturates 1.1g; Cholesterol 64mg; Calcium 163mg; Fibre 7.2g; Sodium 37mg.

Tia Maria Gâteau

SERVES 8

75g/3oz/³/4 cup plain (all-purpose) flour

30ml/2 tbsp instant coffee powder

3 eggs

115g/4oz/¹/2 cup caster (superfine) sugar

coffee beans, to decorate (optional)

FOR THE FILLING

175g/6oz/³/4 cup low-fat soft cheese

15ml/1 tbsp clear honey

15ml/1 tbsp Tia Maria liqueur

50g/2oz/¹/4 cup preserved stem ginger,
   roughly chopped

FOR THE ICING

225g/8oz/1³/4 cups icing (confectioners')
   sugar, sifted

10ml/2 tsp coffee extract

15ml/1 tbsp water

5ml/1 tsp reduced-fat unsweetened
   cocoa powder

1 ▲ Preheat the oven to 190°C/
375°F/Gas 5. Grease a 20cm/8in
deep round cake tin (pan) and line
with baking parchment. Sift the flour
and coffee powder together on to a
sheet of baking parchment.

~ COOK'S TIP ~

When folding in the flour mixture,
be careful not to knock out the
air, as it helps the cake to rise.

2 ▲ Whisk the eggs and sugar in a
bowl with a hand-held electric whisk
until thick and mousse-like (when
the whisk is lifted, a trail should
remain on the surface of the mixture
for at least 15 seconds).

3 ▲ Gently fold in the flour
mixture with a metal spoon. Turn
the batter into the prepared tin.
Bake the sponge for 30–35 minutes
or until it springs back when lightly
pressed. Turn on to a wire rack to
cool completely.

4 ▲ To make the filling, mix the soft
cheese with the honey in a bowl.
Beat until smooth, then stir in the
Tia Maria and chopped stem ginger.

5 ▲ Split the cake in half horizontally and sandwich the two halves
together with the Tia Maria filling.

6 Make the icing. In a bowl, mix the
icing sugar and coffee extract with
enough of the water to make a
consistency that will coat the back of
a wooden spoon. Pour three-quarters
of the icing over the cake, spreading
it evenly to the edges.

7 Stir the cocoa into the remaining
icing until smooth. Spoon into a
piping bag fitted with a writing
nozzle and pipe the mocha icing
over the coffee icing. Decorate with
coffee beans, if liked.

Energy 247kcal/1050kJ; Protein 4.9g; Carbohydrate 54.7g, of which sugars 47.4g; Fat 2.5g, of which saturates 1.5g; Cholesterol 12mg; Calcium 65mg; Fibre 0.5g; Sodium 120mg.

Chocolate Banana Cake

SERVES 8

225g/8oz/2 cups self-raising (self-rising) flour

45ml/3 tbsp reduced-fat unsweetened cocoa powder

115g/4oz/scant ¾ cup light muscovado sugar

30ml/2 tbsp malt extract

30ml/2 tbsp golden (light corn) syrup

2 eggs

60ml/4 tbsp skimmed milk

60ml/4 tbsp sunflower oil

2 large ripe bananas

FOR THE ICING

225g/8oz/2 cups icing (confectioners') sugar, sifted

35ml/7 tsp reduced-fat unsweetened cocoa powder, sifted

15–30ml/1–2 tbsp warm water

1 ▲ Preheat the oven to 160°C/ 325°F/Gas 3. Grease and line a deep round 20cm/8in cake tin (pan).

2 ▲ Sift the flour into a mixing bowl with the cocoa. Stir in the sugar.

3 ▲ Make a well in the centre and add the malt extract, golden syrup, eggs, milk and oil. Mash the bananas thoroughly and stir them into the mixture until well combined.

4 ▲ Pour the cake mixture into the prepared tin and bake for 1–1¼ hours or until the centre of the cake springs back when lightly pressed.

5 ▲ Remove the cake from the tin, remove the lining paper and leave on a wire rack to cool.

6 ▲ Reserve 45ml/3 tbsp icing sugar and 5ml/1 tsp cocoa powder. Make a dark icing by beating the remaining sugar and cocoa powder with enough of the warm water to make a thick icing. Pour it over the cake and spread evenly.

7 Make a light icing by mixing the remaining icing sugar and cocoa powder with a few drops of water. Drizzle this icing across the top of the cake.

Energy 352kcal/1487kJ; Protein 6.5g; Carbohydrate 64.4g, of which sugars 41.9g; Fat 9.4g, of which saturates 2.3g; Cholesterol 48mg; Calcium 145mg; Fibre 2.3g; Sodium 233mg.

Chocolate and Orange Angel Cake

SERVES 10

25g/1oz/¼ cup plain (all-purpose) flour

15g/½oz/2 tbsp reduced-fat unsweetened cocoa powder

15g/½oz/2 tbsp cornflour (cornstarch)

pinch of salt

5 egg whites

2.5ml/½ tsp cream of tartar

115g/4oz/scant ½ cup caster (superfine) sugar

blanched and shredded rind of 1 orange, to decorate

FOR THE ICING

200g/7oz/1 cup caster (superfine) sugar

1 egg white

1 ▲ Preheat the oven to 180°C/350°F/Gas 4. Sift the flour, cocoa powder, cornflour and salt together three times. Beat the egg whites in a large clean, dry bowl until foamy. Add the cream of tartar, then whisk.

2 ▲ Add the caster sugar to the egg whites a spoonful at a time, whisking after each addition. Sift a third of the flour and cocoa mixture over the meringue and gently fold in. Repeat, sifting and folding in the flour and cocoa mixture two more times.

3 ▲ Spoon the mixture into a non-stick 20cm/8in ring mould and level the top. Bake for 35 minutes or until springy to the touch. Turn upside down on to a wire rack and leave to cool in the mould. Carefully ease out of the mould.

4 ▲ For the icing, mix the sugar with 75ml/5 tbsp cold water. Stir over a low heat until dissolved. Boil until the syrup reaches 120°C/250°F on a sugar thermometer or when a drop of the syrup makes a soft ball when dripped into cold water. Remove from the heat.

5 ▲ Whisk the egg white until stiff. Add the syrup in a thin stream, whisking all the time. Continue to whisk until the mixture is very thick.

~ COOK'S TIP ~

Make sure you do not over-beat the egg whites. They should not be stiff but should form soft peaks, so that the air bubbles can expand further during cooking and help the cake to rise.

6 ▲ Spread the icing over the top and sides of the cooled cake with a palette knife or metal spala. Sprinkle the orange rind over the top of the cake and serve.

Energy 1495kcal/6373kJ; Protein 24.1g; Carbohydrate 364.1g, of which sugars 329.6g; Fat 3.7g, of which saturates 2g; Cholesterol 0mg; Calcium 233mg; Fibre 2.6g; Sodium 535mg.

Eggless Christmas Cake

3 ▲ Lightly grease and line an 18cm/ 7in square cake tin (pan).

4 ▲ Add the hazelnuts, pumpkin seeds, ginger and lemon rind to the fruit. Stir in the milk, oil, sifted flour and spice, and the brandy or rum.

SERVES 12

75g/3oz/¹/₂ cup sultanas (golden raisins)

75g/3oz/¹/₂ cup raisins

75g/3oz/¹/₂ cup currants

75g/3oz/¹/₃ cup glacé (candied) cherries, halved

50g/2oz/¹/₃ cup cut mixed (candied) peel

250ml/8fl oz/1 cup apple juice

25g/1oz/¹/₄ cup toasted hazelnuts

30ml/2 tbsp pumpkin seeds

2 pieces preserved stem ginger, chopped

finely grated rind of 1 lemon

120ml/4fl oz/¹/₂ cup skimmed milk

50ml/2fl oz/¹/₄ cup sunflower oil

225g/8oz/2 cups wholemeal self-raising (whole-wheat self-rising) flour

10ml/2 tsp mixed (apple pie) spice

45ml/3 tbsp brandy or dark rum

apricot jam, for brushing

glacé (candied) fruits, to decorate

1 ▲ Place the sultanas, raisins, currants, halved cherries and mixed peel in a bowl and stir in the apple juice. Cover the fruit and leave to soak overnight.

2 Preheat the oven to 150°C/300°F/ Gas 2.

5 ▲ Spoon into the tin and bake for 1½ hours, or until golden brown and firm to the touch. Turn out and cool. Brush with sieved apricot jam and decorate with glacé fruits, if desired.

Energy 2366kcal/9987kJ; Protein 44.8g; Carbohydrate 393.4g, of which sugars 253.8g; Fat 68.1g, of which saturates 8.6g; Cholesterol 7mg; Calcium 628mg; Fibre 30.3g; Sodium 291mg.

Fruit and Nut Cake

SERVES 12–14

175g/6oz/1½ cups wholemeal self-raising (whole-wheat self-rising) flour

175g/6oz/1½ cups white self-raising (self-rising) flour

10ml/2 tsp mixed (apple pie) spice

15ml/1 tbsp apple and apricot spread

45ml/3 tbsp clear honey

15ml/1 tbsp molasses

90ml/6 tbsp sunflower oil

175ml/6fl oz/¾ cup orange juice

2 eggs, beaten

675g/1½lb/3 cups mixed dried fruit

45ml/3 tbsp split almonds

50g/2oz/4 tbsp glacé (candied) cherries

3 ▲ Put the apple and apricot spread in a small bowl. Gradually stir in the honey and molasses. Add to the dry ingredients with the oil, orange juice, eggs and dried fruit and mix.

4 ▲ Turn the mixture into the prepared tin and smooth the surface. Halve the cherries and arrange with the almonds in a pattern over the top. Bake for 2 hours or until a skewer comes out clean. Transfer to a wire rack until cold, then lift out of the tin and remove the paper.

1 ▲ Preheat the oven to 160°C/ 325°F/Gas 3. Grease and line a deep round 20cm/8in cake tin (pan). Tie brown paper around the outside.

2 ▲ Sift the flours with the mixed spice. Make a well in the centre.

Energy 327kcal/1384kJ; Protein 5.2g; Carbohydrate 63g, of which sugars 43.8g; Fat 7.8g, of which saturates 1g; Cholesterol 27mg; Calcium 94mg; Fibre 2.2g; Sodium 40mg.

Banana Ginger Parkin

SERVES 12

200g/7oz/1¾ cups plain (all-purpose) flour

10ml/2 tsp bicarbonate of soda (baking soda)

10ml/2 tsp ground ginger

150g/5oz/1¼ cups medium oatmeal

60ml/4 tbsp muscovado (molasses) sugar

75g/3oz/6 tbsp sunflower margarine

150g/5oz/generous ⅓ cup golden (light corn) syrup

1 egg, beaten

3 ripe bananas, mashed

75g/3oz/¾ cup icing (confectioners') sugar

stem ginger, to decorate (optional)

1 Preheat the oven to 160°C/325°F/ Gas 3. Grease and line a 18 × 28cm/ 7 × 11in cake tin (pan).

2 ▲ Sift together the flour, bicarbonate of soda and ginger, then stir in the oatmeal. Melt the sugar, margarine and syrup in a pan, then stir into the flour mixture. Beat in the egg and mashed bananas.

3 ▲ Spoon into the tin and bake for about 1 hour, or until firm to the touch. Allow to cool in the tin, then turn out and cut into squares.

4 ▲ Sift the icing sugar into a bowl and stir in just enough water to make a smooth, runny icing. Drizzle the icing over each square and top with a piece of stem ginger, if desired.

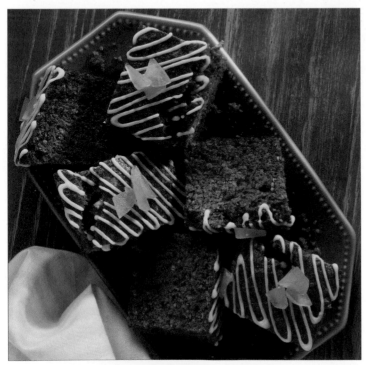

~ COOK'S TIP ~

This is a nutritious, energy-giving cake that is a really good choice for packed lunches as it doesn't break up too easily.

Energy 157kcal/662kJ; Protein 2.4g; Carbohydrate 29.2g, of which sugars 15.8g; Fat 4.2g, of which saturates 0.7g; Cholesterol 10mg; Calcium 25mg; Fibre 1g; Sodium 57mg.

Nectarine Amaretto Cake

SERVES 8

3 eggs, separated

175g/6oz/scant 1 cup caster (superfine) sugar

grated rind and juice of 1 lemon

50g/2oz/¹/₂ cup semolina

40g/1oz/¹/₄ cup ground almonds

25g/1oz/¹/₄ cup plain (all-purpose) flour

2 nectarines, halved and stoned (pitted)

60ml/4 tbsp apricot glaze

FOR THE SYRUP

75g/3oz/6 tbsp caster (superfine) sugar

90ml/6 tbsp water

30ml/2 tbsp Amaretto liqueur

1 ▲ Preheat the oven to 180°C/ 350°F/Gas 4. Grease a 20cm/8in round, loose-bottomed cake tin (pan). Whisk the egg yolks, sugar, lemon rind and juice until tthick and creamy.

2 Fold in the semolina, almonds and flour until smooth.

3 Whisk the egg whites in a bowl until fairly stiff.

4 ▲ Using a metal spoon, stir some of the whites into the semolina mixture, then fold in the rest.

5 Spoon the mixture into the cake tin. Bake for 30–35 minutes until the centre of the cake springs back when pressed lightly. Loosen around the edge. Prick the top with a skewer. Leave to cool in the tin.

6 To make the syrup, heat the sugar and water in a pan, stirring until the sugar is dissolved. Boil without stirring for 2 minutes. Add the Amaretto and drizzle over the cake.

7 ▲ Remove the cake from the tin and transfer to a serving plate. Decorate with sliced nectarines. Brush with warm apricot glaze.

Energy 223kcal/946kJ; Protein 5g; Carbohydrate 42g, of which sugars 35g; Fat 4g, of which saturates 1g; Cholesterol 87mg; Calcium 33mg; Fibre 2g; Sodium 36mg.

Banana and Gingerbread Slices

SERVES 20

275g/10oz/2 cups plain (all-purpose) flour

20ml/4 tsp ground ginger

10ml/2 tsp mixed (apple pie) spice

5ml/1 tsp bicarbonate of soda (baking soda)

115g/4oz/½ cup soft light brown sugar

60ml/4 tbsp sunflower oil

30ml/2 tbsp black treacle (molasses)

30ml/2 tbsp malt extract

2 eggs

60ml/4 tbsp orange juice

3 bananas

115g/4oz/⅔ cup raisins

1 ▲ Preheat the oven to 180°C/350°F/ Gas 4. Grease and line an 18 × 28cm/ 7 × 11in baking tin (pan).

2 ▲ Put the sugar in a bowl. Sift in the flour, spices and bicarbonate of soda.

3 ▲ Make a well in the centre. Mix in the oil, black treacle, malt extract, eggs and orange juice.

4 ▲ Mash the bananas, then add them to the bowl with the raisins and mix together well.

5 ▲ Pour the mixture into the prepared baking tin.

6 Bake for about 35–40 minutes, or until the centre springs back when lightly pressed. Remove from the oven and leave the cake in the tin to cool for 5 minutes

7 ▲ Turn out the cake on to a wire rack, remove the lining paper and leave to cool completely. Cut into 20 slices with a sharp knife.

~ VARIATION ~

To make Spiced Honey and Banana Cake: omit the ground ginger and add another 5ml/1 tsp mixed (apple pie) spice; omit the malt extract and treacle and add 60ml/4 tbsp strong-flavoured clear honey instead; and replace the raisins with either sultanas (golden raisins) or coarsely chopped ready-to-eat dried apricots, or semi-dried pineapple. If you choose to use pineapple, then you could also replace the orange juice with fresh pineapple juice.

~ COOK'S TIP ~

This cake improves as it keeps, so store it for a few days before eating.

Energy 147kcal/619kJ; Protein 2g; Carbohydrate 27g, of which sugars 16g; Fat 4g, of which saturates 1g; Cholesterol 23mg; Calcium 39mg; Fibre 1g; Sodium 71mg.

Apricot and Orange Roulade

3 Fold in the flour, orange rind and juice. Spoon the mixture into the prepared tin and spread it evenly.

4 Bake for about 15–18 minutes, or until the sponge is firm and light golden in colour. Turn out on to a sheet of baking parchment and roll it up Swiss roll-style loosely from one short side. Leave to cool.

5 ▲ For the filling, roughly chop the apricots, and place them in a pan with the orange juice. Cover the pan and leave the fruit to simmer until most of the liquid has been absorbed. Purée the apricots.

SERVES 6

4 egg whites

115g/4oz/generous 1/2 cup golden caster (superfine) sugar

50g/2oz/1/2 cup plain (all-purpose) flour

finely grated rind of 1 small orange

45ml/3 tbsp orange juice

10ml/2 tsp icing (confectioners') sugar and shreds of orange rind, to decorate

FOR THE FILLING

115g/4oz/1/2 cup ready-to-eat dried apricots

150ml/1/4 pint/2/3 cup orange juice

1 Preheat the oven to 200°C/400°F/ Gas 6. Grease a 23 × 33cm/9 × 13in Swiss roll tin (jelly roll pan) and line with baking parchment. Grease.

2 ▲ For the roulade, place the egg whites in a large bowl and whisk them until they hold peaks. Gradually add the sugar, whisking hard between each addition.

6 ▲ Unroll the roulade and spread the inside with the apricot mixture. Roll up the sponge tightly, then arrange strips of paper diagonally across the top. Sprinkle the surface of the roulade lightly with icing sugar, remove the paper and scatter with orange zest to serve.

Energy 1145kcal/4878kJ; Protein 29.1g; Carbohydrate 270.4g, of which sugars 232.3g; Fat 1.5g, of which saturates 0.1g; Cholesterol 0mg; Calcium 271mg; Fibre 9g; Sodium 427mg.

Strawberry Roulade

SERVES 6

4 egg whites

115g/4oz/scant ³/₄ cup golden caster
(superfine) sugar, plus extra
for sprinkling

75g/3oz/²/₃ cup plain (all-purpose) flour

30ml/2 tbsp orange juice

115g/4oz strawberries, chopped

150ml/¹/₄ pint/²/₃ cup low-fat
fromage frais

strawberries, to decorate

6 Unroll and remove the paper. Stir
the strawberries into the fromage
frais and spread over the sponge.
Re-roll and serve immediately
decorated with strawberries.

5 ▲ Roll up the sponge loosely from
one short side, with the paper inside.
Leave to cool.

1 Preheat the oven to 200°C/400°F/
Gas 6. Oil a 23 × 33 cm/9 × 13in
Swiss roll tin (jelly roll pan) and line
with non-stick baking parchment.

2 ▲ Place the egg whites in a large,
scrupulously clean bowl and whisk
until they form soft peaks. Gradually
whisk in the sugar. Fold in half of the
flour, then fold in the rest with the
orange juice.

3 Spoon the mixture into the
prepared tin, spreading it evenly
without removing too much air. Bake
for 15–18 minutes, or until golden
brown and firm to the touch.

4 Meanwhile, spread out a sheet of
non-stick baking parchment and
sprinkle with caster sugar. Turn out
the cake on to this and remove the
lining paper.

Energy 72kcal/305kJ; Protein 5g; Carbohydrate 13g, of which sugars 3g; Fat 0g, of which saturates 0g; Cholesterol 0mg; Calcium 44mg; Fibre 1g; Sodium 51mg.

Peach Swiss Roll

SERVES 6–8

3 eggs

115g/4oz/scant ³/4 cup caster (superfine) sugar, plus extra for sprinkling

75g/3oz/²/3 cup plain (all-purpose) flour, sifted

15ml/1 tbsp boiling water

90ml/6 tbsp peach jam

icing (confectioners') sugar, for dusting (optional)

1 Preheat the oven to 200°C/400°F/ Gas 6. Grease a 30 × 20cm/12 × 8in Swiss roll tin (jelly roll pan) and line with non-stick baking parchment.

2 ▲ Combine the eggs and sugar in a bowl. Beat with an electric whisk until thick and mousse-like (when the whisk is lifted, a trail should remain on the surface of the mixture for 15 seconds).

3 ▲ Carefully fold in the flour with a large metal spoon, then add the boiling water in the same way.

4 ▲ Spoon into the prepared tin, spread evenly to the edges and bake for about 10–12 minutes until the cake springs back when lightly pressed in the centre.

5 ▲ Spread a sheet of baking parchment on a flat surface, sprinkle it generously with caster sugar, then carefully invert the cake on top. Peel off the paper.

6 ▲ Neatly trim the edges of the cake. Make a cut two-thirds of the way through the cake, about 1cm/¹/2in from the short edge nearest you.

7 ▲ Spread the cake with the peach jam and roll up quickly from the partially cut end. Hold in position for a minute, making sure the join is underneath. Cool on a wire rack.

8 Decorate with piped glacé icing (see Cook's Tip) or dust with icing sugar before serving.

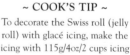

~ COOK'S TIP ~

To decorate the Swiss roll (jelly roll) with glacé icing, make the icing with 115g/4oz/2 cups icing (confectioners') sugar and enough warm water to make a thin glacé icing. Put in a piping bag fitted with a small writing nozzle and pipe lines over the top.

Energy 146kcal/618kJ; Protein 3.4g; Carbohydrate 30.1g, of which sugars 22.9g; Fat 2.2g, of which saturates 0.6g; Cholesterol 71mg; Calcium 33mg; Fibre 0.3g; Sodium 31mg.

Chestnut and Orange Roulade

SERVES 8

3 eggs, separated

115g/4oz/scant ¾ cup caster
(superfine) sugar

225g/8oz canned unsweetened
chestnut purée

grated rind and juice of 1 orange

icing (confectioners') sugar,
for dusting

FOR THE FILLING

225g/8oz/1 cup low-fat soft cheese

15ml/1 tbsp clear honey

1 orange

1 Preheat the oven to 180°C/350°/
Gas 4. Grease a 30 ×20cm/12 × 8in
Swiss roll tin (jelly roll pan) and line
with non-stick baking parchment.

2 ▲ Whisk the egg yolks and sugar
in a bowl until thick.

~ COOK'S TIP ~

Do not whisk the egg whites too
stiffly or it will be difficult to fold
them into the mixture and they
will form lumps in the roulade.

3 ▲ Put the chestnut purée in a
separate bowl. Whisk in the orange
rind and juice, then whisk the
chestnut purée into the egg mixture.

4 ▲ Whisk the egg whites in a
grease-free bowl until fairly stiff.
Using a metal spoon, stir a generous
spoonful of the whites into the
chestnut mixture to lighten it, then
fold in the rest.

5 Spoon into the prepared tin and
bake for 30 minutes until firm.
Cool for 5 minutes, then cover
with a clean damp tea towel until
completely cold.

6 ▲ Meanwhile, make the filling.
Mix the soft cheese with the honey.
Add the orange rind, finely grated.
Peel away all the pith from the
orange, cut the fruit into segments,
chop roughly and set aside. Add any
juice to the cheese mixture, then
beat until smooth. Mix in the orange.

7 ▲ Dust a sheet of non-stick baking
parchment thickly with icing sugar.
Carefully turn the roulade out on to
the paper, then peel off the lining
paper. Spread the filling over the
roulade and roll up like a Swiss roll.
Transfer to a plate and dust with
some more icing sugar.

Energy 176kcal/741kJ; Protein 7.2g; Carbohydrate 28.1g, of which sugars 19.9g; Fat 5.1g, of which saturates 2.2g; Cholesterol 78mg; Calcium 64mg; Fibre 1.1g; Sodium 154mg.

Chocolate, Date and Walnut Pudding

3 ▲ Separate the eggs and place the yolks in a bowl with the vanilla extract and sugar. Place the bowl over a pan of hot water and whisk until the mixture is thick and pale.

4 ▲ Sift the flour and cocoa into the mixture and fold them in with a metal spoon. Stir in the milk. Whisk the egg whites until they hold soft peaks and fold them in.

SERVES 4

30ml/2 tbsp chopped walnuts
30ml/2 tbsp chopped dates
2 eggs
5ml/1 tsp vanilla extract
30ml/2 tbsp golden caster (superfine) sugar
45ml/3 tbsp plain (all-purpose) flour
15ml/1 tbsp unsweetened cocoa powder
30ml/2 tbsp skimmed milk

1 ▲ Preheat the oven to 180°C/350°F/Gas 4.

2 ▲ Grease a 1.2 litre/2 pint/5 cup heatproof bowl and place a small circle of baking parchment in the base. Spoon in the walnuts and dates.

5 ▲ Spoon into the bowl and bake for 40–45 minutes, until risen and firm to the touch. Run a knife around the pudding, turn it out and serve.

Energy 192kcal/809kJ; Protein 7g; Carbohydrate 24g, of which sugars 13g; Fat 8g, of which saturates 2g; Cholesterol 116mg; Calcium 60mg; Fibre 1g; Sodium 62mg.

Feather-light Peach Pudding

SERVES 4

400g/14oz canned peach slices

50g/2oz/¹/₄ cup low-fat spread

40g/1¹/₂oz/3 tbsp soft light brown sugar

1 egg, beaten

50g/2oz/¹/₂ cup wholemeal plain
(whole-wheat all-purpose) flour

50g/2oz/¹/₂ cup plain (all-purpose) flour

5ml/1 tsp baking powder

2.5ml/¹/₂ tsp ground cinnamon

60ml/4 tbsp skimmed milk

2.5ml/¹/₂ tsp vanilla extract

10ml/2 tsp icing (confectioners') sugar

3 ▲ Spoon the sponge mixture over the peaches and level the top evenly. Cook in the oven for 35–40 minutes, or until springy to the touch.

4 ▲ Lightly dust the top with icing sugar before serving hot with custard.

> **~ COOK'S TIP ~**
>
> For a simple sauce, blend 5ml/
> 1 tsp arrowroot with 15ml/1 tbsp
> peach juice in a small pan. Stir in
> the remaining peach juice from the
> can and simmer for 1 minute.

1 ▲ Preheat the oven to 180°C/
350°F/Gas 4. Drain the peaches and
put into a 1 litre/1¾ pint/4 cup dish
with 30ml/2 tbsp of the juice.

2 ▲ Put all the remaining ingredients,
except the icing sugar into a mixing
bowl. Beat for 3–4 minutes, until
thoroughly combined.

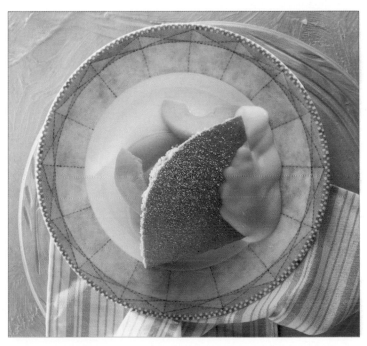

Energy 239kcal/1008kJ; Protein 7g; Carbohydrate 40g, of which sugars 22g; Fat 7g, of which saturates 2g; Cholesterol 59mg; Calcium 75mg; Fibre 2g; Sodium 243mg.

Snowballs

MAKES ABOUT 20

2 egg whites

115g/4oz/scant ³/4 cup caster
   (superfine) sugar

15ml/1 tbsp cornflour
   (cornstarch), sifted

5ml/1 tsp white wine vinegar

1.25ml/¹/4 tsp vanilla extract

1 ▲ Preheat the oven to 150°C/
300°F/Gas 2. Line two baking sheets
with non-stick baking parchment.
Whisk the egg whites in a grease-free
bowl until stiff, using an electric whisk.

2 ▲ Add the sugar, whisking until
the meringue is very stiff. Whisk in the
cornflour, vinegar and vanilla.

3 ▲ Drop teaspoonfuls of the
meringue mixture on to the baking
sheets, shaping them into mounds.
Place in the preheated oven and
bake for 30 minutes until crisp.

4 ▲ Remove from the oven and
leave the meringues to cool on the
baking sheet. When the snowballs
are cold, remove them from the baking parchment with a palette knife or
metal spatula.

Energy 26kcal/113kJ; Protein 0.3g; Carbohydrate 6.7g, of which sugars 6g; Fat 0g, of which saturates 0g; Cholesterol 0mg; Calcium 3mg; Fibre 0g; Sodium 7mg.

Muscovado Meringues

MAKES ABOUT 20

115g/4oz/scant ¾ cup light
  muscovado sugar

2 egg whites

5ml/1 tsp finely chopped walnuts

1 ▲ Preheat the oven to 160°C/
325°F/Gas 3. Line two baking sheets
with non-stick baking parchment.
Press the muscovado sugar through
a metal sieve (strainer).

2 ▲ Whisk the egg whites in a
clean, dry bowl, until very stiff and
dry, then whisk in the sugar, about
15ml/1 tbsp at a time, until the
meringue is very thick and glossy.

3 ▲ Drop teaspoonfuls of the
meringue mixture on to the baking
sheets, shaping them into mounds
with your finger.

4 ▲ Sprinkle the meringues with the
chopped walnuts. Bake for 30 minutes.
Cool for 5 minutes on the baking
sheets, then leave on a wire rack.

Energy 23kcal/97kJ; Protein 0g; Carbohydrate 6g, of which sugars 6g; Fat 0g, of which saturates 0g; Cholesterol 0mg; Calcium 3mg; Fibre 0g; Sodium 8mg.

Coffee Sponge Drops

MAKES 12

50g/2oz/¹/₂ cup plain (all-purpose) flour

15ml/1 tbsp instant coffee powder

2 eggs

75g/3oz/6 tbsp caster (superfine) sugar

FOR THE FILLING

115g/4oz/¹/₂ cup low-fat soft cheese

45ml/3 tbsp chopped preserved
    stem ginger

~ VARIATION ~

As an alternative to preserved
stem ginger in the filling, try the
same amount of very finely
chopped walnuts.

1 ▲ Preheat the oven to 190°C/
375°F/Gas 5. Line two baking sheets
with non-stick baking parchment.
Beat the soft cheese and stem ginger
together. Chill until required. Sift
the flour and coffee powder together.

3 ▲ Carefully add the sifted flour
and coffee mixture to the whisked
egg whites and gently fold in with a
metal spoon, being careful not to
knock out any air.

2 ▲ Combine the eggs and caster
sugar in a clean, grease-free bowl.
Beat with a hand-held electric whisk
until thick and mousse-like. (When
the whisk is lifted, a trail should
remain on the surface of the mixture
for at least 15 seconds.)

4 ▲ Spoon the mixture into a piping
bag fitted with a 1cm/¹/₂in plain
nozzle. Pipe 4cm/1¹/₂in rounds on the
baking sheets. Bake for 12 minutes.
Cool on a wire rack, then sandwich
together with the filling.

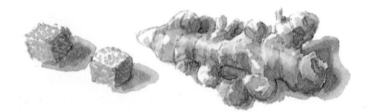

Energy 33kcal/138kJ; Protein 1.5g; Carbohydrate 5.2g, of which sugars 3.6g; Fat 0.9g, of which saturates 0.4g; Cholesterol 17mg; Calcium 13mg; Fibre 0.1g; Sodium 27mg.

Raspberry Vacherin

SERVES 6

3 egg whites

175g/6oz/³/₄ cup caster (superfine) sugar

5ml/1 tsp chopped almonds

icing (confectioners') sugar, for dusting

raspberry leaves, to decorate (optional)

FOR THE FILLING

175g/6oz/³/₄ cup low fat soft cheese

15–30ml/1–2 tbsp clear honey

15–30ml/1–2 tbsp Cointreau

120ml/4fl oz/¹/₂ cup low-fat
    fromage frais

225g/8oz raspberries

~ COOK'S TIP ~

When making the meringue,
whisk the egg whites until they
are so stiff that you can turn the
bowl upside down without them
falling out.

1 ▲ Preheat the oven to 140°C/
275°F/Gas 1. Draw a 20cm/8in circle
on two pieces of non-stick baking
parchment. Turn the paper over so
the marking is on the underside and
use it to line two heavy baking sheets.

2 ▲ Whisk the egg whites in a
grease-free bowl until very stiff, then
gradually whisk in the caster sugar to
make a stiff meringue mixture.

3 ▲ Spoon on to the circles on the
baking sheets, spreading the meringue
to the edges. Sprinkle one meringue
round with the chopped almonds.

4 ▲ Bake for 1½–2 hours, then
carefully lift the meringue rounds off
the baking sheets, peel away the
paper and cool on a wire rack.

5 ▲ To make the filling, cream the
cheese with the honey and liqueur.
Add the fromage frais and raspberries,
reserving three for decoration.

6 ▲ Place the plain meringue round
on a board, spread with the filling
and top with the nut-covered round.
Dust with icing sugar, transfer to a
plate and decorate with raspberries
and a sprig of raspberry leaves, if liked.

Energy 187kcal/796kJ; Protein 6g; Carbohydrate 42g, of which sugars 42g; Fat 0g, of which saturates 0g; Cholesterol 0mg; Calcium 57mg; Fibre 3g; Sodium 50mg.

Baked Blackberry Cheesecake

SERVES 5

175g/6oz/³⁄₄ cup cottage cheese

150g/5oz/²⁄₃ cup low-fat natural (plain) yogurt

15ml/1 tbsp wholemeal plain (whole-wheat all-purpose) flour

30ml/2 tbsp golden caster (superfine) sugar

1 egg

1 egg white

finely grated rind and juice of ¹⁄₂ lemon

200g/7oz/scant 2 cups blackberries

1 ▲ Preheat the oven to 180°C/350°F/ Gas 4. Lightly grease and line base of an 18cm/7in sandwich tin (pan).

2 ▲ Place the cottage cheese in a food processor and process until smooth. Alternatively, rub it through a sieve (strainer) to achieve a smooth texture.

3 ▲ Add the yogurt, flour, sugar, egg and egg white and mix. Add the lemon rind, juice and blackberries, reserving a few for decoration.

4 ▲ Tip the mixture into the tin and bake for 30–35 minutes, or until it is just set. Turn off the oven and leave for a further 30 minutes.

5 ▲ Run a knife around the edge of the cheesecake, then turn it out. Remove the lining paper and place the cheesecake on a warm serving plate.

6 Decorate the cheesecake with the reserved blackberries and serve it warm.

~ COOK'S TIP ~

If you prefer to use canned blackberries when fresh ones are not in season, choose those canned in natural juice and drain the fruit well before adding it to the cheesecake mixture. The juice can be served with the cheesecake, but this will increase the total calories.

Energy 88kcal/368kJ; Protein 7g; Carbohydrate 9.9g, of which sugars 7.8g; Fat 2.4g, of which saturates 1.1g; Cholesterol 37mg; Calcium 108mg; Fibre 1.1g; Sodium 142mg.

Mango and Amaretti Strudel

SERVES 4

1 large mango

grated rind of 1 lemon

2 amaretti biscuits (cookies)

30ml/2 tbsp demerara (raw) sugar

60ml/4 tbsp wholemeal
  (whole-wheat) breadcrumbs

2 sheets filo pastry, each
  48 × 28cm/19 × 11in

15ml/1 tbsp soft margarine, melted

15ml/1 tbsp chopped almonds

icing (confectioners') sugar, for dusting

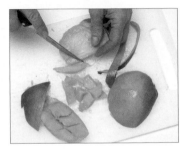

1 ▲ Preheat the oven to 190°C/
375°F/Gas 5. Lightly grease a large
baking sheet. Halve, stone (pit) and
peel the mango (*see* Cook's Tip). Cut
the flesh into cubes, then place them
in a bowl, and sprinkle with grated
lemon rind.

~ COOK'S TIP ~

The easiest way to prepare a
mango is to cut horizontally
through the fruit, keeping the
knife blade close to the stone
(pit). Repeat on the other side of
the stone and peel off the skin.
Remove the remaining skin and
flesh from around the stone.

2 ▲ Place the amaretti biscuits in a
strong plastic bag and crush them
with a rolling pin. Transfer them to
a bowl with the demerara sugar and
wholemeal breadcrumbs and stir to
combine well.

3 ▲ Lay one sheet of filo on a flat
surface and brush with a quarter of
the margarine. Top with the second
sheet, brush with one-third of the
remaining margarine, then fold both
sheets over to make a rectangle
28 × 23cm/11 × 9in. Brush
with half the remaining margarine.

4 ▲ Sprinkle the filo with the
amaretti mixture, leaving a 5cm/2in
border on each long side. Arrange
the mango cubes over the top.

5 ▲ Roll up the filo from one of the
long sides. Lift the strudel on to
the baking sheet with the join
underneath. Brush the filo with the
remaining melted margarine and
sprinkle with the chopped almonds.

6 ▲ Bake for 20–25 minutes until
golden brown, then transfer to a
board. Dust with the icing sugar,
slice diagonally and serve warm.

Energy 136kcal/573kJ; Protein 2g; Carbohydrate 17g, of which sugars 10g; Fat 7g, of which saturates 1g; Cholesterol 0mg; Calcium 20mg; Fibre 2g; Sodium 62mg.

Blueberry and Orange Crêpe Baskets

SERVES 6

FOR THE PANCAKES

150g/5oz/1¼ cups plain (all-purpose) flour

pinch of salt

2 egg whites

200ml/7fl oz/scant 1 cup skimmed milk

150ml/¼ pint/⅔ cup orange juice

FOR THE FILLING

4 medium-size oranges

225g/8oz/2 cups blueberries

1 ▲ Preheat the oven to 200°C/400°F/Gas 6. To make the pancakes, sift the flour and salt into a bowl. Make a well in the centre of the flour and add the egg whites, milk and orange juice. Whisk hard, until all the liquid has been incorporated and the batter is smooth and bubbly.

2 ▲ Lightly grease a heavy or non-stick pancake pan and heat until it is very hot. Pour in just enough batter to cover the base of the pan, swirling it to cover the pan evenly.

3 ▲ Cook until the pancake has set and is golden, and then turn it to cook the other side. Remove the pancake to a sheet of kitchen paper, and then cook the remaining batter, to make a total of 6–8 pancakes.

4 ▲ Place six small ovenproof bowls or moulds on a baking sheet and arrange the pancakes over these. Bake in the oven for 10 minutes, until they are crisp and set into the shape of the moulds. Lift off.

5 ▲ For the filling, pare a thin piece of orange rind from one orange and cut it in fine strips. Blanch the strips in boiling water for 30 seconds, then rinse in cold water. Cut the peel and white pith from the oranges.

6 ▲ Segment the oranges, catching the juice, combine with the blueberries and warm them gently. Spoon the fruit into the baskets and scatter the shreds of rind over the top.

~ COOK'S TIP ~

Don't fill the pancake baskets until you're ready to serve them because they will absorb the fruit juice and begin to soften.

Energy 181kcal/768kJ; Protein 6g; Carbohydrate 36g, of which sugars 17g; Fat 13g, of which saturates 0g; Cholesterol 1mg; Calcium 129mg; Fibre 3g; Sodium 108mg.

Filo and Apricot Purses

MAKES 12

115g/4oz/¹/₂ cup dried apricots

45ml/3 tbsp apricot compote
  or conserve

3 amaretti biscuits, crushed

3 sheets filo pastry

20ml/4 tsp soft margarine, melted

icing (confectioners') sugar,
  for dusting

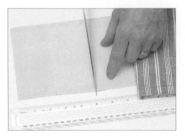

1 ▲ Preheat the oven to 180°C/
350°F/Gas 4. Grease two baking
sheets. Chop the apricots, put them
in a bowl and stir in the apricot
compote. Add the crushed amaretti
biscuits and mix well.

2 ▲ Cut the filo pastry into 24
13cm/5in squares, pile the squares on
top of each other and cover with a
clean dish towel.

3 ▲ Lay one pastry square on a flat
surface, brush with melted margarine
and lay another square diagonally on
top. Brush the top square with melted
margarine. Spoon a small mound of
apricot mixture in the centre of the
pastry, bring up the edges and pinch
together in a money-bag shape.
Repeat with the remaining squares
to make 12 purses.

4 ▲ Arrange on the baking sheets
and bake for 5–8 minutes until golden
brown. Dust with icing sugar and serve.

Energy 62kcal/264kJ; Protein 0.9g; Carbohydrate 11.3g, of which sugars 7.1g; Fat 1.8g, of which saturates 0.2g; Cholesterol 0mg; Calcium 17mg; Fibre 0.8g; Sodium 24mg.

Filo Scrunchies

MAKES 6

5 apricots or plums

4 sheets filo pastry

20ml/4 tsp soft margarine, melted

50g/2oz/4 tbsp demerara (raw) sugar

30ml/2 tbsp flaked (sliced) almonds

icing (confectioners') sugar,
    for dusting

1 Preheat the oven to 190°C/375°F/
Gas 5. Halve the apricots or plums,
remove the stones (pits) and cut the
fruit into slim slices .

2 ▲ Cut the filo pastry into 12
18cm/7in squares. Pile the squares on
top of each other and cover with a
clean dish towel.

3 ▲ Remove one square of filo pastry
and brush it with a little melted
margarine. Lay a second filo pastry
square on top, then, using your
fingers, mould the pastry into folds.
Make five more filo pastry scrunchies
in the same way, working quickly so
that the pastry does not dry out.

3 ▲ Arrange a few slices of fruit in
the folds of each scrunchie, then
sprinkle generously with the
demerara sugar and flaked almonds.

4 ▲ Place the scrunchies on a baking
sheet. Bake for 8–10 minutes until
golden brown, then loosen the
scrunchies from the baking sheet
with a palette knife and transfer to a
wire rack. Dust with icing sugar and
serve immediately.

Energy 127kcal/534kJ; Protein 2.2g; Carbohydrate 18g, of which sugars 11.5g; Fat 5.7g, of which saturates 0.2g; Cholesterol 0mg; Calcium 33mg; Fibre 1.2g; Sodium 29mg.

Plum Filo Pockets

2 ▲ Sandwich the plum halves back together with a spoonful of the cheese mixture in each plum.

3 Spread out the pastry and cut into 16 pieces, about 23cm/9in square. Brush one lightly with oil and place a second at a diagonal on top. Repeat with the remaining squares.

SERVES 4

115g/4oz/¹/₂ cup skimmed milk soft cheese

15ml/1 tbsp light muscovado (brown) sugar

2.5ml/¹/₂ tsp ground cloves

8 large, firm plums, halved and stoned (pitted)

8 sheets filo pastry, thawed if frozen

sunflower oil, for brushing

icing (confectioners') sugar, to sprinkle

1 ▲ Preheat the oven to 220°C/425°F/Gas 7. Mix together the cheese, sugar and cloves.

4 ▲ Place a plum on each pastry square, and gather the corners together. Place on a baking sheet. Bake for 15–18 minutes, until golden, then dust with icing sugar.

Energy 147kcal/624kJ; Protein 4g; Carbohydrate 27g, of which sugars 16g; Fat 3g, of which saturates 0g; Cholesterol 0mg; Calcium 40mg; Fibre 3g; Sodium 12mg.

Glazed Apricot Sponge

SERVES 4

10ml/2 tsp golden (light corn) syrup

400g/14oz can apricot halves in
fruit juice

150g/5oz/1¼ cups self-raising
(self-rising) flour

75g/3oz/1½ cups fresh breadcrumbs

90g/3½oz/⅔ cup light muscovado
(brown) sugar

5ml/1 tsp ground cinnamon

30ml/2 tbsp sunflower oil

175ml/6fl oz/¾ cup skimmed milk

1 ▲ Preheat the oven to 180°C/
350°F/Gas 4. Lightly oil a 900ml/
1½ pint/3¾ cups heatproof bowl.
Spoon in the syrup.

2 ▲ Drain the apricots and reserve
the juice. Arrange about eight halves
in the bottom of the bowl.

3 Purée the rest of the apricots with
the juice and set aside.

4 ▲ Mix the flour, breadcrumbs,
sugar and cinnamon, then beat in
the oil and milk. Spoon into the
bowl and bake for 50–55 minutes, or
until firm and golden. Turn out and
serve with the puréed fruit as a sauce.

Energy 376kcal/1595kJ; Protein 7g; Carbohydrate 74g, of which sugars 37g; Fat 9g, of which saturates 1g; Cholesterol 1mg; Calcium 283mg; Fibre 3g; Sodium 275mg.

Latticed Peaches

SERVES 6

FOR THE PASTRY

115g/4oz/1 cup plain (all-purpose) flour

45ml/3 tbsp butter or margarine

45ml/3 tbsp low-fat natural
(plain) yogurt

30ml/2 tbsp orange juice

skimmed milk, for brushing

FOR THE FILLING

3 ripe peaches or nectarines

45ml/3 tbsp ground almonds

30ml/2 tbsp low-fat natural
(plain) yogurt

finely grated rind of 1 small orange

1.25ml/¹/₄ tsp almond extract

FOR THE SAUCE

1 ripe peach or nectarine

45ml/3 tbsp orange juice

1 ▲ For the pastry, sift the flour into a bowl and rub in the butter or margarine. Stir in the yogurt and orange juice to bind the mixture.

2 ▲ Roll out about half the pastry thinly and stamp out rounds slightly larger than the circumference of the peaches. Place on a baking sheet.

3 ▲ Skin the peaches or nectarines, halve and remove the stones (pits). Mix together the almonds, yogurt, rind and almond extract. Spoon into each peach half and place, cut-side down, on to the pastry rounds.

4 ▲ Roll out the remaining pastry thinly and cut into thin strips. Arrange the strips over the peaches to form a lattice, brushing with milk to secure firmly. Trim off the ends.

5 ▲ Chill for 30 minutes. Preheat the oven to 200°C/400°F/Gas 6. Brush with milk and bake for 15–18 minutes, until golden brown.

6 ▲ For the sauce, skin the peach or nectarine and remove the stone. Purée the flesh in a food processor with the orange juice until smooth. Serve with the hot peaches.

~ COOK'S TIP ~

This dessert is best eaten fairly fresh from the oven, as the pastry can toughen slightly if left to stand. However, you can assemble the peaches in their pastry cases on a baking sheet, chill in the refrigerator, and bake just before serving.

Energy 196kcal/822kJ; Protein 4.7g; Carbohydrate 21.6g, of which sugars 6.8g; Fat 10.8g, of which saturates 4.3g; Cholesterol 16mg; Calcium 75mg; Fibre 1.9g; Sodium 59mg.

EVERYDAY BREADS

THOUGH THE PACE OF TODAY'S LIFE
LEAVES LITTLE TIME FOR BAKING,
BREADMAKING CAN BE VERY
THERAPEUTIC. THE PROCESS IS
SIMPLE YET INFINITELY VARIABLE,
AS THE LOAVES THAT FOLLOW
PROVE. ROLL UP YOUR SLEEVES AND
CREATE A TRADITION.

White Bread

MAKES 2 LOAVES

60ml/4 tbsp lukewarm water
15ml/1 tbsp active dried yeast
30ml/2 tbsp sugar
475ml/16fl oz/2 cups lukewarm milk
25g/1oz/2 tbsp butter or margarine, at room temperature
10ml/2 tsp salt
850–900g/1lb 14 oz–2 lbs/7¹/₄–8 cups strong white bread flour

1 Combine the water, dried yeast and 15ml/1 tbsp of sugar in a measuring jug (cup) and leave to stand for 15 minutes until the mixture is frothy.

2 ▼ Pour the milk into a large bowl. Add the remaining sugar, the butter or margarine, and salt. Stir in the yeast mixture.

3 Stir in the flour, 150g/5oz/1¹/₄ cups at a time, until a stiff dough forms. Alternatively, use a food processor.

4 ▲ Transfer the dough to a floured surface. To knead, push the dough away from you with the palm of your hand, then fold it towards you, and push it away again. Repeat until the dough is smooth and elastic.

5 Place the dough in a large greased bowl, cover with a plastic bag or a dish towel, and leave to rise in a warm place until doubled in volume, 2–3 hours. Grease two 23 × 13cm/ 9 × 5in tins (pans).

7 ▲ Punch down the risen dough with your fist and divide in half. Form into a loaf shape and place in the tins, seam-side down. Cover and let rise in a warm place until almost doubled in volume, about 45 minutes.

8 Preheat a 190°C/375°F/Gas 5 oven.

9 Bake until firm and brown, 45–50 minutes. Turn out and tap the bottom of a loaf: if it sounds hollow the loaf is done. If necessary, return to the oven and bake a few minutes more. Let cool on a wire rack.

Energy 1796kcal/7623kJ; Protein 50.6g; Carbohydrate 376.6g, of which sugars 33.7g; Fat 20.2g, of which saturates 10g; Cholesterol 41mg; Calcium 925mg; Fibre 14g; Sodium 193mg.

Country Bread

MAKES 2 LOAVES

350g/12oz/3 cups strong wholemeal (whole-wheat) bread flour

350g/12oz/3 cups plain (all-purpose) flour

150g/5oz/1¼ cups strong white bread flour

10ml/4 tsp salt

50g/2oz/¼ cup butter, at room temperature

450ml/¾ pint/scant 2 cups lukewarm milk

FOR THE STARTER

15ml/1 tbsp active dried yeast

250ml/8fl oz/1 cup lukewarm water

150g/5oz/1¼ cups strong white bread flour

1.25ml/¼ tsp caster (superfine) sugar

1 ▲ For the starter, combine the yeast, water, flour and sugar in a bowl and stir with a fork. Cover and leave in a warm place for 2–3 hours, or leave overnight in a cool place.

2 Place the flours, salt and butter in a food processor and process just until blended, 1–2 minutes.

3 Stir together the milk and starter, then slowly pour into the processor, with the motor running, until the mixture forms a dough. If necessary, add more water. Alternatively, the dough can be mixed by hand. Transfer to a floured surface and knead until smooth and elastic.

4 Place in an ungreased bowl, cover with a plastic bag, and leave to rise in a warm place until doubled in volume, about 1½ hours.

5 Transfer to a floured surface and knead briefly. Return to the bowl and leave to rise until tripled in volume, about 1½ hours.

6 ▲ Divide the dough in half. Cut off one-third of the dough from each half and shape into balls. Shape the larger remaining portion of each half into balls. Grease a baking sheet.

7 ▲ For each loaf, top the large ball with the small ball and press the centre with the handle of a wooden spoon to secure. Cover with a plastic bag, slash the top, and leave to rise.

8 Preheat a 200°C/400°F/Gas 6 oven. Dust the dough with flour and bake until the top is browned and the bottom sounds hollow when tapped, 45–50 minutes. Cool on a rack.

Energy 1760kcal/7482kJ; Protein 60.9g; Carbohydrate 375.5g, of which sugars 19.7g; Fat 12.1g, of which saturates 3.7g; Cholesterol 14mg; Calcium 807mg; Fibre 25.8g; Sodium 2082mg.

Split Tin

4 ▲ Place on a lightly floured surface and knead for about 10 minutes until smooth and elastic. Place in a lightly oiled bowl, cover with lightly oiled clear film (plastic wrap) and leave to rise, in a warm place, for 1–1¼ hours, or until nearly doubled in bulk.

5 Knock back the dough and turn out on to a lightly floured surface. Shape it into a rectangle. Roll up lengthways, tuck the ends under and place the dough seam-side down in the tin. Cover and leave to rise for about 20–30 minutes, or until nearly doubled in bulk.

6 ▲ Using a sharp knife, make one deep central slash the length of the bread; dust with flour. Leave for 10–15 minutes to rise further.

7 Preheat the oven to 230°C/450°F/Gas 8. Bake the bread for 15 minutes, then reduce the oven temperature to 200°C/400°F/Gas 6. Bake for 20–25 minutes, or until the bread is golden and sounds hollow when tapped.

MAKES 1 LOAF

500g/1¼lb/4⅔ cups strong white bread flour, plus extra for dusting
10ml/2 tsp salt
15ml/1 tbsp fresh yeast
300ml/½ pint/1¼ cups lukewarm water
60ml/4 tbsp lukewarm milk

1 Lightly grease a 900g/2lb/8 cups loaf tin (pan). Sift the flour and salt together into a large bowl and make a well in the centre.

2 Mix the yeast with half the water, then stir in the remaining water. Pour the yeast mixture into the centre of the flour and using your fingers, mix in a little flour. Gradually mix in more of the flour from around the edge of the bowl to form a batter.

3 Sprinkle a little more flour from around the edge over the batter and leave in a warm place to 'sponge'. Bubbles will appear in the batter after about 20 minutes. Add the milk and remaining flour; mix to a firm dough.

Energy 1733kcal/7367kJ; Protein 49g; Carbohydrate 391.3g, of which sugars 10.3g; Fat 7.5g, of which saturates 1.6g; Cholesterol 4mg; Calcium 773mg; Fibre 15.5g; Sodium 3971mg.

Plaited Loaf

MAKES 1 LOAF

15ml/1 tbsp active dried yeast

5ml/1 tsp honey

250ml/8fl oz/1 cup lukewarm water

50g/2oz/¼ cup butter, melted

425g/15oz/3⅔ cups strong white
  bread flour

5ml/1 tsp salt

1 egg, lightly beaten

1 egg yolk beaten with 5ml/1 tsp milk,
  for glazing

1 ▼ Combine the yeast, honey, milk and butter. Stir and leave for 15 minutes to dissolve.

2 In a large bowl, mix together the flour and salt. Make a well in the centre and add the yeast mixture and egg. With a wooden spoon, stir from the centre, incorporating flour with each turn, to obtain a rough dough.

3 Transfer to a floured surface and knead until smooth and elastic. Place in a clean bowl, cover and leave to rise in a warm place until doubled in volume, about 1½ hours.

4 Grease a baking sheet. Punch down the dough and divide into three equal pieces. Roll to shape each piece into a long thin strip.

5 ▲ Begin plaiting with the centre strip, tucking in the ends. Cover loosely and leave to rise in a warm place for 30 minutes.

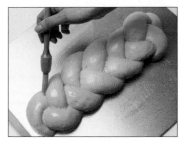

6 ▲ Preheat the oven to 190°C/375°F/Gas 5 oven. Place the bread in a cool place while the oven heats. Brush with the glaze and bake until golden, 40–45 minutes. Cool on a rack.

Energy 2033kcal/8584kJ; Protein 55g; Carbohydrate 348.4g, of which sugars 24.5g; Fat 56.4g, of which saturates 31.1g; Cholesterol 312mg; Calcium 933mg; Fibre 13.2g; Sodium 494mg.

Sourdough Bread

MAKES 1 LOAF

350g/12oz/3 cups strong white bread flour

15ml/1 tbsp salt

250ml/8fl oz/1 cup Sourdough Starter

120ml/4fl oz/¹/₂ cup) lukewarm water

1 ▲ Combine the flour and salt in a large bowl. Make a well in the centre and add the starter and water. With a wooden spoon, stir from the centre, incorporating more flour with each turn, to obtain a rough dough.

2 ▲ Transfer the dough to a floured surface. To knead, push the dough away from you with the palm of your hand, then fold it towards you, and push it away again. Repeat the process until the dough has become smooth and elastic.

3 Place in a clean bowl, cover, and leave to rise in a warm place until doubled in volume, about 2 hours.

4 Lightly grease a 20 × 10cm/ 8 × 4in bread tin (pan).

5 ▼ Punch down the dough with your fist. Knead briefly, then form into a loaf shape and place in the tin, seam-side down. Cover with a plastic bag, and leave to rise in a warm place, for about 1¹/₂ hours.

6 Preheat the oven to 220°C/425°F/ Gas 7. Dust the top of the loaf with flour, then score lengthways. Bake for 15 minutes. Lower the heat to 190°C/ 375°F/Gas 5 and bake for about 30 minutes more, or until the bottom sounds hollow when tapped.

Sourdough Starter

MAKES 750ML/1¹/₄ PINTS/3 CUPS

5ml/1 tsp active dried yeast

175ml/6fl oz/³/₄ cup lukewarm water

50g/2oz/¹/₂ cup strong white bread flour

~ COOK'S TIP ~

After using, feed the starter with a handful of flour and enough water to restore it to a thick batter. The starter can be refrigerated for up to 1 week, but must be brought back to room temperature before using.

1 ▲ For the starter, combine the yeast and water, stir and leave for 15 minutes to dissolve.

2 ▼ Sprinkle over the flour and whisk until it forms a batter. Cover and leave to rise in a warm place for at least 24 hours or preferably 2–4 days, before using.

Bread: Energy 253kcal/5329kJ; Protein 35g; Carbohydrate 6g, of which sugars 5g; Fat 1g, of which saturates 0g; Cholesterol 0mg; Calcium 515mg; Fibre 13g; Sodium 197mg.
Starter: Energy 176kcal/747kJ; Protein 6g; Carbohydrate 39g, of which sugars 1g; Fat 1g, of which saturates 0g; Cholesterol 0mg; Calcium 72mg; Fibre 2g; Sodium 3mg.

Rye Bread

MAKES 2 LOAVES

350g/12oz/3 cups strong wholemeal (whole-wheat) bread flour

225g/8oz/2 cups rye flour

115g/4oz/1 cup strong white bread flour

7.5ml/1½ tsp salt

30ml/2 tbsp caraway seeds

475ml/16fl oz/2 cups warm water

10ml/2 tsp active dried yeast

pinch of sugar

30ml/2 tbsp black treacle (molasses)

1 ▲ Put the flours and salt in a bowl. Set aside 5ml/1 tsp of the caraway seeds and add the rest to the bowl.

2 ▲ Put half the water in a jug (pitcher). Sprinkle the yeast on top. Add the sugar, mix and leave for 10 minutes.

3 ▲ Make a well in the flour mixture, then add the yeast mixture with the black treacle and the remaining water. Gradually incorporate the flour and mix to a soft dough, adding a little extra water, if necessary.

4 ▲ Transfer to a floured surface and knead for 5 minutes until smooth and elastic. Return to the clean bowl, cover and leave for 2 hours until doubled in bulk. Grease a baking sheet.

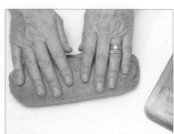

5 ▲ Turn the dough on to a floured surface and knead for 2 minutes. Divide the dough in half, then shape into two 23cm/9in long oval loaves. Flatten the loaves slightly and place them on the baking sheet.

6 ▲ Brush with water and sprinkle with the remaining caraway seeds. Cover and leave in a warm place for about 40 minutes, until well risen. Preheat the oven to 200°C/400°F/Gas 6. Bake the loaves for 30 minutes or until they sound hollow when tapped underneath. Cool on a wire rack.

~ COOK'S TIP ~

To make caraway-seed bread rolls, divide each of the two flattened loaves into eight equal portions. Place them on the baking sheet, brush with water and sprinkle with caraway seeds. Vary the topping by using poppy seeds, if you prefer.

Energy 4323kcal/18332kJ; Protein 98.1g; Carbohydrate 893.3g, of which sugars 93.3g; Fat 64.4g, of which saturates 33.6g; Cholesterol 128mg; Calcium 1926mg; Fibre 49.8g; Sodium 6502mg.

Pecan Rye Bread

Makes 2 loaves

22.5ml/1½ tbsp active dried yeast
700ml/24fl oz/scant 3 cups lukewarm water
700g/1½lb/6 cups strong white bread flour
500g/1¼lb/4⅔ cups rye flour
30ml/2 tbsp salt
15ml/1 tbsp honey
10ml/2 tsp caraway seeds, (optional)
115g/4oz/½ cup butter, at room temperature
225g/8oz/1½ cups pecans, chopped

1 Combine the yeast and 120ml/4fl oz/1 cup of the water. Stir and leave for 15 minutes to dissolve.

2 In the bowl of an electric mixer, combine the flours, salt, honey, caraway seeds and butter. With the dough hook, mix on low speed until well blended.

3 Add the yeast mixture and the remaining water and mix on medium speed until the dough forms a ball.

4 ▲ Transfer to a floured surface and knead in the pecans.

5 Return the dough to a bowl, cover with a plastic bag and leave in a warm place until doubled, about 2 hours.

6 Grease two 21.5 × 11.5cm/8½ × 4½in bread tins (pans).

7 ▲ Punch down the risen dough.

8 Divide the dough in half and form into loaves. Place in the tins, seam side down. Dust the tops with flour.

9 Cover with plastic bags and leave to rise in a warm place until doubled in volume, about 1 hour.

10 Preheat a 190°C/375°F/Gas 5 oven.

11 ▼ Bake until the bottoms sound hollow when tapped, 45–50 minutes. Cool on wire racks.

Energy 3274kcal/13766kJ; Protein 80g; Carbohydrate 465g, of which sugars 16g; Fat 134g, of which saturates 38g; Cholesterol 123mg; Calcium 693mg; Fibre 21g; Sodium 2339mg.

Sourdough Rye Bread

MAKES 2 LOAVES

10ml/2 tsp active dried yeast
120ml/4fl oz/^{1}/$_2$ cup lukewarm water
25g/1oz/2 tbsp, melted
15ml/1 tbsp salt
115g/4oz/1 cup wholemeal (whole-wheat) flour
400–450g/14–16oz/3^1/$_2$–4 cups plain (all-purpose) flour
1 egg mixed with 15ml/1 tbsp water, for glazing

FOR THE STARTER

15ml/1 tbsp active dried yeast
350ml/12fl oz/1^1/$_2$ cups lukewarm water
45ml/3 tbsp black treacle (molasses)
30ml/2 tbsp caraway seeds
250g/9oz/2^1/$_4$ cups rye flour

1 For the starter, combine the dried yeast and water, stir and leave for 15 minutes to dissolve.

2 ▲ Stir in the black treacle, caraway seeds and rye flour. Cover and leave in a warm place for 2–3 days.

3 In a large bowl, combine the dried yeast and water, stir and leave for 10 minutes. Stir in the melted butter, salt, wholemeal flour and 400g/14oz/ 3^1/$_2$ cups of the plain flour.

4 ▲ Make a well in the centre and pour in the starter.

5 Stir to obtain a rough dough, then transfer to a floured surface and knead until smooth and elastic. Return to the bowl, cover and leave to rise in a warm place until doubled in volume, about 2 hours.

6 Grease a large baking sheet. Knock back the dough and knead briefly. Cut the dough in half and form each half into log-shaped loaves.

7 ▼ Place the loaves on the baking sheet and score the tops with a sharp knife. Cover and leave to rise in a warm place until almost doubled, about 50 minutes.

8 Preheat the oven to 190°C/375°F/ Gas 5. Brush the loaves with the egg wash to glaze them, then bake until the bottoms sound hollow when tapped, about 50–55 minutes. If the tops brown too quickly, place a sheet of foil over the tops to protect them. Cool on a wire rack.

Energy 1555kcal/6598kJ; Protein 43g; Carbohydrate 317g, of which sugars 25g; Fat 23g, of which saturates 10g; Cholesterol 148mg; Calcium 602mg; Fibre 13g; Sodium 198mg.

Buttermilk Graham Bread

SERVES 8

10ml/2 tsp active dried yeast

120ml/4fl oz/¹/₂ cup lukewarm water

225g/8oz/2 cups graham or wholemeal (whole-wheat) flour

350g/12oz/3 cups plain (all-purpose) flour

125g/4¹/₂oz/1¹/₄ cups cornmeal

10ml/2 tsp salt

30ml/2 tbsp sugar

50g/2oz/¹/₄ cup butter, at room temperature

457ml/16fl oz/2 cups lukewarm buttermilk

1 beaten egg, for glazing

sesame seeds, for sprinkling

1 Combine the yeast and water, stir, and leave for 15 minutes to dissolve.

2 ▲ Mix together the two flours, cornmeal, salt and sugar in a large bowl. Make a well in the centre and pour in the yeast mixture, then add the butter and the buttermilk.

3 ▲ Stir from the centre, mixing in the flour until a rough dough is formed. If too stiff, use your hands.

4 ▲ Transfer to a floured surface and knead until smooth. Place in a clean bowl, cover, and leave in a warm place for 2–3 hours.

5 ▲ Grease two 20cm/8in square baking tins (pans). Punch down the dough. Divide into eight pieces and roll them into balls. Place four in each tin. Cover and leave for about 1 hour.

6 Preheat the oven to 190°C/375°F/ Gas 5. Brush with the glaze, then sprinkle over the sesame seeds. Bake for about 50 minutes, or until the bottoms sound hollow when tapped.

Energy 385kcal/1625kJ; Protein 12g; Carbohydrate 67g, of which sugars 4g; Fat 9g, of which saturates 4g; Cholesterol 46mg; Calcium 150mg; Fibre 5g; Sodium 583mg.

Bread Stick

MAKES 2 LOAVES

10ml/2 tsp active dry yeast
475ml/16fl oz/2 cups lukewarm water
5ml/1 tsp salt
675–900g/1½–2lb/6–8 cups plain (all-purpose) flour
cornmeal, for sprinkling

1 Combine the yeast and water, stir, and leave for 15 minutes to dissolve. Stir in the salt.

2 Add the flour, 115g/4oz/1 cup at a time. Beat in with a wooden spoon, adding just enough flour to obtain a dough. Alternatively, use an electric mixer with a dough hook attachment, following manufacturer's instructions.

3 Transfer to a floured surface and knead until smooth and elastic.

4 Shape into a ball, place in a lightly greased bowl, and cover with a plastic bag. Leave to rise in a warm place until doubled in volume, 2–4 hours.

5 ▲ Transfer the dough to a lightly floured board and knock it back. Halve the dough and shape into two long loaves. Place the loaves on a baking sheet liberally sprinkled with cornmeal, and leave to rise for 5 minutes.

6 ▲ Score the tops in several places with a very sharp knife. Brush with water and place in a cold oven. Set a pan of boiling water on the bottom of the oven and set the oven to 200°C/400°F/Gas 6. Bake for about 40 minutes. Cool on a wire rack.

Energy 1344kcal/5713kJ; Protein 37g; Carbohydrate 306g, of which sugars 6g; Fat 5g, of which saturates 1g; Cholesterol 0mg; Calcium 552mg; Fibre 14g; Sodium 994mg.

Three Grain Bread

MAKES 1 LOAF

475ml/16fl oz/2 cups warm water
10ml/2 tsp dried yeast
pinch of sugar
225g/8oz/2 cups strong white white flour
7.5ml/1½ tsp salt
25g/8oz/2 cups malted brown bread flour
25g/8oz/2 cups rye flour
30ml/2 tbsp linseed
75g/3oz/²/₃ cup medium oatmeal
45ml/3 tbsp sunflower seeds
30ml/2 tbsp malt extract

1 ▲ Mix half the water, the yeast and sugar together; leave for 10 minutes.

2 ▲ Sift the white flour and salt into a bowl and add the other flours. Set aside 5ml/1 tsp of the linseed and add the rest to the flour mixture with the oatmeal and sunflower seeds. Add the yeast mixture to the bowl with the malt extract and the remaining water.

3 Gradually incorporate the flour.

4 ▲ Mix to a soft dough, adding extra water if necessary. Turn out on to a floured surface and knead for 5 minutes until smooth and elastic. Return to the clean bowl, cover with a damp dish towel and leave to rise for about 2 hours until doubled in bulk.

5 ▲ Grease a baking sheet. Turn the dough on to a floured surface, knead for 2 minutes, then divide in half. Roll each half into a 30cm/12in sausage.

6 ▲ Twist the two sausages together, dampen the ends and press to seal.

7 Lift the twist on to the prepared baking sheet. Brush the plait with water, sprinkle with the remaining linseed and cover loosely with a large plastic bag. Leave in a warm place until well risen. Preheat the oven to 220°C/425°F/Gas 7.

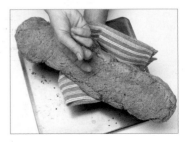

8 ▲ Bake the loaf for 10 minutes, then lower the oven temperature to 200°C/400°F/Gas 6 and cook for 20 minutes more, or until the loaf sounds hollow when it is tapped underneath. Transfer to a wire rack to cool.

Energy 3021kcal/12801kJ; Protein 96g; Carbohydrate 568g, of which sugars 27g; Fat 56g, of which saturates 6g; Cholesterol 0mg; Calcium 791mg; Fibre 32g; Sodium 3005mg.

Multi-Grain Bread

MAKES 2 LOAVES

15ml/1 tbsp active dried yeast
60ml/4 tbsp lukewarm water
75ml/5 tbsp rolled oats
475ml/16fl oz/2 cups milk
10ml/2 tsp salt
60ml/4 tbsp oil
50g/2oz/4 tbsp light brown sugar
30ml/2 tbsp honey
2 eggs, lightly beaten
25g/1oz/¼ cup wheat germ
175g/6oz/1½ cups soya flour
350g/12oz/3 cups wholemeal (whole-wheat) flour
425–500g/15–18oz/3²/₃–4²/₃ cups strong white bread flour

1   Combine the yeast and water, stir, and leave for 15 minutes to dissolve.

2   ▲   Place the oats in a large bowl. Scald the milk, then pour over the rolled oats.

3   Stir in the salt, oil, sugar and honey. Leave until lukewarm.

~ **VARIATION** ~

Different flours may be used in this recipe, such as rye, barley, buckwheat or cornmeal. Try replacing the wheat germ and the soya flour with one or two of these, using the same total amount.

4   ▲   Stir in the yeast mixture, eggs, wheat germ, soya and wholemeal flours. Gradually stir in enough strong flour to obtain a rough dough.

5   Transfer the dough to a floured surface and knead, adding flour if necessary, until smooth and elastic. Return to a clean bowl, cover and leave to rise in a warm place until doubled in volume, about 2½ hours.

6   Grease two 21.5 × 11.5cm/ 8½ × 4½in bread tins (pans). Punch down the dough and knead briefly.

7   Divide the dough into quarters. Roll each quarter into a cylinder 3cm/1½in thick. Twist together two cylinders and place in a tin; repeat for remaining cylinders.

8   Cover and leave to rise until doubled in size, about 1 hour.

9   Preheat a 190°C/375°F/Gas 5 oven.

10   ▲   Bake the bread for 45–50 minutes, until the bottoms sound hollow when tapped lightly. Cool on a wire rack.

Energy 1511kcal/6403kJ; Protein 48.9g; Carbohydrate 286.5g, of which sugars 22.9g; Fat 26.9g, of which saturates 12.9g; Cholesterol 52mg; Calcium 350mg; Fibre 32.1g; Sodium 2187mg.

Sesame Seed Bread

MAKES 1 LOAF

10ml/2 tsp active dry yeast
300ml/¹/₂ pint/1¹/₄ cups lukewarm water
200g/7oz/1³/₄ cups strong white bread flour
200g/7oz/1³/₄ cups strong wholemeal (whole-wheat) bread flour
10ml/2 tsp salt
75g/5 tbsp toasted sesame seeds
milk, for glazing
30ml/2 tbsp sesame seeds, for sprinkling

1   Combine the yeast and 75ml/ 5 tbsp of the water and leave to dissolve. Mix the flours and salt in a large bowl. Make a well in the centre and pour in the yeast and water.

2 ▲ With a wooden spoon, stir from the centre, incorporating flour with each turn, to obtain a rough dough.

3 ▲ Transfer to a lightly floured surface. Knead the dough for about 10 minutes, until smooth and elastic. Lightly grease the bowl, then return the dough to it and cover with a plastic bag. Leave the dough in a warm place for about 1¹/₂–2 hours, until doubled in volume.

4 ▲ Grease a 23cm/9in cake tin (pan). Punch down the dough and knead in the sesame seeds. Divide the dough into 16 balls and place in the pan. Cover with a plastic bag and leave in a warm place until risen above the rim of the tin.

5 ▼ Preheat a 220°C/425°F/Gas 7 oven. Brush the loaf with milk and sprinkle with the sesame seeds. Bake for 15 minutes. Lower the heat to 190°C/375°F/Gas 5 and bake until the bottom sounds hollow when tapped, about 30 minutes more. Cool on a rack.

Energy 1691kcal/7142kJ; Protein 56g; Carbohydrate 283.8g, of which sugars 7.5g; Fat 44.7g, of which saturates 6.4g; Cholesterol 0mg; Calcium 793mg; Fibre 29.3g; Sodium 3955mg.

Granary Cob

MAKES 1 LOAF

450g/1lb/4 cups Granary (whole-wheat)
or malthouse flour

10ml/2 tsp salt

15g/1/2oz fresh yeast

350ml/12fl oz/1½ cups lukewarm water
or milk and water mixed

FOR THE TOPPING

30ml/2 tbsp water

2.5ml/1/2 tsp salt

wheat flakes or cracked wheat,
to sprinkle

1 Lightly flour a baking sheet. Sift the flour and salt together in a bowl and make a well in the centre. Place in a very low oven for 5 minutes.

2 ▲ Mix the yeast with a little of the water or milk mixture then blend in the rest. Add the yeast mixture to the centre of the flour and mix to a dough.

3 Turn out on to a floured surface and knead for about 10 minutes.

4 Place in a lightly oiled bowl, cover with lightly oiled clear film (plastic wrap) and leave to rise for 1¼ hours, or until doubled in bulk.

5 ▲ Turn the dough out on to a lightly floured surface and knock back. Knead for 2–3 minutes, then roll into a plump, round ball.

6 Place the dough in the centre of the prepared baking sheet. Cover with an inverted bowl or a clean dish towel and leave to rise, in a warm place, for 30–45 minutes.

7 Mix the water and salt and brush over the bread. Sprinkle with wheat flakes or cracked wheat.

8 Meanwhile, preheat the oven to 230°C/450°F/Gas 8. Bake the bread for 15 minutes, then reduce the oven temperature to 200°C/400°F/Gas 6 and bake for a further 20 minutes, or until the loaf is firm to the touch and sounds hollow when tapped on the base. Leave to cool on a wire rack.

Energy 1395kcal/5931kJ; Protein 57.1g; Carbohydrate 287.6g, of which sugars 9.4g; Fat 9.9g, of which saturates 1.4g; Cholesterol 0mg; Calcium 172mg; Fibre 40.5g; Sodium 4926mg.

Oatmeal Bread

MAKES 2 LOAVES

475ml/16fl oz/2 cups milk
25g/1oz/2 tbsp butter
50g/2oz/4 tbsp dark brown sugar
10ml/2 tsp salt
15ml/1 tbsp active dried yeast
60ml/4 tbsp lukewarm water
390g/13³/4oz/4 cups rolled oats (not quick-cooking)
700–850g/1lb 8oz–1lb 14oz/6–7¹/4 cups strong white bread flour

1 ▲ Scald the milk. Remove from the heat and stir in the butter, brown sugar and salt. Leave until lukewarm.

2 Combine the yeast and warm water in a large bowl and leave until the yeast is dissolved and the mixture is frothy. Stir in the milk mixture.

3 ▲ Add 275g/10oz/3 cups of the oats and enough flour to obtain a soft dough.

4 Transfer to a floured surface and knead until smooth and elastic.

5 ▲ Place in a greased bowl, cover with a plastic bag, and leave until doubled in volume, 2–3 hours.

6 Grease a large baking sheet. Transfer the dough to a lightly floured surface and divide in half.

7 ▼ Shape into rounds. Place on the baking sheet, cover with a dish towel and leave to rise until doubled in volume, about 1 hour.

8 Preheat a 200°C/400°F/Gas 6 oven. Score the tops and sprinkle with the remaining oats. Bake until the bottoms sound hollow when tapped, 45–50 minutes. Cool on wire racks.

Energy 2254kcal/9556kJ; Protein 64.8g; Carbohydrate 445.2g, of which sugars 42.4g; Fat 36.1g, of which saturates 9.8g; Cholesterol 41mg; Calcium 883mg; Fibre 24.1g; Sodium 256mg.

Granary Baps

MAKES 8

300ml/¹/₂ pint/1¹/₄ cups warm water
5ml/1 tsp dried yeast
pinch of sugar
450g/1lb/4 cups malted brown flour
5ml/1 tsp salt
15ml/1 tbsp malt extract
15ml/1 tbsp rolled oats

1 ▲ Put half the warm water in a jug (pitcher). Sprinkle in the yeast. Add the sugar, mix and leave for 10 minutes.

2 ▲ Put the malted brown flour and salt in a mixing bowl and make a well in the centre. Add the yeast mixture with the malt extract and the remaining water. Gradually mix in the flour to make a soft dough.

3 ▲ Turn the dough on to a lightly floured surface and knead for about 5 minutes, until smooth and elastic. Return to the clean lightly oiled bowl, cover with a damp dish towel or a plastic bag and leave in a warm place to rise for about 2 hours until doubled in bulk.

4 ▲ Lightly grease two large baking sheets. Turn the dough on to a floured surface, knead for 2 minutes, then divide into eight pieces. Shape the pieces into balls and flatten them to make neat 10cm/4in rounds.

5 ▲ Place the rounds on the baking sheets, cover loosely with a large plastic bag or dish towel and leave to stand in a warm place for about 20 minutes, until well risen. Preheat the oven to 220°C/425°F/Gas 7.

6 ▲ Brush the baps with water, sprinkle with the oats and bake for about 20–25 minutes or until they sound hollow when tapped underneath. Cool on a wire rack, then serve with the filling of your choice.

~ COOK'S TIP ~

To make a large loaf, shape the dough into a round, flatten it slightly and bake for 30–40 minutes. Test by tapping the base of the loaf – if it sounds hollow, it is cooked.

Energy 195kcal/834kJ; Protein 7.3g; Carbohydrate 41.4g, of which sugars 2.4g; Fat 1.3g, of which saturates 0.2g; Cholesterol 0mg; Calcium 75mg; Fibre 3.7g; Sodium 254mg.

Brown Soda Bread

MAKES 1 LOAF

450g/1lb/4 cups plain (all-purpose) flour
450g/1lb/4 cups wholemeal (whole-wheat) flour
10ml/2 tsp salt
15ml/1 tbsp bicarbonate of soda (baking soda)
20ml/4 tsp cream of tartar
10ml/2 tsp sugar
50g/2oz/¼ cup butter
up to 900ml/1½ pints/3¾ cups buttermilk or skimmed milk
extra wholemeal flour, to sprinkle

1 Lightly grease a baking sheet. Preheat the oven to 190°C/375°F/Gas 5.

2 ▲ Sift all the dry ingredients into a large bowl, tipping any bran from the flour back into the bowl.

3 ▲ Rub the butter into the flour mixture, then add enough buttermilk or milk to make a soft dough.

4 ▲ Knead until smooth, then transfer to the baking sheet and shape to a large round about 5cm/2in thick.

5 ▲ Using the floured handle of a wooden spoon, make a large cross on top of the dough. Sprinkle over a little extra wholemeal flour. Bake for 40–50 minutes until risen and firm. Leave to cool for 5 minutes before transferring to a wire rack.

Energy 3340kcal/14198kJ; Protein 130g; Carbohydrate 693g, of which sugars 72g; Fat 20g, of which saturates 5g; Cholesterol 18mg; Calcium 1883mg; Fibre 55g; Sodium 7747mg.

Sage Soda Bread

MAKES 1 LOAF

175g/6oz/1¹/₂ cups wholemeal
(whole-wheat) flour

115g/4oz/1 cup strong white
bread flour

2.5ml/¹/₂ tsp salt

5ml/1 tsp bicarbonate of soda
(baking soda)

30ml/2 tbsp shredded fresh sage or
10ml/2 tsp dried sage

300–450ml/¹/₂–³/₄ pint/1¹/₄–scant 2 cups
buttermilk

1 ▲ Preheat the oven to 220°C/
425°F/Gas 7. Sift the dry ingredients
into a mixing bowl.

2 ▲ Stir in the sage and add enough
buttermilk to make a soft dough.

~ VARIATION ~

Try using either finely chopped
rosemary or thyme instead of sage.

3 ▲ Shape the dough into a round
loaf with your hands and place on a
lightly oiled baking sheet.

4 ▲ Cut a deep cross in the top.
Bake in the preheated oven for about
40 minutes, until the loaf is well
risen and sounds hollow when tapped
on the bottom. Leave to cool on a
wire rack.

Energy 1186kcal/5041kJ; Protein 49.6g; Carbohydrate 246.3g, of which sugars 19.6g; Fat 7.3g, of which saturates 1.3g; Cholesterol 11mg; Calcium 613mg; Fibre 23.8g; Sodium 1125mg.

Rosemary Bread

MAKES 1 LOAF

10g/¹/₄oz easy-blend (rapid-rise)
  dried yeast

175g/6oz/1¹/₂ cups wholemeal
  (whole-wheat) flour

175g/6oz/1¹/₂ cups self-raising
  (self-rising) flour

10ml/2 tsp butter, melted

50ml/2fl oz/¹/₄ cup warm water

250ml/8fl oz/1 cup skimmed milk,
  at room temperature

15ml/1 tbsp sugar

5ml/1 tsp salt

15ml/1 tbsp sesame seeds

15ml/1 tbsp dried chopped onion

15ml/1 tbsp fresh rosemary leaves,
  plus extra to decorate

115g/4oz Cheddar cheese, cubed

coarse salt, to decorate

1 ▲ Mix the yeast with the flours in
a mixing bowl. Add the butter. Stir
in the warm water, milk, sugar, salt,
sesame seeds, onion and rosemary.
Knead until quite smooth.

2 ▲ Flatten the dough, then add the
cheese cubes.

3 Quickly knead in the cheese cubes
until they are well combined.

4 Place the dough in a lightly
greased bowl. Cover with a clean, dry
dish cloth. Leave to rise in a warm
place for about 1¹/₂ hours, or until the
dough has risen and doubled in size.

5 Grease a 23 × 13cm/9 × 5in loaf
tin (pan). Knock down the dough to
remove some of the air, and shape it
into a loaf. Put the loaf into the tin,
cover with the clean cloth and leave
for about 1 hour until it has doubled
in size once again. Preheat the oven
to 190°C/375°F/Gas 5.

6 Bake in the preheated oven for
about 40 minutes, until the loaf is
well risen and sounds hollow when
tapped on the bottom. During the
last 5–10 minutes of baking, cover
the loaf with foil to prevent it
becoming too dark in colour. Remove
from the tin and cool on a wire rack.
Decorate with rosemary leaves and
coarse salt scattered on top.

Energy 1999kcal/8422kJ; Protein 77.3g; Carbohydrate 280.2g, of which sugars 37.4g; Fat 68.7g, of which saturates 41.5g; Cholesterol 180mg; Calcium 1489mg; Fibre 22g; Sodium 3069mg.

Spiral Herb Bread

MAKES 2 LOAVES

30ml/2 tbsp active dried yeast
600ml/1 pint/2½ cups lukewarm water
425g/15oz/3⅔ cups strong white bread flour
500g/1¼lb/4⅔ cups wholemeal (whole-wheat) flour
15ml/3 tsp salt
50g/2oz/¼ cup butter
1 large bunch of parsley, finely chopped
1 bunch of spring onions (scallions), finely chopped
1 garlic clove, finely chopped
salt and freshly ground black pepper
1 egg, lightly beaten
milk, for glazing

1 Combine the yeast and 60ml/4 tbsp of the water and leave for 15 minutes.

2 Combine the flours and salt in a large bowl. Make a well and pour in the yeast mixture and the remaining water. Stir from the centre, working outwards to obtain a rough dough.

3 Transfer the dough to a floured surface and knead until smooth and elastic. Return to the bowl, cover with a plastic bag, and leave until doubled in volume, about 2 hours.

4 ▲ Meanwhile, combine the butter, parsley, spring onions and garlic in a large frying pan. Cook over low heat, stirring, until softened. Season and set aside.

5 Grease two 23 × 13cm/9 × 5in tins (pans). When the dough has risen, cut it in half and roll each half into a rectangle about 35 × 23cm/14 × 9in in size.

6 ▼ Brush both rectangles with the beaten egg. Divide the herb mixture between the two, spreading just up to the edges.

7 ▲ Roll up to enclose the filling and pinch the short ends to seal. Place in the tins, seam-side down. Cover, and leave in a warm place until the dough rises above the rim of the tins.

8 Preheat a 190°C/375°F/Gas 5 oven. Brush with milk and bake until the bottoms sound hollow when tapped, about 55 minutes. Cool on a rack.

Energy 1726kcal/7323kJ; Protein 58.3g; Carbohydrate 345.9g, of which sugars 10.3g; Fat 21.9g, of which saturates 8.6g; Cholesterol 122mg; Calcium 465mg; Fibre 30.6g; Sodium 3077mg.

Dill Bread

MAKES 2 LOAVES

20ml/4 tsp active dried yeast
475ml/16fl oz/2 cups lukewarm water
30ml/2 tbsp sugar
1kg/2¼lb/9 cups strong white bread flour
½ onion, chopped
60ml/4 tbsp oil
1 large bunch of dill, finely chopped
2 eggs, lightly beaten
150g/5oz/generous ½ cup cottage cheese
10ml/4 tsp salt
milk, for glazing

1 Mix together the yeast, water and sugar in a large bowl and leave for 15 minutes to dissolve.

2 ▼ Stir in about half of the flour. Cover and leave to rise in a warm place for 45 minutes.

3 ▲ Cook the onion in 15ml/1 tbsp of the oil until soft. Cool, then stir into the yeast with the dill, eggs, cheese, salt and remaining oil. Add the flour until the mixture is too stiff to stir.

4 ▲ Transfer to a floured surface and knead until smooth and elastic. Place in a bowl, cover and leave to rise until doubled in volume, 1–1½ hours.

5 ▲ Grease a large baking sheet. Cut the dough in half and shape into 2 rounds. Leave to rise in a warm place for 30 minutes.

6 Preheat a 190°C/375°F/Gas 5 oven. Score the tops, brush with the milk and bake until browned, for about 50 minutes. Cool on a rack.

Energy 2207kcal/9346kJ; Protein 65.5g; Carbohydrate 428.3g, of which sugars 27.6g; Fat 37.4g, of which saturates 6.9g; Cholesterol 202mg; Calcium 874mg; Fibre 16.7g; Sodium 313mg.

Cheese Bread

MAKES 1 LOAF

15ml/1 tbsp active dried yeast
250ml/8fl oz/1 cup lukewarm milk
25g/1oz/2 tbsp butter
425g/15oz/3²/₃ cups strong white bread flour
10ml/2 tsp salt
115g/4oz/1 cup mature (sharp) cheddar cheese, grated

1 Combine the yeast and milk. Stir and leave for 15 minutes to dissolve.

2 Melt the butter, let cool, and add to the yeast mixture.

3 Mix the flour and salt together in a large bowl. Make a well in the centre and pour in the yeast mixture.

4 With a wooden spoon, stir from the centre, incorporating flour with each turn, to obtain a rough dough. If the dough seems too dry, add 30–45ml/2–3 tbsp water.

5 Transfer to a floured surface and knead until smooth and elastic. Return to the bowl, cover and leave to rise in a warm place until doubled in volume, 2–3 hours.

6 ▲ Grease a 23 × 13cm/9 × 5in bread tin (pan). Punch down the dough with your fist. Knead in the cheese, distributing it evenly.

7 ▼ Twist the dough, form into a loaf shape and place in the tin, tucking the ends under. Leave in a warm place until the dough rises above the rim of the tin.

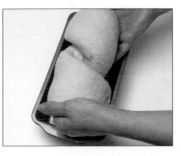

8 ▲ Preheat a 200°C/400°F/Gas 6 oven. Bake for 15 minutes, then lower to 190°C/375°F/Gas 5 and bake until the bottom sounds hollow when tapped, about 30 minutes more.

Energy 2125kcal/8967kJ; Protein 71.5g; Carbohydrate 342.2g, of which sugars 18.4g; Fat 59.8g, of which saturates 36.1g; Cholesterol 155mg; Calcium 1565mg; Fibre 13.2g; Sodium 2887mg.

Sun-Dried Tomato Plait

MAKES 1 LOAF

300ml/¹/₂ pint/1¹/₄ cups warm water
5ml/1 tsp active dried yeast
pinch of sugar
225g/8oz/2 cups wholemeal (whole-wheat) flour
225g/8oz/2 cups strong white bread flour
5ml/1 tsp salt
1.25ml/¹/₄ tsp freshly ground black pepper
115g/4oz drained sun-dried tomatoes in oil, chopped, plus 15ml/1 tbsp oil from the jar
30ml/2 tbsp freshly grated Parmesan cheese
30ml/2 tbsp red pesto
5ml/1 tsp coarse sea salt

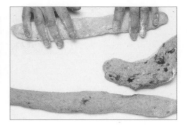

1 ▲ Put half the warm water in a jug (pitcher). Sprinkle the yeast on top. Add the sugar, mix and leave for 10 minutes.

2 ▲ Mix the flours, salt and pepper in a bowl. Add the yeast mixture, sun-dried tomatoes, oil, Parmesan, pesto and the remaining water. Gradually incorporate the flour and mix to a soft dough, adding a little extra water if necessary.

3 ▲ Transfer the dough to a floured surface and knead for 5 minutes until smooth and elastic. Return to the clean bowl, cover with a damp dish towel and leave in a warm place for about 2 hours until doubled in bulk. Lightly grease a baking sheet.

4 ▲ Transfer the dough on to a lightly floured surface and knead for a few minutes. Divide the dough into three equal pieces and shape each into a 30cm/12in-long sausage.

5 ▲ Dampen one end of the sausages, press them together, plait them loosely, then dampen and press them together at the other end. Place on the baking sheet, cover and leave for 30 minutes until well risen. Preheat the oven to 220°C/425°F/Gas 7.

6 ▲ Sprinkle with the salt. Bake for 10 minutes, then lower the temperature to 200°C/400°F/Gas 6 and bake for a further 15–20 minutes, or until the loaf sounds hollow when tapped underneath. Cool on a wire rack.

~ VARIATION ~

If you are unable to locate red pesto, use 30ml/2 tbsp chopped fresh basil mixed with 15ml/1 tbsp sun-dried tomato paste.

Energy 190kcal/804kJ; Protein 7.7g; Carbohydrate 33.5g, of which sugars 2.4g; Fat 3.7g, of which saturates 1.4g; Cholesterol 6mg; Calcium 110mg; Fibre 3g; Sodium 89mg.

Proscuitto and Parmesan Bread

MAKES 1 LOAF

225g/8oz/2 cups self-raising wholemeal (self-rising whole-wheat) flour

225g/8oz/2 cups self-raising (self-rising) flour

5ml/1 tsp baking powder

5ml/1 tsp salt

5ml/1 tsp black pepper

75g/3oz prosciutto, finely chopped

30ml/2 tbsp freshly grated Parmesan cheese

30ml/2 tbsp chopped fresh parsley

45ml/3 tbsp Meaux mustard

350ml/12fl oz/1½ cups buttermilk

skimmed milk, to glaze

1 ▲ Preheat the oven to 200°C/ 400°F/Gas 6. Flour a baking sheet. Place the wholemeal flour in a bowl and sift in the white flour, baking powder and salt. Add the pepper and the prosciutto. Set aside 15ml/1 tbsp of the grated Parmesan and stir the rest into the flour mixture with the parsley. Make a well in the centre.

2 ▲ Mix the mustard and buttermilk, pour into the flour and quickly mix to a soft dough.

3 ▲ Transfer the dough to a floured surface and knead briefly. Shape into an oval loaf, brush with milk and sprinkle with the reserved Parmesan. Place on the prepared baking sheet.

4 ▲ Bake the loaf for 25–30 minutes, or until it sounds hollow when tapped underneath. Allow to cool before serving.

Energy 229kcal/972kJ; Protein 11.1g; Carbohydrate 42.4g, of which sugars 3.5g; Fat 2.9g, of which saturates 1g; Cholesterol 10mg; Calcium 146mg; Fibre 3.4g; Sodium 334mg.

Courgette Yeast Bread

MAKES 1 LOAF

450g/1lb courgettes (zucchini), grated

30ml/2 tbsp salt

10ml/2 tsp active dried yeast

300ml/¹/₂ pint/1¹/₄ cups lukewarm water

400g/14oz/3¹/₂ cups strong white
  bread flour

olive oil, for brushing

1 ▲ In a colander or large sieve
(strainer), alternate layers of grated
courgettes and salt. Leave for 30
minutes, then squeeze out the
moisture with your hands.

2 Combine the yeast with 45ml/
3 tbsp of the lukewarm water, stir
and leave for 15 minutes to dissolve
the yeast.

3 ▲ Place the courgettes, yeast and
flour in a bowl. Stir together and add
just enough of the remaining water
to obtain a rough dough.

4 Transfer the dough to a floured
surface and knead for about 10
minutes, until smooth and elastic.

5 Put the dough in a lightly oiled
bowl, cover with a plastic bag, and
leave to rise in a warm place until
doubled in volume, for about
1¹/₂ hours.

6 Grease a baking sheet. Punch
down the risen dough with your fist
and knead into a tapered cylinder.
Place on the baking sheet, cover
with a dish towel and leave to rise
in a warm place until doubled in
volume, for about 45 minutes.

7 ▲ Preheat the oven to 220°C/
425°F/Gas 7. Brush the bread with
olive oil and bake for about 40–45
minutes, or until the loaf is a golden
colour. Cool on a rack before serving.

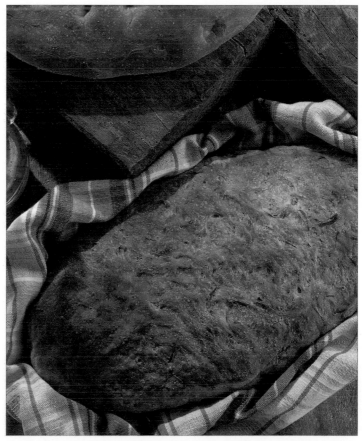

Energy 1445kcal/6133kJ; Protein 46g; Carbohydrate 319g, of which sugars 14g; Fat 7g, of which saturates 1g; Cholesterol 0mg; Calcium 673mg; Fibre 14g; Sodium 1982mg.

Spinach and Bacon Bread

MAKES 2 LOAVES

450ml/³/4 cup/scant 2 cups warm water
10ml/2 tsp dried yeast
pinch of sugar
15ml/1 tbsp olive oil
1 onion, chopped
115g/4oz rindless smoked bacon rashers (strips), chopped
225g/8oz chopped spinach, thawed if frozen
675g/1¹/2lb/6 cups strong white bread flour
7.5ml/1¹/2 tsp salt
7.5ml/1¹/2 tsp grated nutmeg
30g/2 tbsp grated reduced-fat Cheddar cheese

1 ▲ Put the water in a bowl. Sprinkle the yeast on top and add the sugar. Mix, and leave for 10 minutes. Grease two 23cm/9in cake tins (pans).

2 ▲ Heat the oil in a frying pan and fry the onion and bacon for 10 minutes until golden brown. If using frozen spinach, drain it thoroughly.

3 ▲ Sift the flour, salt and nutmeg into a mixing bowl and make a well in the centre. Add the yeast mixture. Tip in the fried bacon and onion (with the oil), then add the spinach. Gradually incorporate the flour mixture and mix to a soft dough. Transfer the dough to a floured surface and knead for 5 minutes.

4 ▲ Return to the clean bowl, cover with a damp dish towel and leave in a warm place to rise for about 2 hours, until doubled in bulk.

5 ▲ Transfer the dough to a floured surface, knead briefly, then divide it in half. Shape each half into a ball, flatten slightly and place in a tin, pressing the dough to the edges. Mark each loaf into eight wedges and sprinkle with the cheese. Cover loosely with a plastic bag and leave in a warm place until well risen. Preheat the oven to 200°C/400°F/Gas 6.

6 ▲ Bake the loaves for 25–30 minutes, or until they sound hollow when they are tapped underneath. Transfer to a wire rack to cool.

~ COOK'S TIP ~

If using frozen spinach, be sure to squeeze out any excess liquid or the resulting dough will be too sticky.

Energy 160kcal/680kJ; Protein 5.8g; Carbohydrate 32.6g, of which sugars 1.2g; Fat 1.6g, of which saturates 0.3g; Cholesterol 1mg; Calcium 98mg; Fibre 1.7g; Sodium 216mg.

Walnut Bread

MAKES 1 LOAF

425g/15oz/3²/₃ cups wholemeal (whole-wheat) flour

150g/5oz/1¹/₄ cups strong white bread flour

12.5ml/2¹/₂ tsp salt

550ml/18fl oz/2¹/₄ cups lukewarm water

15ml/1 tbsp honey

15ml/1 tbsp active dried yeast

150g/5oz/scant 1 cup walnut pieces, plus extra for decorating

1 beaten egg, for glazing

1 Combine the flours and salt in a large bowl. Make a well in the centre and add 250ml/8fl oz/1 cup of the water, the honey and the yeast.

2 Set aside until the yeast dissolves and the mixture is frothy.

3 Add the remaining water to the flour mixture. With a wooden spoon, stir from the centre, incorporating flour from the edges with each turn, to obtain a smooth dough. Add more flour if the dough is too sticky and use your hands if the dough becomes too stiff to stir.

4 Transfer to a floured board and knead, adding flour if necessary, until the dough is smooth and elastic. Place in a greased bowl and roll the dough around in the bowl to coat thoroughly on all sides.

5 ▲ Cover with a plastic bag and leave in a warm place until doubled in volume, about 1¹/₂ hours.

6 ▲ Punch down the dough and knead in the walnuts evenly.

7 Grease a baking sheet. Shape into a round loaf and place on the baking sheet. Press in walnut pieces to decorate the top. Cover loosely with a damp cloth and leave to rise in a warm place until doubled, 25–30 minutes.

8 Preheat a 220°C/425°F/Gas 7 oven.

9 ▲ With a sharp knife, score the top. Brush with the glaze. Bake for 15 minutes. Lower the heat to 190°C/375°F/Gas 5 and bake until the bottom sounds hollow when tapped, about 40 minutes. Cool on a rack.

Energy 2786kcal/11722kJ; Protein 87.1g; Carbohydrate 393.2g, of which sugars 26g; Fat 107g, of which saturates 9.4g; Cholesterol 0mg; Calcium 489mg; Fibre 47g; Sodium 4941mg.

Courgette and Walnut Loaf

MAKES 1 LOAF

3 eggs
75g/3oz/6 tbsp soft light brown sugar
50ml/2fl oz/¼ cup sunflower oil
225g/8oz/2 cups wholemeal (whole-wheat) flour
5ml/1 tsp baking powder
5ml/1 tsp bicarbonate of soda (baking soda)
5ml/1 tsp ground cinnamon
2.5ml/½ tsp ground allspice
7.5ml/½ tbsp green cardamoms, seeds removed and crushed
150g/5oz grated courgette (zucchini)
45ml/3 tbsp walnuts, chopped
45ml/3 tbsp walnuts sunflower seeds

1 ▲ Preheat the oven to 180°C/ 350°F/Gas 4. Grease and line a 900g/ 2lb loaf tin (pan). Beat the eggs and sugar together and add the oil.

2 ▲ Sift the flour together with the baking powder, bicarbonate of soda, cinnamon and allspice.

3 ▲ Mix the flour and spices into the egg mixture with the rest of the ingredients, reserving 15ml/1 tbsp of the seeds.

4 Spoon into the loaf tin, level off the top, and sprinkle with the reserved sunflower seeds.

5 ▲ Bake for about 1 hour or until a skewer inserted in the centre comes out clean. Leave to cool slightly, then turn out on to a wire cooling rack.

Energy 2356kcal/9855kJ; Protein 72g; Carbohydrate 235g, of which sugars 85g; Fat 133g, of which saturates 18g; Cholesterol 695mg; Calcium 506mg; Fibre 22g; Sodium 1862mg.

Prune Bread

MAKES 1 LOAF

225g/8oz/1 cup dried prunes
15ml/1 tbsp active dried yeast
75g/3oz/²/₃ cup wholemeal (whole-wheat) flour
375–425g/13–15oz/3¹/₄–3²/₃ cups strong white bread flour
2.5ml/¹/₂ tsp bicarbonate of soda (baking soda)
5ml/1 tsp salt
5ml/1 tsp pepper
25g/1oz/2 tbsp butter, at room temperature
175ml/6fl oz/³/₄ cup milk buttermilk
50g/2oz/¹/₃ cup walnuts, chopped
milk, for glazing

1 Simmer the prunes with enough water to cover until soft, or soak overnight. Drain, reserving 60ml/ 4 tbsp of the soaking liquid. Pit and chop the prunes.

2 Combine the yeast and the reserved prune liquid, stir and leave for 15 minutes to dissolve.

3 In a large bowl, stir together the flours, bicarbonate of soda, salt and pepper. Make a well in the centre.

4 ▲ Add the chopped prunes, butter, and buttermilk. Pour in the yeast mixture. With a wooden spoon, stir from the centre, incorporating more flour with each turn, to obtain a rough dough.

5 Transfer to a floured surface and knead until smooth and elastic. Return to the bowl, cover with a plastic bag and leave to rise in a warm place until doubled in volume, about 1¹/₂ hours.

6 Grease a baking sheet.

7 ▲ Punch down the dough with your fist, then knead in the walnuts.

8 Shape the dough into a cylindrical loaf. Place on the baking sheet, cover, and leave to rise for 45 minutes.

9 Preheat a 220°C/425°F/Gas 7 oven.

10 ▼ Score the top deeply. Brush with milk and bake for 15 minutes. Lower to 190°C/375°F/ Gas 5 and bake until the bottom sounds hollow when tapped, about 35 minutes more. Cool.

Energy 2520kcal/10639kJ; Protein 65.6g; Carbohydrate 433.3g, of which sugars 93.2g; Fat 70.4g, of which saturates 19.9g; Cholesterol 70mg; Calcium 915mg; Fibre 33.4g; Sodium 2266mg.

Orange Wheat Loaf

MAKES 1 LOAF

275g/10oz/2½ cups wholemeal
  (whole-wheat) flour

2.5ml/½ tsp salt

25g/1oz/2 tbsp butter butter

30ml/2 tbsp soft light brown sugar

½ sachet easy-blend (rapid-rise)
  dried yeast

grated rind and juice of ½ orange

1 ▲ Sift the flour into a large bowl
and add any wheat flakes from the
sieve (strainer). Add the salt and rub
in the butter with your fingertips.

2 ▲ Stir in the sugar, yeast and
orange rind. Pour the orange juice
into a measuring jug (cup) and make
up to 200ml/7fl oz/scant 1 cup with
hot water (not more than hand hot).

3 ▲ Stir the liquid into the flour
and mix to a ball of dough. Knead on
a floured surface until smooth.

4 Place the dough in a greased 450g/
1lb loaf tin (pan) and leave in a warm
place until doubled in size. Preheat
the oven to 220°C/425°F/Gas 7.

5 ▲ Bake the bread for 30–35
minutes, or until it sounds hollow
when you tap the bottom. Remove
from the tin and leave to cool on a
wire rack.

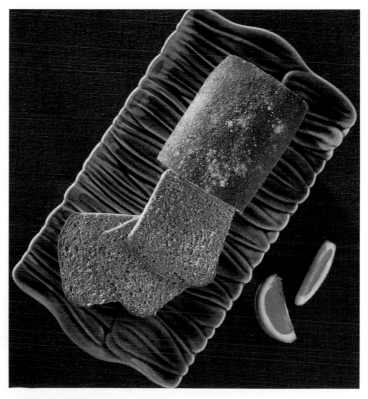

Energy 1329kcal/5602kJ; Protein 35g; Carbohydrate 205g, of which sugars 35g; Fat 47g, of which saturates 27g; Cholesterol 107mg; Calcium 132mg; Fibre 24g; Sodium 1306mg.

Corn Bread

MAKES 1 LOAF

115g/4oz/1 cup plain (all-purpose) flour,

75g/3oz/6 tbsp caster (superfine) sugar

5ml/1 tsp salt

15ml/1 tbsp baking powder

175g/6oz/1½ cups cornmeal or polenta

350ml/12fl oz/1½ cups milk

2 eggs

75g/3oz/6 tbsp butter, melted

115g/4oz/½ cup margarine, melted

1 Preheat a 200°C/400°F/Gas 6 oven.
Line a 23 × 13cm/9 × 5in loaf tin (pan)
with baking parchment and grease.

2 Sift the flour, sugar, salt and baking
powder into a mixing bowl.

3 ▼ Add the cornmeal and stir to
blend. Make a well in the centre.

4 ▲ Whisk together the milk,
eggs, butter and margarine. Pour the
mixture into the well. Stir until just
blended; do not overmix.

5 Pour into the tin and bake until a
skewer inserted in the centre comes
out clean, about 45 minutes. Serve
hot or at room temperature.

Spicy Corn Bread

MAKES 9 SQUARES

3–4 whole canned chilli peppers,
    drained

2 eggs

475ml/16fl oz/2 cups buttermilk

50g/2oz/¼ cup butter, melted

50g/2oz/½ cup plain (all-purpose) flour

5ml/1 tsp bicarbonate of soda (baking soda)

10ml/2 tsp salt

175g/6oz/1½ cups cornmeal or polenta

350g/12oz canned corn or frozen
    corn, thawed

1 Preheat a 200°C/400°F/Gas 6
oven. Line the bottom and sides of a
23cm/9in square cake tin (pan) with
baking parchment and grease lightly.

2 ▲ With a sharp knife, finely chop
the chillies and set aside.

3 ▲ In a large bowl, whisk the eggs
until frothy, then whisk in the
buttermilk. Add the melted butter.

4 In another large bowl, sift together
the flour, bicarbonate of soda and salt.
Fold into the buttermilk mixture in
three batches, then fold in the cornmeal in three batches.

5 ▲ Fold in the chopped chillies and
the corn.

6 Pour the mixture into the prepared
tin and bake in the centre of the oven
until a skewer inserted in the middle
comes out clean, 25–30 minutes.
Let stand for 2–3 minutes before
unmoulding. Cut into squares and
serve warm.

Corn: Energy 3008kcal/12539kJ; Protein 52.7g; Carbohydrate 303.3g, of which sugars 87.7g; Fat 179.8g, of which saturates 46.1g; Cholesterol 561mg; Calcium 696mg; Fibre 7.4g; Sodium 1672mg.
Spicy: Energy 213kcal/892kJ; Protein 6.7g; Carbohydrate 31.2g, of which sugars 6.2g; Fat 7.1g, of which saturates 3.4g; Cholesterol 56mg; Calcium 82mg; Fibre 1.1g; Sodium 614mg.

Onion Focaccia

MAKES 2 ROUND LOAVES

675g/1¹/₂lb/6 cups strong white bread flour
2.5ml/¹/₂ tsp salt
2.5ml/¹/₂ tsp caster (superfine) sugar
15ml/1 tbsp easy-blend (rapid-rise) dried yeast
60ml/4 tbsp extra virgin olive oil
450ml/³/₄ cup/scant 2 cups hand-hot water

TO FINISH

2 red onions, thinly sliced
45ml/3 tbsp extra virgin olive oil
15ml/1 tbsp coarse salt

1 Sift the flour, salt and sugar into a large bowl. Stir in the yeast, oil and water and mix to a dough. (Add a little extra water if the dough is dry.)

2 ▲ Turn out on to a floured surface and knead for 10 minutes until smooth and elastic. Put in a clean, lightly oiled bowl and cover with clear film (plastic wrap). Leave to rise in a warm place until doubled in bulk.

3 ▲ Place two 25cm/10in metal flan rings on baking sheets. Oil the sides of the rings and the baking sheets.

4 ▲ Preheat the oven to 200°C/ 400°F/Gas 6. Halve the dough and roll each piece to a 25cm/10in round. Press into the rings, cover with a dampened dish towel and leave for 30 minutes to rise.

5 ▲ Make deep holes, about 2.5cm/ 1in apart, in the dough. Cover and leave for a further 20 minutes.

6 ▲ Scatter with the onions and drizzle over the oil. Sprinkle with the salt, then a little cold water, to stop a crust from forming.

7 ▲ Bake for about 25 minutes, sprinkling with water again during cooking. Cool on a wire rack.

Energy 1677kcal/7059kJ; Protein 34g; Carbohydrate 274g, of which sugars 13g; Fat 57g, of which saturates 8g; Cholesterol 0mg; Calcium 510mg; Fibre 14g; Sodium 997mg.

Saffron Focaccia

MAKES 1 ROUND LOAF

pinch of saffron threads
150ml/¹/₄ pint/²/₃ cup boiling water
225g/8oz/2 cups plain (all-purpose) flour
2.5ml/¹/₂ tsp salt
5ml/1 tsp easy-blend (rapid-rise) dried yeast
15ml/1 tbsp olive oil
FOR THE TOPPING
2 garlic cloves, sliced
1 red onion, cut into thin wedges
rosemary sprigs
12 black olives, pitted and coarsely chopped
15ml/1 tbsp olive oil

1 ▲ Infuse the saffron in the boiling water. Leave until cooled to lukewarm.

2 ▲ Place the flour, salt, yeast and olive oil in a food processor. Turn on and gradually add the saffron and its liquid until the dough forms a ball.

3 ▲ Transfer to a floured board and knead for 10–15 minutes. Place in a bowl, cover and leave to rise for about 30–40 minutes, until doubled in size.

4 ▲ Punch down the risen dough on a lightly floured surface and roll out into an oval shape, 1cm/¹/₂in thick. Place on a lightly greased baking sheet and leave to rise for 20–30 minutes.

5 Preheat the oven to 200°C/400°F/ Gas 6. Press indentations in the dough.

6 ▲ Cover with the topping ingredients, brush lightly with olive oil, and bake for about 25 minutes or until the loaf sounds hollow when tapped on the bottom. Leave to cool.

Energy 1135kcal/4779kJ; Protein 24g; Carbohydrate 188g, of which sugars 12g; Fat 37g, of which saturates 5g; Cholesterol 0mg; Calcium 376mg; Fibre 12g; Sodium 822mg.

Cheese and Onion Sticks

MAKES 2 STICKS

300ml/½ pint/1¼ cups warm water

5ml/1 tsp dried yeast

pinch of sugar

15ml/1 tbsp sunflower oil

1 red onion, finely chopped

450g/1lb/4 cups strong white bread flour

5ml/1 tsp salt

5ml/1 tsp dry mustard powder

45ml/3 tbsp chopped fresh herbs, such as thyme, parsley, marjoram or sage

75g/3oz/¾ cup grated reduced-fat Cheddar cheese

~ COOK'S TIP ~

To make Onion and Coriander Sticks, omit the Cheddar cheese, herbs and mustard. Add 15ml/ 1 tbsp ground coriander and 45ml/3 tbsp chopped fresh coriander (cilantro) instead.

1 ▲ Put the water in a jug. Sprinkle the yeast on top. Add the sugar, mix well and leave for 10 minutes.

2 ▲ Heat the oil in a frying pan and fry the onion until it is well coloured.

3 ▲ Stir the flour, salt and mustard into a mixing bowl, then add the chopped herbs. Set aside 30ml/2 tbsp of the cheese. Stir the rest into the flour mixture and make a well in the centre.

4 Add the yeast mixture with the fried onions and oil, then gradually incorporate the flour from around the edges and mix to a soft dough, adding extra water if necessary.

5 ▲ Transfer the dough to a floured surface and knead for 5 minutes until smooth and elastic. Return to the clean bowl, cover and leave to rise for 2 hours, until doubled in bulk. Lightly grease two baking sheets.

6 ▲ Knead briefly, then divide the mixture in half and roll each piece into a 30cm/12in long stick. Place on a baking sheet and make diagonal cuts along the top.

7 ▲ Sprinkle with the reserved cheese. Cover and leave for 30 minutes until well risen. Preheat the oven to 220°C/425°F/Gas 7. Bake the sticks for 25 minutes or until they sound hollow when tapped underneath.

Energy 972kcal/4117kJ; Protein 40g; Carbohydrate 176g, of which sugars 7g; Fat 17g, of which saturates 5g; Cholesterol 16mg; Calcium 663mg; Fibre 10g; Sodium 1244mg.

Saffron and Basil Breadsticks

MAKES 32 STICKS

generous pinch of saffron strands

30ml/2 tbsp hot water

450g/1lb/4 cups strong white bread flour

5ml/1 tsp salt

10ml/2 tsp easy-blend (rapid-rise)
  dried yeast

300ml/½ pint/1¼ cups lukewarm water

45ml/3 tbsp olive oil

45ml/3 tbsp chopped fresh basil

1 ▲ Infuse the saffron strands in the hot water for 10 minutes.

2 ▲ Sift the flour and salt into a large mixing bowl. Stir in the yeast, then make a well in the centre of the dry ingredients. Pour in the lukewarm water and saffron liquid.

3 ▲ Add the oil and basil and mix to a soft dough.

4 ▲ Knead the dough for 10 minutes until smooth and elastic. Place in a greased bowl, cover and leave for 1 hour or until it has doubled in size.

5 ▲ Knock back and knead the dough for 2–3 minutes.

6 ▲ Preheat the oven to 220°C/425°F/Gas 7. Divide the dough into 32 pieces and shape into long sticks. Place well apart on greased baking sheets, then leave for a further 15–20 minutes. Bake for about 15 minutes until crisp and golden. Serve warm.

~ VARIATION ~

Use powdered saffron if saffron strands are not available. Turmeric is an inexpensive alternative: it imparts a lovely gold colour, but its flavour is not as delicate.

Energy 61kcal/256kJ; Protein 2g; Carbohydrate 11g, of which sugars 0g; Fat 2g, of which saturates 0g; Cholesterol 0mg; Calcium 20mg; Fibre 1g; Sodium 62mg.

Flat Bread with Sage

MAKES 1 ROUND LOAF

10ml/2 tsp active dried yeast
250ml/8fl oz/1 cup lukewarm water
350g/12oz/3 cups plain (all-purpose) flour
10ml/2 tsp salt
75ml/5 tbsp extra virgin olive oil
12 fresh sage leaves, chopped

1 Combine the yeast and water, stir and leave for 15 minutes to dissolve.

2 Mix the flour and salt in a large bowl, and make a well in the centre.

3 Stir in the yeast mixture and 60ml/4 tbsp of the oil. Stir gently with a wooden spoon from the centre, incorporating flour with each turn, to obtain a rough dough.

4 ▲ Transfer to a floured surface and knead until smooth and elastic. Place in a lightly oiled bowl. Cover with clear film (plastic wrap) and leave to rise in a warm place until doubled in volume, about 2 hours.

5 ▲ Preheat the oven to 200°C/ 400°F/Gas 6 and place a baking sheet in the centre of the oven.

6 ▲ Punch down the dough. Knead in the sage, then roll into a 30cm/ 12in round. Leave to rise slightly.

7 ▲ Dimple the surface of the dough all over with your finger. Drizzle the remaining oil on top. Slide a floured board under the bread, carry to the oven, and slide off on to the hot baking sheet. Bake for about 35 minutes or until golden brown. Cool on a wire rack, wrapped in a dish towel.

Energy 1953kcal/8210kJ; Protein 35g; Carbohydrate 291g, of which sugars 6g; Fat 80g, of which saturates 11g; Cholesterol 0mg; Calcium 526mg; Fibre 14g; Sodium 3941mg.

Sweet Sesame Loaf

MAKES 1 OR 2 LOAVES

90ml/6 tbsp sesame seeds
275g/10oz/2½ cups plain (all-purpose) flour
12.5ml/2½ tsp baking powder
5ml/1 tsp salt
50g/2oz/¼ cup butter or margarine, at room temperature
130g/4½oz/scant ¾ cup sugar
2 eggs, at room temperature
grated rind of 1 lemon
350ml/12fl oz/1½ cups milk

1 Preheat a 180°C/350°F/Gas 4 oven. Line a 23 × 13cm/9 × 5in loaf tin (pan) with baking parchment and grease.

2 ▲ Reserve 30ml/2 tbsp of the sesame seeds. Spread the rest on a baking sheet and bake until lightly toasted, about 10 minutes.

3 Sift the flour, salt and baking powder into a bowl.

4 ▲ Stir in the toasted sesame seeds and set aside.

5 With an electric mixer, cream the butter or margarine and sugar together until light and fluffy. Beat in the eggs, then stir in the lemon rind and milk.

6 ▼ Pour the milk mixture over the dry ingredients and fold in with a large metal spoon until just blended.

7 ▲ Pour into the tin and sprinkle over the reserved sesame seeds.

8 Bake until a skewer inserted in the centre comes out clean, about 1 hour. Let cool in the tin for about 10 minutes. Turn out onto a wire rack to cool completely.

Energy 1339kcal/5625kJ; Protein 28g; Carbohydrate 192g, of which sugars 76g; Fat 56g, of which saturates 23g; Cholesterol 83mg; Calcium 928mg; Fibre 5g; Sodium 3600mg.

Apricot Nut Loaf

MAKES 1 LOAF

115g/4oz/¹/₂ cup dried apricots
1 large orange
75g/3oz/¹/₂ cup raisins
150g/5oz/³/₄ cup caster (superfine) sugar
90ml/6 tbsp oil
2 eggs, lightly beaten
250g/9oz/2¹/₄ cups plain (all-purpose) flour
10ml/2 tsp baking powder
2.5ml/¹/₂ tsp salt
5ml/1 tsp bicarbonate of soda (baking soda)
50g/2oz/¹/₃ cup chopped walnuts

1 Preheat a 180°C/350°F/Gas 4 oven. Line a 23 × 13cm/9 × 5in loaf tin (pan) with baking parchment and grease.

2 Soak the apricots with lukewarm water to cover for 30 minutes.

3 ▲ With a vegetable peeler, remove the orange rind, leaving the pith.

4 With a sharp knife, finely chop the orange rind strips.

5 Drain the apricots and chop coarsely. Place in a bowl with the orange rind and raisins. Set aside.

6 Squeeze the peeled orange. Measure the juice and add enough hot water to obtain 175ml/6fl oz/¾ cup liquid.

7 ▼ Pour the orange juice mixture over the apricot mixture. Stir in the sugar, oil and eggs. Set aside.

8 In another bowl, sift together the flour, baking powder, salt and bicarbonate of soda. Fold the flour mixture into the apricot mixture in three batches.

9 ▲ Stir in the walnuts.

10 Spoon the mixture into the prepared tin and bake until a skewer inserted in the centre comes out clean, 55–60 minutes. If the loaf browns too quickly, protect the top with a sheet of foil. Let cool in the pan for 10 minutes before transferring to a rack to cool completely.

Energy 3267kcal/13734kJ; Protein 57g; Carbohydrate 474g, of which sugars 279g; Fat 140g, of which saturates 17g; Cholesterol 464mg; Calcium 845mg; Fibre 46g; Sodium 3573mg.

Apple-sauce Bread

MAKES 1 LOAF

1 egg
250ml/8fl oz/1 cup apple sauce
50ml/4 tbsp butter or margarine, melted
75g/3oz/6 tbsp soft dark brown sugar, firmly packed
50g/2oz/¼ cup sugar
225g/8oz/2 cups plain (all-purpose) flour
10ml/2 tsp baking powder
2.5ml/½ tsp bicarbonate of soda (baking soda)
2.5ml/½ tsp salt
5ml/1 tsp ground cinnamon
2.5ml/½ tsp grated nutmeg
75g/3oz/½ cup currants or raisins
175g/6oz/1 cup pecans, chopped

1 Preheat the oven to 180°C/350°F/Gas 4. Grease and line a 23 × 13cm/9 × 5in loaf tin (pan) with baking parchment.

2 ▲ Break the egg into a bowl and beat lightly. Stir in the apple sauce, butter or margarine, and both sugars.

3 In another bowl, sift together the flour, baking powder, bicarbonate of soda, salt, cinnamon and nutmeg. Fold the dry ingredients into the apple-sauce mixture in three batches.

4 ▲ Stir in the currants or raisins and chopped pecans.

5 Pour into the prepared tin and bake for about 1 hour, or until a skewer inserted in the centre comes out clean. Allow to stand for 10 minutes before transferring to a cooling rack.

Energy 3349kcal/14030kJ; Protein 58g; Carbohydrate 405g, of which sugars 229g; Fat 179g, of which saturates 43g; Cholesterol 360mg; Calcium 817mg; Fibre 27g; Sodium 3122mg.

Banana and Cardamom Bread

MAKES 1 LOAF

150ml/¼ pint/⅔ cup warm water

5ml/1 tsp dried yeast

pinch of sugar

10 cardamom pods

400g/14oz/3½ cups strong white
bread flour

5ml/1 tsp salt

30ml/2 tbsp malt extract

2 ripe bananas, mashed

5ml/1 tsp sesame seeds

1 ▲ Put the warm water in a bowl.
Sprinkle the yeast on top. Add the
sugar, mix and leave for 10 minutes.

2 ▲ Split the cardamom pods.
Remove the seeds and chop finely.

3 ▲ Sift the flour and salt into a
mixing bowl and make a well in the
centre. Add the yeast mixture with
the malt extract, chopped cardamom
seeds and bananas.

4 ▲ Gradually incorporate the flour
and mix to a soft dough, adding extra
water if necessary. Turn on to a
floured surface and knead for about
5 minutes. Return to the clean bowl,
cover and leave to rise for 2 hours,
until doubled in bulk.

5 ▲ Grease a baking sheet. Turn the
dough on to a floured surface, knead
briefly, then divide into three and
shape into a plait. Place on the baking
sheet and cover loosely with a plastic
bag. Leave until well risen. Preheat
the oven to 220°C/425°F/Gas 7.

6 ▲ Brush lightly with water and
sprinkle with the sesame seeds. Bake
for 10 minutes, then lower the oven
temperature to 200°C/400°F/Gas 6.
Cook for 15 minutes more, or until
the loaf sounds hollow when tapped.

~ COOK'S TIP ~

Make sure the bananas are really
ripe so that they impart maximum
flavour to the bread. If you prefer,
place the dough in one piece in a
450g/1lb loaf tin (pan) and bake
for an extra 5 minutes. As well as
being low in fat, bananas are a
good source of potassium,
therefore making an ideal
nutritious, low-fat snack.

Energy 1618kcal/6876kJ; Protein 49g; Carbohydrate 358g, of which sugars 56g; Fat 9g, of which saturates 1g; Cholesterol 0mg; Calcium 631mg; Fibre 21g; Sodium 1985mg.

Whole-wheat Banana Nut Loaf

MAKES 1 LOAF

115g/4oz/¹/₂ cup butter, at room temperature

115g/4oz/scant ³/₄ cup caster (superfine) sugar

2 eggs, at room temperature

115g/4oz/1 cup plain (all-purpose) flour,

5ml/1 tsp bicarbonate of soda (baking soda)

1.25ml/¹/₄ tsp salt

5ml/1 tsp ground cinnamon

50g/2oz/¹/₂ cup wholemeal (whole-wheat) flour

3 large ripe bananas

5ml/1 tsp vanilla extract

2 oz (55 g) chopped walnuts

1 Preheat a 180°C/350°F/Gas 4 oven. Line a 23 × 13cm/ 9 × 5in loaf tin (pan) with baking parchment and grease the paper.

2 With an electric mixer, cream the butter and sugar together until light and fluffy.

3 ▲ Add the eggs, one at a time, beating well after each addition.

4 Sift the plain flour, bicarbonate of soda, salt and cinnamon over the butter mixture and stir to blend.

5 ▲ Stir in the wholemeal flour.

6 ▲ With a fork, mash the bananas to a purée, then stir into the mixture. Stir in the vanilla and nuts.

7 ▲ Pour the mixture into the prepared tin and spread level.

8 Bake for about 50–60 minutes, until a skewer inserted in the centre comes out clean. Let stand 10 minutes before transferring to a rack.

Energy 2542kcal/10631kJ; Protein 44g; Carbohydrate 275g, of which sugars 149g; Fat 148g, of which saturates 67g; Cholesterol 709mg; Calcium 336mg; Fibre 16g; Sodium 1874mg.

Date and Pecan Loaf

MAKES 1 LOAF

175g/6oz/generous 1 cup pitted
  dates, chopped

175ml/6fl oz/³/₄ cup boiling water

50g/2oz/¹/₄ cup unsalted butter,
  at room temperature

50g/2oz/4 tbsp soft dark brown sugar

50g/2oz/¹/₄ cup caster (superfine) sugar

1 egg, at room temperature

30ml/2 tbsp brandy

175g/6oz/1¹/₂ cups plain (all-purpose) flour

10ml/2 tsp baking powder

2.5ml/¹/₂ tsp salt

3.75ml/³/₄ tsp freshly grated nutmeg

90ml/6 tbsp chopped pecans or walnuts

1 ▲ Place the dates in a heatproof
bowl and pour over the boiling water.
Set aside to cool.

2 Preheat a 180°C/350°F/Gas 4 oven.
Line a 23 × 13cm/9 × 5in loaf tin (pan)
with baking parchment and grease.

3 ▲ With an electric mixer, cream
the butter and sugars until light and
fluffy. Beat in the egg and brandy,
then set aside.

4 Sift the flour, baking powder, salt
and nutmeg together, three times.

5 ▼ Fold the dry ingredients into
the sugar mixture in three batches,
alternating with the dates and water.

6 ▲ Fold in the nuts.

7 Pour the mixture into the prepared
tin and bake for 45–50 minutes, until
a skewer inserted in the centre comes
out clean. Allow to cool in the tin for
10 minutes before transferring to a
rack to cool completely.

Energy 3431kcal/14431kJ; Protein 45g; Carbohydrate 363g, of which sugars 234g, Fat 212g, of which saturates 102g; Cholesterol 634mg; Calcium 577mg; Fibre 24g; Sodium 2079mg.

Raisin Bread

MAKES 2 LOAVES

15ml/1 tbsp active dried yeast
450ml/³/4 cup/scant 2 cups lukewarm milk
150g/5oz/scant 1 cup raisins
75ml/5 tbsp currants
15ml/1 tbsp sherry or brandy
2.5ml/¹/2 tsp grated nutmeg
grated rind of 1 large orange
60ml/4 tbsp sugar
15ml/1 tbsp salt
115g/4oz/¹/2 cup butter, melted
675–850g/1lb 8oz–1lb 14oz/6–7¹/2 cups strong white bread flour
1 egg beaten with 15ml/1 tbsp cream, for glazing

1 Stir together the yeast and 120ml/4fl oz/1 cup of the milk and let stand for 15 minutes to dissolve.

2 ▲ Mix the raisins, currants, sherry or brandy, nutmeg and orange rind together and set aside.

3 In another bowl, mix the remaining milk, sugar, salt and half the butter. Add the yeast mixture. With a wooden spoon, stir in half the flour, 150g/5oz/1¹/4 cups at a time, until blended. Add the remaining flour as needed for a stiff dough.

4 Transfer to a floured surface and knead until smooth and elastic. Place in a greased bowl, cover and leave to rise in a warm place until doubled in volume, about 2¹/2 hours.

5 Punch down the dough, return to the bowl, cover and leave to rise in a warm place for 30 minutes.

6 Grease two 21.5 × 11.5cm/8¹/2 × 4¹/2in bread tins (pans). Divide the dough in half and roll each into a 50 × 8cm/20 × 7in rectangle.

7 ▲ Brush the rectangles with the remaining melted butter. Sprinkle over the raisin mixture, then roll up tightly, tucking in the ends slightly as you roll. Place in the tins, cover, and leave to rise until doubled in volume.

8 ▲ Preheat the oven to 200°C/400°F/Gas 6. Brush the loaves with the glaze. Bake for 20 minutes, then lower the temperature to 180°C/350°F/Gas 4 and bake until golden, for about 25–30 minutes more. Cool on racks.

Energy 2345kcal/9899kJ; Protein 58g; Carbohydrate 406g, of which sugars 120g; Fat 65g, of which saturates 37g; Cholesterol 270mg; Calcium 905mg; Fibre 21g; Sodium 3495mg.

Sweet Potato and Raisin Bread

MAKES 1 LOAF

225–275g/8–10oz/2–2¹/₂ cups plain (all-purpose) flour
10ml/2 tsp baking powder
2.5ml/¹/₂ tsp salt
5ml/1 tsp ground cinnamon
2.5ml/¹/₂ tsp grated nutmeg
450g/1lb mashed cooked sweet potatoes
75g/3oz/6 tbsp soft light brown sugar
115g/4oz/¹/₂ cup butter, melted
3 eggs, beaten
75ml/5 tbsp raisins

1 ▲ Preheat the oven to 180°C/ 350°F/Gas 4. Grease a 23 × 13cm/ 9 × 5in loaf tin (pan).

2 Sift the flour, baking powder, salt, cinnamon and nutmeg into a small bowl. Set aside.

3 ▲ With an electric mixer, beat the mashed sweet potatoes with the brown sugar, butter and eggs until well mixed.

4 ▲ Add the flour mixture and the raisins. Stir with a wooden spoon until the flour is just mixed in.

5 ▲ Transfer the batter to the prepared tin. Bake for 1–1¼ hours, or until a skewer inserted in the centre comes out clean.

6 Cool in the pan on a wire rack for 15 minutes, then turn the bread on to the wire rack and cool completely.

Energy 2871kcal/12063kJ; Protein 55g; Carbohydrate 421g, of which sugars 173g; Fat 119g, of which saturates 67g; Cholesterol 941mg; Calcium 798mg; Fibre 23g; Sodium 3331mg.

Sultana Bread

MAKES 1 LOAF

150ml/¼ pint/²⁄₃ cup warm water

5ml/1 tsp dried yeast

15ml/1 tbsp clear honey

225g/8oz/2 cups wholemeal
(whole-wheat) flour

225g/8oz/2 cups strong white
bread flour

5ml/1 tsp salt

115g/4oz/8 tbsp sultanas

50g/2oz/⅓ cup walnuts, finely chopped

175ml/6fl oz/¾ cup warm skimmed milk,
plus extra for glazing

1 ▲ Put the water in a jug (pitcher).
Sprinkle the yeast on top. Add a few
drops of the honey, mix well and
leave to stand for 10 minutes.

2 ▲ Put the flours in a mixing bowl,
with the salt and sultanas. Set aside
15ml/1 tbsp of the walnuts and add
the rest to the bowl. Mix lightly and
make a well in the centre.

3 ▲ Add the yeast and honey
mixture to the flour mixture with the
milk and remaining honey. Gradually
incorporate the flour, mixing to a
soft dough; add a little extra water if
the dough feels too dry to work with.

4 ▲ Knead for 5 minutes until
smooth and elastic. Return to the
clean bowl, cover with a dish towel
and leave to rise for 2 hours until
doubled in bulk. Grease a baking sheet.

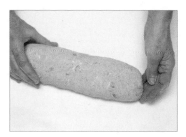

5 ▲ Turn the dough on to a floured
surface and form into a 28cm/11in
sausage shape. Place on the baking
sheet. Make cuts down the loaf.

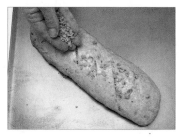

6 ▲ Brush with milk, sprinkle with
the reserved walnuts and leave to rise
for 40 minutes. Preheat the oven to
220°C/425°F/ Gas 7. Bake for
10 minutes. Lower the temperature to
200°C/400°F/Gas 6 and bake for
about 20 minutes more, or until the
loaf sounds hollow when tapped.

> **~ VARIATION ~**
> To make Apple and Hazelnut
> Bread, replace the sultanas with
> two chopped eating apples and use
> chopped toasted hazelnuts instead
> of the walnuts. Add 5ml/1 tsp
> ground cinnamon with the flour.

Energy 2239kcal/9479kJ; Protein 71g; Carbohydrate 418g, of which sugars 112g; Fat 43g, of which saturates 4g; Cholesterol 5mg; Calcium 736mg; Fibre 38g; Sodium 2083mg.

Plaited Prune Bread

MAKES 1 LOAF

15ml/1 tbsp active dry yeast
50ml/2fl oz/¹/4 cup lukewarm water
50ml/2fl oz/¹/4 cup lukewarm milk
50g/2oz/¹/4 cup caster (superfine) sugar
2.5ml/¹/2 tsp salt
1 egg
50g/2oz/¹/4 cup butter, at room temperature
425–500g/15oz–1lb 2oz/3²/3–4²/3 cups plain (all-purpose) flour
1 egg beaten with 10ml/2 tsp water, for glazing

FOR THE FILLING

200g/7oz/1³/4 cups cooked prunes
10ml/2 tsp grated lemon rind
5ml/1 tsp grated orange rind
1.25ml/¹/4 tsp freshly grated nutmeg
40g/1¹/2oz/3 tbsp butter, melted
50g/2oz/¹/3 cup finely chopped walnuts
30ml/2 tbsp caster (superfine) sugar

1 In a large bowl, combine the yeast and water, stir and leave for 15 minutes to dissolve.

2 Stir in the milk, sugar, salt, egg and butter. Gradually stir in 350g/12oz/ 3 cups of the flour to obtain a dough.

3 Transfer to a floured surface and knead in just enough flour to obtain a dough that is smooth and elastic. Put into a clean bowl, cover and leave to rise in a warm place until doubled in volume, about 1¹/2 hours.

> ### ~ VARIATION ~
>
> For Plaited Apricot Bread, replace the prunes with the same amount of dried apricots. It is not necessary to cook them, but to soften, soak them in hot tea and discard the liquid before using.

4 ▲ Meanwhile, for the filling, combine the prunes, lemon and orange rinds, nutmeg, butter, walnuts and sugar and stir together to blend. Set aside.

5 Grease a large baking sheet. Punch down the dough and transfer to a lightly floured surface. Knead briefly, then roll out into a 38 × 25cm/ 15 × 10in rectangle. Carefully transfer to the baking sheet.

6 ▲ Spread the filling in the centre.

7 ▲ With a sharp knife, cut 10 strips at an angle on either side of the filling, cutting just to the filling.

8 ▲ For a plaited pattern, fold up one end neatly, then fold over the strips from alternating sides until all the strips are folded over. Tuck excess dough underneath at the ends.

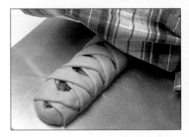

9 ▲ Cover loosely with a tea towel and leave to rise in a warm place until almost doubled in volume.

10 ▲ Preheat a 190°C/375°F/Gas 5 oven. Brush with the glaze. Bake until browned, about 30 minutes. Transfer to a wire rack to cool.

Energy 3530kcal/14844kJ; Protein 75g; Carbohydrate 52g, of which sugars 169g; Fat 142g, of which saturates 61g; Cholesterol 686mg; Calcium 939mg; Fibre 45g; Sodium 1831mg.

CLASSIC BREADS FROM AROUND THE WORLD

THIS COLLECTION FEATURES SAVOURY AND SWEET CLASSICS FROM AROUND THE WORLD, INCLUDING A GOOD SELECTION OF LESSER-KNOWN SPECIALITIES.

British Cottage Loaf

MAKES 1 LOAF

675g/1½lb/6 cups unbleached strong
  white bread flour

10ml/2 tsp salt

20g/¾oz fresh yeast

400ml/14fl oz/1⅔ cups lukewarm water

~ COOK'S TIPS ~
• To ensure a good-shaped
cottage loaf the dough needs to
be firm enough to support the
weight of the top ball.
• Do not over-prove the dough
on the second rising or the loaf
may topple over.

1 Lightly grease two baking sheets.
Sift the flour and salt into a large bowl
and make a well in the centre.

2 Mix the yeast in 150ml/¼ pint/⅔ cup
of the water until dissolved. Pour into
the flour with the remaining water
and mix to a firm dough.

3 Knead on a lightly floured surface
for 10 minutes until smooth and elastic.
Place in a lightly oiled bowl, cover
with lightly oiled clear film (plastic
wrap) and leave to rise for 1 hour,
until doubled in bulk.

4 ▲ Turn out on to a lightly floured
surface and knock back. Knead for
2–3 minutes then divide the dough
into two-thirds and one-third; shape
each to a ball. Transfer to the baking
sheets. Cover with inverted bowls and
leave to rise, in a warm place, for about
30 minutes (see Cook's Tips).

5 Gently flatten the top of the larger
round of dough and cut a cross in the
centre, about 4cm/1½in across. Brush
with a little water and place the
smaller round on top.

6 ▲ Press a hole through the middle
of the top ball, down into the lower
part, using the thumb and first two
fingers of one hand. Cover with oiled
clear film and leave in a warm place
for 10 minutes. Preheat the oven to
220°C/425°F/Gas 7 and place the
bread on the lower shelf. Bake for
35–40 minutes, or until it is golden
brown and sounds hollow when
tapped. Cool on a wire rack.

Energy 2302kcal/9794kJ; Protein 78g; Carbohydrate 508g, of which sugars 9g; Fat 9g, of which saturates 1g; Cholesterol 0mg; Calcium 946mg; Fibre 25g; Sodium 1985mg.

British Grant Loaves

1 Grease three loaf tins (pans), 21 × 12 × 6cm/8½ × 4½ × 2½in and set aside in a warm place. Sift the flour and salt in a large bowl and warm slightly to take off the chill.

2 Sprinkle the dried yeast over 150ml/¼ pint/⅔ cup of the water. After a couple of minutes stir in the sugar. Leave for 10 minutes.

3 Make a well in the centre of the flour and stir in the yeast mixture and remaining water. The dough should be slippery. Mix for about 1 minute, working the sides into the middle until all the flour is incorporated.

4 ▲ Divide among the prepared tins, cover with oiled clear film (plastic wrap) and leave to rise, in a warm place, for 30 minutes, or until the dough has risen by about a third.

MAKES 3 LOAVES

1.3kg/3lb/12 cups wholemeal (whole-wheat) bread flour
15ml/1 tbsp salt
15ml/1 tbsp easy-blend (rapid-rise) dried yeast
1.2 litres/2 pints/4 cups warm water
15ml/1 tbsp muscovado (molasses) sugar

5 Meanwhile, preheat the oven to 200°C/400°F/Gas 6. Bake for 40 minutes, or until the loaves are crisp and sound hollow when tapped. Turn out on to a wire rack to cool.

Energy 1550kcal/6590kJ; Protein 64g; Carbohydrate 320g, of which sugars 11g; Fat 11g, of which saturates 2g; Cholesterol 0mg; Calcium 191mg; Fibre 43g; Sodium 1980mg.

British Poppy-Seeded Bloomer

MAKES 1 LOAF

675g/1½lb/6 cups unbleached strong
white bread flour

10ml/2 tsp salt

15g/½oz fresh yeast

450ml/¾ cup/scant 2 cups water

FOR THE TOPPING

2.5ml½ tsp salt

30ml/2 tbsp water

poppy seeds, for sprinkling

1 Lightly grease a baking sheet. Sift the flour and salt together into a large bowl and make a well in the centre.

2 ▲ Mix the yeast and 150ml/¼ pint/ ⅔ cup of the water in a jug (pitcher) or bowl. Mix in the remaining water. Add to the centre of the flour. Mix, incorporating the flour, until the mixture forms a firm dough.

~ COOK'S TIP ~

The traditional cracked, crusty appearance of this loaf is hard to achieve in a domestic oven. However, you can get a similar result by spraying the oven with water before baking. If the underneath of the loaf is not very crusty at the end of baking, turn the loaf over on the baking sheet, switch off the heat and leave it in the oven for a further 5–10 minutes.

3 ▲ Turn out on to a lightly floured surface and knead the dough very well, for at least 10 minutes, until smooth and elastic. Place the dough in a lightly oiled bowl, cover with lightly oiled clear film (plastic wrap) and leave to rise, at cool room temperature, about 15–18°C/60–65°F, for 5–6 hours, or until doubled in bulk.

4 Knock back the dough, turn out on to a lightly floured surface and knead it quite hard for about 5 minutes. Return the dough to the bowl, and re-cover. Leave to rise, at cool room temperature, for a further 2 hours.

5 ▲ Knock back again and repeat the thorough kneading. Leave to rest for 5 minutes, then roll out on a lightly floured surface into a rectangle 2.5cm/1in thick. Roll the dough up from one long side and shape it into a square-ended thick baton shape about 33 × 13cm/13 × 5in.

6 ▲ Place it seam-side up on a lightly floured baking sheet, cover and leave to rest for 15 minutes. Turn the loaf over and place on the greased baking sheet. Plump up by tucking the dough under the sides and ends, then cut six diagonal slashes on the top. Leave to rest, covered, in a warm place, for 10 minutes. Meanwhile preheat the oven to 230°C/450°F/Gas 8.

7 ▲ Mix the salt and water together and brush this glaze over the bread. Sprinkle with poppy seeds.

8 Spray the oven with water, bake the bread immediately for 20 minutes, then reduce the oven temperature to 200°C/400°F/Gas 6; bake for 25 minutes more, or until golden. Transfer to a wire rack to cool.

British Harvest Festival Sheaf

MAKES 1 LARGE LOAF

900g/2lb/8 cups strong white bread flour
15ml/1 tbsp salt
15g/½oz fresh yeast
75ml/5 tbsp lukewarm milk
400ml/14fl oz/1⅔ cups cold water

FOR THE GLAZE

1 egg
15ml/1 tbsp milk

1 Lightly grease a large baking sheet, at least 38 × 33cm/15 × 13in. Sift the flour and salt together into a large bowl and make a well in the centre.

2 Cream the yeast with the milk in a jug (pitcher). Add to the centre of the flour with the water and mix to a dough. Turn out on to a lightly floured surface and knead for about 10–15 minutes until smooth and elastic.

3 Place in a lightly oiled bowl, cover with oiled clear film (plastic wrap) and leave to rise, at room temperature, for 2 hours, or until doubled in bulk.

4 Turn the dough out on to a lightly floured surface, knock back and knead for about 1 minute. Cover and leave to rest for 10 minutes.

5 ▲ Divide the dough in two. Roll out one piece to a 35 × 25cm/14 × 10in oblong. Fold in half lengthways. Cut out a half mushroom shape for the sheaf (leave the folded edge uncut). Make the 'base' 18cm/7in long.

6 Place the dough on the baking sheet and open out. Prick with a fork and brush with water to prevent a skin from forming. Reserve 75g/3oz of the trimmings for the tie. Cover and set aside. Divide the remaining dough in two and mix the rest of the trimmings with one half. Cover and set aside. Beat together the egg and milk for the glaze.

7 ▲ Roll out the remaining dough on a lightly floured surface to a rectangle, 28 × 18cm/11 × 7in, and cut into 30–35 thin strips 18cm/7in long. Place side by side lengthways on the base, as close as possible, to represent wheat stalks. Brush with some glaze.

8 Take the larger piece of reserved dough and divide into four. Divide each piece into 25 and shape into oblong rolls to make 100 wheat ears. Make each roll pointed at one end.

9 ▲ Holding one roll at a time, snip along each side towards the centre, using scissors, to make wheat ears.

10 Preheat the oven to 220°C/425°F/Gas 7. Arrange the ears around the outer edge of the top of the mushroom shape, overlapping on to the baking sheet. Make a second row lower down, placing it between the first ears. Repeat until they are all used. Brush with glaze as you work to stop the dough from drying out.

11 ▲ Divide the smaller piece of reserved dough into six pieces and roll each to a 43cm/17in strip. Make two plaits each with three strips. Place across the wheat stalks to make a tied bow. Brush with some glaze. Prick between the wheat ears and stalks using a sharp knife and bake the sheaf for 15 minutes.

12 Reduce the oven temperature to 180°C/350°F/Gas 4. Brush the bread with the remaining glaze and bake for a further 30–35 minutes, or until golden and firm. Leave to cool on the baking sheet.

> **~ COOK'S TIP ~**
> Harvest loaves are often baked for display, rather than for eating. If you'd like to do this, then leave the baked loaf in the oven, reduce the temperature to very low, 120°C/250°F/Gas ½, for several hours until the dough dries out.

Energy 3218kcal/13670kJ; Protein 95g; Carbohydrate 703g, of which sugars 18g; Fat 22g, of which saturates 6g; Cholesterol 244mg; Calcium 1404mg; Fibre 32g; Sodium 6046mg.

British Lardy Cake

MAKES 1 LOAF

575g/1lb 4oz/5 cups unbleached strong white bread flour

5ml/1 tsp salt

15g/¹/₂oz/1 tbsp lard or white cooking fat

30ml/2 tbsp caster (superfine) sugar

20g/³/₄oz fresh yeast

300ml/¹/₂ pint/1¹/₄ cups lukewarm water

FOR THE FILLING

75g/3oz/6 tbsp lard

75g/3oz/6 tbsp soft light brown sugar

115g/4oz/8 tbsp currants, slightly warmed

75g/3oz/¹/₂ cup sultanas (golden raisins), slightly warmed

25g/1oz/¹/₃ cup mixed chopped (candied) peel

5ml/1 tsp mixed (apple pie) spice

FOR THE GLAZE

10ml/2 tsp sunflower oil

15–30ml/1–2 tbsp caster (superfine) sugar

1 Grease a 25 × 20cm/10 × 8in shallow roasting pan. Sift the flour and salt into a bowl and rub in the lard. Add the sugar. Make a well in the centre.

2 Cream the yeast with half of the water, then blend in the rest. Add to the flour and mix to a smooth dough.

3 Turn out on to a lightly floured surface and knead for about 10 minutes until smooth and elastic. Place in a lightly oiled bowl, cover with oiled clear film (plastic wrap) and leave to rise, in a warm place, for 1 hour, or until doubled in bulk.

4 Turn the dough out on to a lightly floured surface and knock back. Knead for 2–3 minutes. Roll into a rectangle about 5mm/¼in thick.

5 ▲ Using half the lard for the filling, cover the top two-thirds of the dough with flakes of lard. Sprinkle over half the sugar, half the dried fruits and peel and half the mixed spice. Fold the bottom third up and the top third down, sealing the edges with the rolling pin.

6 Turn the dough by 90 degrees. Repeat the rolling and cover with the remaining lard, fruit and peel and mixed spice. Fold, seal and turn as before. Roll out to fit the prepared tin. Cover with oiled clear film and leave to rise, in a warm place, for 30–45 minutes, until doubled in size.

7 Meanwhile, preheat the oven to 200°C/400°F/Gas 6. Brush the cake with oil and sprinkle with caster sugar.

8 ▲ Score a criss-cross pattern on top, then bake for 30–40 minutes until golden. Turn out on to a wire rack to cool slightly. Serve warm in slices.

Energy 3322kcal/14033kJ; Protein 47g; Carbohydrate 620g, of which sugars 277g; Fat 91g, of which saturates 32g; Cholesterol 70mg; Calcium 865mg; Fibre 28g; Sodium 2106mg.

British Malted Currant Bread

MAKES 2 LOAVES

50g/2oz malt extract
30ml/2 tbsp golden (light corn) syrup
50g/2oz/¹/4 cup butter
450g/1lb/4 cups strong white bread flour
5ml/1 tsp mixed (apple pie) spice
20g/³/4oz fresh yeast
175ml/6fl oz/³/4 cup lukewarm milk
175g/6oz/1 cupcurrants, slightly warmed
FOR THE GLAZE
30ml/2 tbsp milk
30ml/2 tbsp caster (superfine) sugar

4 Turn the dough out on to a floured surface, knock back, then knead in the currants. Divide the dough in two and shape into two loaves. Place in the prepared tins. Cover with oiled clear film and leave to rise, in a warm place, for 2–3 hours, or until the dough reaches the top of the tins.

5 ▲ Meanwhile, preheat the oven to 200°C/400°F/Gas 6. Bake for 35–40 minutes or until golden. While the loaves are baking, heat the milk and sugar for the glaze in a small pan. Turn out the loaves on to a wire rack, then invert them, so that they are the right way up. Brush the glaze evenly over the loaves and leave to cool.

1 ▲ Lightly grease two 450g/1lb loaf tins (pans). Place the malt extract, golden syrup and butter in a pan and heat gently until the butter has melted. Set aside to cool completely.

2 Sift the flour and mixed spice together into a large bowl and make a well in the centre. Cream the yeast with a little of the milk, then blend in the remaining milk. Add the yeast mixture and cooled malt mixture to the centre of the flour and blend together to form a dough.

3 Turn out the dough on to a floured surface and knead for about 10 minutes until smooth and elastic. Place in a lightly oiled bowl, cover with lightly oiled clear film (plastic wrap) and leave to rise, in a warm place, for 1½–2 hours, or until doubled in bulk.

Energy 1250kcal/5327kJ; Protein 31g; Carbohydrate 282g, of which sugars 113g; Fat 8g, of which saturates 3g; Cholesterol 14mg; Calcium 575mg; Fibre 13g; Sodium 127mg.

Welsh Bara Brith

MAKES 1 LOAF

20g/³/₄oz fresh yeast
200ml/7fl oz/scant 1 cup lukewarm milk
450g/1lb/4 cups strong white bread flour
75g/3oz/6 tbsp butter or lard
5ml/1 tsp mixed (apple pie) spice
2.5ml/¹/₂ tsp salt
50g/2oz/4 tbsp soft light brown sugar
1 egg, lightly beaten
115g/4oz/8 tbsp seedless raisins, warmed
75g/3oz/¹/₂ cup currants, slightly warmed
50g/2oz/²/₃ cup mixed chopped (candied) peel
15–30ml/1–2 tbsp clear honey, for glazing

1 Grease a baking sheet. In a jug (pitcher), blend the yeast with a little of the milk, then stir in the remainder. Set aside for 10 minutes.

2 ▲ Sift the flour into a large bowl and rub in the butter or lard until the mixture resembles breadcrumbs. Stir in the mixed spice, salt and sugar and make a well in the centre.

3 Add the yeast mixture and beaten egg to the centre of the flour and mix to a rough dough.

4 Turn out the dough on to a lightly floured surface and knead for 10 minutes until smooth and elastic. Place in an oiled bowl, cover with oiled clear film (plastic wrap) and leave to rise for 1½ hours, or until doubled in bulk.

5 ▲ Turn out the dough on to a floured surface, knock back, and knead in the dried fruits and peel. Shape into a round and place on the baking sheet. Cover with oiled clear film and leave to rise, in a warm place, for 1 hour, or until doubled in size.

6 Meanwhile, preheat the oven to 200°C/400°F/Gas 6. Bake for 30 minutes or until the bread sounds hollow when tapped on the base. If the bread starts to over-brown, cover loosely with foil for the last 10 minutes. Transfer the bread to a wire rack, brush with honey and leave to cool.

~ VARIATION ~

The bara brith can be baked in a 1.5–1.75 litre/2½–3 pint loaf tin (pan) or deep round or square cake tin, if you prefer.

Energy 330kcal/13950kJ; Protein 72g; Carbohydrate 604g, of which sugars 271g; Fat 84g, of which saturates 47g; Cholesterol 421mg; Calcium 1169mg; Fibre 30g; Sodium 1842mg.

Welsh Clay Pot Loaves

MAKES 2 LOAVES

115g/4oz/1 cup strong wholemeal (whole-wheat) bread flour
350g/12oz/3 cups strong white bread flour
7.5ml/1½ tsp salt
15g/½oz fresh yeast
150ml/¼ pint/⅔ cup lukewarm milk
50ml/2fl oz/¼ cup lukewarm water
50g/2oz/¼ cup butter, melted
15ml/1 tbsp chopped fresh chives
15ml/1 tbsp chopped fresh parsley
5ml/1 tsp chopped fresh sage
1 garlic clove, crushed
beaten egg, for glazing
fennel seeds, for sprinkling (optional)

1 ▲ Lightly grease two clean 14cm/ 5½in diameter, 12cm/4½in high clay flower pots. Sift the flours and salt into a bowl and make a well in the centre. Blend the yeast with a little of the milk until smooth, then stir in the remaining milk. Pour into the centre of the flour and sprinkle over a little of the flour from around the edge. Cover and leave in a warm place for 15 minutes.

2 ▲ Add the water, melted butter, herbs and garlic to the flour mixture and blend together to form a dough. Turn out on to a floured surface and knead for 10 minutes until the dough is smooth and elastic.

3 Place in a lightly oiled bowl, cover with oiled clear film (plastic wrap) and leave to rise, in a warm place, for 1¼–1½ hours, or until doubled in bulk.

4 Turn the dough out on to a floured surface and knock back. Divide in two. Shape and fit into the flower pots. They should about half fill the pots. Cover with oiled clear film and leave to rise for 30–45 minutes, in a warm place, or until the dough is 2.5cm/1in from the top of the pots.

5 ▲ Meanwhile, preheat the oven to 200°C/400°F/Gas 6. Brush the tops with beaten egg and sprinkle with fennel seeds, if using. Bake for 35–40 minutes or until golden. Turn out on to a wire rack to cool.

Energy 1057kcal/4463kJ; Protein 34g; Carbohydrate 172g, of which sugars 7g; Fat 30g, of which saturates 16g; Cholesterol 180mg; Calcium 381mg; Fibre 11g; Sodium 1707mg.

Scottish Morning Rolls

MAKES 10 ROLLS

450g/1lb/4 cups unbleached strong white bread flour, plus extra for dusting
10ml/2 tsp salt
20g/³/₄oz fresh yeast fresh yeast
150ml/¹/₄ pint/²/₃ cup lukewarm milk
150ml/¹/₄ pint/²/₃ cup lukewarm water
30ml/2 tbsp milk) milk

1 Grease two baking sheets. Sift the flour and salt into a bowl and make a well in the centre. Mix the yeast with the milk, then mix in the water. Add to the flour and mix to a soft dough.

2 Knead the dough in the bowl, then cover with oiled clear film (plastic wrap) and leave to rise for 1 hour, or until doubled in bulk. Turn out on to a floured surface and knock back.

3 ▲ Divide the dough into 10 equal pieces. Knead lightly and, using a rolling pin, shape each piece to a flat oval 10 × 7.5cm/4 × 3in or a flat round 9cm/3½in.

4 Place on the baking sheets and cover with oiled clear film. Leave to rise, in a warm place, for about 30 minutes.

5 ▲ Meanwhile, preheat the oven to 200°C/400°F/Gas 6. Press each roll in the centre with the three middle fingers to equalize the air bubbles and to help prevent blistering. Brush with milk and dust with flour.

6 Bake for 15–20 minutes or until lightly browned. Dust with more flour and cool slightly. Serve warm.

Energy 165kcal/702kJ; Protein 5g; Carbohydrate 36g, of which sugars 1g; Fat 1g, of which saturates 1g; Cholesterol 3mg; Calcium 84mg; Fibre 2g; Sodium 402mg.

Cornish Saffron Breads

MAKES 2 LOAVES

300ml/¹/₂ pint/1¹/₄ cups milk
2.5ml/¹/₂ tsp saffron strands
400g/14oz/3¹/₂ cups unbleached strong white bread flour
25g/1oz fresh yeast
50g/2oz/¹/₂ cup ground almonds
2.5ml/¹/₂ tsp grated nutmeg
2.5ml/¹/₂ tsp ground cinnamon
50g/2oz/¹/₄ cup caster (superfine) sugar
2.5ml/¹/₂ tsp salt
75g/3oz/6 tbsp butter, softened
50g/2oz/4 tbsp sultanas
50g/2oz/4 tbsp currants
extra milk and sugar, to glaze

1 Grease two 900g/2lb loaf tins (pans). Heat half the milk until almost boiling.

2 ▲ Place the saffron strands in a small heatproof bowl and pour over the milk. Stir gently, then leave to infuse for 30 minutes.

3 Heat the remaining milk in the same pan until it is just lukewarm.

4 Place 50g/2oz/¹/₂ cup flour in a small bowl or jug (pitcher), crumble in the yeast and stir in the lukewarm milk. Mix well, then leave for about 15 minutes until the yeast starts to ferment and goes frothy.

5 Mix the remaining flour, ground almonds, spices, sugar and salt together in a large bowl and make a well in the centre. Add the saffron infusion, yeast mixture and softened butter to the centre of the flour and mix to a very soft dough.

6 Turn out on to a floured surface and knead for 5 minutes until smooth and elastic. Place in an oiled bowl, cover with oiled clear film (plastic wrap) and leave to rise, in a warm place, for 1¹/₂–2 hours, or until doubled in bulk.

7 ▲ Turn the dough out on to a lightly floured surface, knock back, and knead in the sultanas and currants. Divide in two and shape into two loaves. Place in the tins. Cover with oiled clear film and leave to rise, in a warm place, for 1¹/₂ hours, or until the dough reaches the top of the tins.

8 Preheat the oven to 220°C/425°F/ Gas 7. Bake the loaves for 10 minutes, then reduce the oven temperature to 190°C/375°F/Gas 5 and bake for 15–20 minutes or until golden.

9 To make the glaze, heat the milk and sugar in a pan. When the loaves are cooked, brush them with the glaze, leave in the tins for 5 minutes, then turn out on to a wire rack to cool.

Energy 1447kcal/6091kJ; Protein 35g; Carbohydrate 220g, of which sugars 71g; Fat 54g, of which saturates 25g; Cholesterol 101mg; Calcium 584mg; Fibre 14g; Sodium 802mg.

French Kugelhopf

MAKES 1 LOAF

150g/5oz/10 tbsp unsalted butter, softened
12 walnut halves
675g/1½lb/6 cups unbleached strong white bread flour
7.5ml/1½ tsp salt
20g/¾oz fresh yeast
300ml/½ pint/1¼ cups milk
115g/4oz smoked bacon, diced
1 onion, finely chopped
15ml/1 tbsp vegetable oil
5 eggs, beaten
freshly ground black pepper

~ VARIATION ~

Replace nuts, bacon and onion
with 115g/4oz/8 tbsp raisins and
45ml/3 tbsp mixed (candied) peel.
Add 45ml/3 tbsp sugar in step
2 and omit the pepper.

1 ▲ Use 25g/1oz/2 tbsp of the butter
to grease a 23cm/9in kugelhopf
mould. Place eight walnut halves
around the base and chop the remainder.

2 Sift the flour and salt into a bowl
and season with pepper. Make a well
in the centre. Cream the yeast with
45ml/3 tbsp of the milk. Add to the
flour with the remaining milk. Mix in
a little flour to make a thick batter.
Sprinkle a little flour over the top,
cover and leave for 20–30 minutes
until the mixture bubbles.

3 ▲ Fry the bacon and onion in the
oil until the onion is golden.

4 Add the eggs to the flour mixture
and gradually beat in the flour, using
your hand. Beat in the remaining
butter to form a soft dough. Cover with
oiled clear film and leave to rise, in a
warm place, for 45–60 minutes, or
until almost doubled in bulk. Preheat
the oven to 200°C/400°F/Gas 6.

5 ▲ Knock back the dough and
gently knead in the bacon, onion and
nuts. Place in the mould, cover with
oiled clear film and leave to rise, in a
warm place, for about 1 hour.

6 Bake for 40–45 minutes, or until
the loaf has browned and sounds
hollow when tapped on the base.
Cool in the mould for 5 minutes, then
on a wire rack.

Energy 4689kcal/19654kJ; Protein 143g; Carbohydrate 552g, of which sugars 34g; Fat 227g, of which saturates 103g; Cholesterol 1588mg; Calcium 1588mg; Fibre 29g; Sodium 6003mg.

French Pain Polka

MAKES 1 LOAF

225g/8oz 6–15-hours-old French baguette dough
OR FOR THE STARTER
10g/¹/₄oz fresh yeast
120ml/4fl oz/¹/₂ cup lukewarm water
115g/4oz/1 cup plain (all-purpose) flour
FOR THE DOUGH
10g/¹/₄oz fresh yeast
300ml/¹/₂ pint/1¹/₄ cups lukewarm water
450g/1lb/4 cups unbleached strong white bread flour, plus extra for dusting
15ml/1 tbsp salt

> **~ COOK'S TIP ~**
> The piece of previously made dough can be kept covered in the refrigerator for up to 2 days, or frozen for up to a month. Just let it come back to room temperature and allow it to rise for an hour before using.

1 ▲ Flour a baking sheet. If you have French baguette dough, proceed to step 2. Make the starter. Mix the yeast with the water, then stir in sufficient flour to form a batter. Beat, then add the remaining flour and mix to a soft dough. Knead for 5 minutes. Place in a bowl, cover with oiled clear film (plastic wrap), and leave at room temperature for 4–5 hours, or until well risen and starting to collapse.

2 In a bowl, mix the yeast for the dough with half of the water, then stir in the remainder. Add the previously made dough (step 1) and knead to dissolve the dough. Gradually add the flour and salt and mix to a dough. Turn out on to a lightly floured surface and knead for 8–10 minutes until the dough is smooth and elastic.

3 Place the dough in an oiled bowl, cover with oiled clear film and leave to rise, in a warm place, for about 1½ hours, or until doubled in bulk.

4 Turn out the dough on to a lightly floured surface, knock back and shape into a round ball. Flatten slightly and place on the prepared baking sheet. Cover with oiled clear film and leave to rise, in a warm place, for 1 hour.

5 ▲ Dust the top of the loaf with flour and cut the top fairly deeply in a criss-cross pattern. Leave to rest for 10 minutes. Meanwhile, preheat the oven to 230°C/450°F/Gas 8.

6 Bake for 25–30 minutes, or until browned. Spray the inside of the oven with water as soon as the bread goes into the oven, and three times during the first 10 minutes of baking. Transfer to a wire rack to cool.

Energy 1927kcal/8198kJ; Protein 65g; Carbohydrate 425g, of which sugars 8g; Fat 8g, of which saturates 1g; Cholesterol 0mg; Calcium 793mg; Fibre 21g; Sodium 5921mg.

French Pain Bouillie

MAKES 2 LOAVES

10g/¼oz fresh yeast

30ml/2 tbsp lukewarm water

5ml/1 tsp caraway seeds, crushed

10ml/2 tsp salt

350g/12oz/3 cups unbleached strong white bread flour

olive oil, for brushing

FOR THE PORRIDGE

225g/8oz/2 cups rye flour

450ml/¾ cup/scant 2 cups boiling water

5ml/1 tsp clear honey

1 ▲ Lightly grease a 23.5 × 13cm/ 9¼ × 5in loaf tin (pan). Place the rye flour for the porridge in a large bowl. Pour over the boiling water and leave for 5 minutes. Stir in the honey. Cover with clear film (plastic wrap) and leave in a warm place for 12 hours.

2 ▲ Make the dough. Put the yeast in a jug (pitcher) and blend in the water. Stir into the porridge with the caraway seeds and salt. Add the white flour a little at a time, mixing first with a spoon and then with your hands, until the mixture forms a firm dough.

3 Turn out on to a lightly floured surface and knead for 6–8 minutes until smooth and elastic. Return to the bowl, cover with oiled clear film and leave to rise, in a warm place, for 1½ hours, until doubled in bulk.

4 ▲ Turn out the dough on to a floured surface and knock back. Cut and roll into rectangles 38 × 12cm/ 15 × 4½in. Fold the bottom third up and the top third down and seal the edges. Turn over.

5 Brush one side of each piece of folded dough with olive oil and place side by side in the prepared tin, oiled edges next to each other. Cover with lightly oiled clear film and leave to rise, in a warm place, for 1 hour, or until the dough reaches the top of the tin.

6 Meanwhile, preheat the oven to 220°C/425°F/Gas 7. Brush the tops with olive oil and, using a sharp knife, slash with one or two cuts. Bake for 30 minutes, then reduce the oven temperature to 190°C/375°F/Gas 5 and bake for a further 25–30 minutes. Turn out on to a wire rack to cool.

> **~ COOK'S TIP ~**
> Serve thickly sliced, with a little butter.

Energy 1996kcal/8500kJ; Protein 59g; Carbohydrate 447g, of which sugars 18g; Fat 9g, of which saturates 1g; Cholesterol 0mg; Calcium 564mg; Fibre 13g; Sodium 3945mg.

French Epi

MAKES 2 LOAVES

10g/¼oz fresh yeast
275ml/9fl oz/generous 1 cup lukewarm water
115g/4oz 6–10-hours-old French baguette dough
225g/8oz/2 cups strong white bread flour
75g/3oz/⅔ cup fine French plain flour
5ml/1 tsp salt

> ### ~ COOK'S TIP ~
> You can use any amount up to 10 per cent of previously made French baguette dough for this recipe. The épi can also be shaped into a circle.

1 ▲ Sprinkle a baking sheet with flour. Mix the yeast with the water in a jug (pitcher). Place the French bread dough in a large bowl and break up. Add a little of the yeast water to soften the dough. Mix in a little of the bread flour, then alternate the additions of yeast water and both flours until incorporated. Sprinkle the salt over the dough and knead in. Turn out on to a floured surface and knead for 5 minutes until smooth and elastic.

2 Place in an oiled bowl, cover with oiled clear film (plastic wrap) and leave for about 1 hour, or until the dough has doubled in bulk.

3 ▲ Knock back the dough, then cover with the oiled clear film and leave to rise for about 1 hour.

4 Divide the dough in half, place on a lightly floured surface and stretch each piece into a baguette.

5 Let the dough rest between rolling for a few minutes, if necessary, to avoid tearing. Pleat a floured dish towel on a baking sheet to make two moulds for the loaves. Place them between the pleats of the towel, cover with lightly oiled clear film and leave to rise, in a warm place, for 30 minutes.

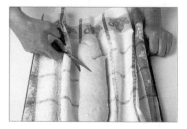

6 ▲ Preheat the oven to 230°C/450°F/Gas 8. Using scissors, make diagonal cuts halfway through the dough about 5cm/2in apart, alternating the cuts along the loaf. Gently pull the dough in the opposite direction.

7 Place on the baking sheet and bake for 20 minutes, until golden. Spray inside the oven with water 2–3 times during the first 5 minutes of baking.

Energy 962kcal/4092kJ; Protein 32g; Carbohydrate 212g, of which sugars 4g; Fat 4g, of which saturates 1g; Cholesterol 0mg; Calcium 395mg; Fibre 10g; Sodium 1973mg.

French Pain de Campagne Rustique

MAKES 1 LOAF

FOR THE CHEF

50g/2oz/¹/₂ cup wholemeal (whole-wheat) bread flour

45ml/3 tbsp warm water

FOR THE 1ST REFRESHMENT

60ml/4 tbsp warm water

75g/3oz/²/₃ cup wholemeal (whole-wheat) bread flour

FOR THE 2ND REFRESHMENT

4 fl oz (120 ml) lukewarm water

4 oz (115 g) strong white bread flour

1 oz (25 g) wholemeal bread flour

FOR THE DOUGH

120ml/4fl oz/¹/₂ cup lukewarm water

350g/12oz/3 cups unbleached strong white bread flour

10ml/2 tsp salt

~ COOK'S TIPS ~
• Start making this bread four days before you'd like to eat it.
• To make another loaf, keep the piece of starter dough (see step 6) in the refrigerator for up. to three days. Use dough for the 2nd refreshment in place of the *levain* in step 3, gradually mix in the water, then the flours and leave to rise as described.

1 ▲ To make the *chef*, place the flour in a bowl, add the water and knead for 3–4 minutes to form a dough. Cover and leave in a warm place for 2 days.

2 Pull off the crust and discard, then remove 30ml/2 tbsp of the moist centre. Place in a bowl and gradually mix in the water for the 1st refreshment. Mix in the flour and knead for 3–4 minutes to form a dough or *levain*, cover with clear film (plastic wrap) and leave in a warm place for a day.

3 ▲ Discard the crust from the *levain* and gradually mix in the water for the 2nd refreshment. Mix in the flours a little at a time, mixing well after each addition to form a firm dough. Cover with lightly oiled clear film and leave to rise, in a warm place, for about 10 hours, or until doubled in bulk.

4 Lightly flour a baking sheet. For the final stage in the preparation of the dough, gradually mix the water into the *levain* in the bowl, then gradually mix in the flour, then the salt. Turn out the dough on to a lightly floured surface and knead for about 5 minutes until smooth and elastic.

5 Place the dough in a large lightly oiled bowl, cover with lightly oiled clear film and leave to rise, in a warm place, for 1¹/₂–2 hours, or until the dough has almost doubled in bulk.

6 Knock back the dough and cut off 115g/4oz. Set aside for making the next loaf. Shape the remaining dough into a ball – you should have about 350g/12oz.

7 Line a 10cm/4in high, 23cm/9in round basket or large bowl with a dish towel and dust with flour.

8 ▲ Place the dough ball seam side up in the prepared basket or bowl. Cover with lightly oiled clear film and leave to rise, in a warm place, for 2–3 hours, or until almost doubled in bulk.

9 Preheat the oven to 230°C/450°F/ Gas 8. Invert the loaf on to the baking sheet and sprinkle with flour.

10 ▲ Slash the top of the loaf, using a sharp knife, four times at right angles to each other, to form a square pattern.

11 Sprinkle with a little more flour, if you like, then bake for 30–35 minutes, or until the loaf has browned and sounds hollow when tapped on the base. Transfer to a wire rack to cool.

Energy 1973kcal/8395kJ; Protein 69g; Carbohydrate 430g, of which sugars 9g; Fat 9g, of which saturates 1g; Cholesterol 0mg; Calcium 700mg; Fibre 28g; Sodium 3948mg.

French Fougasse

MAKES 2 LOAVES

450g/1lb/4 cups unbleached strong white bread flour

5ml/1 tsp salt

20g/³/₄oz fresh yeast

275ml/9fl oz/generous 1 cup lukewarm water

15ml/1 tbsp extra virgin olive oil

FOR THE FILLING

50g/2oz Roquefort cheese, crumbled

45ml/3 tbsp walnut pieces, chopped

25g/1oz drained, canned anchovy fillets, soaked in milk for 20 minutes, and drained again, chopped

olive oil, for brushing

~ VARIATION ~

To make a sweet fougasse, replace 15ml/1 tbsp of the water with orange flower water. Include 45ml/3 tbsp chopped candied orange peel and 30ml/2 tbsp sugar.

1 ▲ Lightly grease two baking sheets. Sift the flour and salt together into a large bowl and make a well in the centre. In a measuring jug (cup), cream the yeast with 60ml/4 tbsp of the water. Pour the yeast mixture into the centre of the flour with the remaining water and the olive oil and mix to a soft dough. Turn out on to a floured surface and knead for 8–10 minutes until smooth and elastic.

2 Place the dough in an oiled bowl, cover with oiled clear film (plastic wrap) and leave for about 1 hour, or until doubled in bulk.

3 ▲ Turn out on to a floured surface and knock back. Divide in half and flatten one piece. Sprinkle over the cheese and walnuts and fold the dough over on itself two or three times to incorporate. Repeat with the other piece of dough, this time incorporating the anchovies. Shape each piece of flavoured dough into a ball.

4 Flatten each ball of dough and fold the bottom third up and the top third down, to make an oblong. Roll the cheese dough into a rectangle measuring about 28 × 15cm/ 11 × 6in. Make four diagonal cuts almost to the edge. Stretch the dough evenly, so that it resembles a ladder.

5 Shape the anchovy dough into an oval with a flat base, about 25cm/10in long. Make three diagonal slits on each side towards the flat base, and pull to open the cuts. Transfer to the baking sheets, cover with oiled clear film and leave to rise, in a warm place, for about 30–45 minutes, or until nearly doubled in bulk.

6 Meanwhile, preheat the oven to 220°C/425°F/Gas 7. Brush both loaves with a little olive oil and bake for 25 minutes, or until golden. Transfer to a wire rack to cool.

Energy 1090kcal/4597kJ; Protein 37g; Carbohydrate 170g, of which sugars 4g; Fat 34g, of which saturates 8g; Cholesterol 30mg; Calcium 504mg; Fibre 10g; Sodium 1899mg.

French Pain aux Noix

MAKES 2 LOAVES

50g/2oz/¼ cup butter
350g/12oz/3 cups strong wholemeal (whole-wheat) bread flour
115g/4oz/1 cup unbleached strong white bread flour
15ml/1 tbsp light muscovado (brown) sugar
7.5ml/1½oz salt
20g/¾oz fresh yeast
275ml/9fl oz/generous 1 cup lukewarm milk
175g/6oz/1 cup walnut pieces

3 Knead on a floured surface for 6–8 minutes. Place in an oiled bowl, cover with oiled clear film (plastic wrap) and leave for 1 hour, until doubled in bulk.

4 ▲ Turn out the dough on to a floured surface and knock back. Press or roll out to flatten and then sprinkle over the nuts. Gently press the nuts into the dough, then roll it up. Return to the oiled bowl, re-cover and leave, in a warm place, for 30 minutes.

5 Turn out on to a floured surface, divide in half and shape each piece into a ball. Place on the baking sheets, cover with oiled clear film and leave to rise, in a warm place, for 45 minutes, until doubled in bulk.

6 Preheat the oven to 220°C/425°F/ Gas 7. Slash the top of each loaf three times. Bake for 35 minutes, or until they sound hollow when tapped. Transfer to a wire rack to cool.

1 ▲ Grease two baking sheets. Place the butter in a small pan and heat until melted and starting to brown, then set aside to cool. Mix the flours, sugar and salt in a bowl and make a well in the centre. Cream the yeast with half the milk. Add to the centre of the flour with the remaining milk.

2 ▲ Pour the cool melted butter through a fine strainer into the centre of the flour so that it joins the liquids already there. Using your hand, mix the liquids together in the bowl and gradually mix in small quantities of the flour to make a batter. Continue until the mixture forms a moist dough.

Energy 2979kcal/12433kJ; Protein 80g; Carbohydrate 280g, of which sugars 39g; Fat 179g, of which saturates 44g; Cholesterol 145mg; Calcium 763mg; Fibre 36g; Sodium 3397mg.

French Baguettes

Makes 3 loaves

500g/1¼lb/4⅔ cups unbleached strong
  white bread flour

115g/4oz/1 cup fine French plain flour

10ml/2 tsp salt

15g/½oz fresh yeast

550ml/18fl oz/2¼ cups lukewarm water

~ VARIATION ~

If you make baguettes regularly
you may want to purchase
baguette frames to hold and
bake the breads in, or long
bannetons in which to prove
this wonderful bread.

---

1 Sift the flours and salt into a bowl.
Add the yeast to the water in another
bowl and stir to dissolve. Gradually
beat in half the flour mixture to form
a batter. Cover with clear film (plastic
wrap) and leave at room temperature
for 3 hours, or until nearly trebled in
size and starting to collapse.

2 Add the remaining flour a little at a
time, beating with your hand. Turn
out on to a floured surface and knead
for 8–10 minutes to form a moist
dough. Place in an oiled bowl, cover
with oiled clear film and leave to rise,
in a warm place, for 1 hour.

3 When the dough has almost doubled in bulk, knock it back, turn out
on to a floured surface and divide into
3. Shape each into a rectangle 15 ×
7.5cm/6 × 3in.

4 Fold the bottom third up lengthways and the top third down and press
down to make sure the pieces of
dough are in contact. Seal the edges.
Repeat two or three more times until
each loaf is an oblong. Leave to rest in
between folding for a few minutes, if
necessary, to avoid tearing the dough.

5 ▲ Gently stretch each piece of
dough lengthways into a 33–35cm/
13–14in long loaf. Pleat a floured dish
towel on a baking sheet to make three
moulds for the loaves.

6 Place the breads between the pleats
of the towel to help hold their shape
while rising. Cover with lightly oiled
clear film and leave to rise, in a warm
place, for about 45–60 minutes.

7 Preheat the oven to maximum, at
least 230°C/450°F/Gas 8. Roll the
loaves on to a baking sheet, spaced
well apart. Slash the top of each loaf
several times with long diagonal slits.

8 Bake at the top of the oven for
20–25 minutes, or until golden. Spray
inside the oven with water two or
three times during the first 5 minutes
of baking. Transfer to a wire rack to
cool before serving.

Energy 699kcal/2973kJ; Protein 19.3g; Carbohydrate 159.3g, of which sugars 3.1g; Fat 2.7g, of which saturates 0.4g; Cholesterol 0mg; Calcium 287mg; Fibre 6.4g; Sodium 1316mg.

French Brioche

1 Sift the flour and salt together into a large bowl and make a well in the centre. Put the yeast in a measuring jug (cup) and stir in the milk.

2 ▲ Add the yeast mixture to the centre of the flour with the eggs and mix together to form a soft dough.

3 ▲ Using your hand, beat the dough for 4–5 minutes, until it is smooth and elastic. Cream the butter and sugar together in a separate bowl. Gradually add the butter mixture to the dough, ensuring it is incorporated before adding more. Beat until smooth, shiny and elastic.

MAKES 1 LOAF

350g/12oz/3 cups strong white bread flour
2.5ml/¹/₂ tsp salt
15g/¹/₂oz fresh yeast
60ml/4 tbsp lukewarm milk
3 eggs
175g/6oz/³/₄ cup butter, softened
30ml/2 tbsp caster sugar
FOR THE GLAZE
1 egg yolk
15ml/1 tbsp milk

4 Cover with lightly oiled clear film (plastic wrap) and leave to rise for 1–2 hours or until doubled in bulk.

5 Lightly knock back the dough, then cover and place in the refrigerator for 8–10 hours or overnight.

6 Lightly grease a 1.6 litre/2¾ pint/ 6¾ cup brioche mould. Turn the dough out on to a floured surface. Cut off almost a quarter and set aside. Shape the rest into a ball and place in the prepared mould. Shape the reserved dough into an elongated egg shape. Using two or three fingers, make a hole in the centre of the large ball of dough. Gently press the narrow end of the egg-shaped dough into the hole.

7 Mix together the egg yolk and milk for the glaze, and brush a little over the brioche. Cover with oiled clear film and leave to rise, in a warm place, for 1½–2 hours, or until the dough nearly reaches the top of the mould.

8 Meanwhile, preheat the oven to 230°C/450°F/Gas 8. Brush the brioche with the remaining glaze and bake for 10 minutes. Reduce the oven temperature to 190°C/375°F/Gas 5 and bake for a further 20–25 minutes, or until golden. Turn out on to a wire rack to cool.

Energy 2974kcal/12430kJ; Protein 70g; Carbohydrate 294g, of which sugars 36g; Fat 177g, of which saturates 101g; Cholesterol 1281mg; Calcium 744mg; Fibre 13g; Sodium 2352mg.

French Croissants

MAKES 14 CROISSANTS

350g/12oz/3 cups unbleached strong
white bread flour

115g/4oz/1 cup fine French plain flour

5ml/1 tsp salt

30ml/2 tbsp caster sugar

15g/½oz fresh yeast

250ml/8fl oz/1 cup lukewarm milk

1 egg, lightly beaten

225g/8oz/1 cup butter

FOR THE GLAZE

1 egg yolk

15ml/1 tbsp milk

~ COOK'S TIP ~

Make sure that the block
of butter and the dough are
about the same temperature
when combining, to ensure
the best results.

1 ▲ Sift the flours and salt into a
bowl. Stir in the sugar. Make a well
in the centre. Cream the yeast with
45ml/3 tbsp of the milk, then stir in
the rest. Add the yeast mixture to the
centre of the flour, then add the egg and
beat in the flour until it forms a dough.

2 Turn out on to a floured surface and
knead for 3–4 minutes. Place in an
oiled bowl, cover with oiled clear film
(plastic wrap) and leave to rise, in a
warm place, for about 45–60 minutes,
or until doubled in bulk.

3 Knock back, re-cover and chill in
the refrigerator for 1 hour. Flatten the
butter into a block about 2cm/¾in
thick. Knock back the dough and turn
out on to a floured surface. Roll out
into a rough 25cm/10in square, with
edges thinner than the centre.

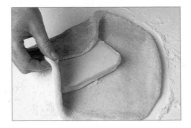

4 ▲ Place the block of butter
diagonally in the centre and fold the
corners of the dough over the butter
like an envelope, tucking in the edges
to completely enclose the butter.

5 ▲ Roll the dough into a rectangle
about 2cm/¾in thick, twice as long as
it is wide. Fold the bottom third up
and the top third down and seal the
edges. Chill for 20 minutes.

6 Repeat the rolling, folding and
chilling the dough twice more,
turning it by 90 degrees each time.
Roll out the chilled dough on a lightly
floured surface into a 62 × 33cm/
25 × 13in rectangle; trim to leave a
60 × 30cm/24 × 12in rectangle. Cut
in half lengthways. Cut crossways into
14 equal triangles with bases that
measure 15cm/6in.

7 Place the dough triangles on
two baking sheets, cover with clear
film and chill for 10 minutes.

8 ▲ To shape the croissants, place
each with the wide end at the top, hold
each side and pull gently to stretch the
top of the triangle a little, then roll
towards the point, finishing with the
pointed end tucked underneath.
Curve the ends towards the pointed
end to make a crescent. Place on two
baking sheets, spaced well apart.

9 Mix together the egg yolk and milk
for the glaze. Lightly brush a little
glaze over the croissants, avoiding the
cut edges of the dough. Cover the
croissants loosely with lightly oiled
clear film and leave to rise, in a warm
place, for about 30 minutes, or until
they are nearly doubled in size.

10 Meanwhile, preheat the oven to
220°C/425°F/Gas 7. Brush the
croissants with the remaining glaze
and bake for 15–20 minutes, or until
crisp and golden. Transfer to a wire
rack to cool slightly. Serve warm.

~ VARIATION ~

To make chocolate-filled
croissants, place a small square
of chocolate at the wide end
of each triangle before rolling
up as in step 8.

Energy 262kcal/1095kJ]; Protein 5g; Carbohydrate 28g, of which sugars 3g; Fat 15g, of which saturates 9g; Cholesterol 68mg; Calcium 74mg; Fibre 1g; Sodium 253mg.

French Petits Pains au Lait

MAKES 12 ROLLS

450g/1lb/4 cups unbleached strong white bread flour

10ml/2 tsp salt

15ml/1 tbsp caster (superfine) sugar

50g/2oz/1/4 cup butter, softened

15g/1/2oz fresh yeast

275ml/9fl oz/generous 1 cup lukewarm milk, plus 15ml/1 tbsp extra milk, for glazing

---

~ VARIATION ~

These can also be made into long rolls. To shape, flatten each ball of dough and fold in half. Roll back and forth, using your hand to form a 13cm/5in long roll, tapered at either end.

---

1 Lightly grease two baking sheets. Sift the flour and salt together into a large bowl. Stir in the sugar. Rub the softened butter into the flour.

2 Cream the yeast with 60ml/4 tbsp of the milk. Stir in the remaining milk. Pour into the flour mixture and mix to a soft dough.

3 Turn out on to a floured surface and knead for 8–10 minutes until smooth and elastic. Place in an oiled bowl, cover with oiled clear film (plastic wrap) and leave to rise, in a warm place, for 1 hour, or until doubled in bulk.

4 Turn out the dough on to a lightly floured surface and gently knock back. Divide into 12 pieces, shape these into balls and space well apart on the baking sheets.

5 ▲ Using a sharp knife, cut a cross in the top of each roll. Cover with lightly oiled clear film and leave to rise, in a warm place, for about 20 minutes, or until doubled in size.

6 Preheat the oven to 200°C/400°F/Gas 6. Brush the rolls with milk and bake for 20–25 minutes, or until golden. Transfer to a wire rack to cool.

French Dimpled Rolls

MAKES 10 ROLLS

400g/14oz/3½ cups unbleached strong white bread flour

7.5ml/1½ tsp salt

15ml/1 tbsp caster sugar

15g/1/2oz fresh yeast

120ml/4fl oz/1/2 cuplukewarm milk

175ml/6fl oz/3/4 cup lukewarm water

1 Grease two baking sheets. Sift the flour and salt into a bowl. Stir in the sugar and make a well in the centre.

2 Cream the yeast with the milk until dissolved, then pour into the centre of the flour mixture. Sprinkle over a little of the flour from around the edge. Leave at room temperature for 15–20 minutes, or until the mixture starts to bubble.

3 Add the water and gradually mix in the flour to form a fairly moist, soft dough. Turn out on to a lightly floured surface and knead for 8–10 minutes until smooth and elastic. Place in a lightly oiled bowl, cover with oiled clear film (plastic wrap) and leave to rise, at room temperature, for about 1½ hours, or until doubled in bulk.

4 Turn out on to a floured surface and knock back. Re-cover and leave to rest for 5 minutes. Divide the dough into 10 pieces. Shape into balls by rolling under your hand, then roll until oval. Lightly flour the tops.

5 Place the rolls, spaced well apart, on the baking sheets, cover with oiled clear film and leave to rise, at room temperature, for about 30 minutes, until almost doubled in size.

6 ▲ Oil the side of your hand and press the centre of each roll to make a deep split. Re-cover and leave to rest for 15 minutes.

7 Place a roasting pan in the bottom of the oven and preheat it to 230°C/450°F/Gas 8. Pour 250ml/8fl oz/ 1 cup water into the pan and bake on a higher shelf for 15 minutes, until golden.

Pains: Energy 179kcal/755kJ; Protein 5g; Carbohydrate 31g, of which sugars 3g; Fat 5g, of which saturates 3g; Cholesterol 12mg; Calcium 81mg; Fibre 1g; Sodium 364mg.
Rolls: Energy 146kcal/622kJ; Protein 5g; Carbohydrate 31g, of which sugars 2g; Fat 1g, of which saturates 0g; Cholesterol 2mg; Calcium 70mg; Fibre 1g; Sodium 301mg.

Swiss Braid

3 Add the yeast mixture and egg to the centre of the flour and mix to a dough. Beat in the softened butter.

4 ▲ Turn out on to a floured surface and knead for 5 minutes until smooth and elastic. Place in an oiled bowl, cover with oiled clear film (plastic wrap) and leave in a warm place, for 1½ hours, or until doubled in size.

5 Turn out on to a floured surface and knock back. Cut in half and shape each piece of dough into a long rope about 35cm/14in in length.

6 To make the braid, place the two pieces of dough on top of each other to form a cross. Starting with the bottom rope, fold the top end over and place between the two bottom ropes. Fold the remaining top rope over so that all four ropes are pointing down. Starting on the left, plait the first rope over the second, and the third over the fourth.

7 Continue plaiting to form a tapered bread. Tuck under the ends and place on the baking sheet. Cover with oiled clear film and leave to rise, in a warm place, for about 40 minutes.

8 Meanwhile, preheat the oven to 190°C/375°F/Gas 5. Mix the egg yolk and water for the glaze, and brush over the loaf. Bake the bread for 30–35 minutes, or until golden. Cool on a wire rack.

MAKES 1 LOAF

350g/12oz/3 cups unbleached strong white bread flour

5ml/1 tsp salt

20g/³/₄oz fresh yeast

30ml/2 tbsp lukewarm water

150ml/¹/₄ pint/²/₃ cup sour cream

1 egg, lightly beaten

50g/2oz/¹/₄ cup butter, softened

FOR THE GLAZE

1 egg yolk

15ml/1 tbsp water

1 Grease a baking sheet. Sift the flour and salt together into a large bowl and make a well in the centre. Mix the yeast and water in a jug (pitcher).

2 ▲ Gently warm the sour cream in a small pan until it reaches blood heat (35–38°C/95–100.4°F). Add to the yeast mixture and mix together.

Energy 1870kcal/7858kJ; Protein 37.5g; Carbohydrate 277.6g, of which sugars 10.9g; Fat 75.3g, of which saturates 46.5g; Cholesterol 205mg; Calcium 638mg; Fibre 10.9g; Sodium 2412mg.

German Sourdough Bread

MAKES 1 LOAF
FOR THE SOURDOUGH STARTER
75g/3oz/²/₃ cup rye flour
75ml/5 tbsp warm water
pinch caraway seeds
FOR THE DOUGH
15g/¹/₂oz fresh yeast
315ml/11fl oz/generous 1¹/₄ cups lukewarm water
275g/10oz/2¹/₂ cups rye flour
150g/5oz/1¹/₄ cups wholemeal strong (whole-wheat) bread flour
150g/5oz/1¹/₄ cups strong white bread flour
10ml/2 tsp salt

1 ▲ Mix the rye flour, warm water and caraway for the starter together in a large bowl with your fingertips, to make a soft paste. Cover with a damp dish towel and leave in a warm place for about 36 hours. Stir after 24 hours.

2 Lightly grease a baking sheet. In a measuring jug (cup), blend the yeast for the dough with the water. Add to the starter and mix thoroughly.

3 ▲ Mix the rye flour, wholemeal bread flour and unbleached white bread flour for the dough with the salt in a large bowl; make a well in the centre. Pour in the yeast liquid and gradually incorporate the surrounding flour to make a smooth dough.

4 Turn out the dough on to a lightly floured surface and knead for 8–10 minutes until smooth and elastic. Place in an oiled bowl, cover with lightly oiled clear film (plastic wrap) and leave to rise, in a warm place, for 1½ hours, or until nearly doubled in bulk.

5 ▲ Turn out on to a lightly floured surface, knock back and knead gently. Shape into a round and place in a floured basket or *couronne*, with the seam side up. Cover with lightly oiled clear film and leave to rise, in a warm place, for 2–3 hours.

6 Meanwhile, preheat the oven to 200°C/400°F/Gas 6. Turn out the loaf on to the baking sheet and bake for 35–40 minutes. Cool on a wire rack before serving.

> ~ COOK'S TIP ~
> Proving the dough in a floured basket gives it its characteristic patterned crust.

Energy 2065kcal/8793kJ; Protein 59.8g; Carbohydrate 459.1g, of which sugars 5.4g; Fat 11.7g, of which saturates 1.7g; Cholesterol 0mg; Calcium 372mg; Fibre 56.2g; Sodium 3942mg.

German Stollen

MAKES 1 LOAF

75g/3oz/¹/₂ cup sultanas (golden raisins)

50g/2oz/4 tbsp currants

45ml/3 tbsp rum

375g/13oz/3¹/₄ cups unbleached strong white bread flour

2.5ml/¹/₂ tsp salt

45ml/3 tbsp caster (superfine) sugar

1.25ml/¹/₄ tsp ground cardamom

2.5ml/¹/₂ tsp ground cinnamon

40g/1¹/₂oz fresh yeast

120ml/4fl oz/¹/₂ cup lukewarm milk

50g/2oz/¹/₄ cup butter, melted

1 egg, lightly beaten

50g/2oz/²/₃ cup mixed chopped (candied) peel

50g/2oz/¹/₃ cup blanched whole almonds, chopped

melted butter, for brushing

icing (confectioners') sugar, for dusting

FOR THE ALMOND FILLING

115g/4oz/1 cup ground almonds

50g/2oz/¹/₄ cup caster (superfine) sugar

50g/2oz/¹/₂ cup icing (confectioners') sugar

2.5ml/¹/₂ tsp lemon juice

¹/₂ egg, lightly beaten

1 ▲ Grease a baking sheet. Preheat the oven to 180°C/350°F/Gas 4. Put the sultanas and currants in a heatproof bowl and warm for 3–4 minutes. Pour over the rum and set aside.

2 Sift the flour and salt into a large bowl. Stir in the sugar and spices.

3 ▲ Mix the yeast with the milk until creamy. Pour into the flour and mix in a little of the flour from around the edge to make a thick batter. Sprinkle some of the remaining flour over the top of the batter, then cover with clear film (plastic wrap) and leave in a warm place for 30 minutes.

4 Add the melted butter and egg and mix to a soft dough. Turn out the dough on to a floured surface and knead for 8–10 minutes until smooth and elastic. Place in an oiled bowl, cover with lightly oiled clear film and leave to rise, in a warm place, for 2–3 hours, until doubled in bulk.

5 ▲ Mix the ground almonds and sugars for the filling. Add the lemon juice and enough egg to make a smooth paste. Shape into a 20cm/8in sausage, cover and set aside.

6 Turn out the dough on to a lightly floured surface and knock back.

7 Pat out the dough into a rectangle about 2.5cm/1in thick and sprinkle over the sultanas, currants, peel and almonds. Fold and knead to incorporate the fruit and nuts.

8 ▲ Roll out the dough into an oval about 30 × 23cm/12 × 9in. Roll the centre slightly thinner than the edges. Place the almond paste filling along the centre and fold over the dough to enclose it, making sure that the top of the dough doesn't completely cover the base. The top edge should be slightly in from the bottom edge. Press down to seal.

9 Place the loaf on the prepared baking sheet, cover with lightly oiled clear film and leave to rise, in a warm place, for 45–60 minutes, or until doubled in size.

10 Meanwhile, preheat the oven to 200°C/400°F/Gas 6. Bake the loaf for about 30 minutes, or until it sounds hollow when tapped on the base. Brush the top with melted butter and transfer to a wire rack to cool. Dust with icing sugar just before serving.

> **~ COOK'S TIP ~**
>
> Dust the stollen with cinnamon and icing (confectioners') sugar, or drizzle over glacé icing.

Energy 3919kcal/16493kJ; Protein 89g; Carbohydrate 581g, of which sugars 291g; Fat 153g, of which saturates 40g; Cholesterol 469mg; Calcium 1296mg; Fibre 42g; Sodium 1671mg.

German Pumpernickel

MAKES 2 LOAVES

450g/1lb/4 cups rye flour

225g/8oz/2 cup wholemeal
(whole-wheat) flour

115g/4oz/²/₃ cup bulgur wheat

10ml/2 tsp salt

30ml/2 tbsp molasses

150ml/¹/₄ pint/²/₃ cup warm water

15ml/1 tbsp vegetable oil

1 Lightly grease two 18 × 9cm/7 ×
3½in loaf tins (pans). Mix the rye
flour, wholemeal flour, bulgur wheat
and salt together in a large bowl.

2 Mix the molasses with the warm
water and add to the flours with the
oil. Mix to form a dense mass.

3 ▲ Place in the tins, pressing well
into the corners. Cover with lightly
oiled clear film (plastic wrap) and
leave in a warm place for 18–24 hours.

4 Preheat the oven to 110°C/225°F/
Gas ¼. Cover the tins tightly with
foil. Fill a roasting pan with boiling
water and place a rack on top.

5 Place the tins on top of the rack
and transfer very carefully to the
oven. Bake the loaves for 4 hours.
Increase the oven temperature to
160°C/325°F/Gas 3. Top up the water
in the roasting pan if necessary,
uncover the loaves and bake for a
further 30–45 minutes, or until the
loaves feel firm and the tops are crusty.

6 Leave the loaves to cool in the tins
for 5 minutes, then turn out on to a
wire rack to cool completely. Serve
cold, very thinly sliced.

Energy 1426kcal/6046kJ; Protein 38g; Carbohydrate 300g, of which sugars 14g; Fat 15g, of which saturates 2g; Cholesterol 0mg; Calcium 183mg; Fibre 10g; Sodium 1981mg.

Swedish Vört Limpa

MAKES 1 LOAF

350g/12oz/3 cups rye flour
350g/12oz/3 cups unbleached strong white bread flour
2.5ml/^{1}/2 tsp salt
30ml/2 tbsp caster (superfine) sugar
5ml/1 tsp grated nutmeg
5ml/1 tsp ground cloves
5ml/1 tsp ground ginger
40g/1^1/2oz fresh yeast
300ml/^{1}/2 pint/1^1/4 cups light ale
120ml/4fl oz/^{1}/2 cup port
15ml/1 tbsp molasses
25g/1oz/2 tbsp butter, melted
15ml/1 tbsp grated orange rind
75g/3oz/^{1}/2 cup raisins
15ml/1 tbsp malt extract, for glazing

5 Turn out the dough on to a floured surface and knock back. Gently knead in the orange rind and raisins. Roll into a 30cm/12in square.

6 ▲ Fold the bottom third of the dough up and the top third down, sealing the edges. Place in the loaf tin, cover with oiled clear film and leave to rise, in a warm place, for 1 hour, or until it reaches the top of the tin.

7 Meanwhile, preheat the oven to 190°C/375°F/Gas 5. Bake for 35–40 minutes, or until browned. Turn out on to a wire rack, brush with malt extract and leave to cool.

1 Lightly grease a 30 × 10cm/12 × 4in loaf tin (pan). Mix together the rye and white flours, salt, sugar, nutmeg, cloves and ginger in a large bowl.

2 In another large bowl, using a wooden spoon, blend the yeast into the ale until dissolved, then stir in the port, molasses and melted butter.

3 Gradually add the flour mixture to the yeast liquid, beating to make combine the ingredients to a smooth batter. Continue adding the flour a little at a time and mixing until the mixture forms a soft dough.

4 ▲ Turn out on to a floured surface. Knead for 8–10 minutes until smooth and elastic. Place in an oiled bowl, cover with oiled clear film (plastic wrap) and leave to rise, in a warm place, for 1 hour, or until doubled in size.

Energy 2978kcal/12652kJ; Protein 72g; Carbohydrate 624g, of which sugars 98g; Fat 33g, of which saturates 15g; Cholesterol 53mg; Calcium 813mg; Fibre 18g; Sodium 1232mg.

Swedish Knackerbröd

MAKES 8 CRISPBREADS

450g/1lb/4 cups rye flour

5ml/1 tsp salt

50g/2oz/¹/₄ cup butter

20g/³/₄oz fresh yeast

275ml/9fl oz/generous 1 cup
  lukewarm water

75g/3oz/³/₄ cup wheat bran

~ COOK'S TIP ~
The hole in the centre of these
crispbreads is a reminder of the
days when breads were strung
on a pole, which was hung
across the rafters to dry. Make
smaller crispbreads, if you like,
and tie them together with
bright red ribbon for an
unusual Christmas gift.

1 ▲ Lightly grease two baking sheets.
Preheat the oven to 230°C/450°F/
Gas 8. Mix the rye flour and salt in
a large bowl. Rub in the butter, then
make a well in the centre.

2 Cream the yeast with a little water,
then stir in the remainder. Pour into
the centre of the flour, mix to a
dough, then mix in the bran. Knead
on a lightly floured surface for 5
minutes until smooth and elastic.

3 Divide the dough into eight pieces
and roll each one out on a floured
surface, to a 20cm/8in round.

4 ▲ Place two rounds on each baking
sheet and prick with a fork. Cut a hole
in the centre, using a 4cm/1½in cutter.

5 Bake for 15–20 minutes, or until
golden and crisp. Transfer to a wire
rack to cool. Repeat with the
remaining crispbreads.

Finnish Barley Bread

MAKES 1 LOAF

225g/8oz/2 cups barley flour

5ml/1 tsp salt

10ml/2 tsp baking powder

50g/2oz/¹/₄ cup butter, melted

120ml/4fl oz/¹/₂ cup single (light) cream

60ml/4 tsbp milk

~ COOK'S TIPS ~
• This flat bread tastes good
with cottage cheese, especially
cottage cheese with chives.
• For a citrusy tang,
add 10–15ml/2–3 tsp finely
grated lemon, lime or orange
rind to the flour mixture
in step 1.

1 ▲ Grease a baking sheet. Preheat
the oven to 200°C/400°F/Gas 6. Sift
the dry ingredients into a large mixing
bowl. Add the wet ingredients. Stir to
a dough.

2 Turn out the dough on to a lightly
floured surface and shape into a flat
round about 1cm/½in thick using
your hands.

3 ▲ Transfer the dough round to the
prepared baking sheet and, using a
sharp knife, lightly mark the top into
six sections.

4 Prick the surface of the round
evenly with a fork. Bake for about
15–18 minutes, or until pale golden.
Leave to cool slightly, then cut into
wedges and serve warm.

Swedish: Energy 277kcal/1170kJ; Protein 7g; Carbohydrate 47g, of which sugars 2g; Fat 8g, of which saturates 4g; Cholesterol 18mg; Calcium 70mg; Fibre 4g; Sodium 301mg.
Finnish: Energy 1147kcal/4827kJ; Protein 30g; Carbohydrate 153g, of which sugars 10g; Fat 51g, of which saturates 29g; Cholesterol 128mg; Calcium 386mg; Fibre 19g; Sodium 3128mg.

Swedish Lusse Bröd

MAKES 12 BUNS

120ml/4fl oz/¹/₂ cup milk
pinch of saffron threads
400g/14oz/3¹/₂ cups unbleached strong white bread flour
45ml/3 tbsp ground almonds
2.5ml/¹/₂ tsp salt
75g/3oz/6 tbsp caster (superfine) sugar
25g/1oz fresh yeast
120ml/4fl oz/¹/₂ cup lukewarm water
few drops of almond extract
50g/2oz/¹/₄ cup butter, softened
FOR THE GLAZE
1 egg, beaten with 15ml/1 tbsp water

1 ▲ Lightly grease two baking sheets. Place the milk in a small pan and bring to the boil. Add the saffron, remove from the heat and leave to infuse for about 15 minutes. Meanwhile, mix the flour, ground almonds, salt and sugar in a bowl.

2 Cream the yeast with the water. Add the saffron liquid, yeast mixture and almond extract to the flour mixture and mix to a dough. Gradually beat in the softened butter.

3 Turn out on to a lightly floured surface and knead for 5 minutes until smooth and elastic. Place in an oiled bowl, cover with oiled clear film (plastic wrap) and leave for about 1 hour, or until doubled in bulk.

4 ▲ Turn out the dough on to a lightly floured surface and knock back. Divide into 12 equal pieces and make into different shapes: roll into a long rope and shape into an 'S' shape; to make a star, cut a dough piece in half and roll into two ropes, cross one over the other and coil the ends; make an upturned 'U' shape and coil the ends to represent curled hair; divide a dough piece in half, roll into two thin ropes and twist together to make a rope.

5 Place the rolls on the prepared baking sheets, spaced well apart, cover with lightly oiled clear film and leave to rise, in a warm place, for about 30 minutes.

6 Meanwhile, preheat the oven to 200°C/400°F/Gas 6. Brush the glaze over the rolls. Bake for 15 minutes, or until golden. Transfer to a wire rack to cool. Serve warm or cold.

Energy 215kcal/908kJ; Protein 6g; Carbohydrate 33g, of which sugars 8g; Fat 8g, of which saturates 3g; Cholesterol 31mg; Calcium 85mg; Fibre 2g; Sodium 125mg.

Savoury Danish Crown

1 Lightly grease a baking sheet. Sift the flour and salt together into a large bowl. Rub in 45ml/3 tbsp of the butter. Mix the yeast with the milk and water. Add to the flour with the egg and mix to a soft dough.

2 Turn out on to a floured surface and knead for 10 minutes until smooth and elastic. Place in an oiled bowl, cover with oiled clear film (plastic wrap) or slide into an oiled polythene bag and leave to rise for about 1 hour, or until doubled in bulk.

3 Knock back and turn out on to a lightly floured surface. Roll out into an oblong about 1cm/½in thick.

4 ▲ Dot half the remaining butter over the top two-thirds of the dough. Fold the bottom third up and the top third down and seal the edges. Turn by 90 degrees and repeat with the remaining butter. Fold and seal as before. Cover with oiled clear film and leave to rest for 15 minutes.

5 Turn by a further 90 degrees. Roll and fold again without any butter. Repeat once more. Wrap in oiled clear film and chill for 30 minutes.

6 Meanwhile, heat the oil for the filling. Add the onions and cook for 10 minutes until golden. Remove from the heat and add the breadcrumbs, almonds, Parmesan and seasoning.

7 Mix half the beaten egg into the breadcrumb mixture.

8 Roll out the dough on a floured surface into a rectangle 56 × 23cm/ 22 × 9in. Spread with the filling to within 2cm/¾in of the edges, then roll up like a Swiss roll (jelly roll) from one long side. Cut in half lengthways. Plait together with the cut sides up and shape into a ring.

9 Place on the baking sheet, cover with oiled clear film and leave to rise, in a warm place, for 30 minutes.

10 Meanwhile, preheat the oven to 200°C/400°F/Gas 6. Brush the remaining beaten egg over the dough. Sprinkle with sesame seeds and Parmesan cheese and bake in the centre of the preheated oven for 40–50 minutes, or until golden. Transfer to a wire rack to cool. Serve warm or cold, cut into slices.

MAKES 1 LOAF

350g/12oz/3 cups strong white bread flour
5ml/1 tsp salt
185g/6½oz/generous ¾ cup butter, softened
20g/¾oz fresh yeast
200ml/7fl oz/scant 1 cup mixed lukewarm milk and water
1 egg, lightly beaten
FOR THE FILLING
30ml/2 tbsp sunflower oil
2 onions, finely chopped
45ml/3 tbsp fresh breadcrumbs
30ml/1 tbsp ground almonds
50g/2oz/⅔ cup freshly grated Parmesan cheese
1 egg, lightly beaten
salt and freshly ground black pepper
FOR THE TOPPING
15ml/1 tbsp sesame seeds
15ml/1 tbsp freshly grated Parmesan cheese

Energy 3660kcal/15276kJ; Protein 85.2g; Carbohydrate 333.5g, of which sugars 29.2g; Fat 230.2g, of which saturates 121.5g; Cholesterol 687mg; Calcium 1734mg; Fibre 19g; Sodium 2551mg.

Danish Julekage

MAKES 1 LOAF

25g/1oz fresh yeast
75ml/5 tbsp lukewarm milk
450g/1lb/4 cups unbleached strong white bread flour
10ml/2 tsp salt
75g/3oz/6 tbsp butter
15 cardamom pods
2.5ml/½ tsp vanilla extract
50g/2oz/4 tbsp soft light brown sugar
grated rind of ½ lemon
2 eggs, lightly beaten
50g/2oz/¼ cup ready-to-eat dried apricots, chopped
50g/2oz/¼ cup glacé (candied) pineapple pieces, chopped
50g/2oz/¼ cup red and green glacé (candied) cherries, chopped
25g/1oz/⅙ cup dried dates, chopped
25g/1oz/⅙ cup crystallized stem ginger, chopped

FOR THE GLAZE

1 egg white
10ml/2 tsp water

FOR THE DECORATION

15ml/1 tbsp caster sugar
2.5ml/½ tsp ground cinnamon
8 pecan nuts or whole blanched almonds

~ VARIATIONS ~

• You can vary the fruits for this loaf. Try glacé (candied) peaches, yellow glacé cherries, sultanas, raisins, candied angelica, dried mango or dried pears and use in place of some or all of the fruits in the recipe. Use a mixture of colours and make sure that the total weight is the same as above.

• Use walnuts in place of the pecan nuts or almonds.

---

1 Lightly grease a 23 × 13cm/9 × 5in loaf tin (pan). In a measuring jug (cup), cream the yeast with the milk.

2 ▲ Sift the flour and salt together into a large bowl. Add the butter and rub in. Make a well in the centre. Add the yeast mixture to the centre of the flour and butter mixture and stir in sufficient flour to form a thick batter. Sprinkle over a little of the remaining flour and set aside in a warm place for 15 minutes.

3 Remove the seeds from the cardamom pods. Put them in a mortar and crush with a pestle. Add the crushed seeds to the flour with the vanilla extract, sugar, lemon rind and eggs, then mix to a soft dough.

4 ▲ Turn out on to a floured surface and knead for 8–10 minutes until smooth and elastic. Place in an oiled bowl, cover with oiled clear film (plastic wrap) and leave to rise in a warm place for 1–1½ hours, or until doubled in bulk.

5 Knock back the dough and turn it out on to a lightly floured surface. Flatten into a rectangle and sprinkle over half of the apricots, pineapple, cherries, dates and ginger. Fold the sides into the centre and then fold in half to contain the fruit. Flatten into a rectangle again and sprinkle over the remaining fruit. Fold and knead gently to distribute the fruit.

6 Cover the fruited dough with lightly oiled clear film and leave to rest in a warm place for 10 minutes.

7 Roll the fruited dough into a rectangle 38 × 25cm/15 × 10in. With a short side facing you, fold the bottom third up lengthways and the top third down, tucking in the sides, to form a 23 × 13cm/9 × 5in loaf.

8 Place in the prepared tin, seam side down. Cover with lightly oiled clear film and leave to rise, in a warm place, for 1 hour, or until the dough has reached the top of the tin.

9 Meanwhile, preheat the oven to 180°C/350°F/Gas 4. Using a sharp knife, slash the top of the loaf lengthways and then make diagonal slits on either side.

10 Mix together the egg white and water for the glaze, and brush over the top. Mix the sugar and cinnamon in a bowl, then sprinkle over the top. Decorate with pecan nuts or almonds. Bake for 45–50 minutes, or until risen and browned. Transfer to a wire rack to cool.

~ COOK'S TIP ~

If the top of the loaf starts to brown too quickly during cooking, cover loosely with foil.

Energy 2703kcal/11407kJ; Protein 59.2g; Carbohydrate 468.3g, of which sugars 125.4g; Fat 78.6g, of which saturates 44.6g; Cholesterol 553mg; Calcium 814mg; Fibre 20g; Sodium 4685mg.

Scandinavian Sunshine Loaf

3 Mix the yeast for the dough with 60ml/4 tbsp of the water until creamy, then stir in the remaining water. Gradually mix into the starter to dilute it. Gradually mix in the rye flour to form a smooth batter. Cover with lightly oiled clear film and leave in a warm place, for 3–4 hours, or until well risen.

4 Stir the bread flour and salt into the batter to form a dough. Turn on to a floured surface and knead for 5 minutes until smooth and elastic. Place in an oiled bowl, cover with oiled clear film and leave to rise, in a warm place, for 1 hour, until doubled in bulk.

5 ▲ Knock back on a floured surface. Cut the dough into five pieces. Roll one piece into a 50cm/20in 'sausage' and roll up into a spiral shape.

6 Cut the remaining pieces in half and shape each one into a 20cm/8in rope. Place in a circle on a baking sheet, spaced equally apart, like rays of the sun, and curl the ends round, leaving a small gap in the centre. Place the spiral shape on top, in the centre. Cover with oiled clear film and leave to rise, in a warm place, for 30 minutes.

7 Preheat the oven to 230°C/450°F/ Gas 8. Brush the bread with milk, sprinkle with caraway seeds and bake for 30 minutes, or until lightly browned. Cool on a wire rack.

MAKES 1 LARGE LOAF

FOR THE STARTER

60ml/4 tbsp lukewarm milk

60ml/4 tbsp lukewarm water

10g/¼oz fresh yeast

100g/3¾oz/generous ⅔ cup unbleached strong white bread flour

FOR THE DOUGH

15g/½oz fresh yeast

500ml/17fl oz/generous 2 cups lukewarm water

450g/1lb/4 cups rye flour

225g/8oz/2 cups unbleached strong white bread flour

15ml/1 tbsp salt

milk, for glazing

caraway seeds, for sprinkling

1 ▲ Combine the milk and water for the starter in a bowl. Mix in the yeast until dissolved. Gradually stir the flour with a metal spoon.

2 Cover the bowl with clear film (plastic wrap) and leave in a warm place for 3–4 hours, or until well risen, bubbly and starting to collapse.

Energy 2665kcal/11347kJ; Protein 77g; Carbohydrate 590g, of which sugars 8g; Fat 16g, of which saturates 4g; Cholesterol 11mg; Calcium 689mg; Fibre 12g; Sodium 5942mg.

Spanish Pan de Cebada

MAKES 1 LOAF

FOR THE SOURDOUGH STARTER

175g/6oz/1½ cups maize meal

550ml/18fl oz/2¼ cups water

225g/8oz/2 cups wholemeal (whole-wheat)
  bread flour

75g/3oz/⅔ cup barley flour

FOR THE DOUGH

20g/¾oz fresh yeast

45ml/3 tbsp lukewarm water

225g/8oz/2 cups wholemeal (whole-wheat)
  bread flour

15ml/1 tbsp salt

maize meal, for dusting

1 ▲ In a pan, mix the maize meal for the sourdough starter with half the water, then blend in the remainder. Cook over a gentle heat, stirring until thickened. Transfer to a large bowl and set aside to cool.

2 Mix in the wholemeal flour and barley flour. Turn out on to a floured surface and knead for 5 minutes. Return to the bowl, cover with oiled clear film (plastic wrap) and leave the starter in a warm place for 36 hours.

5 ▲ Knock back the dough and turn out on to a lightly floured surface. Shape into a plump round. Sprinkle with a little maize meal.

6 Place the shaped bread on the prepared baking sheet. Cover with an upturned bowl. Leave to rise, in a warm place, for about 1 hour, or until nearly doubled in bulk. Meanwhile, place a roasting pan in the bottom of the oven. Preheat the oven to 220°C/425°F/Gas 7.

7 Pour 300ml/½ pint/1¼ cups water into the roasting pan. Remove the bowl and bake the bread for 10 minutes. Remove the pan, reduce the oven temperature to 90°C/375°F/Gas 5 and bake for 20 minutes. Cool on a rack.

3 ▲ Dust a baking sheet with maize meal. In a small bowl, cream the yeast with the water for the dough. Mix the yeast mixture into the starter with the wholemeal flour and salt and work to a dough. Turn out on to a lightly floured surface and knead for 4–5 minutes until smooth and elastic.

4 Transfer the dough to a lightly oiled bowl, cover with oiled clear film or an oiled polythene bag and leave, in a warm place, for 1½–2 hours to rise, or until nearly doubled in bulk.

Energy 2365kcal/10014kJ; Protein 80g; Carbohydrate 498g, of which sugars 9g; Fat 15g, of which saturates 1g; Cholesterol 0mg; Calcium 512mg; Fibre 38g; Sodium 5911mg.

Spanish Twelfth Night Bread

MAKES 1 LOAF

450g/1lb/4 cups unbleached strong white bread flour
2.5ml/½ tsp salt
25g/1oz fresh yeast
150ml/¼ pint/⅔ cup mixed lukewarm milk and water
75g/3oz/6 tbsp butter
75g/3oz/6 tbsp caster sugar
10ml/2 tsp finely grated lemon rind
10ml/2 tsp finely grated orange rind
2 eggs
15ml/1 tbsp brandy
15ml/1 tbsp orange flower water
silver coin or dried bean (optional)
1 egg white, lightly beaten, for glazing

FOR THE DECORATION

a mixture of candied and glacé (candied) fruit slices
flaked (sliced) almonds

~ COOK'S TIP ~

If you like, this bread can be baked in a 24cm/9½in ring-shaped cake tin (pan).

1 ▲ Lightly grease a large baking sheet. Sift the flour and salt together into a large bowl. Make a well in the centre.

2 In a bowl, mix the yeast with the milk and water until the yeast has dissolved. Pour the yeast mixture into the centre of the flour and stir in enough of the flour from around the sides of the bowl to make a thick batter.

3 Sprinkle a little of the remaining flour over the top of the batter and leave to 'sponge', in a warm place, for about 15 minutes or until frothy.

4 Using an electric whisk or a wooden spoon, beat the butter and sugar together in a bowl until soft and creamy, then set aside.

5 Add the citrus rinds, eggs, brandy and orange flower water to the flour mixture and mix to a sticky dough.

6 ▲ Using one hand, beat the mixture until it forms a smooth dough. Gradually beat in the reserved butter mixture and beat for a few minutes until the dough is smooth and elastic. Cover with oiled clear film and leave to rise, in a warm place, for 1½ hours, or until doubled in bulk.

7 Knock back the dough and turn out on to a floured surface. Gently knead for 2 or 3 minutes, incorporating the lucky coin or bean, if using.

8 Using a rolling pin, roll out the dough into a long strip measuring about 65 × 13cm/26 × 5in.

9 ▲ Roll up the dough from one long side like a Swiss roll (jelly roll) to make a sausage shape. Place seam-side down on the baking sheet and seal the ends. Cover with oiled clear film (plastic wrap) and leave to rise for 1–1½ hours, or until doubled in size.

10 ▲ Meanwhile, preheat the oven to 180°C/350°F/Gas 4. Brush the dough ring with lightly beaten egg white and decorate with candied and glacé fruit slices, pushing them slightly into the dough. Sprinkle with flaked almonds and bake for 30–35 minutes, or until risen and golden. Turn out on to a wire rack to cool.

Energy 2751kcal/11597kJ; Protein 76g; Carbohydrate 434g, of which sugars 101g; Fat 91g, of which saturates 46g; Cholesterol 633mg; Calcium 865mg; Fibre 18g; Sodium 1774mg.

Pan Gallego

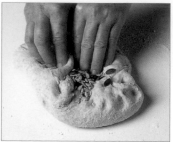

3 ▲ Knock back the dough and turn out on to a lightly floured surface. Gently knead in the pumpkin seeds, sunflower seeds and millet. Re-cover and leave to rest for 5 minutes.

4 ▲ Shape into a ball; twist the centre to make a cap. Transfer to the baking sheet and dust with maize meal. Cover with an upturned bowl and leave to rise, in a warm place, for 45 minutes, or until doubled in bulk.

5 Place a roasting pan in the bottom of the oven. Preheat the oven to 220°C/425°F/Gas 7. Pour about 300ml/½ pint/1¼ cups water into the pan. Remove the bowl and place the loaf in the oven, above the roasting pan. Bake the bread for 10 minutes.

6 Remove the pan of water and bake the bread for a further 25–30 minutes, or until well browned and sounding hollow when tapped on the base. Transfer to a wire rack to cool.

MAKES 1 LOAF

350g/12oz/3 cups unbleached strong white bread flour
115g/4oz/1 cup wholemeal (whole-wheat) bread flour
10ml/2 tsp salt
20g/¾oz fresh yeast
275ml/9fl oz/generous 1 cup lukewarm water
30ml/2 tbsp olive oil, or melted lard or white cooking fat
30ml/2 tbsp pumpkin seeds
30ml/2 tbsp sunflower seeds
15ml/1 tbsp millet
maize meal, for dusting

1 Sprinkle a baking sheet with maize meal. Mix the flours and salt together in a large bowl.

2 ▲ In a bowl, mix the yeast with the water. Add to the centre of the flours with the olive oil or melted fat and mix to a firm dough. Turn out on to a lightly floured surface and knead for about 10 minutes until smooth and elastic. Place in an oiled bowl, cover with oiled clear film (plastic wrap) and leave to rise for 1½–2 hours, or until doubled in bulk.

Energy 1668kcal/7038kJ; Protein 47g; Carbohydrate 276.1g, of which sugars 6.9g; Fat 49.1g, of which saturates 6g; Cholesterol 0mg; Calcium 443mg; Fibre 20.8g; Sodium 12mg.

Portuguese Corn Bread

MAKES 1 LOAF

20g/³/₄oz fresh yeast
250ml/8fl oz/1 cup lukewarm water
225g/8oz/2 cups maize meal
225g/8oz/2 cups unbleached strong white bread flour
150ml/¹/₄ pint/²/₃ cup lukewarm milk
30ml/2 tbsp olive oil
7.5ml/1¹/₂ tsp salt
polenta, for dusting

1 ▲ Dust a baking sheet with a little maize meal. Put the yeast in a bowl and gradually mix in the water until smooth. Stir in half the maize meal and 45ml/3 tbsp of the flour and mix to a batter, with a wooden spoon.

2 ▲ Cover the bowl with lightly oiled clear film (plastic wrap) and leave the batter undisturbed in a warm place for about 30 minutes, or until bubbles start to appear on the surface. Remove the clear film.

3 Stir the milk into the batter, then stir in the olive oil. Gradually mix in the remaining maize meal, flour and salt to form a pliable dough.

4 Turn out the dough on to a lightly floured surface and knead for about 10 minutes until smooth and elastic. Place in a lightly oiled bowl, cover with lightly oiled clear film and leave to rise for 1½–2 hours, or until doubled in bulk.

5 ▲ Turn out the dough on to a floured surface and knock back. Shape into a ball, flatten slightly and place on the prepared baking sheet. Dust with polenta, cover with a large upturned bowl and leave to rise, in a warm place, for 1 hour, or until doubled in size. Preheat the oven to 230°C/450°F/Gas 8.

6 Bake the bread for 10 minutes, spraying the inside of the oven with water a few times. Reduce the oven temperature to 190°C/375°F/ Gas 5 and bake for a further 20–25 minutes, or until golden and hollow-sounding when tapped. Cool on a rack.

Energy 3008kcal/12539kJ; Protein 52.7g; Carbohydrate 303.3g, of which sugars 87.7g; Fat 179.8g, of which saturates 46.1g; Cholesterol 561mg; Calcium 696mg; Fibre 7.4g; Sodium 1672mg.

Mallorcan Ensaimadas

MAKES 16 ROLLS

225g/8oz/2 cups unbleached strong white bread flour
2.5ml/1/2 tsp salt
50g/2oz/1/4 cup caster sugar
15g/1/2oz fresh yeast
75ml/5 tbsp lukewarm milk
1 egg
30ml/2 tbsp sunflower oil
50g/2oz/1/4 cup butter, melted
icing (confectioners') sugar, for dusting

1 Grease two baking sheets. Sift the flour and salt into a bowl. Stir in the sugar and make a well in the centre.

2 Cream the yeast with the milk, pour into the centre of the flour mixture, then sprinkle a little of the flour over the top of the liquid. Leave for about 15 minutes, or until frothy.

3 Beat the egg with the oil. Add to the flour and mix to a smooth dough.

4 Turn out on to a floured surface and knead for 8–10 minutes until smooth and elastic. Place in an oiled bowl, cover with oiled clear film (plastic wrap) and leave to rise for 1 hour, or until doubled in bulk.

5 ▲ Turn out the dough on to a lightly floured surface. Knock back and divide the dough into 16 equal pieces. Shape each piece into a thin rope about 38cm/15in long. Pour the melted butter on to a plate and dip the ropes into the butter to coat.

6 ▲ On the baking sheets, curl each rope into a loose spiral, spacing well apart. Tuck the ends under to seal. Cover with oiled clear film and leave to rise, in a warm place, for about 45 minutes, or until doubled in size.

7 Meanwhile, preheat the oven to 190°C/375°F/Gas 5. Brush the rolls with water and dust with icing sugar. Bake for 10 minutes, or until light golden brown. Leave to cool on a wire rack. Dust again with icing sugar and serve warm.

Energy 327kcal/1371kJ; Protein 8.7g; Carbohydrate 38.6g, of which sugars 4.3g; Fat 16.1g, of which saturates 9.3g; Cholesterol 117mg; Calcium 172mg; Fibre 1.4g; Sodium 162mg.

Italian Olive Bread

1 Lightly grease a baking sheet. Mix the flours, yeast and salt in a large bowl and make a well in the centre.

2 ▲ Add the water and oil to the centre of the flour and mix to a soft dough. Knead the dough on a lightly floured surface for 8–10 minutes until smooth and elastic. Place in a lightly oiled bowl, cover with oiled clear film (plastic wrap) and leave to rise for 1 hour, or until doubled in bulk.

3 Turn out on to a floured surface and knock back. Flatten out and sprinkle over the olives. Knead to distribute the olives. Leave to rest for 5 minutes, then shape into an oval loaf. Place on the baking sheet.

4 ▲ Make six deep cuts in the top, and gently push the sections over. Cover with oiled clear film and leave to rise, in a warm place, for 30–45 minutes, or until doubled in size.

MAKES 1 LOAF

275g/10oz/2¹/₂ cups unbleached strong white bread flour
50g/2oz/¹/₂ cup wholemeal (whole-wheat) bread flour
10g/¹/₄oz easy-blend (rapid-rise) dried yeast
2.5ml/¹/₂ tsp salt
200ml/7fl oz/scant 1 cup lukewarm water
15ml/1 tbsp extra virgin olive oil, plus extra, for brushing
115g/4oz/1 cup pitted black and green olives, coarsely chopped

~ VARIATION ~
Add some hazelnuts or pine nuts.

5 Meanwhile, preheat the oven to 200°C/400°F/Gas 6. Brush the bread with olive oil and bake for 35 minutes. Transfer to a wire rack to cool.

Energy 1346kcal/5689kJ; Protein 39g; Carbohydrate 239g, of which sugars 5g; Fat 33g, of which saturates 5g; Cholesterol 0mg; Calcium 474mg; Fibre 19g; Sodium 3580mg.

Italian Polenta Bread

MAKES 1 LOAF

50g/2oz/¹/₂ cup polenta
300ml/¹/₂ pint/1¹/₄ cups lukewarm water
15g/¹/₂oz fresh yeast
2.5ml/¹/₂ tsp clear honey
225g/8oz/2 cups unbleached strong white bread flour
25g/1oz/2 tbsp butter
45ml/3 tbsp pine nuts
7.5ml/1¹/₂ tsp salt
FOR THE TOPPING
1 egg yolk
15ml/1 tbsp water
pine nuts, for sprinkling

1 ▲ Grease a baking sheet. Mix the polenta and 250ml/8fl oz/1 cup of the water together in a pan and slowly bring to the boil, stirring continuously. Reduce the heat and simmer for 2–3 minutes, stirring occasionally. Set aside to cool until just warm.

2 In a small bowl, mix the yeast with the remaining water and honey until creamy. Sift 115g/4oz/1 cup of the flour into a large bowl. Gradually beat in the yeast mixture, then gradually stir in the polenta mixture to combine. Turn out on to a lightly floured surface and knead for 5 minutes until smooth and elastic.

3 Cover the bowl with lightly oiled clear film (plastic wrap). Leave to rise, in a warm place, for about 2 hours, or until it has doubled in bulk.

4 ▲ Meanwhile, melt the butter in a small pan, add the pine nuts and cook over a medium heat, stirring, until pale golden. Set aside to cool.

5 Add the remaining flour and the salt to the polenta dough and mix to a soft dough. Knead in the pine nuts. Turn out on to a lightly floured surface and knead the dough for 5 minutes until smooth and elastic.

6 Place in an oiled bowl, cover with clear film and leave to rise, in a warm place, for 1 hour, until doubled in bulk.

7 ▲ Knock back the dough and turn it out on to a floured surface. Cut the dough into two equal pieces and roll each piece into a fat sausage about 38cm/15in long. Plait together and place on the baking sheet. Cover with lightly oiled clear film and leave to rise, in a warm place, for 45 minutes. Preheat the oven to 200°C/400°F/Gas 6.

8 Mix the egg yolk and water and brush over the loaf. Sprinkle with pine nuts and bake for 30 minutes, or until golden and sounding hollow when tapped. Cool on a wire rack.

Energy 1347kcal/5569kJ; Protein 36g; Carbohydrate 210g, of which sugars 7g; Fat 45g, of which saturates 16g; Cholesterol 255mg; Calcium 348mg; Fibre 11g; Sodium 3115mg.

Italian Prosciutto Loaf

1 Grease a baking sheet. Sift the flour and salt into a large mixing bowl and make a well in the centre. Cream the yeast with 30ml/2 tbsp of the water, then gradually mix in the rest of the water. Pour into the centre of the flour.

2 ▲ Gradually beat in most of the flour with a wooden spoon to make a batter. Beat gently to begin with and then more vigorously as the batter thickens. When most of the flour is incorporated, mix in the rest with your hand to form a moist dough.

3 Turn out the dough on to a lightly floured surface and knead for 5 minutes, until smooth and elastic. Place in an oiled bowl, cover with lightly oiled clear film (plastic wrap) and leave to rise for 1½ hours, or until doubled in bulk.

4 ▲ Turn out the dough on to a floured surface, knock back and knead for 1 minute. Flatten to a round, then sprinkle with half the prosciutto and pepper. Fold in half and repeat with the remaining ham and pepper. Roll up, tucking in the sides.

MAKES 1 LOAF

350g/12oz/3 cups unbleached strong white bread flour
7.5ml/1½ tsp salt
15g/½oz fresh yeast
250ml/8fl oz/1 cup lukewarm water
40g/1½oz prosciutto, torn into small pieces
5ml/1 tsp freshly ground black pepper

~ VARIATION ~

To make pesto bread, spread 45ml/3 tbsp pesto over the flattened dough in step 4.

5 Place on the baking sheet, cover with oiled clear film and leave to rise, in a warm place, for about 30 minutes. On a floured surface, roll into an oval, fold in half and seal the edges. Flatten and fold again. Seal and fold again to make a long loaf.

6 Roll into a stubby long loaf. Draw out the edges by rolling the dough under the palms of your hands. Place on the baking sheet, cover with oiled clear film and leave to rise, in a warm place, for 45 minutes, or until the loaf has doubled in size. Preheat the oven to 200°C/400°F/Gas 6.

7 ▲ Slash the top of the loaf diagonally and bake for 30 minutes, or until golden. Cool on a wire rack.

Energy 1283kcal/5451kJ; Protein 51g; Carbohydrate 264g, of which sugars 5g; Fat 10g, of which saturates 2g; Cholesterol 0mg; Calcium 491mg; Fibre 13g; Sodium 3758mg.

Italian Focaccia

MAKES 2 LOAVES

20g/³/₄oz fresh yeast

315–350ml/11–12fl oz/1¹/₄–1¹/₂ cups
   lukewarm water

45ml/3 tbsp extra virgin olive oil

500g/1¹/₄lb/4²/₃ cups unbleached strong
   white bread flour

10ml/2 tsp salt

15ml/1 tbsp chopped fresh sage

FOR THE TOPPING

60ml/4 tbsp extra virgin olive oil

4 garlic cloves, chopped

12 fresh sage leaves

4 ▲ Knock back the dough and turn
out on to a floured surface. Gently
knead in the chopped sage. Divide the
dough into two equal pieces. Shape
each into a ball, roll out into 25cm/
10in circles and place in the tins.

1 ▲ Lightly oil two 25cm/10in
shallow round cake tins (pans) or
pizza pans. Cream the yeast with
60ml/4 tbsp of the water in a small
bowl, then stir in the remaining
water. Stir in the oil.

2 Sift the flour and salt together into
a large bowl and make a well in the
centre. Pour the yeast mixture into
the well and incorporate the flour to
make a soft dough.

3 Turn out the dough on to a lightly
floured surface and knead for 8–10
minutes until smooth and elastic.
Place in a lightly oiled bowl, cover
with lightly oiled clear film (plastic
wrap), and leave to rise, in a warm
place, for about 1–1½ hours, or until
the dough has doubled in bulk.

5 ▲ Cover the dough with lightly
oiled clear film and leave to rise in a
warm place for about 30 minutes.
Uncover, and using your fingertips,
poke the dough to make deep dimples
over the entire surface. Replace the
clear film cover and leave to rise until
doubled in bulk.

6 Meanwhile, preheat the oven to
200°C/400°F/Gas 6. Sprinkle the
loaves with olive oil and garlic for
the topping and dot with sage leaves.
Bake for 25–30 minutes, or until
both loaves are golden. Immediately
remove the focaccia from the tins and
transfer them to a wire rack to cool
slightly. These loaves are best
served warm.

Energy 1334kcal/5608kJ; Protein 29g; Carbohydrate 190g, of which sugars 4g; Fat 56g, of which saturates 8g;
Cholesterol 0mg; Calcium 370mg; Fibre 9g; Sodium 1973mg.

Italian Panini all'Olio

MAKES 16 ROLLS

450g/1lb/4 cups unbleached strong white
   bread flour

10ml/2 tsp salt

15g/¹/₂oz fresh yeast

250ml/8fl oz/1 cup lukewarm water

60ml/4 tbsp extra virgin olive oil,
   plus extra for brushing

1 Oil three baking sheets. Sift the
flour and salt together in a bowl and
make a well in the centre. Cream the
yeast with half of the water, then stir in
the remainder. Add to the centre of the
flour with the oil and mix to a dough.

2 Turn the dough out on to a lightly
floured surface and knead for 8–10
minutes until smooth and elastic.
Place in an oiled bowl, cover with
oiled clear film (plastic wrap) and
leave to rise for 1 hour, or until the
dough has nearly doubled in bulk.

3 Turn on to a lightly floured surface
and knock back. Divide into 12 equal
pieces of dough and shape into rolls as
described in steps 5, 6 and 7.

4 ▲ For *tavalli* (twisted spiral rolls):
roll each piece of dough into a strip
about 30cm/12in long and 4cm/1½in
wide. Twist into a spiral and join the
ends together to make a circle. Place
on the baking sheets, well spaced.
Brush the *tavalli* with olive oil, cover
with oiled clear film and leave to rise,
in a warm place, for 20–30 minutes.

5 ▲ For *filoncini* (finger-shaped rolls):
flatten each piece of dough into an
oval and roll to about 23cm/9in in
length without changing the basic
shape. Make it 5cm/2in wide at one
end and 10cm/4in wide at the other.
Roll up, starting from the wider end.
Gently stretch the roll to 20–23cm/
8–9in long. Cut in half. Place on the
baking sheets, well spaced. Brush with
olive oil, cover with oiled clear film
and leave to rise, in a warm place, for
20–30 minutes.

6 ▲ For *carciofi* (artichoke-shaped
rolls): shape each piece of dough into
a ball and space well apart on the
baking sheets. Brush with olive oil,
cover with oiled clear film and leave
to rise, in a warm place, for about
20–30 minutes. Preheat the oven to
200°C/400°F/Gas 6. Using scissors,
snip several 5mm/¼in deep cuts in a
circle on the top of each *carciofi*, then
make five larger horizontal cuts
around the sides. Bake for 15 minutes.
Transfer to a wire rack to cool.

Energy 130kcal/546kJ; Protein 3g; Carbohydrate 22g, of which sugars 0g; Fat 4g, of which saturates 1g; Cholesterol 0mg; Calcium 39mg; Fibre 1g; Sodium 246mg.

Italian Ciabatta

1 Cream the yeast for the *biga* starter with a little of the water. Sift the flour into a bowl. Gradually mix in the yeast mixture and enough of the remaining water to form a firm dough.

2 Turn out the *biga* starter dough on to a lightly floured surface and knead for about 5 minutes until smooth and elastic. Return the dough to the bowl, cover with lightly oiled clear film (plastic wrap) and leave in a warm place for 12–15 hours, until the dough has risen and is starting to collapse.

3 Sprinkle three baking sheets with flour. Mix the yeast for the dough with a little of the water until creamy, then mix in the remainder. Add the yeast mixture to the *biga* and mix in.

4 Mix in the milk, beating thoroughly with a wooden spoon. Using your hand, gradually mix in the flour, lifting the dough as you mix. Mixing the dough will take 15 minutes or more and form a very wet mix, impossible to knead on a work surface.

5 Beat in the salt and olive oil. Cover with lightly oiled clear film and leave to rise, in a warm place, for 1½–2 hours, or until doubled in bulk.

6 ▲ Using a spoon, tip one-third of the dough at a time on to the baking sheets, trying to avoid knocking back the dough in the process.

7 ▲ Using floured hands, shape into oblong loaf shapes, about 2.5cm/1in thick. Flatten slightly. Sprinkle with flour and leave to rise in a warm place for 30 minutes.

8 Meanwhile, preheat the oven to 220°C/425°F/Gas 7. Bake for 25–30 minutes, or until golden brown and sounding hollow when tapped on the base. Transfer to a wire rack to cool.

MAKES 3 LOAVES

FOR THE BIGA STARTER
10g/¼oz fresh yeast
175–200ml/6–7fl oz/³/₄–scant 1 cup lukewarm water
350g/12oz/3 cups strong white bread flour, plus extra for dusting

FOR THE DOUGH
15g/½oz fresh yeast
400ml/14fl oz/1²/₃ cups lukewarm water
60ml/4 tbsp lukewarm milk
500g/1¼lb/4²/₃ cups strong white bread flour
10ml/2 tsp salt
45ml/3 tbsp extra virgin olive oil

> **~ VARIATION ~**
>
> Add 115g/4oz/2 cups chopped sun-dried tomatoes in step 5.

Energy 1101kcal/4666kJ; Protein 33g; Carbohydrate 213g, of which sugars 4g; Fat 19g, of which saturates 3g; Cholesterol 0mg; Calcium 397mg; Fibre 10g; Sodium 1319mg.

Italian Panettone

Makes 1 Loaf

400g/14oz/3¹/₂ cups unbleached strong white bread flour

2.5ml/¹/₂ tsp salt

15g/¹/₂oz fresh yeast

120ml/4fl oz/¹/₂ cup lukewarm milk

2 eggs

2 egg yolks

75g/3oz/6 tbsp caster (superfine) sugar

150g/5oz/10 tbsp butter, softened

115g/4oz/1¹/₃ cups mixed chopped (candied) peel

75g/3oz/¹/₂ cup raisins

melted butter, for brushing

1 Using a double layer of baking parchment, line and butter a 15cm/6in deep cake tin (pan). Finish the paper 7.5cm/3in above the top of the tin.

2 Sift the flour and salt into a bowl. In a jug (pitcher), cream the yeast with 60ml/4 tbsp of the milk, then mix in the remainder.

3 ▲ Pour the yeast mixture into the centre of the flour, add the whole eggs and mix in sufficient flour to make a thick batter. Sprinkle a little flour over the top and leave to 'sponge', in a warm place, for 30 minutes.

4 Add the egg yolks and sugar and mix to a soft dough. Work in the softened butter, then turn out on to a lightly floured surface and knead for 5 minutes until smooth and elastic. Place in a lightly oiled bowl, cover with lightly oiled clear film (plastic wrap) and leave to rise for 1½–2 hours, or until doubled in bulk.

5 ▲ Knock back the dough and turn out on to a floured surface. Gently knead in the peel and raisins. Shape into a ball and place in the tin. Cover with oiled clear film and leave to rise, in a slightly warm place, for about 1 hour, or until doubled.

6 ▲ Meanwhile, preheat the oven to 190°C/375°F/Gas 5. Brush the loaf with melted butter and cut a cross in the top. Bake for 20 minutes, then reduce the oven temperature to 180°C/350°F/Gas 4. Brush the top with butter again and bake for 25–30 minutes more, or until golden. Cool in the tin for 5–10 minutes, then turn out on to a wire rack to cool.

Italian Pane al Cioccolato

MAKES 1 LOAF

350g/12oz/3 cups unbleached strong white bread flour
22.5ml/1¹/₂ tbsp unsweetened cocoa powder
2.5ml/¹/₂ tsp salt
30ml/2 tbsp caster (superfine) sugar
15g/¹/₂oz fresh yeast
250ml/8fl oz/1 cup lukewarm water
25g/1oz/2 tbsp butter, softened
75g/3oz plain (semisweet) continental chocolate, coarsely chopped
melted butter, for brushing

1 ▲ Lightly grease a 15cm/6in round deep cake tin (pan). Sift the flour, cocoa powder and salt together into a large bowl. Stir in the sugar. Make a well in the centre.

2 Cream the yeast with 60ml/4 tbsp of the water, then stir in the rest. Add to the centre of the flour mixture and gradually mix to a dough.

3 Knead in the butter, then knead on a surface until smooth and elastic. Place in an oiled bowl, cover with clear film (plastic wrap) and leave to rise for 1 hour, or until doubled in bulk.

4 ▲ Turn out on to a floured surface and knock back. Knead in the chopped chocolate, cover with oiled clear film and leave to rest for about 5 minutes.

5 Shape the dough into a round and place in the prepared tin. Cover with lightly oiled clear film and leave to rise, in a warm place, for 45 minutes, or until doubled in bulk.

6 ▲ Preheat the oven to 220°C/425°F/Gas 7. Bake for 10 minutes, then reduce the temperature to 190°C/375°F/Gas 5 and bake for 25–30 minutes more. Brush with melted butter and cool on a wire rack.

Energy 1793kcal/7576kJ; Protein 46g; Carbohydrate 312g, of which sugars 52g; Fat 49g, of which saturates 28g; Cholesterol 58mg; Calcium 535mg; Fibre 13g; Sodium 1244mg.

Sicilian Scroll

MAKES 1 LOAF

450g/1lb/4 cups finely ground semolina

115g/4oz/1 cup unbleached strong white bread flour

10ml/2 tsp salt

20g/³/₄oz fresh yeast

350ml/12fl oz/1¹/₂ cups lukewarm water

30ml/2 tbsp extra virgin olive oil

sesame seeds, for sprinkling

4 ▲ Turn out on to a floured surface and knock back. Knead, then shape into a fat roll about 50cm/20in long. Form into an 'S' shape.

1 ▲ Grease a baking sheet. Mix the semolina, white bread flour and salt together and make a well in the centre.

2 In a jug (pitcher), cream the yeast with half the water, then stir in the remainder. Add the creamed yeast to the centre of the semolina mixture with the olive oil and gradually incorporate the semolina and flour to form a firm dough.

3 Turn out the dough on to a lightly floured surface and knead for 8–10 minutes until smooth and elastic. Place in a lightly oiled bowl, cover with lightly oiled clear film (plastic wrap) and leave to rise for 1–1½ hours, or until doubled in bulk.

5 Transfer to the baking sheet, cover with oiled clear film and leave to rise, in a warm place, for 30–45 minutes, or until doubled in size.

6 Meanwhile, preheat the oven to 220°C/425°F/Gas 7. Brush the top of the scroll with water and sprinkle with sesame seeds. Bake for 10 minutes. Spray the inside of the oven with water twice during this time. Reduce the oven temperature to 200°C/400°F/Gas 6 and bake for a further 25–30 minutes, or until golden. Cool on a wire rack.

~ **VARIATION** ~

Although sesame seeds are the traditional topping on this bread, poppy seeds, or even sea salt, could be used instead.

Energy 2344kcal/9922kJ]; Protein 64.4g; Carbohydrate 438.4g, of which sugars 1.8g; Fat 49g, of which saturates 5.9g; Cholesterol 0mg; Calcium 443mg; Fibre 15.4g; Sodium 63mg.

Pane Toscano

MAKES 1 LOAF

500g/1¼lb/4⅔ cups unbleached strong white bread flour
350ml/12fl oz/1½ cups boiling water
15g/½oz fresh yeast
60ml/4 tbsp lukewarm water

6 ▲ Fold the sides of the round into the centre and seal. Place seam side up on the baking sheet. Cover with oiled clear film and leave to rise, in a warm place, for 30–45 minutes, or until doubled in size.

7 ▲ Flatten the loaf to about half its risen height and flip over. Cover with a large upturned bowl and leave to rise, in a warm place, for 30 minutes.

8 Meanwhile, preheat the oven to 220°C/425°F/Gas 7. Slash the top of the loaf, using a sharp knife, if wished. Bake for 30–35 minutes, or until golden. Cool on a wire rack.

1 ▲ First make the starter. Sift 175g/6oz/1½ cups of the flour into a bowl. Pour over the boiling water, leave for a couple of minutes, then mix well. Cover the bowl with a damp dish towel and leave for 10 hours.

2 Lightly flour a baking sheet. Cream the yeast with the lukewarm water. Stir into the starter.

3 Gradually add the remaining flour and mix to form a dough. Turn out on to a floured surface and knead for 5–8 minutes until smooth and elastic.

4 Place in a lightly oiled bowl, cover with lightly oiled clear film (plastic wrap) and leave to rise for 1–1½ hours, or until doubled in bulk.

5 Turn out the dough on to a lightly floured surface, knock back, and shape into a round.

Energy 1876kcal/7975kJ; Protein 51.7g; Carbohydrate 427.4g, of which sugars 8.3g; Fat 7.2g, of which saturates 1.1g; Cholesterol 0mg; Calcium 770mg; Fibre 17.1g; Sodium 17mg.

Tuscan Schiacciata

MAKES 1 LOAF

350g/12oz/3 cups unbleached strong white bread flour

2.5ml/½ tsp salt

15g/½oz fresh yeast

200ml/7fl oz/scant 1 cup lukewarm water

60ml/4 tbsp extra virgin olive oil

FOR THE TOPPING

30ml/2 tbsp extra virgin olive oil, for brushing

30ml/2 tbsp fresh rosemary leaves

coarse sea salt, for sprinkling

1 Oil a baking sheet. Sift the flour and salt into a bowl and make a well in the centre. Cream the yeast with half the water. Add to the flour with the remaining water and olive oil and mix to a soft dough. Turn out on to a floured surface and knead for 10 minutes until smooth and elastic.

2 Place in a lightly oiled bowl, cover with lightly oiled clear film (plastic wrap) and leave to rise for about 1 hour, or until doubled in bulk.

3 ▲ Knock back the dough, turn out on to a lightly floured surface and knead gently. Roll to a 30 × 20cm/ 12 × 8in rectangle and place on the prepared baking sheet. Brush with some of the olive oil for the topping and cover loosely with lightly oiled clear film.

4 ▲ Leave the dough to rise, in a warm place, for about 20 minutes, then brush with the remaining oil, prick all over with a fork and sprinkle with rosemary and sea salt. Leave to rise again in a warm place for 15 minutes.

5 Meanwhile. preheat the oven to 200°C/400°F/Gas 6. Bake the bread for 30 minutes, or until light golden. Leave to cool slightly on a wire rack. Serve warm.

Energy 2003kcal/8405kJ; Protein 40g; Carbohydrate 264g, of which sugars 5g; Fat 95g, of which saturates 14g; Cholesterol 0mg; Calcium 490mg; Fibre 13g; Sodium 993mg.

Moroccan Holiday Bread

MAKES 1 LOAF

275g/10oz/2¹/₂ cups strong white bread flour
50g/2oz/¹/₂ cup maize meal
5ml/1 tsp salt
20g/³/₄oz fresh yeast
120ml/4fl oz/¹/₂ cup lukewarm water
120ml/4fl oz/¹/₂ cup lukewarm milk
15ml/1 tbsp pumpkin seeds
15ml/1 tbsp sesame seeds
30ml/2 tbsp sunflower seeds

5 ▲ Turn out the dough on to a floured surface and knock back. Knead in the seeds. Shape into a round ball and flatten slightly. Place on the prepared baking sheet and cover with oiled clear film. Leave to rise, in a warm place, for about 45 minutes, or until doubled in bulk.

1 Lightly grease a baking sheet. Sift the flours and salt into a large bowl.

2 ▲ Cream the yeast with a little of the water in a jug (pitcher). Stir in the remainder of the water and the milk. Pour into the centre of the flour and mix to a fairly soft dough.

3 Turn out the dough on to a lightly floured surface and knead it for about 5 minutes, or until it is smooth and elastic.

4 Place the dough in a lightly oiled bowl, cover with lightly oiled clear film (plastic wrap) and leave to rise, in a warm place, for about 1 hour, or until doubled in bulk.

> ### ~ VARIATION ~
> For a plainer-looking loaf that is easier to transport, incorporate all the seeds in the dough in step 5 and leave the top of the loaf seedless.

6 ▲ Preheat the oven to 200°C/400°F/ Gas 6. Brush the top of the loaf with water and sprinkle with the sunflower seeds. Bake for 30–35 minutes, or until golden and hollow-sounding when tapped. Transfer to a rack to cool.

Energy 1531kcal/6456kJ; Protein 45.9g; Carbohydrate 262.1g, of which sugars 10.8g; Fat 38.9g, of which saturates 5.6g; Cholesterol 7mg; Calcium 765mg; Fibre 13.8g; Sodium 2046mg.

Greek Christopsomo

MAKES 1 LOAF

15g/¹/₂oz fresh yeast

140ml/scant ¹/₄ pint/generous ¹/₂ cup lukewarm milk

450g/1lb/4 cups unbleached strong white bread flour

2 eggs

75g/3oz/6 tbsp caster (superfine) sugar

2.5ml/¹/₂ tsp salt

75g/3oz/6 tbsp butter, softened

grated rind of ¹/₂ orange

5ml/1 tsp ground cinnamon

1.25ml/¹/₄ tsp ground cloves

pinch of crushed aniseed

8 walnut halves

beaten egg white, for glazing

1 ▲ Grease a large baking sheet. In a bowl, mix the yeast with the milk until the yeast is dissolved, then stir in 115g/4oz/1 cup of the flour to make a thin batter. Cover with oiled clear film (plastic wrap). Leave to 'sponge' in a warm place for 30 minutes.

2 Beat the eggs and sugar until light and fluffy. Beat into the yeast mixture. Gradually mix in the remaining flour and salt. Beat in the butter and knead to a soft but not sticky dough. Knead on a floured surface for 8–10 minutes until smooth and elastic. Place in an oiled bowl, cover with oiled clear film and leave to rise, in a warm place, for 1¹/₂ hours, or until doubled in bulk.

3 Turn out on to a floured surface and gently knock back. Cut off 50g/2oz of dough, cover it with clear film and set aside. Gently knead the orange rind, cinnamon and cloves into the large piece of dough and shape it into a round loaf. Place the loaf on the baking sheet.

4 Knead the crushed aniseed into the remaining dough. Cut in half and shape each piece into a 30cm/12in rope. Cut through each rope at either end by one-third of its length. Place the two ropes in a cross on top of the loaf, then curl each cut end into a circle, in opposite directions.

5 ▲ Place a walnut half inside each circle. Cover the loaf with clear film and leave to rise for 45 minutes, or until doubled in size. Preheat the oven to 190°C/375°F/Gas 5. Brush the bread with the egg white and bake for 40–45 minutes, or until golden. Cool on a wire rack.

Energy 2652kcal/11177kJ; Protein 61g; Carbohydrate 425g, of which sugars 92g; Fat 91g, of which saturates 45g; Cholesterol 180mg; Calcium 926mg; Fibre 18g; Sodium 536mg.

Greek Tsoureki

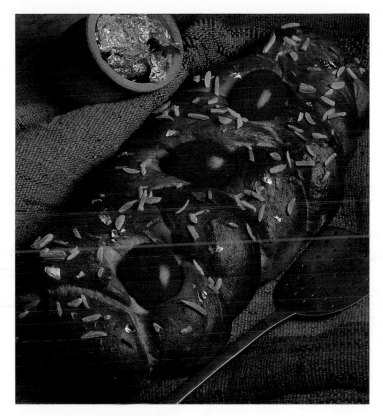

MAKES 1 LOAF

FOR THE EGGS

3 eggs

1.25ml/¼ tsp red food colouring paste

15ml/1 tbsp white wine vinegar

5ml/1 tsp water

5ml/1 tsp olive oil

FOR THE DOUGH

450g/1lb/4 cups unbleached strong
   white bread flour

2.5ml/½ tsp salt

5ml/1 tsp ground allspice

2.5ml/½ tsp ground cinnamon

2.5ml/½ tsp caraway seeds

20g/¾oz fresh yeast

175ml/6fl oz/¾ cup lukewarm milk

50g/2oz/¼ cup butter

45ml/3 tbsp caster (superfine) sugar

2 eggs

FOR THE GLAZE

1 egg yolk

5ml/1 tsp clear honey

5ml/1 tsp water

FOR THE DECORATION

45ml/3 tbsp split almonds, slivered

1 Grease a baking sheet. Place the eggs in a pan of water and bring to the boil. Boil gently for 10 minutes. Meanwhile, mix the red food colouring, vinegar and water in a shallow bowl. Remove the eggs from the boiling water, place on a wire rack for a few seconds to dry then roll in the colouring mixture. Return to the rack to cool and dry.

2 When cold, drizzle the olive oil on to absorbent kitchen paper, lift up each egg in turn and rub all over with the oiled paper.

3 To make the dough, sift the flour, salt, allspice and cinnamon into a large bowl. Stir in the caraway seeds.

4 In a jug (pitcher), mix the yeast with the milk. In a bowl, cream the butter and sugar together, then beat in the eggs. Add the creamed mixture to the flour with the yeast mixture and mix to a dough. Turn out the dough on to a lightly floured surface and knead until smooth and elastic.

5 Place in a lightly oiled bowl, cover with lightly oiled clear film (plastic wrap) and leave to rise for about 2 hours, or until doubled in bulk.

6 Knock back the dough and knead for 2–3 minutes. Return to the bowl, re-cover and leave to rise again, in a warm place, for about 1 hour, or until doubled in bulk.

7 Knock back and turn out on to a floured surface. Divide the dough into three equal pieces and roll each into a 38–50cm/15–20in long rope. Plait together from the centre to the ends.

8 Place on the prepared baking sheet and push the dyed eggs into the loaf. Cover and leave to rise, in a warm place, for about 1 hour.

9 Preheat the oven to 190°C/375°F/ Gas 5. Mix the egg yolk, honey and water for the glaze, and brush over the loaf. Sprinkle with almonds. Bake for 40–45 minutes, or until golden and sounding hollow when tapped. Cool on a wire rack.

Energy 3058kcal/12856kJ; Protein 110g; Carbohydrate 396g, of which sugars 62g; Fat 125g, of which saturates 45g; Cholesterol 1492mg; Calcium 1260mg; Fibre 23g; Sodium 1822mg.

Greek Olive Bread

MAKES 2 LOAVES

675g/1½lb/6 cups unbleached strong
  white bread flour, plus extra for dusting

10ml/2 tsp salt

25g/1oz fresh yeast

350ml/12fl oz/1½ cups lukewarm water

75ml/5 tbsp olive oil

175g/6oz/1½ cups pitted black olives,
  roughly chopped

1 red onion, finely chopped

30ml/2 tbsp chopped fresh coriander
  (cilantro) or mint

1 Lightly grease two baking sheets.
Sift the flour and salt together into a
bowl and make a well in the centre.

2 ▲ In a jug (pitcher), blend the
yeast with half of the water. Add to
the flour with the remaining water
and the olive oil; mix to a soft dough.

3 Turn out the dough on to a lightly
floured surface and knead for 8–10
minutes until smooth. Place in a
lightly oiled bowl, cover with lightly
oiled clear film (plastic wrap) and
leave to rise, in a warm place, for
1 hour, or until doubled in bulk.

4 Turn out on to a lightly floured
surface and knock back. Cut off a
quarter of the dough, cover with
lightly oiled clear film and set aside.

5 ▲ Roll out the large piece of dough
to a round. Sprinkle with the olives,
onion and herbs, then bring up the
sides of the circle and knead together.

6 Cut the dough in half and shape
each piece into a plump oval loaf,
about 20cm/8in long. Place on the
prepared baking sheets.

7 Divide the reserved dough into
four equal pieces and roll each to a
long strand 60cm/24in long. Twist
together and cut in half. Brush the
centre of each loaf with water and
place two pieces of twisted dough
on top of each, tucking the ends
underneath the loaves.

8 Cover with lightly oiled clear film
and leave to rise, in a warm place, for
about 45 minutes, or until the loaves
are plump and nearly doubled in size.

9 Preheat the oven to 220°C/425°F/
Gas 7. Dust the loaves with flour and
bake for 35–40 minutes, or until
golden and sounding hollow when
tapped. Cool on a wire rack.

Energy 1527kcal/6440kJ; Protein 34g; Carbohydrate 270.4g, of which sugars 10.9g; Fat 41.8g, of which saturates 6g; Cholesterol 0mg; Calcium 567mg; Fibre 14.8g; Sodium 3950mg.

Turkish Pitta Bread

MAKES 6 PITTA BREADS

225g/8oz/2 cups unbleached strong
white bread flour

5ml/1 tsp salt

15g/¹/₂oz fresh yeast

150ml/¹/₄ pint/²/₃ cup lukewarm water

10ml/2 tsp extra virgin olive oil

~ VARIATION ~
Replace half the white bread
flour with strong wholemeal
(whole-wheat) bread flour.

5 ▲ Roll out each ball of dough to
an oval 5mm/¹/₄in thick and 15cm/6in
long. Place on a floured dish towel
and cover with oiled clear film.
Leave to rise at room temperature for
about 20–30 minutes. Meanwhile,
preheat the oven to 230°C/450°F/
Gas 8. Place three baking sheets in
the oven to heat.

6 Place two pitta breads on each
baking sheet and bake for 4–6
minutes, or until puffed up; they do
not need to brown. If preferred, cook
the bread in batches. It is important
that the oven has reached the
recommended temperature before
the breads are baked, to ensure that
they puff up.

7 Transfer the pittas to a wire rack to
cool until warm, then cover with a
clean dish towel to keep them soft.

1 Sift the flour and salt together into
a bowl. Mix the yeast with the water
until dissolved, then stir in the olive
oil and pour into a large bowl.

2 Gradually beat the flour into the
yeast mixture, then knead the mixture
to make a soft dough.

3 Turn out on to a floured surface and
knead for 5 minutes until smooth and
elastic. Place in a clean bowl, cover
with oiled clear film (plastic wrap)
and leave to rise, in a warm place, for
1 hour, or until doubled in bulk.

4 ▲ Knock back the dough. On a
floured surface, divide it into six equal
pieces and shape each into a ball.
Cover with oiled clear film and leave
to rest for 5 minutes.

Energy 143kcal/606kJ; Protein 4g; Carbohydrate 28g, of which sugars 1g; Fat 2g, of which saturates 0g; Cholesterol 0mg; Calcium 53mg; Fibre 1g; Sodium 329mg.

Polish Poppy Seed Roll

Makes 1 loaf

350g/12oz/3 cups strong white bread flour

2.5ml/½ tsp salt

30ml/2 tbsp caster (superfine) sugar

20g/¾oz fresh yeast

120ml/4fl oz/½ cup lukewarm milk

1 egg, lightly beaten

50g/2oz/¼ cup butter, melted

15ml/1 tbsp toasted flaked (sliced) almonds

For the filling

115g/4oz poppy seeds

50g/2oz/⅔ cup mixed chopped (candied) peel

50g/2oz/¼ cup butter

75g/3oz/6 tbsp caster (superfine) sugar

75g/3oz/½ cup raisins

50g/2oz/½ cup ground almonds

2.5ml/½ tsp cinnamon

For the icing

115g/4oz/1 cup icing (confectioners') sugar

15ml/1 tbsp lemon juice

10–15ml/2–3 tsp water

1 Lightly grease a baking sheet. Sift the flour and salt into a large bowl. Stir in the sugar. Cream the yeast with the milk in a small bowl. Add to the flour with the egg and melted butter and mix to a dough.

2 Turn out the dough on to a lightly floured surface and knead for 8–10 minutes, or until smooth and elastic. Place in an oiled bowl, cover with oiled clear film (plastic wrap) and leave to rise for 1–1½ hours, or until doubled in size.

3 Pour boiling water over the poppy seeds for the filling, then leave to cool. Drain in a fine sieve (strainer). Finely chop the peel.

4 Melt the butter in a pan, add the poppy seeds and cook, stirring, for 1–2 minutes. Remove from the heat and stir in the sugar, raisins, ground almonds, peel and cinnamon. Set aside to cool.

5 Turn the dough out on to a lightly floured surface, knock back and knead lightly. Roll out into a rectangle 35 × 25cm/14 × 10in. Spread the filling to within 2cm/¾in of the edges.

6 ▲ Roll up the dough, starting from one long edge, like a Swiss roll (jelly roll), tucking in the edges to seal. Place seam side down on the baking sheet. Cover with oiled clear film and leave to rise, in a warm place, for 30 minutes, or until doubled in size.

7 Preheat the oven to 190°C/375°F/ Gas 5. Bake for 30 minutes, or until golden brown. Transfer to a wire rack to cool until just warm.

8 ▲ Mix the icing sugar, lemon juice and sufficient water together in a small pan to make an icing stiff enough to coat the back of a spoon. Heat gently, stirring, until warm. Drizzle the icing over the loaf and sprinkle the flaked almonds over the top. Leave to cool completely, then serve sliced.

Energy 3299kcal/13933kJ; Protein 91g; Carbohydrate 581g, of which sugars 319g; Fat 148g, of which saturates 40g; Cholesterol 355mg; Calcium 2763mg; Fibre 26g; Sodium 1670mg.

Polish Rye Bread

MAKES 1 LOAF

225g/8oz/2 cups rye flour
225g/8oz/2 cups strong white bread flour
10ml/2 tsp caraway seeds
10ml/2 tsp salt
20g/³/₄oz fresh yeast
150ml/¹/₄ pint/²/₃ cup lukewarm milk
5ml/1 tsp clear honey
150ml/¹/₄ pint/²/₃ cup lukewarm water
wholemeal (whole-wheat) flour, for dusting

4 ▲ Turn out on to a floured surface and knock back. Shape into an oval loaf and place on the baking sheet.

5 Dust with wholemeal flour, cover with oiled clear film and leave to rise, in a warm place, for 1–1½ hours, or until doubled in size. Preheat the oven to 220°C/425°F/Gas 7.

1 ▲ Grease a baking sheet. Mix the flours, caraway seeds and salt in a bowl and make a well in the centre.

2 In a bowl or measuring jug (cup), cream the yeast with the milk and honey. Pour into the centre of the flour, add the water and gradually incorporate the surrounding flour and caraway mixture until a dough forms.

3 Turn out the dough on to a floured surface and knead for 8–10 minutes until smooth, elastic and firm. Place in an oiled bowl, cover with oiled clear film (plastic wrap) and leave to rise, in a warm place, for about 3 hours, or until doubled in bulk.

6 ▲ Slash the loaf with two long cuts about 2.5cm/ 1in apart. Bake for 30–35 minutes, or until the loaf sounds hollow when tapped. Cool on a rack.

Energy 1667kcal/7088kJ; Protein 46.4g; Carbohydrate 360.2g, of which sugars 16.2g; Fat 14.6g, of which saturates 3.1g; Cholesterol 8mg; Calcium 567mg; Fibre 33.9g; Sodium 4000mg.

Hungarian Split Farmhouse Loaf

3 ▲ Add the melted butter and gradually mix in with the remaining flour to form a dough. Turn out on to a floured surface and knead for 8–10 minutes until smooth and elastic. Place in an oiled bowl, cover with oiled clear film and leave to rise, in a warm place, for 45–60 minutes, or until doubled in bulk.

4 ▲ Turn out on to a floured surface and knock back. Shape into an oval and place on the baking sheet. Cover with oiled clear film and leave to rise, in a warm place, for 30–40 minutes, or until doubled in size.

MAKES 1 LOAF

450g/1lb/4 cups strong white bread flour
10ml/2 tsp salt
2.5ml/¹/₂ tsp fennel seeds, crushed
15ml/1 tbsp caster (superfine) sugar
20g/³/₄oz fresh yeast
275ml/9fl oz/generous 1 cup lukewarm water
25g/1oz/2 tbsp butter, melted
1 egg white
10ml/2 tsp fennel seeds, for sprinkling

1 Lightly grease a baking sheet. Sift the white bread flour and salt together into a large bowl and stir in the crushed fennel seeds and caster sugar. Make a well in the centre.

2 ▲ Cream the yeast with a little of the water in a small bowl, then stir in the rest. Stir in enough flour to make a runny batter. Sprinkle more of the flour on top of the batter, cover with lightly oiled clear film (plastic wrap) and leave in a warm place for 30 minutes, until the 'sponge' starts to bubble and rise.

5 Meanwhile, preheat the oven to 220°C/425°F/Gas 7. Mix the egg white with a pinch of salt and brush over the loaf. Sprinkle with fennel seeds and then, using a sharp knife, slash along its length. Bake for 20 minutes, then reduce the oven temperature to 180°C/350°F/Gas 4 and bake for 10 minutes more, or until sounding hollow when tapped. Transfer to a wire rack to cool.

Energy 1791kcal/7591kJ; Protein 45.4g; Carbohydrate 365.5g, of which sugars 22.6g; Fat 26.4g, of which saturates 13.9g; Cholesterol 53mg; Calcium 644mg; Fibre 13.9g; Sodium 227mg.

Russian Potato Bread

1 ▲ Lightly grease a baking sheet. Add the potatoes to a pan of boiling water and cook until tender. Drain and reserve 150ml/¼ pint/⅔ cup of the cooking water. Mash and sieve the potatoes and leave to cool.

2 Mix the yeast, bread flours, caraway seeds and salt together in a large bowl. Add the butter and rub in. Mix the reserved potato water and sieved potatoes together. Gradually work this mixture into the flour mixture to form a soft dough.

3 Turn out on to a floured surface and knead for 8–10 minutes until smooth and elastic. Place in an oiled bowl, cover with oiled clear film (plastic wrap) and leave to rise for 1 hour, or until doubled in bulk.

4 ▲ Turn out on to a lightly floured surface, knock back and knead gently. Shape into a plump oval loaf, about 18cm/7in long. Place on the prepared baking sheet and sprinkle with a little wholemeal bread flour.

5 Cover the dough with lightly oiled clear film and leave to rise, in a warm place, for 30 minutes, or until doubled in size. Meanwhile, preheat the oven to 200°C/400°F/Gas 6.

6 ▲ Using a sharp knife, slash the top with three or four diagonal cuts to make a criss-cross effect. Bake for 30–35 minutes, or until golden and sounding hollow when tapped on the base. Transfer to a wire rack to cool.

MAKES 1 LOAF

225g/8oz potatoes, peeled and diced
10g/¼oz easy-blend (rapid-rise) dried yeast
350g/12oz/3 cups unbleached strong white bread flour
115g/4oz/1 cup wholemeal (whole-wheat) bread flour, plus extra for sprinkling
2.5ml/½ tsp caraway seeds, crushed
10ml/2 tsp salt
25g/1oz/2 tbsp

> ### ~ VARIATION ~
> To make a cheese-flavoured potato bread, omit the caraway seeds and knead 115g/4oz/ 1 cup grated Cheddar, Red Leicester or crumbled Stilton into the dough before shaping.

Jewish Challah

MAKES 1 LOAF

500g/1¼lb/4⅔ cups strong white bread flour
10ml/2 tsp salt
20g/¾oz fresh yeast
200ml/7fl oz/scant 1 cup lukewarm water
30ml/2 tbsp caster (superfine) sugar
2 eggs
75g/3oz/6 tbsp butter or margarine, melted
FOR THE GLAZE
1 egg yolk
15ml/1 tbsp water
10ml/2 tsp poppy seeds, for sprinkling

> **~ COOK'S TIP ~**
> If wished, divide the dough in half and make two challah, keeping the plaits quite simple. Reduce the baking time by about 10 minutes.

1 ▲ Lightly grease a baking sheet. Sift the flour and salt into a large bowl and make a well in the centre. Mix the yeast with the water and sugar, add to the flour with the eggs and butter or margarine and gradually mix in the surrounding flour to form a soft dough.

2 Turn out on to a floured surface and knead for 10 minutes until smooth and elastic. Place in an oiled bowl, cover with oiled clear film (plastic wrap) and leave to rise, in a warm place, for 1 hour, or until doubled in bulk.

3 Knock back, re-cover and leave to rise again in a warm place for about 1 hour. Knock back, turn out on to a floured surface and knead gently. Divide into quarters. Roll each piece into a rope 45cm/18in long. Line up next to each other. Pinch the ends together at one end.

4 ▲ Starting from the right, lift the first rope over the second and the third rope over the fourth. Take the fourth rope and place it between the first and second ropes. Repeat, continuing until plaited.

5 Tuck the ends under and place the loaf on the baking sheet. Cover with oiled clear film and leave to rise in a warm place, for about 30–45 minutes, or until doubled in size. Meanwhile, preheat the oven to 200°C/400°F/ Gas 6. Beat together the egg yolk and water for the glaze.

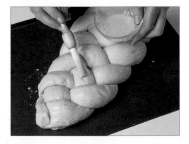

6 ▲ Brush the egg glaze gently over the loaf. Sprinkle evenly with the poppy seeds and bake for 35–40 minutes, or until the challah is a deep golden brown. Transfer to a wire rack and leave to cool.

Energy 2622kcal/11052kJ; Protein 78g; Carbohydrate 408g, of which sugars 39g; Fat 91g, of which saturates 46g; Cholesterol 825mg; Calcium 939mg; Fibre 19g; Sodium 4582mg.

American Pumpkin and Walnut Bread

1 Grease and base line a 21 × 12cm/8½ × 4½in loaf tin (pan). Preheat the oven to 180°C/350°F/Gas 4.

2 ▲ Place the pumpkin in a pan, add water to cover, then bring to the boil. Cover, lower the heat and simmer for 20 minutes, or until the pumpkin is very tender. Drain, then purée in a food processor or blender. Leave to cool.

3 ▲ Place 275g/10oz of the purée in a large bowl. Add the sugar, nutmeg, melted butter and eggs to the purée and mix together. Sift the flour, baking powder and salt into a large bowl and make a well in the centre.

4 Add the pumpkin mixture to the centre of the flour and stir until smooth. Mix in the walnuts.

MAKES 1 LOAF

500g/1¼lb pumpkin, peeled, seeded and cut into chunks
75g/3oz/6 tbsp caster (superfine) sugar
5ml/1 tsp grated nutmeg
50g/2oz/¼ cup butter, melted
3 eggs, lightly beaten
350g/12oz/3 cups unbleached strong white bread flour
10ml/2 tsp baking powder
2.5ml/½ tsp salt
75ml/5 tbsp walnuts, chopped

5 Transfer the dough to the prepared tin and bake for 1 hour, or until it is golden and starting to shrink from the sides of the tin. Leave to cool on a wire rack.

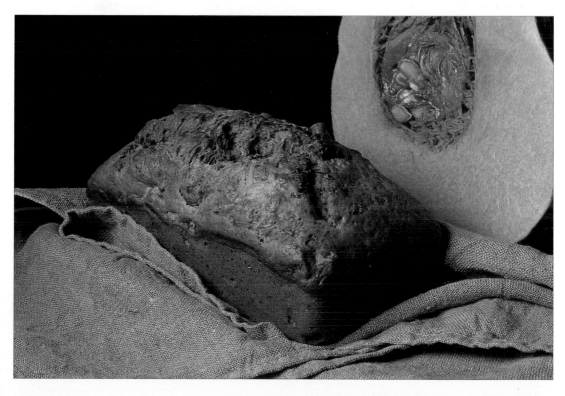

Energy 2724kcal/11446kJ; Protein 79g; Carbohydrate 359g, of which sugars 94g; Fat 118g, of which saturates 37g; Cholesterol 802mg; Calcium 921mg; Fibre 20g; Sodium 25005mg.

San Francisco Sourdough Bread

MAKES 2 LOAVES

FOR THE STARTER

50g/2oz/¹/₂ cup wholemeal
  (whole-wheat) flour

pinch of ground cumin

15ml/1 tbsp milk

15–30ml/1–2 tbsp water

1ST REFRESHMENT

30ml/2 tbsp water

115g/4oz/1 cup wholemeal
  (whole-wheat) flour

2ND REFRESHMENT

60ml/4 tbsp water

115g/4oz/1 cup strong white bread flour

FOR THE BREAD: 1ST REFRESHMENT

75ml/5 tbsp very warm water

75ml/5 tbsp plain (all-purpose) flour

2ND REFRESHMENT

175ml/6fl oz/³/₄ cup lukewarm water

215–225g/7¹/₂–8oz/scant 2–2 cups plain
  (all-purpose) flour

FOR THE SOURDOUGH

275ml/9fl oz/generous 1 cup warm water

500g/1¹/₄lb/4²/₃ cups strong white bread flour

15ml/1 tbsp salt

ice cubes, for baking

1 ▲ Sift the flour and cumin for the starter into a bowl. Add the milk and sufficient water to make a firm but moist dough. Knead for 6–8 minutes. Return to the bowl, cover with a damp dish towel and leave at 24–26°C/75–80°F for about 2 days, until it appears moist and has a crust.

2 Pull off the crust and discard. Scoop out the moist centre (about the size of a hazelnut), which will be aerated and sweet smelling, and place in a clean bowl. Mix in the water for the 1st refreshment. Add the wholemeal flour and mix to a dough.

3 Cover with clear film (plastic wrap). Return to a warm place for 1–2 days. Discard the crust and gradually mix in the water for the 2nd refreshment to the starter, which by now will have a slightly sharper smell. Gradually mix in the plain flour, cover and leave in a warm place for 8–10 hours.

4 ▲ For the bread, mix the sourdough starter with the water for the 1st refreshment. Mix in the flour to form a firm dough. Knead for 6–8 minutes until firm. Cover with a damp dish towel and leave in a warm place for 8–12 hours, until doubled in bulk.

5 Gradually mix in the water for the 2nd refreshment, then mix in enough flour to form a soft, smooth elastic dough. Re-cover and leave in a warm place for 8–12 hours. Gradually stir in the water for the sourdough, then work in the flour and salt. This will take 10–15 minutes.

6 Turn out the dough on to a floured surface and knead until smooth and very elastic. Place in a lightly oiled bowl, cover with oiled clear film and leave to rise, in a warm place, for 8–12 hours.

7 Divide the dough in half and shape into two round loaves by folding the sides over to the centre and sealing.

8 ▲ Place seam-side up in flour-dusted *couronnes*, bowls or baskets lined with flour-dusted dish towels. Re-cover and leave to rise in a warm place for 4 hours.

9 Preheat the oven to 220°C/425°F/Gas 7. Place an empty roasting pan in the bottom of the oven. Dust two baking sheets with flour. Turn out the loaves seam-side down on the prepared baking sheets. Using a sharp knife, cut a criss-cross pattern by slashing the top of the loaves four or five times in each direction.

10 Place the baking sheets in the oven and immediately drop the ice cubes into the hot roasting pan to create steam. Bake the bread for 25 minutes, then reduce the oven temperature to 200°C/400°F/Gas 6 and bake for a further 15–20 minutes, or until the loaves sound hollow when tapped on the bases. Transfer to wire racks to cool.

~ COOK'S TIP ~
If you make sourdough bread regularly, keep a small amount of the starter in a sealed container in the refrigerator. It will keep for several days. Use for the 2nd refreshment.

Energy 1749kcal/7435kJ; Protein 48.2g; Carbohydrate 398.4g, of which sugars 7.7g; Fat 6.7g, of which saturates 1.1g; Cholesterol 0mg; Calcium 718mg; Fibre 15.9g; Sodium 1490mg.

Boston Brown Bread

Makes 1 or 2 loaves

90g/3¹/₂oz/³/₄ cup cornmeal

90g/3¹/₂oz/³/₄ cup plain (all-purpose) or wholemeal (whole-wheat) flour

90g/3¹/₂oz/³/₄ cup rye flour

2.5ml/¹/₂ tsp salt

5ml/1 tsp bicarbonate of soda (baking soda)

90ml/6 tbsp seedless raisins

120ml/4fl oz/¹/₂ cup milk

120ml/4fl oz/¹/₂ cup water

120ml/4fl oz/¹/₂ cup black treacle (molasses)

> ### ~ COOK'S TIP ~
> If you do not have any of the containers listed below, use one or two heatproof bowls.

1 Line the base of a 1.2 litre/2 pint/ 5 cup cylindrical metal or glass container, such as a heatproof coffee jug (pitcher), with greaseproof (waxed) paper. Alternatively, remove the lids from two clean, dry 450g/1lb coffee tins and line with greased greaseproof paper.

2 Mix together the cornmeal, plain or wholemeal flour, rye flour, salt, bicarbonate of soda and raisins in a bowl. Warm the milk and water in a small pan and stir in the black treacle.

3 ▲ Add the molasses mixture to the dry ingredients and mix until it just forms a dough. Do not overmix.

4 ▲ Fill the jug or tins with the dough; they should be about two-thirds full. Cover with foil or greased greaseproof paper and tie securely.

5 Bring water to a depth of 5cm/2in to the boil in a deep, heavy pan large enough to accommodate the jug or tins. Place a trivet in the pan, stand the jug or tins on top, cover the pan and steam for 1½ hours, adding more boiling water to maintain the required level as necessary.

6 Cool the loaves for a few minutes in the jugs or tins, then turn them on their sides and the loaves should slip out. Leave to cool slightly on wire racks. Serve warm, as a teabread or with savoury dishes.

Energy 774kcal/3285kJ; Protein 15.8g; Carbohydrate 176.5g, of which sugars 75.2g; Fat 4.2g, of which saturates 0.8g; Cholesterol 4mg; Calcium 472mg; Fibre 8.6g; Sodium 611mg.

American Bagels

MAKES 10 BAGELS

350g/12oz/3 cups strong white bread flour
10ml/2 tsp salt
10g/¼oz easy-blend (rapid-rise) dried yeast
10ml/2 tsp malt extract
200ml/7fl oz/scant 1 cup lukewarm water
FOR POACHING
2.4 litres/4 pints/10 cups water
15ml/1 tbsp malt extract
FOR THE TOPPING
1 egg white
10ml/2 tsp cold water
30ml/2 tbsp poppy, sesame or caraway seeds

5 Preheat the oven to 220°C/425°F/Gas 7. Place the water and malt extract for poaching in a large pan, bring to the boil, then reduce to a simmer. Add the bagels a few at a time and poach for about 1 minute. They will sink and then rise again.

6 Using a fish slice or draining spoon, turn over and cook for 30 seconds. Remove and drain on a dish towel. Repeat with the remaining bagels.

3 Turn out on to a floured surface and knock back. Knead for 1 minute, then divide into 10 equal pieces. Shape into balls, cover and leave for 5 minutes.

1 ▲ Grease two baking sheets. Sift the flour and salt together into a large bowl. Stir in the dried yeast. Make a well in the centre. Mix the malt extract and water, add to the centre of the flour and mix to a dough. Knead on a floured surface until elastic.

2 Place in a lightly oiled bowl, cover with lightly oiled clear film (plastic wrap) and leave to rise for about 1 hour, or until doubled in bulk.

4 ▲ Gently flatten each ball and make a hole through the centre with your thumb. Enlarge the hole slightly by turning your thumb around. Place on a floured tray; re-cover and leave in a warm place, for 10–20 minutes, or until they begin to rise.

7 ▲ Place five bagels on each baking sheet, spacing them well apart. Beat the egg white with the water for the topping, brush the mixture over the top of each bagel and sprinkle with poppy, sesame or caraway seeds. Bake for 20–25 minutes, or until golden brown. Transfer to a wire rack to cool.

Energy 121kcal/517kJ; Protein 5g; Carbohydrate 27g, of which sugars 1g; Fat 2g, of which saturates 0g; Cholesterol 0mg; Calcium 89mg; Fibre 1g; Sodium 395mg.

American Monkey Bread

MAKES 1 LOAF

10g/¼oz sachet easy-blend (rapid-rise) dried yeast
450g/1lb/4 cups strong white bread flour
2.5ml/½ tsp salt
15ml/1 tbsp caster (superfine) sugar
120ml/4fl oz/½ cup lukewarm milk
120ml/4fl oz/½ cup lukewarm water
1 egg, lightly beaten
FOR THE COATING
75g/3oz/½ cup sultanas
45ml/3 tbsp rum or brandy
115g/4oz/⅔ cup, finely chopped
10ml/2 tsp ground cinnamon
115g/4oz/½ cup soft light brown sugar
50g/2oz/¼ cup butter, melted

1 Grease a 23cm/9in spring-form cake tin (pan). Mix the yeast, flour, salt and sugar in a bowl and make a well.

2 Add the milk, water and egg to the centre of the flour and mix together to a soft dough. Turn out on to a floured surface and knead for about 10 minutes until smooth and elastic. Place in an oiled bowl, cover with oiled clear film (plastic wrap) and leave to rise for 45–60 minutes, until doubled in bulk.

3 ▲ Place the sultanas in a pan, pour over the rum or brandy and heat for 1–2 minutes, or until warm. Remove from the heat and set aside. Mix the walnuts, cinnamon and sugar in a bowl.

4 ▲ Turn out the dough on to a lightly floured surface and knead gently. Divide into 30 equal pieces and shape into small balls. Dip the balls, one at a time into the melted butter, then roll them in the walnut mixture. Place half in the prepared tin, spaced slightly apart. Sprinkle over all the soaked sultanas.

5 ▲ Top with the remaining dough balls, dipping and coating as before. Sprinkle over any remaining walnut mixture and melted butter. Cover with oiled clear film or slide the tin into a lightly oiled large polythene bag and leave to rise, in a warm place, for about 45 minutes, or until the dough reaches the top of the tin.

6 Meanwhile, preheat the oven to 190°C/375°F/Gas 5. Bake for 35–40 minutes, or until well risen and golden. Cool on a wire rack.

Energy 3548kcal/14932kJ; Protein 83g; Carbohydrate 533g, of which sugars 199g; Fat 138g, of which saturates 38g; Cholesterol 355mg; Calcium 1125mg; Fibre 28g; Sodium 1497mg.

New England Fantans

1 Grease a muffin sheet with nine 7.5cm/3in cups or foil cases. Mix the yeast with the buttermilk and sugar and leave to stand for 15 minutes.

2 ▲ In a pan, heat the milk with 45ml/ 3 tbsp of the butter until the butter has melted. Cool until lukewarm.

3 Sift the flour and salt into a bowl. Add the yeast mixture, milk mixture and egg and mix to a soft dough. Turn out on to a floured surface and knead for 5–8 minutes until smooth and elastic. Place in an oiled bowl, cover with oiled clear film (plastic wrap) and leave to rise, in a warm place, for 1 hour, until doubled in size.

4 ▲ Turn out on to a floured surface, knock back and knead until smooth and elastic. Roll into a 45 × 30cm/ 18 × 12in oblong about 5mm/¼in thick. Melt the remaining butter, brush over the dough and cut it lengthways into five equal strips. Stack on top of each other and cut across into nine equal 5cm/2in strips.

5 ▲ Pinch one side of each layered strip together, then place pinched side down into a muffin cup or foil case. Cover with oiled clear film and leave to rise, in a warm place, for 30–40 minutes, or until the fantans have almost doubled in size.

6 Preheat the oven to 200°C/400°F/ Gas 6. Bake the fantans for about 20 minutes, or until golden. Cool on a wire rack.

MAKES 9 ROLLS

15g/½oz fresh yeast

75ml/5 tbsp buttermilk, at room temperature

10ml/2 tsp caster (superfine) sugar

75ml/5 tbsp milk

65g/2½oz/5 tbsp butter

375g/13oz/3¼ cups strong white bread flour

5ml/1 tsp salt

1 egg, lightly beaten

~ VARIATION ~
Add 5ml/1 tsp ground cinnamon to the remaining butter in step 4 before brushing over the dough strips. Sprinkle the rolls with a little icing (confectioners') sugar as soon as they come out of the oven.

Energy 215kcal/905kJ; Protein 5.2g; Carbohydrate 34.4g, of which sugars 2.6g; Fat 7.2g, of which saturates 4.3g; Cholesterol 39mg; Calcium 83mg; Fibre 1.3g; Sodium 291mg.

Mexican 'Bread of the Dead'

2 Sift the flour and salt together into a large bowl. Stir in the sugar and make a well in the centre.

3 In a jug (pitcher), dissolve the yeast in the lukewarm water. Pour into the centre of the flour and mix in a little flour, using your fingers, until a smooth, thick batter forms.

4 Sprinkle over a little of the remaining flour, cover with clear film (plastic wrap) and leave in a warm place for 30 minutes, or until the mixture starts to bubble.

5 Beat the eggs, the reserved liquid flavoured with star anise, orange liqueur and melted butter together. Gradually incorporate into the flour mixture to form a smooth dough.

6 ▲ Turn out the dough on to a lightly floured surface and gently knead in the orange rind. Knead for 5–6 minutes until smooth and elastic. Shape into a 27cm/10½in round and place in the prepared tin.

7 Cover with lightly oiled clear film and leave to rise, in a warm place, for 2–3 hours, or until almost at the top of the tin and doubled in bulk.

8 Meanwhile, preheat the oven to 190°C/375°F/Gas 5. Bake the loaf for 45–50 minutes, or until golden. Turn out on to a wire rack to cool. Dust with icing sugar to serve.

MAKES 1 LOAF

3 star anise

90ml/6 tbsp cold water

700g/1½lb/6 cups unbleached strong white bread flour

5ml/1 tsp salt

115g/4oz/scant ¾ cup caster (superfine) sugar

25g/1oz fresh yeast

175ml/6fl oz/¾ cup lukewarm water

3 eggs

60ml/4 tbsp orange liqueur

115g/4oz/½ cup butter, melted

grated rind of 1 orange

icing (confectioners') sugar, for dusting

1 ▲ Liberally grease a 27cm/10½in fluted round cake tin (pan) with butter. Place the star anise in a pan with the water. Bring to the boil and boil for 3–4 minutes, until the liquid has reduced to 45ml/3 tbsp Discard the star anise and leave the liquid to cool.

Energy 4032kcal/17008kJ; Protein 102g; Carbohydrate 649g, of which sugars 150g; Fat 124g, of which saturates 67g; Cholesterol 941mg; Calcium 1086mg; Fibre 25g; Sodium 2944mg.

Iranian Barbari

1 Lightly dust two baking sheets with flour. Sift the flour and salt into a bowl and make a well in the centre.

2 ▲ Mix the yeast with the water. Pour into the centre of the flour, sprinkle a little flour over and leave in a warm place for 15 minutes. Mix to a dough, then turn out on to a lightly floured surface and knead for 8–10 minutes until smooth and elastic.

3 Place in an oiled bowl, cover with oiled clear film (plastic wrap) and leave for 45–60 minutes, or until doubled.

4 ▲ Knock back the dough and turn out on to a floured surface. Divide into six equal pieces and roll each one out to about 10 × 5cm/4 × 2in and about 1cm/½in thick. Space well apart on the baking sheets, and make four slashes in the tops.

MAKES 6 BARBARI

225g/8oz/2 cups strong white bread flour

5ml/1 tsp salt

15g/½oz fresh yeast

140ml/scant ¼ pint/generous ½ cup lukewarm water

oil, for brushing

~ VARIATION ~
Sprinkle with sesame or caraway seeds before baking.

5 Cover with lightly oiled clear film and leave to rise, in a warm place, for 20 minutes. Preheat the oven to 200°C/400°F/Gas 6. Brush the breads with oil and bake for 12–15 minutes, or until pale golden. Serve warm.

Energy 128kcal/544kJ; Protein 4g; Carbohydrate 28g, of which sugars 1g; Fat 1g, of which saturates 0g; Cholesterol 0mg; Calcium 53mg; Fibre 1g; Sodium 329mg.

Syrian Onion Bread

MAKES 8 BREADS

475g/1lb 2oz/4½ cups unbleached strong white bread flour
5ml/1 tsp salt
20g/¾oz fresh yeast
275ml/9fl oz/generous 1 cup lukewarm water
FOR THE TOPPING
60ml/4 tbsp finely chopped onion
5ml/1 tsp ground cumin
10ml/2 tsp ground coriander
10ml/2 tsp chopped fresh mint
30ml/2 tbsp olive oil

~ COOK'S TIP ~
If you haven't any fresh mint to hand, then add 15ml/1 tbsp dried mint. Use the freeze-dried variety if you can as it has much more flavour.

1 ▲ Lightly flour two baking sheets. Sift the flour and salt together into a large bowl and make a well in the centre. Cream the yeast with a little of the water, then mix in the remainder.

2 Add the yeast mixture to the centre of the flour and mix to a dough. Turn out on to a floured surface; knead for 8–10 minutes until smooth and elastic.

3 Place in a lightly oiled bowl, cover with lightly oiled clear film (plastic wrap) and leave to rise for about 1 hour, or until doubled in size.

4 ▲ Knock back the dough and turn out on to a floured surface. Divide into eight equal pieces and roll into 13–15cm/5–6in rounds. Make them slightly concave. Prick all over and space well apart on the baking sheets. Cover with oiled clear film and leave to rise for 15–20 minutes.

5 ▲ Meanwhile, preheat the oven to 200°C/400°F/Gas 6. Mix the chopped onion, ground cumin, ground coriander and chopped mint in a bowl. Brush the breads with the olive oil for the topping, sprinkle with the spicy onion mixture and bake for 15–20 minutes. Serve warm.

Energy 220kcal/932kJ; Protein 5.5g; Carbohydrate 44.4g, of which sugars 1.3g; Fat 3.5g, of which saturates 0.5g; Cholesterol 0mg; Calcium 85mg; Fibre 1.9g; Sodium 248mg.

Indian Tandoori Rotis

MAKES 6 ROTIS

350g/12oz/3 cups *atta* or fine wholemeal (whole-wheat) flour

5ml/1 tsp salt

250ml/8fl oz/1 cup water

30–45ml/2–3 tbsp melted ghee or butter, for brushing

1 ▲ Sift the flour and salt into a large bowl. Add the water and mix to a soft dough. Knead on a floured surface for 3–4 minutes until smooth. Place in an oiled bowl, cover with oiled clear film (plastic wrap); rest for 1 hour.

2 ▲ Turn out on to a floured surface. Divide the dough into six pieces and shape each piece into a ball. Press out into a larger round with your hand, cover with oiled clear film and leave to rest for 10 minutes.

3 Meanwhile, preheat the oven to 230°C/ 450°F/Gas 8. Place three baking sheets in the oven.

4 Roll the rotis into 15cm/6in rounds, place on the baking sheets and bake for 8–10 minutes. Brush with ghee or butter and serve warm.

Energy 231kcal/981kJ; Protein 7g; Carbohydrate 43g, of which sugars 2g; Fat 5g, of which saturates 3g; Cholesterol 11mg; Calcium 51mg; Fibre 6g; Sodium 381mg.

Indian Naan

MAKES 3 NAAN

225g/8oz/2 cups strong white bread flour
2.5ml/¹/₂ tsp salt
15g/¹/₂oz fresh yeast
60ml/4 tbsp lukewarm milk
15ml/1 tbsp vegetable oil
30ml/2 tbsp natural (plain) yogurt
1 egg
30–45ml/3–4 tbsp melted ghee or butter, for brushing

1 ▲ Sift the flour and salt together into a large bowl. In a smaller bowl, cream the yeast with the milk. Set aside for 15 minutes.

2 ▲ Mix the yeast mixture, oil, yogurt and egg into the flour. Mix to a dough.

3 ▲ Turn out on to a floured surface. Knead for 10 minutes until smooth and elastic. Place in a lightly oiled bowl, cover with lightly oiled clear film (plastic wrap) and leave to rise for 45 minutes, or until doubled in bulk.

4 Preheat the oven to at least 230°C/450°F/Gas 8. Place three heavy baking sheets in the oven to heat.

5 Turn the dough out on to a floured surface and knock back. Divide into three and shape into balls.

6 ▲ Cover two of the balls of dough with oiled clear film and roll out the third into a teardrop shape 25cm/10in long, 13cm/5in wide and with a thickness of about 5–8mm/¹/₄–¹/₃in.

7 Preheat the grill (broiler) to its highest setting. Meanwhile, place the naan on the hot baking sheets and bake for 3–4 minutes, or until puffed up.

8 Remove the naan from the oven and place under the hot grill for a few seconds, or until the top of the naan browns slightly. Wrap the cooked naan in a dish towel to keep warm while rolling out and cooking the remaining naan. Brush with melted ghee or butter and serve warm.

~ VARIATIONS ~

You can flavour naan in numerous different ways:
• To make spicy naan, add 5ml/1 tsp each ground coriander and ground cumin to the flour in step 1. If you would like the naan to be fiery, add 2.5–5ml/½–1 tsp hot chilli powder.
• To make cardamom-flavoured naan, lightly crush the seeds from 4–5 green cardamom pods and add to the flour in step 1.
• To make poppy seed naan, brush the rolled-out naan with a little ghee and sprinkle with poppy seeds. Press lightly to make sure that they stick.
• To make peppered naan, brush the rolled-out naan with a little ghee and dust generously with coarsely ground black pepper.
• To make onion-flavoured naan, add 115g/4oz finely chopped onion to the dough in step 2. You may need to reduce the amount of egg if the onion is very moist to prevent making the dough too soft.
• To make wholemeal (whole-wheat) naan, swap wholemeal bread flour for the white flour.

~ COOK'S TIP ~

To help the dough to puff up and brown, place the baking sheets in an oven preheated to the maximum temperature for at least 10 minutes before baking.

Energy 439kcal/1847kJ; Protein 13g; Carbohydrate 60g, of which sugars 4g; Fat 18g, of which saturates 8g; Cholesterol 104mg; Calcium 196mg; Fibre 3g; Sodium 449mg.

INDEX